THE UNIVERSITY OF CHICAGO
ORIENTAL INSTITUTE PUBLICATIONS
VOLUME XCI

THE UNIVERSITY OF CHICAGO

ORIENTAL INSTITUTE PUBLICATIONS

VOLUME XCI

ARAMAIC RITUAL TEXTS
FROM PERSEPOLIS

BY

RAYMOND A. BOWMAN

THE UNIVERSITY OF CHICAGO PRESS · CHICAGO · ILLINOIS

Library of Congress Catalog Number 68-55148

THE UNIVERSITY OF CHICAGO PRESS, CHICAGO 60637
The University of Chicago Press, Ltd., London, W.C. 1

PREFACE

THE publication of these Aramaic texts found during the excavation of Persepolis in the years 1936 through 1938 is admittedly long overdue. At the conclusion of the excavation, with the onset of World War II, it seemed preferable to leave the artifacts in Iran, where they would presumably be safe, rather than to send them to the United States for study and publication. Indeed, a few specimens that were risked were "lost at sea" through enemy action, and they are so marked in the catalogue of objects in *Persepolis* II. Only two small pieces carried to the United States by Professor Erich Schmidt personally for petrological analysis reached their destination. The remainder, more than two hundred pieces, were crated at Persepolis for shipment to the Teheran Museum.

Fortunately, most of the Aramaic-bearing specimens were photographed by the excavating staff at Persepolis, and they were copied and studied there in 1939 by Professor George Cameron, who was then a member of the Oriental Institute staff at Persepolis. Preliminary publication of his conclusions is found in *Persepolis* II. When I was assigned the task of publishing the Aramaic material from Persepolis, Professor Cameron generously supplied me with the photographs and personal copies as well as the notes he had made in Iran. Without this material publication would now be impossible.

My first independent readings of these texts were made in 1947. Ever since, during a busy schedule of teaching and administration, the study of the artifacts has proceeded on the basis of the secondary materials supplied by Professor Cameron. The difficulties that had to be surmounted in broken, faded, and often stained texts are apparent from the photographs here presented.

Bit by bit the witness of the fragments was extracted. Faded and missing letters were identified wherever possible, and broken words were restored. The essential structure of the texts was determined and the occasional unique, supplementary phrases were given special study. Finally, because of the formulaic character of the texts, broken passages were restored and almost every word could be read with certainty.

But the task then had just begun. Proper names were recognized, but the correct identification and rendering of Iranian names in Aramaic transcription is a continuing problem, especially for one who is not an expert in the subject. The limited and simple vocabulary of Aramaic words found in these texts, too, although easily translated in isolation, was a problem. Attempts to translate the texts by employing the usual and expected meanings of the Aramaic words produced awkward, cumbersome readings that make no sound, consecutive sense. A small but quite clear photograph of one of the more complete and representative texts was published in *Persepolis* II. To my knowledge, only Professor F. Altheim ventured a translation and commentary on that text,[1] an attestation of the difficulty of extracting the sense of such apparently simple texts.

More study was required to discover the syntax of the texts and their proper meaning before a translation could be attempted. On apparently sufficient grounds, Professor Schmidt regarded the vessels as "ritual objects," and, because of their dense concentration within one of the rooms of the Treasury, assumed that the objects had been presented there as memorials.

---

[1] F. Altheim and R. Stiehl, *Die aramäische Sprache unter den Achaemeniden* (Frankfurt am Main, 1936) I 17–21.

In order to arrive at a meaning for the texts that would be intelligible and within the bounds of the accepted assumptions, valid but less usual meanings of the simple Aramaic words had to be tried. The results of such study are apparent in the translations and discussions here presented. Without pretending to have proven a thesis about the texts, I have presented this work simply as what appears to be the most plausible conjecture in harmony with all known facts. It is but a challenge to others to present alternative explanations of these simple yet difficult texts that will be equally true to all of the evidence.

Before publication, an effort was made to collate suspected readings with the original texts in Iran. The result was a continual delay. In 1963 the pieces on exhibition in the museums at Teheran and Persepolis were studied, but determined efforts to locate the bulk of the artifacts were frustrated. Knowledge of their whereabouts was disclaimed everywhere.

After the publication of *Persepolis* II, it was found that not all of the material had been made available for study. A check of the Field Register of the Persepolis Expedition indicated that approximately a third more texts had been found than those represented by the photographs and copies that had been supplied to me for study. A careful search of the effects and records of the late Professor Schmidt produced no further material and publication had to be delayed until another search could be made in Iran.

Attendance at the Congress of Iranologists in Iran in 1966 afforded the needed opportunity to renew the search for the missing artifacts. With the vigorous support and personal assistance of Professor Cameron and with the full cooperation of Iranian officials, an extended, careful search was made in the storage cabinets and storerooms of the archeological museums in Teheran and Persepolis. Only what had been seen previously in 1963 was found at Teheran, and it seemed evident that the artifacts had never reached their destination from Persepolis.

The explanation was finally found by Professor Cameron at Persepolis. The crated objects had been dumped and abandoned in an unused room of the Persepolis Museum. The objects had to be re-excavated there, cleaned, and forwarded to their original destination in Teheran. Some of the objects had been further broken in the interim and in the process of cleaning, the faint Aramaic writing almost disappeared. They were briefly studied and sorted in Teheran and the texts that had never been copied or photographed were sent on loan to the Oriental Institute at Chicago.

The artifacts sent to Chicago from Teheran were generally in such poor condition, presumably as a result of the cleaning process they had undergone, that they were extremely difficult to photograph. Infrared photography produced no satisfactory results, but filters were found that gave passable prints. Hand copies were made of the most difficult examples, using magnification and a slight moistening to bring out the dim letters. Consequently, the copies sometimes show what is not clearly visible in the photographs. In some instances both the copy and photograph are given here so that comparison can be made. Where no presentable photograph is available, copies by Professor Cameron or by me are given (indicated by initials "C" and "B"). In every possible instance, the copies have been checked and rechecked with the almost illegible originals to insure accuracy.[2]

Only part of the missing fragments were recovered in 1966. The remainder were presumably also discarded somewhere and may never be found. It seems imperative now, at long last, to proceed with the publication of the material now available. While the loss of the remainder is deplorable, since the missing texts would doubtless augment the already long list of Iranian names in Aramaic transcription and possibly present variant readings or supplemental material that might cast more light on some of the quite perplexing problems that remain, it

---

[2] All Aramaic texts except those on a few very large objects are shown actual size in the illustrations at the end of this book.

seems unlikely that the missing texts would materially alter the conclusions based on available resources or upset the dating of the texts, which appears to be quite certain.

In the course of this study it has been necessary for me to enter fields of Iranian language and religion that are not normally the province of an Aramaist. I claim no expertise in such areas myself, and I am aware of the differences of opinion that exist among Iranologists, especially in the matter of Achaemenid religion. But an adequate exposition of the nature of these inscribed cultic artifacts demands an examination of the context in which they belong. If the vessels are indeed cultic, as seems likely, religious matters cannot and must not be avoided, even if only for the evidential value of the implements and their texts.

Because the haoma ceremony is an important and continuing aspect of Persian religion and because the praxis of modern Parsi ritual, almost our sole witness to the ancient rite, obviously has ancient survivals as well as subsequent changes, it is both necessary and appropriate to examine the current haoma ritual, at least for comparative purposes. The somewhat extended discussions of religious matters in chapter ii and elsewhere are needed to justify the translations given and to render them intelligible.

Furthermore, since in many of the texts the principal actor in the ritual is a high military official, it seems pertinent to refer to the military Mithraism of much later times in which some substitute for the haoma ceremony seems to have persisted. After conjecturing that the cultic aspects of these Aramaic texts may reflect a Mithraic cult in the Achaemenid army, I was gratified to learn, in a personal communication from Professor Richard N. Frye, of Harvard University, that "It looks more and more that a 'proto-Mithraic' cult existed among the soldiers at Persepolis, for other fragments of information fit in with such a theory."

Because of my obvious deficiencies in Iranian matters, I have sought the assistance of a number of more competent scholars in that area. I am especially grateful to Professor Wilhelm Eilers, of Würzburg, Germany, Professor Janos Harmatta, of Budapest, and Professor Richard N. Frye, of Harvard University, concerning the identifications and etymologies of the many Iranian names in these texts. I must, of course, accept full responsibility for the material that I have used.

Professor E. O. Negahban of the Iran Bastan Museum of Teheran, Iran, has been most helpful during my frustrating periods in Iran and has been an interested and encouraging friend throughout the preparation of this study. Without the assistance of my good friend Professor George G. Cameron, of the University of Michigan, this work could never have been undertaken. Through the years we have discussed the problems involved, and he has carefully read and criticized my manuscript. Although not all of his suggestions have been followed, they are evident in the final draft and this book is, I believe, all the better for his challenges.

Special recognition is due those who have seen this work through the laborious and tedious processes of editing and production. My wife, Marguerite, has patiently and carefully typed seemingly endless copies of my manuscript. Mrs. Jean Eckenfels has carefully edited this work and has seen to the details of production under the supervision of the Editorial Secretary, Mrs. Elizabeth Hauser.

RAYMOND A. BOWMAN

CHICAGO
September, 1968

TABLE OF CONTENTS

LIST OF ILLUSTRATIONS

LIST OF ABBREVIATIONS

Unless otherwise noted, references to classical authors are to the "Loeb Classical Library" editions.

AJSL	American journal of Semitic languages and literature. Chicago, 1884–1941.
Altheim and Stiehl, *Aramäische Sprache*	Franz Altheim and Ruth Stiehl. Die aramäische Sprache unter den Achaemeniden. 1—— vols. Frankfurt am Main, 1936——.
BAiW	Christian Bartholomae. Altiranisches Wörterbuch. 2d ed. Strassburg, 1961.
BLA	Hans Bauer and Pontus Leander. Grammatik des biblisch Aramäischen. Halle [Saale], 1927.
CAD	Chicago. The University. The Oriental Institute. The Assyrian dictionary. 1—— vols. Chicago, 1956——.
Cameron, *PTT*	George G. Cameron. Persepolis Treasury tablets. *OIP* LXV. Chicago, 1948.
Cowley, *AP*	A. Cowley. Aramaic papyri of the fifth century B.C. Oxford, 1923.
Frye, *Heritage*	Richard N. Frye. The heritage of Persia. Cleveland and New York, 1963.
Haug, *Parsis*	Martin Haug. Essays on the sacred language, writings, and religion of the Parsis. London, 1878.
JA	Journal asiatique. Paris, 1822——.
Jastrow, *Dictionary*	Marcus Jastrow. A dictionary of the Targumim, the Talmud Babli, and Yerushalmi, and the Midrashic literature. 2 vols. New York, 1926.
JNES	Journal of Near Eastern studies. Chicago, 1942——.
JRAS	Royal Asiatic Society of Great Britain and Ireland, London. Journal. London, 1834——.
Kent, *Old Persian*	Roland G. Kent. Old Persian: Grammar, texts, and lexicon. American Oriental series XXXIII. 2d ed. New Haven, 1953.
Meillet and Benveniste, *Grammaire*	A. Meillet and E. Benveniste. Grammaire du vieux-Perse. 2d ed. Paris, 1931.
Modi, *Religious Ceremonies*	Jivanji Jamshedji Modi. The religious ceremonies and customs of the Parsees. 2d ed. Bombay, 1937.
Nyberg, *Religionen*	H. S. Nyberg. Die Religionen des alten Irans. Trans. H. H. Schaeder. Mitteilungen der Vorderasiatisch-aegyptische Gesellschaft XLIII. Leipzig, 1938.
OIP	Chicago. The University. The Oriental Institute. Oriental Institute publications. Chicago, 1924——.
Schmidt, *Persepolis* I and II	Erich F. Schmidt. Persepolis. I. Structures, reliefs, inscriptions. *OIP* LXVIII. Chicago, 1953. Persepolis. II. Contents of the Treasury and other discoveries. *OIP* LXIX. Chicago, 1957.
Yadin, *Scroll*	Yigael Yadin. The scroll of the war of the sons of light against the sons of darkness. Trans. Batya and Chaim Rabin. London, 1962.
Zaehner, *Zoroastrianism*	R. C. Zaehner. The dawn and twilight of Zoroastrianism. New York, 1961.
ZATW	Zeitschrift für die alttestamentliche Wissenschaft. Giessen, 1881——.
ZDMG	Deutsche morgenländische Gesellschaft. Zeitschrift. Leipzig, 1847——.

I

THE FIND

URING the excavation of Persepolis by the Oriental Institute of the University of Chicago under the direction of Professor Erich F. Schmidt, in the years 1936 through 1938, the remains of some 269 mortars, pestles, plates, and trays of a distinctive flinty green stone were found in the Treasury building.[1] About 203 of those objects were more or less legibly inscribed in ink in Aramaic writing.[2]

The stone fragments were found scattered on the floors, principally in the complex of rooms and corridors in the northern part of the Treasury (Fig. 1). Schmidt said, "By far the majority of these objects had been stored in the last addition to the building. . . . A small number of specimens occurred in Hall 41 and in other units of the central section of the Treasury, but only three pieces had strayed into the southern and earliest portion of the building."[3] The chief storage place for such objects was the large rectangular room (38) which runs the width of the Treasury at its northern extremity. This room, its roof supported by a hundred columns, was surrounded by seven subsidiary rooms (42 to 48) with entrances from the western and northern sides of the larger room.

Only a few complete vessels were recovered, and those were not found in the room with the great majority of the fragments. Pieces of the objects were found scattered among the pillars of Room 38, but the great mass of them littered the floor to the south and west of the room, especially along the south wall, against which they appear to have been shattered.

After the green stone mortars, pestles, and plates had been interpreted as "ritual objects,"[4] it seemed natural to suppose that their destruction was purposeful, part of the praxis of the religious rite in which they were used. But the recovery of several undamaged pieces[5] and the fact that the royal tableware had been similarly shattered and scattered on the floor among the fragments of the mortars, pestles, and plates made vandalism a more likely explanation of their broken condition.

When Alexander the Great captured Persepolis in 330 B.C., according to Diodorus he permitted his troops to plunder the city, "except the king's palace."[6] It is evident that their looting and vandalism extended to the Treasury of Persepolis on the citadel terrace as well as to the city in the plain below. Everywhere in the Treasury there has been found evidence of plundering and vandalism before the building was burned and of wanton destruction of whatever the looters decided not to carry away.

[1] Schmidt, *Persepolis* II 18, 53, 82, Fig. 7.

Other fragments of damaged green stone mortars and pestles, now at the Oriental Institute, sent by Ernst Herzfeld, who had recovered them earlier at Persepolis, are presumably those mentioned by Schmidt as having been found in the Fratadara Temple and the post-Alexandrian building with the Achaemenid gate (Schmidt, *Persepolis* II 53, n. 55, I 55–56). Schmidt regarded them as vessels, "presumably reused." There is now no trace of writing on any of them.

A similar green chert mortar fragment (NR1 12) was found at Naqsh-i Rustam in the surface layer of BB 14.

[2] Schmidt, *Persepolis* II 55a.   [3] *Ibid.*, p. 53a.

[4] *Ibid.*, I 156–200, Figs. 63–81, II 53–56.

[5] Nos. 33, 43, 76. Illegible or uninscribed pestle (PT5 8) and plates (PT5 536 and PT5 540) were also undamaged; see Plate 1 here and *Persepolis* II, Pl. 23:4.

[6] Diodorus Siculus xvii. 70–71; A. T. Olmstead, *History of the Persian Empire* (Chicago, 1948), pp. 519–24.

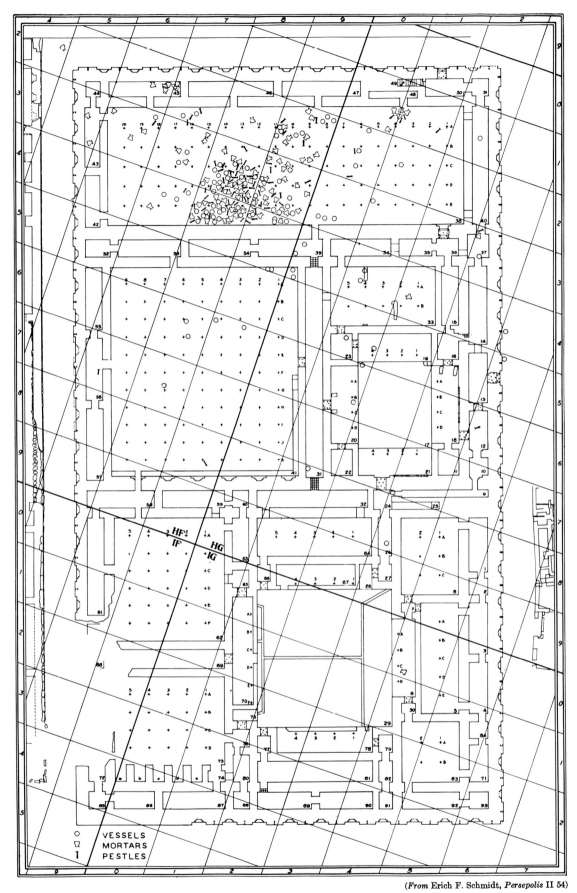

VESSELS
MORTARS
PESTLES

(*From* Erich F. Schmidt, *Persepolis* II 54)

FIG. 1. FIND-SPOT OF RITUAL OBJECTS OF GREEN CHERT IN TREASURY. SCALE OF PLAN, 1:667
(ALL OBJECTS SHOWN AT EXAGGERATED SCALE)

The great conflagration evident elsewhere in the Treasury scarcely touched the large store-room, Room 38, where most of the mortar, pestle, and plate fragments were found. Even its roof seems to have escaped destruction by fire. Only where burning debris fell into the room from outside was there even scorching. It is evident that the material stored there was not flammable. Its contents appear to have been statuary and tableware of stone, composition, and glass. Especially prominent among the finds of this room were the green stone ritual objects scattered on its floor, especially near the base of its south wall.

Rooms 46 and 47, subsidiary to Room 38, which lay beyond the northern wall of that great room, contained no trace of the green stone vessels. In Room 42, entered near the southwestern corner of Room 38, only a single object was found in the debris. Room 43 and, subsidiary to it, Room 44, in the northwestern corner, appear to have been depositories for weapons, principally, but two green stone mortar fragments and one of a plate were found in Room 43; one of the mortar pieces was inscribed.[7]

Room 45, entered from Room 38 near the northwestern corner of its north wall, held fragments of seven green stone objects, four of which were inscribed (Nos. 36, 74, 88, and 125).[8] The finding of so many objects in such a relatively small room has led to the conclusion that at least some cult vessels had been stored there.

A small collection of fragments of such stone vessels lay before the doorless opening in the eastern part of the north wall which led to the long, narrow room (48) below the stairway at the northern exit of the Treasury building. Only one fragment, and that inscribed (No. 117), was found within, at the eastern end of the long room.

A single door in the southern wall of Room 38 linked it with the remainder of the Treasury. Just beyond the door in the south wall, in Room 39, where more than a thousand arrowheads were found, fragments of several green stone plates were recovered. They had probably been kicked or thrown from Room 38. Beyond Room 39 a long corridor (Room 31) extended southward to Room 32 in the southern part of the Treasury. A pestle fragment and part of a green stone plate were found in Room 31 quite near its southern exit.[9]

A doorway in the western wall of the long corridor (31) led to a large square room (41) with a roof supported by 99 columns. There a patched strip of flooring running between the doorway and the entrance to Room 56, on the opposite side, attests to heavy traffic. A considerable number of labels bearing impressions of official seals found in the complex indicate that Room 56 and Rooms 55 and 57, which flank it, were used for the storage of the most valuable things. These three rooms, looted of all major objects, were almost bare, but a fragment of a single stone pestle was found just inside the door to Room 56.[10] It could have been dropped or discarded by a busy plunderer who had found more desirable loot there. Not a trace of a green stone ritual vessel was found in the other subsidiary rooms entered from Room 41 through doors in the north and south walls of the room.

Blackened walls, burnt plaster, and spalled and heat-shattered column bases attest to a violent conflagration of combustible stores in Room 41. But it was also the depository for the most precious royal tableware, which included foreign, pre-Achaemenid objects, spoils of war, as well as vessels of domestic production. In the northern half of the room, fragments of royal tableware were scattered over the floor among the columns, as they were also in Room 38. A heap of fragments was found in the northeastern corner of the room, where the vessels had been shattered against the walls. But few, if any, of the ritual vessels appear to have been stored in Room 41. Fragments of four plates and of a mortar were found in the heap of shattered tableware in the northeastern corner of the room and five fragments of other plates were scattered among the columns near the center. A fragment of a pestle was found near the center

[7] Schmidt, *Persepolis* I 184.

[8] *Ibid.*, p. 184a.

[9] *Ibid.*, p. 177a; plate fragment (PT5 277) and a pestle.

[10] *Ibid.*, p. 180b.

of the south wall. Four of the plates (Nos. 18, 45, 72, and 111)[11] and a mortar fragment (No. 82) found in Room 41 were inscribed.

Across the corridor (31) from Room 41, a door in the east wall led to an open courtyard (17) surrounded by four porticoes, a complex that appears to have been the administrative center of the Treasury. From the courtyard there was access, through Portico 19 and Room 23, to a large rectangular room (33) with a roof supported by ten columns in two rows. The large number of cuneiform tablets found there suggests that Room 33 was the archival headquarters of the local administration.

Only scattered fragments of the stone ritual objects were found in the complex of rooms and corridors east of Corridor 31. A piece of a plate was recovered from the western portico (20); another was in the northwestern corner of the main courtyard (17); still another came from the northwestern portico (19) and another plate fragment (No. 113) was found in the small Room 23.[12] In the archive room (33) there were fragments of two plates and a mortar. Since there is no evidence for storage of such vessels in any of these rooms, the pieces recovered in the administrative complex were apparently brought there by looters from elsewhere, ultimately, perhaps, from Room 38.

A doorway from the south portico (21) of the administrative complex led southward to Room 24, which gave access to a ramp (25) leading eastward by two inclines to the roof of the Treasury. From Room 24 doorways opened to the east and south to corridors of rooms.

Southward Room 24 led to a short corridor (26) in which a fragment of a green stone plate was found,[13] but the room was otherwise completely lacking in objects. Corridor 26 ran southward through Rooms 27 and 28, to a large courtyard (29) in the southern part of the Treasury. There, in the eastern portico (6) off the courtyard, a mortar fragment was found.

Eastward, at the junction of Room 24 and a long, narrow corridor (9), a single fragment of a green stone plate was found. A suite of rooms (10, 12, and 13) off the eastern end of Corridor 9 led to the eastern exit of the Treasury building. Room 10 was simply a barren passageway. Room 12, to the north, had a doorway in its western wall that gave access to the administrative courtyard (17) in the central part of the Treasury already discussed above. In almost the center of Room 12 a green stone pestle fragment was found.[14] To the north of Room 12 a doorway led to Room 13, a guardroom at the eastern exit of the Treasury. An earlier doorway that had continued the passage northward toward the northern exit of the Treasury had been blocked up, making Room 13 a dead end.

The eastern exit of the Treasury opened on "Garrison Street," which faced the soldiers' quarters at the foot of the mountain to the east, Mount Kuh-i-Raḥmat. Near the eastern entrance, both within the guardroom (13) and in the street outside, fragments of tableware were found. In the street, north of the exit, lay fragments of two green stone plates, one of which (No. 112) was inscribed.[15] In a later excavation in 1949, the Archaeological Institute of Persepolis found a beautiful, complete green stone plate (No. 43), inscribed with Aramaic, in the street east of the Hall of the Hundred Columns (Room 38).[16]

At the north end of the portico (18) of the administrative compound mentioned above, a door led to Room 16, which then gave access eastward to another suite of corridor rooms (14, 37, 40, 51, and 50) leading to the northern exit of the Treasury building.

Room 14 was used for the storage of combustible material as well as for traffic, as its scarred walls and the layers of ash and charcoal in its debris show. North of it, Storeroom 37 held a

[11] Only part of plate No. 72 was found in Room 41; the other fragment was in Room 38.

[12] Schmidt, *Persepolis* I 172*b*.   [13] *Ibid.*, p. 188*a*.

[14] *Ibid.*, p. 170*b*.

[15] Schmidt also mentions "pieces of green chert mortars" found there (*Persepolis* I 170*b*).

[16] Ali-Sami, *Persepolis* (*Takht-i-Jamshid*), trans. R. N. Sharp (4th ed.; Shiraz, 1966), pp. 95–96.

heterogeneous collection of objects. A bronze pestle (PT6 123) lay at the opening between Rooms 14 and 37 and a fragment of a green stone plate was found nearby.[17] In the northern end of Room 37, where it opened into Room 40, a mortar and pestle in perfect condition were found.[18] Room 40, a long storeroom running northward along the narrow end of Room 38, shows evidence of violent burning. Midway along its length a fragment of a green stone plate was found, apparently dropped by a looter on his way to the northern exit of the Treasury building.

The door at the northern end of Room 40 led to a small, square room (51) at the northeastern corner of the Treasury which, like Room 40, showed signs of a great conflagration. From Room 51 a door led west to the guardroom (50) at the northern exit of the Treasury. It was used for the storage of tools and other hardware as well as for martial projectiles.

Once a doorway in the western wall of the guardroom had opened to a stairway (49) to the roof. This passage had been blocked by a wall, but the plunderers of the Treasury reopened it with a breach to gain access to the northern exit from the stairway. Schmidt says, "It seems, however, that the despoilers of the Treasury found this convenient means of access to the northern entrance. They breached the southern part of the blocking wall and—after carrying their loot from the interior of the building, up Ramp 25 and across the roof—used Stairway 49 as a passage to Vestibule 50 and its street exit. They enable us to follow their tracks by dropping some of their plunder at two bottlenecks, namely on Ramp 25 . . . and on the stairway."[19] An inscribed fragment of a green stone pestle (No. 123) was found on the stairs, where it apparently had been dropped by a plunderer coming down from above. In the street outside, just beyond the northwestern corner of the building, a fragment of a green stone mortar (No. 124) was recovered.

A few other pieces of inscribed green stone objects were later recovered from the sherd pile of the excavation and their provenance was determined by the general area from which the fragments came.[20]

Thus, the distribution of the stone mortars, pestles, and plates in the Treasury clearly indicates that the bulk of them had been stored in the large Room 38 and its subsidiary Room 45 in the northern part of the Treasury. The remainder was scattered elsewhere, with decreasing frequency toward the southern and older part of the Treasury complex. Scattered pieces were often found in unexpected places, usually along the routes that would be taken by the plunderers into the heart of the Treasury or outward toward its exits.

Apparently some looters, attracted by the beauty or utility of particular pieces, carried them off and were thus responsible for scattering them into the central and even the southern parts of the Treasury, far from Room 38. As more valued items of booty were encountered and as the loot accumulated, the despoilers became more aware of the bulkiness or weight of the stone objects, which they then discarded. Some were purposely smashed and in a few instances others were dropped intact on the way. A complete small mortar and pestle were doubtless carried a long way before they were discarded as a burden, near the northern exit of the building.

[17] Schmidt, *Persepolis* I 185*a*.

[18] Mortar No. 33 and uninscribed pestle PT5 8 (Teheran Museum No. 2208).

[19] Schmidt, *Persepolis* I 186.

[20] Nos. 13, 18, 51, 60, 67, 84, and 98.

II

THE HAOMA CEREMONY

THE excavator of the mortar, pestle, and plate fragments has called them "ritual objects" and has identified them as having been used in the haoma ceremony of the Persian religion.[1] The basis for such an identification was the discovery of a seal impression imperfectly registered on several clay labels of the time of Xerxes which were found in the Treasury at Persepolis.[2]

The seal design portrays two persons standing below a winged sun-disk, the emblem of the Persian god Ahuramazda. The figures flank a fire altar and a stand bearing a mortar and pestle identical in form with the green stone vessels inscribed in Aramaic that were found in the Persepolis Treasury.

The person on the left, bent forward slightly toward the fire altar, seems to be wearing a tiara-like headdress.[3] His face shows a blurred, beardlike projection, which probably represents the expected mouth cloth (*padâm*).[4] His garment is a long, belted coat with long sleeves. He extends several twigs toward the flame, apparently replenishing it.[5]

The figure on the right, standing before the table bearing the mortar and pestle, wears a headdress such as Strabo describes on Magians. It is of felt, with cheek pieces at the sides that come down to cover the lips.[6] His mantle, thrown over his shoulders and falling to his knees, there meets his long, rather tight trousers. In his right hand he holds three "rods," which probably represent the twig bundle (*barsom*) rather than a few haoma twigs.[7] His left hand holds the top of a slender, canelike staff, which appears to rest on his somewhat advanced right foot.[8]

Behind the figure at the right there is an Aramaic legend, *ḥtm dtm* . . . "Seal of *dtm*. . . ," which Cameron once read as "Seal of Datames." He also once identified the owner as the

---

[1] Schmidt, *Persepolis* I 156–200, II 53–56.

[2] The labels bear the field numbers PT3 384 and PT3 363. See Pl. 1 here.

[3] The figure on the left is found in only one impression of the seal (PT3 384), where it is blurred and distorted. Schmidt (*Persepolis* II 26) describes the headdress as "round (mutilated) . . . possibly bashlyk," but it seems to be rather rectangular, more closely resembling the crownlike headdress found elsewhere (Schmidt, *Persepolis* II, Pl. 7, Seal 23). The figure in Seal 23 seems to be similarly clothed. Pausanius (*Description of Greece* v. 27, 6) describes a Magian as putting a tiara on his head before intoning an invocation before the fire altar.

[4] Zaehner, *Zoroastrianism*, Fig. 42; Haug, *Parsis*, p. 243, n. 1.

[5] He doubtless represents the Old Persian **ātarǝvaxša* (Elamite *ḫa-tur-ma-ak-ša*, Greek *pyraithos*), the "fire-watcher."

[6] Strabo *Geography* xv. 15, C 733.

[7] He probably represents the *frabaretar*, who bore the *barsom* to the fire.

[8] Similarly the spear-bearing soldiers on the stairway leading to the Apadana at Persepolis as well as the leaders of the Kashshites, Bactrians, Saka, Indians, and Cilicians: each rests the end of his spear or stave on the toe of his extended foot. Likewise the spear-bearers in the glazed brick reliefs found at Susa.

The rod in the seal impression is perhaps the "reed staff" which Magians carried. Several classical writers mention such a Magian "wand." Strabo (*Geography* xv. 14, C 732) claims that the Magians touched the sacrificial flesh with it. Athenaeus (*Deipnosophistae* xii. 530e) quotes Phoenix as declaring that the Magians kindled the sacred flame by touching "the god" with their wand. Nicander (*Scholia on the Theriaca of Nicander*, ed. O. Schneider, p. 613) cites the first book of Dino's third treatise to the effect that Median soothsayers practiced divination by means of wands.

scribe Daddumania of the time of Darius I, but he later repudiated that association.[9] As the published transcription of the name indicates, the writer has always regarded the name as incomplete. In even the better of the impressions, the lower-right corner of the seal has been registered incompletely and there is space for two more letters. At the very lower edge of the inscription I believe that I can see the short, right-hand stroke of the Aramaic letter *t*. It is probable that the inscription should be read as חתם דתמ[ותר] "Seal of Dāta-Mithra." This seal, showing a scene from a haoma ceremony, probably was the property of the treasurer Dāta-Mithra, who is regularly named among the officials in the Aramaic texts on the green stone ritual objects of the time of Xerxes that were found in the Treasury at Persepolis.[10]

To judge from the procedure in the modern Parsi ceremony, the scene in this seal design probably represents the moment in the haoma ceremony when the priest consecrates the fire (Yasna 9:1) while his colleague, who has just strained the haoma liquid, takes the consecrated *barsom* in his right hand while he recites a religious formula. Shortly thereafter the drinking of the haoma intoxicant takes place.[11]

The use of an intoxicating drink, which is called *soma* by the people of India and *haoma* by the Iranians,[12] is one of the earliest and most persistent elements in the religion of the Indo-Iranian peoples. The importance assigned to the drink by both of those ancient peoples clearly shows that its use must have originated in a common source in prehistoric times.

One tradition ascribes the origin of its use to the primeval man Yima (the Indic Yama), who was believed to have been the first to slaughter oxen as sacrifices to the ancient gods and associated such sacrifices with the drinking of the juice called haoma.[13] Another legend traces its first use to a certain prophet, Haoma-Dūraosha or Haoma-Frāshmi, a learned, pious man of the early period of the Peshdādian dynasty, before the Indians and Iranians separated to become distinct peoples. While meditating on the heights of the Hukairya peak in the Elburz Mountains, he discovered a plant that was nutritious, invigorating, and health-promoting. From it he pressed a golden liquid which ever afterward bore his name, Haoma, and he devised a ritual to accompany its pressing which would teach religion and morality to aid all mankind.[14]

Whatever its origin, soma/haoma at a very early period was freely prepared and drunk by all who sought its life-giving and life-preserving properties. It was the first liquid to pass the lips of the new-born babe and the last draught given to a dying person.[15] According to the Visparad (12:5), it was hoped that the mortar for pounding the plant would be used widely in houses and streets, cities and countries.[16] In India during the Vedic period worshipers could say, "We have drunk soma; we have become immortal,"[17] and among Iranians an epithet for haoma was *dūraoša*, "the averter of death." No special adept was necessary for its making, and long before a special caste of priests was recognized, the householder himself produced the intoxicant. Such practice long continued among the daēva-worshipers, who claimed that, as householders, they were also priests.[18]

---

[9] In Schmidt, *Persepolis* II 26, n. 122.

[10] See p. 28.   [11] Modi, *Religious Ceremonies*, pp. 293–94.

[12] The words *soma* and *haoma* are cognate, originally referring to the same plant and the liquid derived from it. The word, while used to designate a plant, is not in fact a botanical name but a development from an Indo-Iranian verb meaning "press." Thus, as Eilers has indicated, the word is as noncommittal as the "squash" used by the British to indicate any one of a variety of pressed drinks; see W. Eilers and M. Mayrhofer, "Kurdisch *būz* und die indogermanische Buchen-Sippe," *Mitteilungen der Anthropologischen Gesellschaft in Wien* XCII (1962 [= *Festschrift Franz Hančar*]) 60, 67, n. 56, *haoma*.

[13] Yasna 32:14; see Zaehner, *Zoroastrianism*, p. 38.   [14] Modi, *Religious Ceremonies*, pp. 284–85.

[15] J. J. Modi, "Birth Customs and Ceremonies of the Parsees," *Journal of the Anthropological Society of Bombay* XII (1912) 576.

[16] C. E. Pavry, *Iranian Studies* (Bombay, 1927), p. 196.   [17] Rig-Veda, VIII, 48, 3.

[18] Zaehner (*Zoroastrianism*, p. 122) cites a Pahlavi gloss on Yasna 32:11.

It was inevitable that such an important beverage, which created emotional exhilaration and unnatural mental states and was believed to give strength and courage against the foe as well as the promise of immortality, should develop an important role in popular religion. It was regarded as a substance consumed by the gods to ensure their own immortality and to increase their strength against their enemies, and in the Yasna of the Seven Chapters, which may possibly be dated as early as the sixth century B.C., the haoma plant is listed as an object of worship along with the earth, sky, water, fire, and other natural phenomena.[19]

The use of haoma in early Iranian religion was certainly more diversified than we find it in the later cultus. It accompanied sacrifices and presumably was used in a variety of other ways. Plutarch describes a Persian rite which, if genuine, must preserve the praxis of a propitiatory sacrifice used by daēva-worshipers to placate their dreaded gods. Plutarch claims,

> Zoroaster taught them [i.e., the Persians] to make to the one [i.e., to "Horomazes" = Ahuramazda] vows and thank offerings; to the other [i.e., to "Arimanius" = Ahriman] sacrifices for averting evil and the things of depressing appearance. For example, while pounding in a mortar a certain herb called *omōmi* [i.e., haoma], they appeal to Hades and Darkness; then they mix it with the blood of a slaughtered wolf, take it to a place where the sun never shines, and throw it away. The reason for this is because they regard some plants as belonging to the beneficent god and others to the evil demon.[20]

In India, in Vedic times, it was primarily for the daēva Indra, the chief god of the Brahmans, the patron of the warrior bands of the Aryans, that the worshipers squeezed and drank the intoxicating soma and gave the god his share. Naturally, the soma ceremony in India came to be of particular interest to military men.[21]

Among the Iranians the haoma rite became associated principally with the god Mithra, who, after a somewhat varied career, had come to assume the warlike character of the Indic god Indra.[22] It has been said of the Mithra Yasht of the Avesta, "Throughout the poem, Mithra is preeminently a god of battles; he was, therefore, especially fitted to become, as he did in later times, the favorite deity of the Roman soldier."[23] Nyberg has described Mithraism as a religion of warriors and chieftains.[24]

It is probably the use of haoma to which Greek writers refer when they describe royal drunkenness during the Mithraic festival. Athenaeus quotes Ctesias as saying that Persian kings could drink heavily on only one day of the year, the day of their sacrifice to Mithra.[25] He also quotes the seventh book of Duris' *History* to the effect that "at the festival of Mithra alone, of all the festivals celebrated by the Persians, the king gets drunk and dances 'the Persian (dance).' "[26]

---

[19] I. Gershevitch, "Zoroaster's Own Contribution," *JNES* XXIII (1964) 14–15, n. 11.

[20] Plutarch *Moralia; Isis and Osiris* v. 46.
The rite described is "Zoroastrian" only in the sense of being "Persian." One must differentiate between the ancient ceremony used as an illustration and the theological framework in which it is set. Zaehner (*Zoroastrianism*, pp. 124–25) says that Plutarch's Persian theology, which was presumably derived from Theopompus, is "a half-way house between Catholic Zoroastrianism and the Mithraism we meet in the Roman Empire."
The non-Zoroastrian nature of the rite is manifest in the fact that in Zoroastrianism wolves rank as most evil animals (Yasna 9:18) and should be killed (Vendidād 18:65). A wolf must be seen by a man before it spies him, or evil results will follow (Yasna 9:21). Also, the surprising association of haoma with the wolf and Ahriman seems to reflect the ancient usage in which haoma was offered principally to the daēvas in India and presumably also originally in Iranian religion.

[21] Zaehner, *Zoroastrianism*, pp. 97–116.

[22] The question whether Mithra, like Indra, was originally a daēva is debatable. Frye (*Heritage*, pp. 114–15) and Haug (*Parsis*, pp. 272, 288) claim that Mithra was a daēva, while Zaehner (*Zoroastrianism*, pp. 97–116) suggests that he was originally an ahura who attained the warlike characteristics of the daēva Indra.

[23] H. S. Jones, "Mithraism," *Encyclopaedia of Religion and Ethics* VIII (New York, 1916) 753a.

[24] Nyberg, *Religionen*, p. 288.   [25] Athenaeus *Deipnosophiuae* x. 45, 434d–e.

[26] K. Müller, *Fragmenta Historicum Graecorum* (Paris, 1848) II 472–73, Sec. 13.

Great quantities of the sacred intoxicant were consumed in religious services in both India and Persia. In the days of Zoroaster, the daēva priests and prophets of the Brahmans, the *kavi*'s and *karapan*'s,[27] the opponents of the Zoroastrians, prepared solemn soma feasts to secure the assistance of the god Indra and, after the sacrificial feasts, during which they were totally inebriated by soma, they led their people in predatory excursions against the Iranian settlers.[28]

Zoroaster reacted vigorously against such a situation. He execrated the *kavi*'s and *karapan*'s, inquiring of Ahuramazda, "When, O Wise One, will the warriors understand the message? When wilt thou smite this filth of drink through which sacrificers wickedly and the evil masters of the countries of their own will commit their deeds of malice?"[29]

This outburst by the prophet has created controversy among students of Iranian religion. Because of the bitterness of his denunciation, it is often claimed that Zoroaster condemned the use of haoma and ordered its suppression in Persian religion. Gershevitch, for example, calls attention to Herodotus' description of the part played by the worshiper and the Magus during the sacrifice and indicates not only that there is no reference to haoma but that Herodotus expressly states that the Persians "pour no libations,"[30] from which Gershevitch concluded that "no haoma ritual was involved."[31] Furthermore, he indicates that the name of Haoma does not appear in the religious calendar adopted in 441 B.C., during the reign of Artaxerxes I, in which most of the deities of the Zarathustric religion appear as the religious names of each day and each month of the year.[32]

But Zaehner repudiates such a view as extreme and contends that it was only against the abuse of haoma that Zoroaster inveighed. He insists that the prophet was probably disgusted by the drunkenness of the daēva-worshipers because it seemed to him a sacrilege against the plant-god Haoma, "the sacramental center of the cult."[33] He says, "There is nothing in the (Yasna) texts that forces us to conclude that Zoroaster condemned animal sacrifices and the haoma cult as such" and "all that Zoroaster seems to have condemned . . . is a form of animal sacrifice in which the sacrificial flesh was given to laity to consume and in which, perhaps,— to judge from the reference to the burning of the haoma—the sacrificial meat was sprinkled with the sacred fluid and then roasted."[34]

Zaehner recalls that, according to Yasna 3:2, haoma was pressed and offered to the righteous *fravashi* of Zoroaster and he concludes that if, indeed, the prophet had banned haoma, it would be incredible that anyone who claimed to be a true Zoroastrian would insult the prophet, within a generation or two after his death, by offering to his soul what Zoroaster himself had outlawed. He concludes, "So far as we can tell, the haoma rite has been the central liturgical

---

[27] Zaehner (*Zoroastrianism*, p. 37) regards the *karapan*'s as liturgical priests and the *kavi*'s as local rulers; Frye (*Heritage*, p. 36) thinks of the *kavi*'s as "some kind of 'priest-kings' of eastern Iran who upheld the ancient Aryan rites and practices" and the *karapan*'s, "mumblers," as another kind of priest. M. Haug (*Parsis*, pp. 289–91) identifies the *kavi*'s and *karapan*'s, in this context, with the daēva priests of the Brahmans of India (cft. Yasht 32:3, 48:10).

[28] Haug, *Parsis*, pp. 173, 291–92; cf. Yasna 12:2–3; E. B. N. Dhabhar, "The Hôm Yasht and 'The Bacchae' of Euripides: A Contrast," *Essays on Iranian Subjects* (Bombay, 1955), p. 25.

[29] Yasna 48:10 (J. Duchesne-Guillemin, *The Hymns of Zarathustra*, trans. Mrs. M. Henning [London, 1952], p. 39). Zaehner (*Zoroastrianism*, p. 38) translates the passage as "When wilt thou strike down this filthy drunkenness with which the priests evilly delude [the people] as do the wicked rulers of the provinces in [full] consciousness [of what they do]?"

[30] Herodotus i. 132, but compare vii. 43, where he declares that the Magi poured libations, at least to the Trojan Artāvans.

[31] Gershevitch, in *JNES* XXIII 16, n. 16, and 26, n. 43.

[32] *Ibid.*, pp. 21a, 26, n. 43; S. H. Taqizadeh, *Old Iranian Calendars* (London, 1938), pp. 13, 33.

[33] Zaehner, *Zoroastrianism*, p. 87. [34] *Ibid.*, pp. 85–86.

act of Zoroastrianism ever since the religion developed liturgical worship and the central position it enjoys has never at any time been disputed."[35]

It was inevitable that aversion to excessive drunkenness due to the cultic use of the intoxicant should bring reforms in both Indian and Iranian religions. In India, as the cult became more regulated, only the upper three castes were permitted to drink soma, and then only during religious ceremonies.[36] In Iran, in accord with Xenophon's observation that "the Persians consider the employment of professionals far more important in matters of religion than in any other sphere,"[37] the operation of the official cult was put fully into the hands of the Magian priests. In modern Parsi procedure, too, the extracting and mixing of haoma is done only by the priests and, as in India, except for some use for medicinal purposes, the haoma is consumed only by them.

Drastic revisions of the ancient religious rites occurred in Iran, but, because of later reversions and revisions of the cultus,[38] it is difficult to determine Zoroaster's part in the change. All that is certain is that both the Indians and the Iranians abandoned the primitive Aryan manner of preparing the sacred drink and that the Iranians invented a new procedure more in harmony with the spirit of their later religion. Because Zoroaster himself never mentions the reformed haoma ceremony in the Gathas, it seems doubtful whether it existed during his lifetime or if it did, whether he approved of it. But the haoma rite even today is central in the religious ceremonies of the Parsis.

The details of the modern Parsi ceremony, a mixture of ancient and relatively modern elements, are quite well known. The use of dry haoma twigs (*hôm sali*) is now in vogue. The "haoma" twigs are washed, purified, and stored in a special container for thirteen months and thirteen days, with periodic washings and purifications, before they are used in the haoma ceremony. Because of epithets used to describe the haoma twigs, Pavry contends that originally the fresh haoma plant (*haoma jâiri*) was used in the ceremony.[39] The plant then used was called *gaoman*, "full of juice/milk," *huiti*, "juicy," *zairi*, "green," and *uzadât*, "fermenting," as well as *hubaoidhi*, "fragrant," in the ancient records, according to Pavry.[40]

Today the haoma twigs are mixed with milk and the roots of the pomegranate or juice of the pomegranate fruit and are pounded together in the mortar.[41] The present ritual is long and tedious, with each action minutely prescribed and accompanied by a carefully synchronized recitation of the Haoma Yasht (Yasna 9–10) and pious formulae.[42]

The preliminary stage of the ceremony involves a careful purification of the officiating priests and of the implements and materials essential to the ritual. The necessary items are set forth, each in its prescribed place, near the priest who will operate the mortar and pestle. The proper hand to be used at each point in the ritual, the direction of movement during the pounding of the mortar, the number of times for the performance of each repetitive act, and the precise passage of the Haoma Yasht to accompany each action are all carefully prescribed.

---

[35] *Ibid.*

[36] E. W. Hopkins, "Soma," *Encyclopaedia of Religion and Ethics* XI (New York, 1921) 685–86.

Even in modern times in India great quantities of soma are consumed by the priests during the religious ceremonies. Modi (*Religious Ceremonies*, p. 297) indicates that at the *Jyotishṭoma* ceremony each of the Brahman priests must drink some soma and the chief priests, such as the *adhvaryu* and the *hotâ*, must drink a very large quantity.

[37] Xenophon *Cyropaedia* viii. 3, 2.

[38] Gershevitch (in *JNES* XXIII 12–32) has discussed the role of the Magians in the corruption of Zoroastrian religion from the time of Darius I to the Sassanian period through the re-introduction of diverse ancient ideas and practices.

[39] Pavry, *Iranian Studies*, pp. 165, 196.

[40] *Ibid.*, pp. 160, 196.   [41] *Ibid.*, p. 165.

[42] A detailed description of the modern Parsi ceremony is given by Modi, *Religious Ceremonies*, pp. 287–96, 306; cf. Haug, *Parsis*, pp. 394–403.

Sometimes a key word in the ritual is the cue for the beginning of the action and at other times the movement is synchronized with specific words recited during the action. Periodically the pounding of the twigs is interrupted for the pounding of the mortar itself in a set pattern. Such sonorous poundings are doubtless a primitive survival of an ancient practice once intended to frighten away lurking daēvas. The haoma ceremony is now and perhaps from quite ancient times has been associated with the sacred fire and the use of the sacred bundle of twigs.

Tradition persists that the assemblage for the haoma ceremony, now consisting of but two priests, once required eight participants[43] and in some manuscripts of the Vendidād a diagram is given showing their placement for the rite.[44] The members were arranged in a rectangular pattern oriented to the points of the compass in the ceremonial room (*Arvīs gāh*), with a priest at each end of the ceremonial space and three on each side.

The chief priest, who sat at the northern end of the space, was the *zaotar* (1),[45] corresponding to the *hotâ* of the Vedic ceremony, who recited the mantras of the Rig-Veda. The *zaotar* superintended the haoma rite and recited the religious texts that accompanied the ceremonial actions.

At his right hand, in the northwestern corner of the ceremonial space was the *hāvanān* (2), who operated the mortar and pestle in the pressing of the haoma juice. At the left hand of the *zaotar*, opposite the *hāvanān*, in the northeastern corner, was the *frabaretar* (4), who bore the *barsom* to the fire.[46]

To the right of the *hāvanān*, in the west, was the *asnātor* (6), who washed and cleaned the ceremonial implements.[47] Opposite him, in the east and at the left of the *frabaretar*, was the *raēθwiškara* (7), who mixed the haoma with the other ingredients. It is he who has survived, as the *rathwi* or *rāspī*, the modern acolyte of the chief priest in the Parsi ritual.[48]

In the south of the ceremonial space sat the *sraošāvareza* (8), corresponding to the *pratiprasthātā* of the Brahmans. He represented the angel Sroša in the ceremony and bore a sword to drive away the evil spirits. Pavry calls him "the Chastiser, who corrects mistakes."[49]

To the right of the *sraošāvareza*, at the southeastern corner of the ceremonial space, was the *aberetar* (5), whose duty was to transport the ceremonially prepared water (*zor*). Left of the *sraošāvareza*, in the southwestern corner, was the *ātarəvaxša* (3), corresponding to the *agnīdhra* of the Brahmans, who was in charge of the sacred fire.[50]

The modern minimal number of two participants in the ceremony, the principal priest

[43] Vendidād 5:57; Visparad 3:1; Nīrangistān 72 ff., 82; cf. C. P. Tiele, *Geschichte der Religion im Altertum*, trans. G. Gehrich, II (Gotha, 1903) 313.

[44] Haug, *Parsis*, pp. 332, n. 1, 395; cf. Pavry, *Iranian Studies*, pp. 221–24.

[45] The numbers in parentheses after the priestly titles here designate the relative rank of the eight priests according to the ancient valuation.

[46] *BAiW*, col. 985, *frabaretar*. D. D. Kapadia (*Glossary to the Pahlavi Vendidād* [Bombay, 1953], p. 491, *frabartār*) identifies him as "the carrier, i.e., the priest who brings to the Zaotar all the implements required in religious ceremonies." He designates the office as third rank, which conflicts with the valuation given by both Haug and Pavry, who designate the *ātarəvaxša* as third. It is presumably the *frabaretar* who holds the *barsom* in the Dāta-Mithra seal impression.

[47] The chart given by Pavry (*Iranian Studies*, p. 222) varies from Haug's description of the placement of the *asnātor*, *aberetar*, and *frabaretar* in the ceremonial space, but they agree on the rank of the priests.

[48] Pavry (*Iranian Studies*, p. 222) claims that this priest "arranged and placed the ceremonial implements." Such a general function must later have been the reason for assigning this title to the assistant priest of the modern ceremony, although his principal function seems to have been that of the *ātarəvaxša* (see p. 32 and note).

[49] Pavry, *Iranian Studies*, p. 222.

[50] *BAiW*, cols. 318–19, *Ātrə-vaxš/Ātra-vaxš*. This official appears to be the figure tending the fire in the Dāta-Mithra seal impression from Persepolis.

(*zaotar*) and his assistant (*rathwi* or *rāspī*),[51] can be traced back only to the ninth century A.D.,[52] but there is still a recognition of a "shadow company" of eight. During the ritual the officiating priest calls the roll of his seven assistants. His subordinate then leaves his post, assumes the different positions, one after another, and answers, "I am here" each time for himself and his six absent colleagues. Thus, the chief priest of earlier times (*zaotar*) has retained his demanding, specialized role today and the indispensable *ātarəvaxša*, under the old title of the *raēθwiškara*, has absorbed the identities and responsibilities of the other priests of earlier days.[53]

Perhaps the greatest change in the haoma ceremony since ancient times has been the substitution of other plants for the original haoma.[54] The Avesta indicates that the original home of the plant was especially Mount Elburz (Avestan *Hara Berezaiti*), whence it was spread by birds in all directions into the mountains and valleys of Iran. It is described as abundant, having branches and sprigs that are tender and bending, fragrant, juicy, of yellow or golden color, and beautiful in appearance.[55]

In India the Brahmans now use the stalks of the Pūtica plant for their soma,[56] and the Parsis in India, who believe that they are importing the original plant from Persia, now use the *Ephedra gerardiana* (Gnetaceae), which is found in Beluchistan, Afghanistan, Kashmir, and western Tibet. This plant meets many of the specifications of the Avestan description of the ancient haoma plant. It grows as a bush in an upright mass to a height of one or two feet and is leafless, consisting of jointed twigs and branches of somewhat yellowish color. When covered with flowers, the bush appears golden and it often bears the name *zairi-gaona*, "golden color." The juice pressed from its twigs, too, has a golden color, and it has an intoxicating and narcotic effect on the drinker.[57]

Although most modern scholars assume that the Ephedra was the ancient haoma plant, there have been many competing suggestions. Aitchison found that in Beluchistan the *Periploca aphylla* (Asclepiadaceae) was also called *hūm* (haoma).[58] Hopkins and Windischmann have suggested that it might be *Sarcostemma acidum* (Asclepiadaceae) or *S. viminalis*, which are called "soma" and produce a juice with an astringent, narcotic, and intoxicating effect.[59]

[51] E. Edwards, "Priest, Priesthood (Iranian)," *Encyclopaedia of Religion and Ethics* X (New York, 1919) 321*b*. For further discussion, see p. 32 and note.

[52] Tiele (*Geschichte der Religion im Altertum* II 313) agreed with Oldenberg that the reduction in numbers completes a cycle, that originally there must have been a single celebrant, that the number of participants was expanded through the distribution of functions, and that the number was again reduced by the reabsorbing of functions among a smaller number of priests.
The ritual vessel Aramaic texts seem to indicate that in Achaemenid times the number of participants was four.

[53] Pavry, *Iranian Studies*, p. 223; Haug, *Parsis*, p. 332, n. 1.

[54] G. K. Nariman (in Pavry, *Iranian Studies*, p. xvii) indicates that the colophon of the Fravardīn Yasht, written in Iran in 1721, claims that the Parsis in India were no longer in possession of the genuine haoma plant about a thousand years after their migration there.

[55] Modi, *Religious Ceremonies*, pp. 285–86; Pavry, *Iranian Studies*, pp. 160, 165, 196.

[56] Haug, *Parsis*, p. 281. Two plants are called Pūtica in India: *Basella rubra* (Basellaceae) is called Potaki or Pūtica in Sanskrit, while the *Morus acedosa* (Moraceae) is called Pūtica in Telugu; cf. R. N. Chopra, S. L. Naylor, and I. C. Chopra, *Glossary of Indian Medicinal Plants* (New Delhi, 1956), pp. 34*b*, 170*b*.

[57] I. E. Aitchison, "The Botany of the Afghan Delimitation Commission," *Transactions of the Linnean Society*, 1887, p. 112; Sir Aurel Stein, "On the Ephedra, the Hum Plant, and the Soma," *Bulletin of the School of Oriental Studies* VI (1931) 501–14; Chopra, Naylor, and Chopra, *Glossary of Indian Medicinal Plants*, p. 108*a*.

[58] Aitchison, in *Transactions of the Linnean Society*, 1887, p. 112; Chopra, Naylor, and Chopra, *Glossary of Indian Medicinal Plants*, p. 189*a*; Modi, *Religious Ceremonies*, p. 285, n. 1.

[59] Fr. Windischmann, "Ueber den soma Cultus der Arier," *Abhandlungen der Königlich bayerischen Akademie der Wissenschaften* (Philos.-hist. Kl.) IV, No. 2 (München, 1846), 129; Hopkins, in *Encyclopaedia of Religion and Ethics* XI 685*b*; Chopra, Naylor, and Chopra, *Glossary of Indian Medicinal Plants*, p. 222*a*.

Windischmann also recalled that Anquetil identified the *omōmi* mentioned by Plutarch[60] as the *amōmon* which, according to Theophrast and Dioscurides, was an Armenian and Medo-Persian shrub, similar to a grapevine, with a flower like Levkaje and fragrant, bitter-tasting, grape-formed seeds.[61]

It has been noted, too, that the Pahlavi Bundahišn claims that haoma was produced from the *gogard* or *gokern* tree (Avestan *gaōkere naēm*), which bears no fruit but has knotty branches like a grapevine and leaves like jasmine.[62] The plant *Salvia persepolitana*, which grows at Persepolis, has also been suspected of being the ancient haoma plant.[63]

The original plant was early confused with others which served as substitutes when the identity of the original plant was lost. In the Indian Sāma-Veda two kinds of soma, green and yellow, are distinguished but the latter is the more praised type.[64] The Sāma-Veda also mentions a "white" soma[65] and in a later Indian medical treatise as many as twenty-four varieties of soma are listed.[66]

Some, believing that the haoma was used to induce psychic effects resulting in visions and religious ecstasy, have identified the ancient haoma plant with the narcotic *hašīš*, "hemp" (Persian *bangha*, modern Persian *bang*).[67] But Herzfeld contended, "Nothing is known of the use of hemp (*bhang*) as a narcotic prior to the Arsacid period . . . . the use of *hašīš* in Zoroaster's time is an imagination. The mysterious haoma is wine, a reality."[68]

Zaehner notes that the original haoma gave way to wine in western Iran, where the genuine plant was not available.[69] And Cumont indicates that wine was used in the "haoma" ceremony of Mithraism in Europe.[70] Also in the Mithraic cult in the West, where "haoma" was unknown, a species of wild garlic or rue that had a soporific effect was sometimes used as a substitute.[71]

Professor W. Geiger and Sir Aurel Stein have claimed that the ancient haoma plant was simply a wild rhubarb, which grows plentifully in the Persian mountains and satisfies many

---

[60] See p. 8.

[61] Windischmann, in *Abhandlungen der Königlich bayerischen Akademie der Wissenschaften* IV 131; C. Lassen, *Indische Alterthumskunde* (Bonn, 1847) I 281.

[62] Windischmann, in *Abhandlungen der Königlich bayerischen Akademie der Wissenschaften* IV 131.

[63] E. Herzfeld, *Zoroaster and His World* (Princeton, 1947) II 543.

[64] Windischmann, in *Abhandlungen der Königlich bayerischen Akademie der Wissenschaften* IV 130.

[65] *Ibid.*, p. 139; Hopkins, in *Encyclopaedia of Religion and Ethics* XI 685b; Zaehner (*Zoroastrianism*, p. 90) notes that according to the Dātastān-i-Dēnīk, an eschatalogical work of the ninth century A.D., "white" haoma is to be prepared from the fat of the last sacrificial victim, the bull Hadhayans.

[66] Hopkins, in *Encyclopaedia of Religion and Ethics* XI 686a.

[67] A. H. Godbey, "Incense and Poison Ordeals in the Ancient Orient," *AJSL* XLVI (1930) 221; Nyberg, *Religionen*, pp. 177 ff.; compare the contrary view of W. B. Henning, *Zoroaster—Politician or Witch-Doctor?* (London, 1951), pp. 31–34.

[68] Herzfeld, *Zoroaster and His World* II 553. Professor E. Porada has informed me that Herzfeld later abandoned this view.

Pavry (*Iranian Studies*, pp. 162, 165) identifies haoma with a drink called *noshdāru* and claims that another drink, *shāhdāru*, which was obtained from the fermentation of the juice of overripe grapes, was identified with the *noshdāru* of earlier days because their properties were similar.

[69] Zaehner, *Zoroastrianism*, p. 160. Old Persian *bātu*, "wine," is now attested in the compound *bātu-gara*, "wine cup," found on a silver bowl of the time of Artaxerxes I (Kent, *Old Persian*, p. 153, AI, p. 199, *bātugara*). Eilers suggests that the word may appear in the names *Bʾtrt* (No. 98:3) and *Pwrbt* (No. 60:2) in the ritual vessels as well as in the description of a pestle as "a pestle of wine" (No. 29:4) in the sense of "a pestle used for making wine."

[70] Franz Cumont, *Textes et monuments figurés relatifs aux mystères de Mithra* I (Brussels, 1896) 320; *The Mysteries of Mithra*, trans. Thomas J. McCormack (2d ed.; New York, 1956), p. 158.

[71] The Magians in Cappadocia substituted παγάνον ἄγριον, "wild garlic"; Cumont, *Textes et monuments* I 147.

of the specifications of haoma as described in the Avesta.[72] This identification recently has found a number of proponents and is argued with vigor most recently by Hummel.[73]

As a result of experiments, Gordon Wasson has concluded that the original haoma was a species of mushroom fungus which shows considerable potency as an intoxicant when crushed and mixed with water.[74]

Thus, the identity of the original haoma plant is uncertain, and among modern scholars there are widely divergent views regarding it. The product now consumed in the Parsi ceremony certainly differs greatly from the haoma liquid of antiquity. Its potency is greatly reduced, and its effectiveness as an intoxicant has been eliminated. Only a few twigs of a plant are now used in the preparation of haoma, and the juice resulting, greatly diluted by other ingredients, is drunk immediately after mixing, without time for fermentation. Nyberg claims that "haoma," ritually prepared according to the prescription of the later Avesta, contains nothing more than water and pomegranate. In the praxis of the Parsis it is always unfermented plant juice and not an intoxicating drink.[75] In modern times a new-born child is given a token drink of molasses or sugar water instead of the intoxicating haoma used in ancient times.[76]

Details of the modern haoma ceremony are well known, but it is difficult to probe behind it to the earlier forms of the rite. It is entirely probable that, as a result of what was believed to be Zoroaster's teaching, the use of haoma was curbed or possibly even banned, but it was never lost entirely. The use of haoma was a very ancient one with a firm hold on the masses of the people, and they have continued even into modern times to use the substance privately for a variety of purposes. Aitchison reported that "among the Pathans of the Khyber Pass and all over that country, twigs of Ephedra, which are called 'haoma' are made into a decoction with water and used very largely as a household remedy in sickness. It is considered to possess healing and health-promoting properties, as was attributed to the ancient haoma. Moreover, throughout the mountains where Ephedra is found, the ashes of its burned twigs are mixed with snuff 'to make it more irritating.' "[77] People have been reluctant to surrender the precious substance which has long been believed to promote health and promise immortality.

It is now certain that haoma was used in Persepolis in Achaemenid times, at least from the time of Xerxes. The name Haoma-dāta, which has long been known from the Aramaic papyri of the time of Artaxerxes I, is now found also in the ritual texts from Persepolis.[78] Cameron believes that the title of the haoma-mixer (*raēθwiškara*) is found in an Elamite Treasury text of the second year of Xerxes.[79] The seal impressions on labels in the Persepolis Treasury in the time of Xerxes portray a scene from the haoma ceremony[80] and a relatively large number of green stone ritual vessels such as are depicted on the seal impressions attest a rather extensive use of the rite at Persepolis in the days of Xerxes and Artaxerxes I.

It is clear that older forms of religious practice sometimes were re-introduced or persisted clandestinely among the people in Achaemenid times. There is abundant proof of the survival in later Mithraic ritual of the primitive conceptions and practices such as Zoroaster may have

[72] Stein, in *Bulletin of the School of Oriental Studies* VI 511 ff.

[73] K. Hummel, "Aus welcher Pflanzen stellen die arischen Inder den Somatrank her?" *Mitteilungen der Deutschen pharmazeutischen Gesellschaft und der pharmazeutischen Gesellschaft der DDR* (28th year) IV (1959) 57–61; Zaehner, *Zoroastrianism*, p. 88.

[74] R. Gordon Wasson, "Fly Agaric (*Amanita muscaria*)," *Time*, Feb. 10, 1967, p. 85.

[75] Nyberg, *Religionen*, p. 287.

[76] Modi, in *Journal of the Anthropological Society of Bombay* XII 576; cf. p. 7 above.

[77] Modi, *Religious Ceremonies*, p. 285, n. 1; Pavry, *Iranian Studies*, pp. 196–97.

[78] Nos. 14:2, 15:3; Cowley, *AP*, Nos. 8:2 (460 B.C.) and 9:2.

[79] Cameron, *PTT*, pp. 5–6, 101, No. 11.   [80] See Pl. 1.

tried to eradicate or modify. Ghirshman suggests that it may be necessary to distinguish between the official religion and that of the people.[81] Certainly, there was no single religion in Achaemenid times. Cameron regards the court religion of the Achaemenid kings as "a fourth Iranian religion existing at the side of Magism, Mithraism, and Zoroastrianism, independent of all, yet sharer in all." He says, "And in the worship carried out at the court, the cult of haoma, originally a feature of the Mithra community, together with the libation-pourers of the Magian priesthood and the sacred fire, played a full and prominent part."[82]

Because many of those who presented the ritual vessels at the Treasury in Persepolis and in all probability had used them in the haoma ceremony are identified as high military officers, chiliarchs and myriarchs, it seems likely that the haoma ceremony in which the mortars and pestles were used was a Mithraic celebration held by and for the army.

When Mithraism later spread widely in the West, it was propagated principally by the army. Cumont has described later Mithraism as "a branch torn from the ancient trunk" which "has preserved in many respects the characteristics of the ancient worship of the Iranian tribes."[83] The later Mithraic rites also included the preparation and drinking of an intoxicant by the initiates.[84] Cumont declares, "In the Mazdean service, the celebrant consecrated the bread and the water which he mingled with the intoxicating juice of the haoma prepared by him, and he consumed these foods during the performance of his sacrifice. These ancient usages were preserved in the Mithraic initiations, save that for the Haoma, a plant unknown in the Occident, was substituted the juice of the vine."[85]

In the light of all facts at our disposal, it seems likely that in the green stone ritual vessels bearing Aramaic texts from Persepolis, we see evidence that already in Achaemenid times a proto-Mithraic cult was actively operative in the Persian army.

---

[81] R. Ghirshman, *Iran* (Harmondsworth, 1954), p. 155.

[82] Cameron, *PTT*, p. 9a.   [83] Cumont, *Mysteries of Mithra*, p. vi.

[84] A conical mortar of grey sandstone was found in the Mithraeum at Stockstadt, Germany; M. J. Vermaseren, *Corpus Inscriptionum et Monumentorum Religionis Mithriacae* II (The Hague, 1960) 94, No. 1203.

[85] Cumont, *Mysteries of Mithra*, p. 158, and *Textes et monuments* I 146–47, 196–97, 320–21.

III

THE ARAMAIC TEXTS

THE texts inscribed on the green stone ritual objects from the Persepolis Treasury are written in the Aramaic alphabet and language.[1] Although all such objects were probably used for ritual purposes, not all of them are inscribed. Texts on the mortars, plates, and the tray are written on the bottom of the base of the vessel, where there is room for a full or even an expanded text. Those on the pestles are usually found atop the head of the object, but a few writers gained more room by putting the inscription along the shaft of the pestle.[2]

It is not surprising to find Aramaic used in ancient Persia, for there was long preparation for it. By late Assyrian times, Aramaic was already firmly established as an important language of the Near East, where it was used especially in the western areas of the Assyrian empire. But it had a strong hold, too, in Assyria and Babylonia proper, where its use extended into the very palaces of the Assyrian kings. It was not a language imposed on others by a conquering people. In fact, most of the Aramaic that survives was written by non-Aramaean people, many of whom were not even Semitic. It won its way and status as an adaptable and useful tool. In a world using largely a rather complicated cuneiform system of writing (for example, Akkadian, Elamite, Old Persian) which had to be impressed, etched, scratched, or cut into durable materials, a simple alphabet which could not only be scratched or cut into hard surfaces but could also be painted or written in ink upon them or even upon such perishable media as papyrus, leather, or birch bark had much to commend its use. Aramaic was a vigorous competitor. In its wide acceptance in the ancient world it became a language of diplomacy and commerce in the Assyrian and Neo-Babylonian empires.[3]

It was under the Persians that Aramaic reached its zenith as a world language. Its extended employment then was based on the broad foundation of usage already established in the Assyro-Babylonian age. As a means of writing, Aramaic was carried wherever the influence of Persia went. From Abydos on the Hellespont to the most remote frontier of Egypt, Aramaic has been found. There is witness of it from the Caucasus Mountains in the north to the midst of the Syrian Desert and eastward through Kurdistan and the Zagros district to Afghanistan and India.[4]

Achaemenid Persian writings are best known from monumental texts written in the Old Persian alphabet and language, but Nicholas of Damascus, Ctesias, Diodorus Siculus, and others agree that parchment was used for ordinary writing purposes in Persia.[5] A fragment of

---

[1] On the basis of a few linguistic phenomena, the question has been raised whether these texts are in heterographic writing, to be read as Persian. This is a constant and perplexing problem in the field of Persian Aramaic, wherein the number of Persian loanwords gradually increases with time and there is sometimes evidence of Persian syntax.

According to the usual view of Iranologists, the early, Achaemenid date of these texts would argue against a theory of heterographic writing and, although there are Persian loanwords, some evidence of Persian syntax, and even a few troublesome verb forms (see pp. 65–66), the texts can be read rather smoothly as Aramaic.

[2] Nos. 17, 81, 123. [3] R. A. Bowman, "Aramaeans, Aramaic, and the Bible," *JNES* VII (1948) 65–76.

[4] *Ibid.*, pp. 76–84.

[5] R. P. Dougherty, "Writing upon Parchment and Papyrus among the Babylonians and the Assyrians," *Journal of the American Oriental Society* XLVIII (1928) 133 ff.; J. H. Breasted, "The Physical Processes of Writing in the Early Orient and Their Relation to the Origin of the Alphabet," *AJSL* XXXIII (1915) 230–49.

such parchment, inscribed in Aramaic, was found among the Aramaic papyri of Egypt from Achaemenid times.[6] A number of Aramaic letters, dating from the same period, written on parchment and still inclosed in a leather pouch, were also discovered in Egypt. They had been written by the Persian Prince Arsames, the Egyptian satrap, to officials attending his estates in Egypt.[7] In the collection, which was apparently a relic of the famous Persian post, was a document that itself well attests the wide use of Aramaic by Achaemenid Persian officials. It is an Aramaic passport, addressed to Persian authorities at way-stations along the northern route from the East to Cilicia and Egypt, directing the granting of hospitality and rations to its bearers on the way.[8]

An Aramaic journal page, by the placement of its dates, may reflect an early paged book in Achaemenid Egypt.[9] But there certainly were scrolls in that language. Diodorus reports that Ctesias of Cnidus, who served as a physician in the court of Artaxerxes II, saw royal annals there which reported the important events of each year. He claims to have studied and used them in writing his history for the Greeks.[10] The Bible, too, mentions such a "Book of Remembrances" (Ezra 4:15), from which a quotation is made in the Aramaic language.

Later tradition indicates an early interest in libraries in Persia. Pahlavi treatises claim that two great libraries were established there, at Samarkand and Persepolis,[11] and Aulus Gellius indicates that the first "public library," that of Peisistratos of Athens, was taken to Persia by Xerxes and later was returned by Seleucus Nikator.[12]

The witness of the importance of Aramaic in Persia is found in the Persian language itself. The Aramaic alphabet appears to be one of the factors involved in the creation of the Old Persian cuneiform alphabet and Kent declares that Old Persian, "which had no developed literary style at the time of the inscriptions," reflects the written style of Aramaic.[13] It was the widespread use of Aramaic, too, that contributed to the early decay and disappearance of the Old Persian language. Gershevitch notes, "the scribes . . . lost familiarity with the letters and spelling conventions of the Old Persian cuneiform script and could not be expected to do more than to slightly adapt existing patterns to new needs. Even within these limits the scribes were apt to fall back on Aramaic spelling conventions."[14]

A curious spelling error in the cuneiform inscriptions of Darius I and Xerxes near Hamadan led Herzfeld to conjecture that the original text used by the scribes had been written in Aramaic characters in which the sign for both the Old Persian u and v would be expressed by the same Semitic sign *waw*.[15] Gershevitch suggests that it was because of the dominance of Aramaic in Persia that no Achaemenian king later than Xerxes insisted on having his own words inscribed.[16]

[6] E. Sachau, *Aramäische Papyrus und Ostraka* (Leipzig, 1911), pp. xxviii–xxix.

[7] G. R. Driver, *Aramaic Documents of the Fifth Century B.C.* (Oxford, 1954).

[8] *Ibid.*, No. VI, pp. 20–23, Pl. VIII.

[9] R. A. Bowman, "An Aramaic Journal Page," *AJSL* LVIII (1941) 302–13; cf. C. C. McCown, "Codex and Roll in the New Testament," *Harvard Theological Review* XXXIV (1941) 249.

[10] Diodorus Siculus ii. 32, 4 and cf. xvii. 39, 4.

[11] J. J. Modi, "The Cities of Iran as Described in the Old Pahlavi Treatise of Shatroiha-i-Irān," *JRAS* (Bombay Branch) XX (1902) 160–63; Ṭabarī, *Chronique de Abou Djafar-Moḥammed-ben-Djarir-ben-Yezid Ṭabarī*, ed. H. Zotenburg (Paris, 1867) I 675; Maṣʿūdī (*Les prairies d'or*, ed. C. Barbier de Meynard and Pavet de Courteille, II [Paris, 1863] 123–25) also mentions a "Stronghold of Records" (*dazhu-i-napisht*) at Persepolis and Modi (in *JRAS* [Bombay Branch] XX 161) mentions records in the Treasury of the Vaharan fire temple in Samarkand.

[12] Aulus Gellius *Noctes Atticae* vii. 17.

[13] Kent, *Old Persian*, p. 9b, Sec. 12.

[14] Gershevitch, "Zoroaster's Own Contribution," *JNES* XXIII (1964) 20.

[15] E. E. Herzfeld, *Archeological History of Iran* (London, 1935), p. 48; Gershevitch, in *JNES* XXIII 33–34.

[16] Gershevitch, in *JNES* XXIII 20.

A much mutilated inscription is written in Aramaic letters on the tomb of Darius I at Naqsh-i Rustam, but it is almost certainly an addition from a later age. Since the only words that are legible are Iranian, the text is probably in Persian language written in the Aramaic alphabet.[17] Such writing is characteristic of Middle Persian, Pahlavi, which is truly the best evidence of the extent and importance of Aramaic in the earlier period. Persian loanwords are found interspersed in Aramaic texts throughout the Persian period and later; but in Pahlavi common words are spelled as in Aramaic but are regarded as logograms which, when read, are to be pronounced and understood by their Persian equivalents. At times added letters, which distort the Aramaic spelling, give a phonetic clue to the proper identification of their Persian counterparts.[18]

The question of when the system of writing Aramaic with Iranian loanwords changed to one of Iranian written in Aramaic letters with Aramaic ideograms is difficult to determine since it was a gradual development. Haug has asserted that Pahlavi "exhibits a large admixture of Semitic words, which increase as we trace it further back, so that the earliest inscriptions of the Sassanian dynasty may be described as being written in a Semitic language, with some admixture of Iranian words and a prevailingly Iranian construction."[19] Frye has suggested that the transition was made in the farther East (for example, Afghanistan) by about 200 B.C. and in the West (for example, Parthia) in the first century B.C.[20]

Persian texts on leather, papyrus, and other perishable media from the early period have not survived in Persia because of its unfavorable climate.[21] Only that written on durable materials remains. In the storeroom of the Treasury which held the archives of the local administration at Persepolis (Room 33) the final conflagration that destroyed the building was particularly furious, scorching and discoloring the plaster, burning the floor, and baking the mudbrick walls to a considerable depth.[22] The only records recovered from the archive room were clay tablets written in cuneiform Elamite. But with them were found a large number of spheroid lumps of clay or bitumen, each with an oval or rectangular perforation. Such tubes, like napkin rings, could have held rolls of parchment or papyrus. Impressions of strings mark the inner walls and there was sometimes found within them remains of carbonized or decayed material.[23] The parchment or papyrus that they may have contained would have contributed mightily to the intense fire that destroyed the archive room.

Cameron has conjectured that each Elamite tablet in the Treasury was attached to a clay sealing which encircled a parchment or papyrus roll inscribed in the Aramaic language and script, an Aramaic counterpart of the Elamite tablet. He further suggests that every Persian order was translated into Aramaic, "the official language," before its translation into Elamite.[24] He concludes that "over a large part of the empire Aramaic was the language of the government offices (the chancellory) and of communication between master and subject."[25]

---

[17] E. E. Herzfeld, "Reisebericht," *ZDMG* LXXX (1926) 244 ff.; also *Altpersischen Inschriften* (Berlin, 1938), pp. 11–12; Cameron, *PTT*, p. 29; W. B. Henning, "Mitteliranisch," *Handbuch der Orientalistik*, ed. B. Spuler and H. Kees, IV: *Iranistik* (Leiden, 1958), Pt. 1, p. 24.

[18] F. Miller, "Die semitischen Elemente der Pahlawi-Sprache," *Sitzungsberichte der Kaiserliche Akademie der Wissenschaften in Wien* (Philos.-hist. Kl.), CXXXVI, No. 10 (1897), 1–12; F. Rosenthal, *Die aramäistische Forschung* (Leiden, 1939), pp. 72–82; Cameron, *PTT*, pp. 29–30; Henning, in *Handbuch der Orientalistik* IV, Pt. 1, pp. 31 ff.

[19] Haug, *Parsis*, p. 81.   [20] Frye, *Heritage*, pp. 142–43.

[21] But parchments presumably written in Persia have been preserved under more favorable conditions in Egypt; see nn. 6 and 7 above.

[22] Schmidt, *Persepolis* I 173, Fig. 77c; also *The Treasury of Persepolis* ("Oriental Institute Communications," No. 21 [Chicago, 1939]), pp. 27–31, 33 ff.

[23] Cameron, *PTT*, p. 27a.

[24] *Ibid.*, pp. 18, 20, 23.   [25] *Ibid.*, p. 30b.

But actual Aramaic texts written on lasting material were also found at Persepolis. Along with a large number of Elamite tablets found in a storeroom in the Persepolis fortification, there was a number of brief Aramaic texts, incised or written in ink or both, on small clay tablets.[26] There were also Aramaic "dockets," brief abstracts, written on some of the Elamite tablets from the reign of Darius I. References to "skins" and "pens" as rationed items, presumably for scribes, indicate that such media were used in Persia for the writing of Aramaic. Achaemenid seal impressions, some with Aramaic legends, were impressed on both the Elamite and Aramaic tablets. Among the important finds at Persepolis was also a "votive cylinder" bearing four or five lines of Aramaic in addition to a cuneiform text.[27]

Perhaps the most important Aramaic texts from Persepolis are those on the green stone ritual objects here being published. The Aramaic texts they bear all follow a general formula which could be expanded or contracted, usually according to the space available for the writing. With space severely restricted by the small diameter of the pestle heads, parts of the expected formulae were frequently omitted and the resulting text, on some occasions, was reduced to but a few pregnant token words.[28]

Where space was available and the scribe was so inclined, the normal text was expanded to include detail about the size of the object, the character of its stone, its cost or value, or information about the donor or the officers mentioned with him.

In accord with the interpretation of the texts being proposed in this volume the standard text can be read as follows:

In the . . . (ceremony?) . . . of the fortress, beside (*W*) the *segan*, (*X*) used this (object) beside (*Y*) the treasurer (and) opposite (*Z*) the sub-treasurer. *ʾškr* of year (date).[29]

Thus, in the full texts the sequence of essential items is (*a*) a reference to the haoma ceremony or to the place in the fortress in which it was held; (*b*) the name and the title of the *segan*, who was located beside the celebrant during the ceremony; (*c*) the name of the celebrant who used the mortar and pestle and presented them to the Treasury; (*d*) the verb indicating the action of the celebrant in crushing the haoma plant; (*e*) the name of the object being dedicated, which the celebrant had used; (*f*) the names of the treasurer and the sub-treasurer and where they were placed, with relation to the celebrant, during the ceremony; (*g*) the problematic word *ʾškr*; and, finally, (*h*) the year date.

In the pages that follow, the sections of the formula of the Aramaic texts will be treated in the order of their occurrence in the standard formula, except for that of the treasurers (*f*) which will be considered together with the *segan* (*b*).

[26] E. Herzfeld, "Recent Discoveries at Persepolis," *JRAS*, 1934, pp. 226–32; Cameron, *PTT*, p. 23. These will be published by the writer as "Aramaic Tablets from Persepolis."

[27] Schmidt, *Persepolis* II 59, Pl. 25:9 (PT4 99 and PT4 328).

[28] See Nos. 54, 127, 137.

[29] In this translation, aside from the word "and," which is supplied, the variables are placed in parentheses.

IV

THE PLACE

WHEREVER the beginning of the Aramaic text is preserved on the ritual vessels, all but the most abbreviated texts written on pestle heads[1] have *byrtᵓ*, "fortress," as the second word. It is, of course, the Aramaized Akkadian word *bîrtu*, already known from Biblical Aramaic as *birᵉtāᵓ*[2] and from the Aramaic papyri, where it occurs usually as *byrtᵓ*[3] but sometimes as *brtᵓ*.[4]

In a few instances (Nos. 4, 46) the word is written *byrt*, without the final *ᵓaleph* of the determinate state. While that might reflect the syntax of the Persian language, which has no article, at least one such omission is more likely due to the lack of sufficient space on the small pestle head, where the missing letter would be the final letter of the first line. Once (No. 12) the spelling seems to be *byrtm*, but in that text the letter *ᵓaleph* has a peculiar form in other words,[5] and it is probable that despite its appearance the spelling was intended to be the usual *byrtᵓ*. So, too, in a single text (No. 77) where the word seems to be *byrtn*, the final letter, if not an error, must have been intended as an *ᵓaleph*.[6]

Altheim saw in the *byrtᵓ* of these texts a translation of Old Persian **staxra*, "strong," "firm,"[7] but it is clear from the parallels between the Old Persian and the Akkadian and Aramaic texts of the Behistun Inscription that in the Achaemenid period *byrtᵓ* represented Old Persian *didā*, "wall," "stronghold," "fortress."

Normally one expects to find the name of a fortified city before the word *byrtᵓ*. Thus, Altheim misread the word *srk*, which often appears before it, as *prs*, "Parsa," "Persepolis."[8] Despite the error, it seems natural to identify "the fortress" of the ritual vessels with Persepolis, the ritual city,[9] where the objects were found.

The words that appear before the noun *byrtᵓ* in the ritual texts, in the order of frequency of occurrence, are *srk*, *prkn*, and *hst*. There are no known fortresses with such names and none occurs in the Elamite or Aramaic tablets from Persepolis. Because of a reference to Arachosia

---

[1] In a few severely reduced texts (e.g., Nos. 69 and 127) there is no reference to place. Others have simply *bsrk* (Nos. 68, 137), *bsrwk* (No. 54), or *bprkn* (No. 133).

[2] Ezra 6:2. Altheim (Altheim and Stiehl, *Aramäische Sprache* I 17, n. 62) needlessly insists on the Tiberian Biblical vocalization of the word in the Persian period.

[3] Cowley, *AP*, p. 279 (glossary); E. G. Kraeling, *The Brooklyn Museum Aramaic Papyri* (New Haven, 1953), p. 309 (glossary).

[4] Such spelling is usual in the Aramaic copy of the Behistun Inscription (Cowley, *AP*, pp. 251–54), but it is also found in a few papyri (*ibid.*, No. 35:2; Kraeling, *The Brooklyn Museum Aramaic Papyri*, p. 309b, *byrtᵓ*).

[5] *sgnᵓ* (l. 2); *gnzbrᵓ* (l. 3).

[6] Much less likely is the possibility that the word is hybrid, with the Persian affix *-ana*, often used with Persian words to designate a place; cf. Meillet and Benveniste, *Grammaire*, pp. 154–55, Sec. 265.

[7] Altheim and Stiehl, *Aramäische Sprache* I 18.

[8] *Ibid.* His error depends on a single text (No. 39) published by Schmidt (*Persepolis* II, Pl. 23:3). But the word *srk* occurs with such frequency and clarity that there is no question of its spelling.

[9] A. U. Pope, "Persepolis as a Ritual City," *Archeology* X (1957) 123–30.

in these texts,[10] Cameron has suggested that *srk*, *prkn*, and *hst* are perhaps fortresses lying east of Persepolis, probably in Arachosia. He thus assumes that the vessels were brought to Persepolis from remote places by visitors attending the New Year's Festival or by men just passing through who wanted the "ritual capital" to have a memorial of their presence there.

The word *srk* or *srwk*, if a geographical name, might suggest the rather remote Sirōk (Σιρωκ) mentioned by Isidore of Charax,[11] the Sirakene (Σιρακηνή) of Ptolemy,[12] which was later known as Saraḫs (سرخس) and Serkas (سرکۍ).[13] It lay quite far from Persepolis, in Khorasān, midway between Nishapur and Merv, near the ancient Tus, the former capital of Khorasān.[14] The site, rather extensive in later times, was one of the most celebrated fortresses of Khorasān.

It has been suggested that the word *prkn* might represent the Parikani mentioned by Herodotus, a people that he associates with both the Maka and the Yautiyā, who dwelt in Arachosia and Seistan[15] and with the Orthocorybantis of the Median satrapy in the lands east of the Caspian Sea.[16] Because Darius I located the Yautiyā in Parsa,[17] Junge would locate the Parikani in Kerman, in the east of Persis.[18]

But the Parikani are a people and not a fortress, even though their name may be preserved in the city Parikani in Persis, mentioned by Hecataeus (παρικάνη πόλις περσική).[19] Despite the similarity of consonantal structure, it does not seem possible that either the Parikani people or the remote city of Sirōk have anything to do with the *prkn* and *srk/srwk* of the ritual vessels. Nor has it been possible yet to link the word *hst* with any known fortress in Persia.

Although it is tempting, in the interest of consistency, to find the names of scattered fortresses in the words *srk*, *prkn*, and *hst*, there are some important considerations that advise caution. The sites suggested were all a considerable distance from Persepolis, where the relatively large number of vessels was found. Furthermore, the remarkable homogeneity in these ritual objects suggests a place of common origin: All are made of the same green chert material; all have the same pattern and workmanship; all are inscribed in ink, in the same places, in the same language, and with essentially the same formula; all have the same continuing staff of officials, so uniform that they can be used for a close dating of the texts.[20] Moreover, all of the inscribed ritual vessels were found together in the Treasury of the "ritual capital," Persepolis, most of them within the same room.

It seems extremely unlikely that such remarkable uniformity would be found in vessels processed independently in scattered fortresses in the remote East and that such a large number of them, some of considerable bulk and weight, would find their way fortuitously to a common storeroom in the Treasury of the reputed ritual capital of the Persian empire. Furthermore, while it would not be surprising to find high military officials, chiliarchs and myriarchs,

---

[10] See pp. 28–30.

[11] W. H. Schoff, *Parthian Stations by Isadore of Charax* (Philadelphia, 1914), pp. 8–9, Sec. 12; J. Rennell, *The Geographical System of Herodotus* (London, 1830) I 390–91.

[12] Ptolemy *Geography* vi, ix. 5.

[13] C. Barbier de Meynard, *Dictionnaire géographique, historique, et littéraire de la Perse et des contrées adjacentes* (Paris, 1861), pp. 307–8, 311, 635.

[14] F. Wüstenfeld, *Jacut's Geographisches Wörterbuch* III (Leipzig, 1868) 71–72, 82; Shāhnāme 566.

[15] Herodotus iii. 94, vii. 68; Frye, *Heritage*, pp. 49–50.

[16] Herodotus vii. 86. [17] Behistun Inscription, Sec. 40.

[18] P. J. Junge, "Parikanioi," in Pauly-Wissowa, *Real-Encyclopädie der classischen Altertumswissenschaft* XXXVI, 3 (Waldsee [Württ.], 1949) 1482.

[19] K. Müller, *Fragmenta Historicum Graecorum* (Paris, 1848) II, Frag. 180.

[20] Three texts (Nos. 36, 119, and 120) which have unique *segan*'s and sub-treasurers may be apparent rather than real exceptions since they also have Baga-pāta as the treasurer.

at Persepolis, it is improbable that more than a dozen of them would be found in three minor, hitherto unknown "fortresses" in the East.

It is probable that the word *byrt*ᵓ in the ritual vessels does refer to Persepolis. It seems likely, too, that the haoma ritual was performed in or near the ritual capital, perhaps in connection with the New Year's Festival, during which, according to al-Bīrūnī,[21] the third session was for the warriors, or during the other great festival dedicated to Mithra, the later *Mihrajān*.[22]

The words *srk*, *prkn*, and *hst* must have a meaning other than geographical. Admittedly a geographical name usually precedes *byrt*ᵓ, but another construction is also possible in Aramaic. The words *srk*, *prkn*, and *hst* could stand in construct relationship with "the fortress," referring either to the haoma rite itself or to some place at Persepolis where the haoma twigs were pressed in the mortars.

While it is conceivable that the word *prkn* might represent the Iranian *paragnah*, the term used to describe the part of the haoma ceremony during which the liquid is extracted from the twigs, prior to the drinking ceremony,[23] the rendering of the Persian phoneme *g* by the Aramaic *k* would be unusual and unlikely in the Aramaic of Persepolis. Some other explanation is preferable.

It is probable that the word *prkn* is Semitic and related to other words found in diverse circumstances in the ritual texts but all related to the Semitic root *prk*, meaning in Aramaic, "to rub," "to pulverize," or "to grind"—the very actions involved in the use of a mortar and pestle.[24] A word *pyrk* is sometimes used to indicate the "crushing" function of the pestle[25] and a substantive *prk* is found (No. 5) in a context in which it seems to indicate a ceremony of crushing haoma[26] or a place in which such an operation was performed.

Since the word *prkn* is not found elsewhere in Aramaic, its vocalization is still a matter of conjecture. As a purely Aramaic word the final *-n* might be expected to indicate the Aramaic affix *-ân* for an abstract substantive or one of adjectival character. It could thus be an expression for the act of crushing and might be rendered as "the (haoma-)crushing ceremony," as is done here in the translations of these texts.[27]

The word *srk*, which occurs before *byrt*ᵓ with the greatest frequency in these ritual texts, has been extremely perplexing. Although usually spelled *srk*, a single example (No. 54:1) has *srwk*, which seems to indicate that the letter *w* represents a vowel rather than a consonant.

A possible clue to its meaning may be found in a word spelled similarly and also used in a religio-military context in the so-called War Scroll from the Jewish community at Qumran.[28] Because Yadin relates the word to the Jewish word *sérek*, "habit," "custom," from a root meaning "to cling," "to hold fast," "to adhere,"[29] he renders the word as *sérekh*. He ignores the one instance (col. v, l. 5) in which the word was spelled *srwk*, which would agree with the single variant in a Persepolis ritual text.[30]

---

[21] Al-Bīrūnī, *Chronology of Ancient Nations*, trans. E. Sachau (London, 1879), pp. 203 ff.; D. F. Karaka, *History of the Parsis* I (London, 1884) 145 f.

[22] Al-Bīrūnī, *Chronology of Ancient Nations*, pp. 207–9; Masʿūdī, *Les prairies d'or*, ed. C. Barbier de Meynard and Pavet de Courteille, III (Paris, 1864) 404.

[23] Modi, *Religious Ceremonies*, pp. 288, 294; Haug, *Parsis*, pp. 394, 403.

[24] Jastrow, *Dictionary* II 1228–29; in late Hebrew, too, the *Piʿel* stem means "to crush," "to grind," "to crack," "to crumble."

[25] Nos. 9:3, 13:3, 14:3, 17:5.

[26] Such *prk* seems parallel in meaning to another text (No. 112:5) where the word used is עיד, "festival."

[27] Less likely is the possibility that *prkn* is a hybrid with the Persian affix *-ana* denoting place (cf. Meillet and Benveniste, *Grammaire*, pp. 154–55, Sec. 265), to indicate the ceremonial space (*Arvīs-gāh* or *Dar-i-Meher*) wherein the ritual objects were used. Zaehner (*Zoroastrianism*, Fig. 42) presents a picture of such a Parsi room in Bombay.

[28] Yadin, *Scroll*.   [29] Jastrow, *Dictionary* II 1027–28.

[30] No. 54:1. In the Qumran text the word was later altered to *sdwr* (*siddûr*) meaning "order," "arrangement"; cf. Yadin, *Scroll*, p. 144.

The term *srk* as used in Qumran is somewhat complex in meaning and difficult to define. Yadin finds it in two related senses which he designates as the "Battle Serekh" and the "Ritual Serekh."[31] The former, concerned with organizational and tactical affairs of the army,[32] seems irrelevant to the use of the word *srk* in the ritual vessels of Achaemenid Persepolis.

The Ritual Serekh involves the religious or, more precisely, the cultic aspects of military affairs. In the Qumran context it is concerned with the method of fulfilling the laws of the Jewish Torah within the context of war, especially with the "Prayer for the Appointed Time of Battle."[33] Yadin claims, "The regulations or *serekh* must specify in detail the laws of the Torah and the laws of tactics and strategy and the interrelation between them."[34]

Since the haoma rite at Persepolis, with its set recitations and minutely prescribed movements, was performed by military officials, perhaps for military as well as personal reasons,[35] the *srk* at Persepolis may refer to the cultic pressing and drinking of haoma as a realistic and practical military phenomenon,[36] as valid for the Persians as the "Prayer for the Appointed Time of Battle" was for the Jews.

Still another aspect of the Ritual Serekh is encountered at Qumran. Yadin notes, "Special interest attaches, however, to the numerous instances in which the word *serekh* occurs in this scroll to indicate the actual body or unit, as arranged into a formation or acting according to a prescribed order."[37] With such usage he compares one of the meanings of the Greek τάξις, as "a congregation or group of people making up a religious or political body."[38] Thus, the Qumran text mentions "the men of the *serekh*" (col. iii, l. 1), "the elders of the *serekh*" (col. xiii, sec. 17, l. 1), and "the *serekh* of god" (col. iii, l. 3). Yadin therefore sees in the *serekh* as used at Qumran, "at least among its members, one of the official names of the sect,"[39] the members of the order in general, as organized in a military structure.

Thus, as used at Qumran, *srk* had a quite complex meaning. It could signify disciplinary rule, custom, order, and prescription. But its use extended as well to the men responsible for carrying out the prescribed orders and even to an actual body of men as arranged in a prescribed formation or acting according to a prescribed order.

At Persepolis, too, the term *srk/srwk* appears to have cultic rather than geographical significance. The haoma ceremony in antiquity was of military value in its promise of divine support leading to victory over the foe, just as the Jewish prayers and prescribed ritual were believed to have military effectiveness. As we know it and as it must have been also in earlier times, the haoma ceremony was a rigidly prescribed performance. The celebrants mentioned in the Persepolis texts who bear high military titles doubtless sought both personal and military values in the haoma ceremony.

In the ritual texts the term *srk/srwk* is as difficult to define as it is at Qumran. It might mean several things. It could signify the prescribed ritual with an emphasis on the orderliness of the procedure. Or, since the haoma rite was observed by a relatively small group of participants at a time, the *srk* might refer more narrowly to the celebrants seated at their closely prescribed posts, following the rigid order of service.[40]

Because of the limited context in which it is found in the ritual texts and because of the complexity of the concept there, it is impossible to be even as precise at Persepolis as at

---

[31] Yadin, *Scroll*, p. 6.

[32] *Ibid.*, pp. 149–50.

[33] *Ibid.*, pp. 6, 303.

[34] *Ibid.*, p. 5.

[35] See pp. 36–37.

[36] Historically, in earlier days at least, the haoma ceremony preceded military expeditions; cf. Haug, *Parsis*, pp. 173, 291–92 and Yasna 12:2–3.

[37] Yadin, *Scroll*, p. 148.

[38] H. S. Jones, *A Greek-English Lexicon* (*Liddell & Scott*) (Oxford, 1961), p. 1756*b*, τάξις IV, 1.

[39] Yadin, *Scroll*, p. 150.

[40] See pp. 10–12, 32.

Qumran in defining the term *srk*. If "regulations" or praxis alone were intended, we should expect the Aramaic text to be *ksrk*, "according to the *srk*." Lacking a simple single word to translate the complex and rather ambiguous *srk*, where *srk/srwk* appears in these texts it is, for the moment at least, rendered by the equally complex term "the ritual."

The third word used with the noun *byrt*, "the fortress," *hst* is found in only three texts, all of which involve the same celebrant.[41] Professor R. Emmerick has suggested as a possible meaning, "a place where something is beaten,"[42] and Professor J. Harmatta has suggested simply, "haoma feast."[43]

[41] Nos. 36, 119, 120.

[42] Professor Emmerick has proposed as a solution to *hst* the Persian form **hŭsta* in the sense of "a place where something is beaten." He explains the form **hŭsta* as a "proper" past participle of *hvah*, "to beat," although only *hvasta-* is attested. The form *hvasta* must be secondary, with the vocalism of the present, as the Indo-European system of forming past participles requires. Professor Emmerick compares the situation with that of **hvax*, "to sleep." We have Avestan *xᵛax*, past participle *xᵛaxta-*, whereas in Old Indian we have *svax-*, past participle, *suxta-*. The expected Iranian past participle **hufta-* may, however, be seen in Sogdian *ˀωβτ-* (see I. Gershevitch, *A Grammar of Manichean Sogdian* [Oxford, 1954], § 397, p. 61).

On this basis, the word *hst*, *hŭsta*, would be an Iranian parallel to the Semitic *prkn*, "crushing ceremony," found under identical circumstances.

[43] In a letter of April 23, 1968, Professor Harmatta has written, "I can reassuringly establish the sense of the term *hst* as 'haoma-feast.' " Presumably he will present his views more fully after this book appears in print.

V

THE OFFICIALS

Except on a number of pestle tops where lack of space has resulted in the omission of all officials,[1] the celebrant is always associated with at least one and often two or three of the officials mentioned in the green chert ritual vessels, the *segan*, the treasurer (*gnzbr*ᵓ), and the sub-treasurer (ᵓ*pgnzbr*ᵓ).

The *segan* appears with greater frequency than the others. Except in two texts (Nos. 22 and 116), whenever only one official is mentioned, it is always the *segan*.[2] In a single abbreviated text (No. 54), where a name appears without a title, the reference is probably to the *segan*. In one of the exceptional texts mentioned above (No. 22) only the treasurer is named and in the other (No. 116) the treasurer and sub-treasurer are found without the *segan*.

Principally on mortars and plates, where more room is available for writing, but also on a few pestles where the writing is quite small, all three officials are named with the celebrant.[3] Seven plates mention all three officials.[4] One pestle that has its text written along its shaft (No. 81) also has three, but of the many inscribed on the top of the head only three (Nos. 7, 23, and 39) have that many.

Of texts that name two officials beside the celebrant, twenty-nine mention the *segan* and treasurer[5] and eleven have the *segan* and sub-treasurer.[6]

It is impossible to determine why the number of officials in the texts should vary. One might surmise that the availability of officers at the time determined their number and identity, but it is probable that the number of officers participating in the ceremony was constant, despite the number mentioned in the text. From the statistics given above, it appears that there is some correlation between the number of officers mentioned and the amount of space available for the text. This seems supported by the following circumstance. The celebrant Haoma-dāta presented a set of objects in the nineteenth year of Xerxes. A full corps of three officers is mentioned on the mortar (No. 14), where adequate space was available for the text, but only two are found on the pestle (No. 15), where space is at a premium.

THE *Segan*

The title *sᵉgan* is a loanword in Aramaic from the Akkadian title *šaknu*. Although it is vocalized as *sāgān* or *ségen* in Hebrew[7] and *sᵉgan* in Aramaic,[8] what is probably the earlier

---

[1] Nos. 57, 59–63, 66–71, 126–29, 131, 133, 134, 137. Figures given here are tabulated only from texts complete enough for the facts to be determined without question.

[2] Nos. 2–4, 27, 29, 37, 49, 55, 58, 65, 77, 78, and 120.

[3] Nos. 13, 14, 30–32, 36, 41, and 94, and probably Nos. 74, 79, 80, 82, 91, 97, and 122.

[4] Nos. 18, 47, 51, 119, and probably Nos. 50, 92, and 98.

[5] Nos. 1, 6, 8–12, 15, 17, 19, 21, 24, 25, 34, 42–44, 46, 48, 51, 52, 73, 95, and probably Nos. 99, 106, 110, 113, 117, and 123.

[6] Nos. 5, 26, 28, 33, 38, 40, 64, 72, 87, and probably Nos. 56 and 124.

[7] Koehler and Baumgartner, *Lexicon in Veteris Testamenti Libros* (Leiden, 1948), p. 649a.

[8] Jastrow, *Dictionary* II 955b.

25

Aramaic spelling of the title as *saganu* has been noted in a cuneiform letter of the Neo-Babylonian period.[9]

In Akkadian the title meant, etymologically, "one who is set (or 'placed') in a position of authority" and originally it signified a powerful person, a royal appointee who served as vice-regent. Johns declares, "It is clear that the *šaknu's* position was properly that of *locum tenens* for the king; a 'delegate,' a 'deputy,' the forerunner and closely similar parallel of the Persian satrap."[10] The *šaknu* in Assyria was the official most frequently named and he is always named first when mentioned with other officers.

The early importance of the title is reflected in Biblical Aramaic by its listing immediately after that of the satrap (Dan. 3:2), and in one instance (Dan. 6:8) it even precedes that title. In the Aramaic papyri of the Achaemenid period officers of relatively high rank were called *segan* and their function, like that of the judge, was to hear cases at law.[11] In such a capacity the *segan* leads in the series of magistrates, "*segan*, lord, and judge" (*sgn wmrᵓ wdyn*),[12] as it does also when it stands alone with either "lord" or "judge."[13] If, as Cowley believes, "the lord" in the papyri always refers to Prince Arsames, the satrap of Egypt,[14] the *segan* associated with him must have been a person of relatively high rank indeed.[15] Johns indicates that in Assyria the *šaknu* was often mentioned with the *ḫazanu*, "the chief civil magistrate of the city" and that the *šaknu* was "the representative of the central authority and very likely, as such, the chief military authority."[16]

In the Biblical books of Ezra and Nehemiah, which portray events of the Achaemenid period, the *segan*'s in Palestine are constantly associated with the local Jewish rulers (*ḥorîm*, "nobles"[17]), apparently as secular Persian officials in the government while the Jewish nobles functioned as religious leaders.[18] Frye recognizes the *šaknu/segan* as "an important official" but finds his role in the Achaemenid economy to be particularly that of a tax collector.[19] In these ritual texts, however, this is certainly not the case.

Important titles sometimes deteriorated and became ambiguous with overuse, as the titles *paḫâtu* and *satrap* show.[20] Even while the title *segan* could still refer to an important official, it too was sometimes degraded to signify simply "foreman." Aramaic dockets on cuneiform tablets of the time of Darius sometimes use the title *sgn* for those who in the cuneiform texts of

---

[9] A. T. Clay, *Neo-Babylonian Letters from Erech* ("Yale Oriental Series: Babylonian Texts" III [New Haven, 1919]), No. 142:26; E. Ebeling, *Glossar zu den neubabylonischen Briefen* ("Sitzungsberichte der Bayerischen Akademie der Wissenschaften," Philos.-hist. Kl., I [München, 1953]), p. 201, *sagânu*.

[10] C. H. W. Johns, *Assyrian Deeds and Documents* II (Cambridge and London, 1901) 132–33, Secs. 177–78 and III (1901) 319–22; E. Klauber, *Assyrisches Beamtentum* (Leipzig, 1910), p. 100.

[11] Cowley, *AP*, Nos. 8:13, 10:13 and 18, 47:2 and 7; E. G. Kraeling, *The Brooklyn Museum Aramaic Papyri* (New Haven, 1953), No. 12:28.

[12] Kraeling, *The Brooklyn Museum Aramaic Papyri*, No. 12:28.

[13] Cowley, *AP*, Nos. 10:13 and 18 (*sgn wmrᵓ*), and 8:13 (*sgn wdyn*).

[14] *Ibid.*, pp. xxix and 152 (on No. 47:2); cf. Dan. 6:8. For Prince Arsames see G. R. Driver, *Aramaic Documents of the Fifth Century B.C.* (Oxford, 1954), pp. 44–56.

[15] Cowley, *AP*, p. 25, renders *sgn* as "magistrate," "deputy," and "representative of the king." The Greek translators of Daniel translate it as "consul" (*hupatos*) or "general" (*strategos*).

[16] Johns, *Assyrian Deeds and Documents* III 322.

[17] J. Van der Ploeg, "Les nobles israelites," *Oudtestamentische Studien* IX (1951) 49–64.

[18] Such a relationship between *segan*'s and nobles is also described in the Midrash Rabbah to the Book of Numbers (cf. Jastrow, *Dictionary* II 955, *sāgān*). Could the nobles have functioned in Palestine like the Assyrian *ḫazânu?*

[19] Frye, *Heritage*, pp. 108–9.

[20] F.-M. Abel, *Géographie de la Palestine* II (2d ed.; Paris, 1933) 115, n. 3.

the tablets are called simply *ḥaṭru*, "overseer,"[21] and an Aramaic papyrus mentions a *"segan of the carpenters"* who must have been their foreman.[22] The *segan* in the ritual texts from Persepolis, however, appears to be still quite important. It is he who is mentioned first among the officers named in the texts and he who is most frequently mentioned when only one official is named.

Perhaps it is because of its sensitivity as a royal appointment that the office of *segan* is more subject to change than those of the treasurers. It is probable, too, that some of those who bear the title *segan* are but aides to a superior *segan* who functions more regularly. As in the Bible (Dan. 2:48), where it is reported that Daniel became *rb sgnyn*, "the chief of the *segan*'s," it is probable that in one instance (No. 2) Mithra-pāta is called the *sgn⁾ rb⁾*, "chief *segan*."[23]

A single text (No. 94) which appears to give a geographical designation to the *segan* may indicate that they, like the treasurers, could come from outside of Persepolis to function there beside resident officials.[24]

From the dated texts of Persepolis it is clear that Mithra-pāta, "the chief *segan*," is mentioned as early as the eighth year of Xerxes (478/77 B.C.) and that he functions, with but few interruptions, until the nineteenth year of Xerxes (467/66 B.C.). Ama-dāta, who is mentioned as *segan* in the seventh, sixteenth, and seventeenth years of Xerxes (479/78 B.C. and 470–468 B.C.) and Arta-dāta in the eleventh year of that reign (475/74 B.C.) were presumably his subordinates.

In the nineteenth year of Xerxes (467/66 B.C.), when a general change of officers occurred, both Mithra-pāta and his successor Mithraka appear as *segan*'s.[25] Thereafter Mithraka served constantly as the principal *segan* down to the seventh year of Artaxerxes I (458/57 B.C.).

Apparently Mithraka's subordinates were Mazza-farnah in the second year of Artaxerxes I (463/62 B.C.), Āraya(t)-vahuš in the third (462/61 B.C.), Vinda(t)-farnah in the seventh year (458/57 B.C.) and Ari-bānu in the tenth (455/54 B.C.). Ama-dāta, who had served during the reign of Xerxes, reappears in the tenth year of Artaxerxes I (455/54 B.C.), presumably still a subordinate.

Another major change in the office of *segan* is reflected in the eleventh year of Artaxerxes I (454/53 B.C.), when Āraya(t)-vahuš, who appeared as a subordinate of Mithraka in the third year of Artaxerxes I, became the principal *segan* and served at least until the twenty-ninth year of Artaxerxes I (436/35 B.C.). Only Suxra-raθa, called *segan* in the thirteenth year of Artaxerxes I (452/51 B.C.), a year in which Āraya(t)-vahuš also served in that office (Nos. 43 and 44), appears to have been his subordinate.

In an undated text (No. 116) Āraya(t)-vahuš, normally called *segan*, is designated as "subtreasurer." If the *segan*'s post is the higher, this would appear to be a demotion after long service or possibly a temporary return after retirement.[26]

Segan's found in undated texts include Vahu-farnah (No. 119), *Bḥprt* (No. 121), who apparently was a *segan* during the reign of Artaxerxes I, and *Srby*, who served with treasurer

---

[21] A. T. Clay, *Business Documents of Murashû Sons of Nippur* (University of Pennsylvania "Babylonian Expedition" X [Philadelphia, 1904]), Nos. 115:7–8, 126:6 and 9; L. Delaporte, *Épigraphes Araméens* (Paris, 1912), Nos. 70 and 73.

[22] Cowley, *AP*, No. 26:9 and 21.

[23] The word "chief" (*rb⁾*) is written as an addition to the text in small letters between the regular lines.

[24] See p. 29 below.

[25] Nos. 15, 16, 17, and 18. Although the name Mithraka could be an abbreviation for such a name as Mithra-pāta, from the consistent spelling of Mithraka thereafter it is apparent that a new official is intended.

[26] A similar shift in office possibly may be seen in the case of *Mzprn*, who is called *segan* in the second year of Artaxerxes I (Nos. 21, 118), if he, as *Mdzprn*, can be the sub-treasurer in the undated text No. 54. This assumes that the two unique names represent the same name, probably Mazda-farnah.

Arta-čanah (No. 122). A broken text (No. 58) contains a partial name of a *segan* that cannot be identified. The name *Šwrty*, which is listed as a *segan* in No. 120, is probably a scribal error.

THE TREASURER

The spelling of the Persian title "treasurer" in the Aramaic ritual texts closely approximates the consonantal structure of the word in its Old Persian (*ganzabara*)[27] and Akkadian (*ganzabaru*) forms. The title, which occurs regularly in the Aramaic ritual texts, is also encountered at least once in the Aramaic fortification tablets from Persepolis.[28]

In contrast to the *segan*'s, relatively few treasurers are named in the ritual vessels. Only in the nineteenth year of Xerxes do two treasurers appear as contemporaries.[29]

The earliest dated Aramaic text in the ritual vessels (No. 1, the seventh year of Xerxes, 479/78 B.C.) names Dāta-Mithra as treasurer, and he is the only such officer mentioned in the texts until the nineteenth year of Xerxes (467/66 B.C.) when, apparently in a general change of officers, Baga-pāta is found as treasurer for the first time. It is probably the seal of Dāta-Mithra that was found impressed on several clay labels dating from the time of Xerxes.[30]

Both Dāta-Mithra and Baga-pāta are found as treasurers during the nineteenth year of Xerxes, but thereafter it is only Baga-pāta who is named in the dated texts, at least through the twenty-ninth year of Artaxerxes I (436/35 B.C.), when the dated texts cease. He is also mentioned, of course, in many broken, undateable texts. His successor may have been the Arta-čanah of No. 122, the only other person named as treasurer in the ritual texts. Because of the incompleteness of the text in which he is mentioned, however, it is impossible to date him.

Because there is a quite different group of treasurers named in the Elamite Treasury texts and because only one treasurer is found at a time in the Persepolis Treasury tablets,[31] Cameron originally denied that the treasurers of the Elamite texts and those of the Aramaic texts on the ritual vessels could be contemporary and he concluded that the Aramaic texts were later than the time of Xerxes.[32]

But with evidence that at least some of the ritual texts were inscribed in the time of Xerxes,[33] Cameron has shifted his point of view. He now accepts the dating proposed here, but he holds that the treasurers were not contemporary at Persepolis, that the sphere of activity of the treasurers of the ritual vessels is to be sought elsewhere.

A supplementary statement attached to the title of the treasurers in some of the texts on the cult vessels might be expected to shed some light on the relationship between the two groups of treasurers, but it actually makes the problem even more perplexing.

Both Dāta-Mithra and Baga-pāta are sometimes clearly designated as "the treasurer who is in Arachosia."[34] A single text of the nineteenth year of Xerxes (No. 14) identifies Dāta-Mithra as "the treasurer who is in *Ghštk*." While *Ghštk* might represent a district or town in

[27] Meillet and Benveniste, *Grammaire*, pp. 149–50, Sec. 255; W. Eilers, "Iranische Beamtennamen in der keilschriftlichen Überlieferung," *Abhandlungen für die Kunde des Morgenlandes* XXV, No. 5 (1940), p. 123.

In Biblical Aramaic (Ezra 7:12) and in Jewish Aramaic (Jastrow, *Dictionary* I 228; F. E. Peiser, "Miscellen," *ZATW* XVII [1897] 347 [Ezra 1:8; גִּזְבָּר]) the letter *n* is elided (*gizbār*) and in Syriac (J. Payne Smith, *A Compendious Syriac Dictionary* [Oxford, 1957], p. 67a) the letter *-n* is assimilated to the following letter *-z* (*gizzabᵉrāʾ*).

[28] Tablet 2 (519/18 B.C.) and perhaps also in Nos. 59:3 and 90:2.

[29] Nos. 14–18.

[30] See pp. 6–7.

[31] Cameron, *PTT*, p. 10a.

[32] Schmidt, *Persepolis* II 55, n. 69.

[33] See pp. 56–57.

[34] For Dāta-Mithra Nos. 9 and 13; for Baga-pāta Nos. 19, 43–45, 47, 48, 51, 52, 95, 110. A broken text in which the name of the treasurer is lost (No. 119) probably belongs to the time of Baga-pāta. Some incomplete texts also refer to Arachosia (Nos. 79, 123, 132, 155, and 162).

Arachosia, more closely identifying the proper sphere of Dāta-Mithra's activity, it is probable that the place name refers to his new post of assignment, since in that year he was replaced by Baga-pāta.

It is likely that the words "who is in Arachosia," when they occur, do not indicate a change in status for the treasurer. The full title is perhaps to be understood always, even when the simple title "the treasurer" is used. Possibly the supplementary text "who is in Arachosia" is to be regarded as similar to the full title "treasurer of Parsa" found in some of the Elamite Treasury texts or to the words "in the fortress" that occur in two Treasury texts when the title of the treasurer is omitted.[35]

The meaning of the words "who is in Arachosia" is problematical. Because of them Cameron now insists that the relatively large number of ritual vessels bearing Aramaic texts all came from the East, probably from Arachosia and that the words *srk*, *prkn*, and *hst* that occur at the beginning of the Aramaic texts are the names of places, fortresses from which the objects were brought to Persepolis.[36] That would be an obvious and easy solution to the problem of the two sets of treasurers at Persepolis, but it is not without great difficulties that make its acceptance impossible.

There is a remarkable homogeneity about the cult vessels bearing the Aramaic texts that calls for explanation. The objects are structurally quite uniform in type, style, and material. The texts have the same formula, each part written in exactly the same sequence. The officials named in the texts form a group so uniform that the names can be used for arriving at an exact date for the texts and objects. Moreover, it would be rather difficult to explain the presence of the unusually large number of the highest military officers, chiliarchs and myriarchs, in apparently scattered, possibly insignificant and certainly otherwise unknown "fortresses" in remote Arachosia. They might rather be expected in Persepolis. Furthermore, it seems highly improbable that the numerous stone vessels, some of which at least were quite heavy and bulky, would have gravitated fortuitously from scattered remote places in the East to the same room in the Persepolis Treasury where they were found as a single collection.

Such considerations make it improbable that the place of origin of the ritual objects is to be sought far from Persepolis. It is most likely that they were used and presented at Persepolis, which has been called the "ritual capital" of the Persian empire.[37]

If this be so, then the officers mentioned in the Aramaic texts must have functioned at Persepolis and there must have been two groups of treasurers there contemporaneously. Could the occasional use of the words "of Parsa" and "in the fortress" in the Elamite Treasury texts and the "who is in Arachosia" of the Aramaic texts indicate a deliberate attempt to distinguish between the two separate sets of treasurers who presumably had quite separate functions? Unless there were good reasons for doing otherwise, the local officials would be designated simply as "the treasurer" as most of them, of both groups, normally were at Persepolis.

If, as seems likely, the treasurers of the Aramaic texts functioned at Persepolis, the words "in Arachosia" must have had some other significance. If the treasurers were simply visitors at Persepolis, we might expect the Aramaic to read "who is *from* Arachosia." But that might have been regarded as ambiguous, possibly suggesting Arachosia as a natal place. It would certainly not indicate specifically that their assignment as treasurers was there. Perhaps the additional "who is in Arachosia" is to be understood as meaning "the treasurer who normally functions in Arachosia."

But why Arachosia? That province lay far to the east of Persepolis, beyond Drangiana, with its eastern frontier along the Indus River. During the earliest Indo-Iranian invasions the

---

[35] Cameron, *PTT*, p. 9b.   [36] See pp. 20–21.

[37] A. U. Pope, "Persepolis as a Ritual City," *Archeology* X (1957) 123–30; cf. Frye, *Heritage*, p. 97.

region, like Punjab, was settled by people who were the future folk of India.[38] The land was always subject to Indianization, from both the North and East. Through its fertile, well-watered fields ran the great road linking Persia with India. Arachosia always formed a connecting link between the pure Indian and the Iranian peoples. In later days the region was known as "White India" and its people as "White Indians."[39]

Tiele has suggested that in all probability the oldest home of the soma/haoma cultus lay between the streams which bore the similar sounding names, Harahuvati/Śarasvatī, southeast of Iran and northwest of India, in the border region between the two related folk.[40] Moreover, if we may judge from the facts that the Mithra Yasht exhibits an eastern Iranian geographical horizon and is written in eastern Iranian language,[41] the cult of Mithra, which always had close association with the use of haoma, was more prevalent and popular in the East where the mixed population could more readily support the cult, without the interference of Zoroastrian reforms that were more prevalent in the West.

Then we might conjecture that the treasurers mentioned in the ritual vessels may have been brought to Persepolis seasonally, perhaps during the New Year's Festival, to officiate as experts or adepts in the rite as celebrated by the army officers. One of the texts (No. 112) indicates that the vessel presented was used "in a festival." It was perhaps not by chance that the seal of Dāta-Mithra depicted an episode in the haoma ceremony.[42]

THE SUB-TREASURER

In the Aramaic ritual texts there is found, for the first time, an official called the ʾpgnzbrʾ, whom Eilers identified as the *upa-ganzabara*, "the sub-treasurer."[43] Such an officer apparently does not appear in the Elamite texts from Persepolis.

The earliest dateable sub-treasurer in the ritual texts is Māh(a)-dāta, who is mentioned in the eighteenth and nineteenth years of Xerxes (468–466 B.C.), at the time of the general change of officials. Perhaps the Arzarātayna named in an undateable text (No. 74) as a contemporary of the treasurer Dāta-Mithra comes from an even earlier date.

In the nineteenth year of Xerxes a sub-treasurer Mazda-dāta appears beside the earlier Māh(a)-dāta (Nos. 14 and 18), and he continues into the reign of Artaxerxes I, when he is found with considerable frequency as sub-treasurer from the fourth to the eleventh years (461–453 B.C.), more often than any of the others mentioned. In the sixth and seventh years of Artaxerxes I (459–457 B.C.) a person whose name appears to be *Mbm* is found in the office (Nos. 33 and 38). Mazda-dāta does not occur in dated texts after the eleventh year of Artaxerxes I (454/53 B.C.).

In the fifteenth year (450/49 B.C.) Artamaka occurs as a sub-treasurer (No. 47) and Čithra-farnah appears in the twenty-first year (No. 50) and also in still another text (No. 53) which is probably later than the twentieth year of Artaxerxes I.

A sub-treasurer *Šrwn* is mentioned in an undateable text (No. 119) while Baga-pāta was treasurer, and in a single text written while Baga-pāta was still treasurer (No. 116) Āraya(t)-vahuš, who previously appeared frequently as the *segan*, is designated as the sub-treasurer.[44]

The role of the officials named in the Persepolis ritual objects is somewhat perplexing. Erich Schmidt viewed the treasurers in the Elamite Treasury texts as warehouse personnel who,

[38] R. Ghirshman, *Iran* (Harmondsworth, 1954), p. 74.

[39] W. H. Schoff, *Parthian Stations by Isadore of Charax* (Philadelphia, 1914), p. 9, Sec. 19.

[40] C. P. Tiele, *Geschichte der Religion im Altertum*, trans. G. Gehrich, II (Gotha, 1903) 234.

[41] Frye, *Heritage*, p. 118.   [42] See pp. 6–7.

[43] Cameron, *PTT*, p. 10, n. 64; Schmidt, *Persepolis* II 55, n. 69.

[44] See above p. 27.

with their assistants, "received incoming stores which had to be verified, labeled, and sealed."[45] If the function of those treasurers was to receive objects for deposit in the Treasury, it is surprising that the treasurers of the Elamite texts are not those in the ritual vessels presented in Persepolis.

Persian records of the Achaemenid period offer scant information about the titles and functions of the Persian priests. Most conceptions that now prevail are reflections from later classical sources or deductions from references made in later Persian literature.

Since Magian priests were regarded as indispensable in religious ceremonials of the Achaemenid period, one might have expected priestly titles in the Aramaic texts. Ghirshman notes that "no sacrifice could be accomplished without the ministrations of the Magi, a fraternity, probably Median in origin, which held certain political and religious privileges. Their functions were very important under the Achaemenians. . . . The Magi accompanied the army to celebrate the sacrifices, they interpreted dreams, and took part in the coronation of the new king. . . ."[46] The chance occurrence of two Magian witnesses in an Aramaic business document from Egypt fully attests their presence in a military context.[47]

The presence of Magians in the Achaemenid community at Persepolis is well attested both by the Elamite Treasury texts[48] and the Aramaic fortification tablets.[49] The seal impression of Dāta-Mithra represents the participants in the haoma rite in Magian dress.[50]

If the hypothesis proposed here is acceptable, it would appear from the context of the Aramaic ritual texts that despite their titles, which appear to be secular, the officers named in the Aramaic texts participated in the haoma ceremony, functioning as priests. If the inscribed ritual objects were those used in the haoma ceremony, as the Dāta-Mithra seal impression indicates, and if, as seems likely, the military officers named on the vessels *used* them, as celebrants, in the haoma rite, then the officials named with them must stand in some peculiar relationship to the celebrant and the ceremony.

It is quite clear from the Aērpatastān that at least in somewhat later times the participation of priests in secular pursuits was legalized in Persia. Many priests bore the otherwise secular title "judge" (*dātabara*)[51] and at least one priest was "king" (*šāh*).[52]

Admittedly it is dangerous to draw parallels from differing cultures, but the Jews of the Achaemenid period were greatly influenced by the language and culture of the Persians. It might be doubted that the "treasurer" Mithra-dāta of the time of Cyrus, who returned the sacred vessels to the Jews (Ezra 1:8), was a priest, but it is clear that Nehemiah, who served in the royal palace at Susa, appointed priests as "treasurers" in charge of the cultic supplies in the Second Temple at Jerusalem (Neh. 13:13),[53] and it is probable that the priests who received the temple treasures in the time of Ezra (Ezra 8:33–34) are also to be regarded as "treasurers" in the same sense. One might suggest that the officers mentioned as "treasurers" in the Aramaic ritual texts may have been priests bearing "secular" titles who received, guarded, and dispensed the cultic vessels and other materials used in the ritual and, as the texts suggest, also assisted in the performance of the rites.

[45] Schmidt, *Persepolis* I 172.　　　　　[46] Ghirshman, *Iran*, p. 156.

[47] Kraeling, *The Brooklyn Museum Aramaic Papyri*, No. 4:24.

[48] Cameron, *PTT*, pp. 5–6; cf. Ghirshman, *Iran*, p. 188.

[49] Tablet 208 (unpublished).　　　　　[50] See p. 6.

[51] E. Edwards, "Priest, Priesthood (Iranian)," *Encyclopaedia of Religion and Ethics* X (New York, 1919) 321; Edwards cites *Aērpatastān*, ed. S. J. Bulsara (Bombay, 1915), which is not available to me.

[52] Nyberg, *Religionen*, p. 406.

[53] The verse uses the Hebrew rather than the Persian word for "treasurer," possibly under the influence of the Chronicler, but the function of the treasurer as priest is apparent.

It is instructive and perhaps significant that the Jews borrowed from the Persians and used for priests both the titles *segan* and treasurer (*gzbr* < *gnzbr, ganzabara*). The Talmud indicates that in the organization of the Second Temple the *segan* was the foremost of three priestly officers who stood over the "treasurers" of the temple and that it was mandatory for one to serve as a *segan* before becoming the high priest.[54]

A more precise relationship of the officers named in the ritual texts to the haoma ceremony may be indicated, perhaps, by the prepositions that regularly appear before their names. Normally the preposition used before both the *segan* and the treasurer is *lyd*, which may be read as "at the hand of" or "beside."[55] The sub-treasurer is regularly introduced by the preposition *qdm*, "in front of," "before," or "opposite."[56] The prepositions used could thus indicate the relative positions of the participants during the ceremony. The clue to the arrangement is found in the description of the ceremony when it involved eight persons as participants and in the sketch of the positioning of people during the ceremony as sometimes found in the Vendidād.[57] The participants are therein described both by numbered rank and by titles descriptive of their functions.

Since the celebrant in the ritual texts *used* the mortar and pestle, he served as the *hāvanān*, who sat at the northwestern corner of the ceremonial arrangement. He was second in rank during the ceremony. "Beside him," at his left hand, was the *zaotar*, the most important officer in the ceremony, for he was the priest of first rank, the one who quoted the Haoma Yasht during the ceremony. He was probably the *segan*, who is mentioned first and separately in the ritual texts. The *zaotar* sat at the north end of the group facing south. "Opposite" the celebrant, at the northeastern corner of the arrangement, was the priest of fourth rank, the *frabaretar*, who handled the sacred twig-bundle (*barsom*). "Beside" the celebrant, at his right, was the fourth officer, whose identity and function are somewhat difficult to describe.[58] He was doubtless the priest who was third in rank, the *ātaravaxša*, who was in charge of the sacred fire, which was indispensable in religious ceremonies.

Thus, the officers mentioned in the ritual texts were probably professional priests, except for the celebrant. Those mentioned in the Aramaic texts seem to have represented the four top-ranking priests, constituting the assembly for the haoma rite. Seated in a hollow square, each of the participants represented a side, a point of the compass. Such distribution of personnel seems natural since the haoma ceremony of today is still strongly oriented to the points of the compass during the operation of the mortar and in all other essential actions of the ceremony.

[54] Sheqalīm 5:2; cf. Eilers, in *Abhandlungen für die Kunde des Morgenlandes* XXV, No. 5, p. 43.

[55] Such usage is attested in Hebrew (e.g., I Sam. 19:3, I Chron. 18:17, Prov. 8:3, Ps. 140:6; cf. Koehler and Baumgartner, *Lexicon in Veteris Testamenti Libros*, p. 363a), and it is found in an Aramaic fortification tablet from Persepolis with that meaning (Tablet 109, l. 3, *lydh*, "beside him"). See also Akkadian *ana idi, ana i-di-šu* in *CAD* VII 13–14, *idu* A, 2b–2′ and 4′.

[56] In only two texts (Nos. 25 and 113), however, *qdm* introduces the treasurer, as though he were serving as a substitute for the sub-treasurer.

[57] Vendidād 5:57; Haug, *Parsis*, p. 332, n. 1, and p. 395; cf. C. E. Pavry, *Iranian Studies* (Bombay, 1927), p. 222; see p. 11.

[58] The difficulty arises from the fact that the name *raēθwiškara*, the seventh-ranked priest of the larger ceremony, is preserved today for the acolyte who served the *zaotar*, the officiating priest. But Edwards (in *Encyclopaedia of Religion and Ethics* X 321b) says of the secondary priest in the modern ceremony, "Though taking his name from the Avestan *raēθwiškara*, his chief functions correspond more nearly to those of the *ātravaxša*," and Pavry (*Iranian Studies*, p. 223) calls the supporting priest "the *ātaravaxša*."

VI

THE CELEBRANT

IN most of the Aramaic texts the prime actor, the subject of the verb ʿbd, is mentioned just after the naming of the *segan*. In only one complete text (No. 137) is the name not given. In abbreviated texts in which the *segan* is not mentioned the name of the chief actor either follows the usual introduction[1] or it begins the Aramaic text itself.[2] Invariably the name stands before the verb, as in Persian syntax.[3]

In this discussion of the ritual texts the subject of the verb ʿbd is called "the celebrant" because it is assumed that he used the object in the haoma ceremony and later presented it, inscribed, as a memorial of the event, in the Persepolis Treasury.

In a unique, badly damaged text (No. 33) the distribution of the text suggests that the paternity of the celebrant was given. Two other vessels, both of which are also unfortunately damaged, have texts that indicate that two celebrants were involved with the same vessel (Nos. 88 and 95). In one of them (No. 88) there are traces of two names and the title *plg* appears twice. Since haoma is prepared twice in the modern Parsi ceremony,[4] apparently reflecting an older ritual, presumably two men participated in turn, using the same equipment, and then shared the cost of the object presented in the Treasury.

Sometimes the name of the celebrant is followed by a single, short, vertical stroke, the numeral "one," which may be understood as representing an indefinite article.[5] It suggests the so-called *ištên* wedge used in cuneiform texts, including Old Persian, before masculine names.[6] Since the phenomenon is found only with the celebrant and not with the names of the officials on the ritual vessels, it is always the indicator of the name of the celebrant in broken texts. A similar vertical stroke is used with nouns in these texts, where it may represent an indefinite article.[7] Although such a unit stroke was once used in ancient Hebrew lists[8] and in lists in the Aramaic papyri,[9] there is no example of it elsewhere in Aramaic after single personal names.

---

[1] Nos. 22, 54, 57, 59–63, 66–68, 116, 126, 128, 131, 133, 134, and probably Nos. 70 and 71.

[2] Nos. 69, 127, and 129.

[3] Normal Semitic word order calls for the verb to precede the subject unless there is special stress on the subject. But W. Baumgartner ("Das Aramäischen im Buche Daniel," *ZATW* XLV [1927] 128 ff.) has shown that in both Ezra and Daniel the proportion of sentences in which the subject precedes the verb is greater than the reverse order (in Daniel 120 as compared with 80 and in Ezra 30 as compared with 15). Bauer and Leander (*BLA*, p. 332, Sec. 99a) conjecture that the change in order in Biblical Aramaic is probably due to the influence of Akkadian, but it is more likely patterned after Persian syntax, in which the subject normally precedes; cf. Meillet and Benveniste, *Grammaire*, p. 239, Secs. 397–98; Kent, *Old Persian*, p. 96a, Sec. 310.

[4] Modi, *Religious Ceremonies*, pp. 296, 306; C. E. Pavry, *Iranian Studies* (Bombay, 1927), p. 199, n. 1.

[5] Nos. 8:2, 14:2, 15:3, 18:2, 19:2, etc.

[6] An Aramaic text on a clay tablet (L. Delaporte, *Epigraphes araméens* [Paris, 1912], pp. 44–45, No. 26) has such an imitation cuneiform wedge before the name of each witness, but its significance was not recognized, and it was read as the conjunction "and."

[7] Nos. 5:3, 14:3, 18:2, 21:4, 23:5, 56:3, etc.

[8] Josh. 12:9–14. As usual in the Bible, the earlier figure was displaced by a written numeral.

[9] Cowley, *AP*, No. 33.

At times the name of the celebrant is followed by the Aramaic *šmh*, "his name,"[10] which reproduces the Old Persian *nāma*, "by name."[11] This, like the unit stroke, is used only with the celebrant and never with the officials. When both the *šmh* and the unit stroke are found with the name of the celebrant,[12] the usage is a calque for the Old Persian expression 1 *martiya . . . nāma*, "1 man, . . . by name."[13]

In a number of the Aramaic texts a title is given after the celebrant's name. The titles indicate that many, if not all, of the celebrants were military men of very high rank. In two examples the celebrant bears the Aramaic title *ʾlp*.[14] Although the vocalization of *ʾlp* is uncertain here, one thinks at once of the Hebrew *ʾallûf*, "chief," "chiliarch."[15] It represents the Greek chiliarch and the Old Persian *hazarapat*, the commander of a thousand men.[16] According to Yadin, the *ʾlp* at Qumran commanded a *degel*, a military unit mentioned in the Aramaic papyri,[17] the Aramaic fortification texts,[18] and in the much later War Scroll from Qumran.[19]

In thirteen texts the celebrant has the Aramaic title *plg*.[20] The nature of that title and its relative rank are clarified by a single text (No. 118:3) in which the celebrant is called an *ʾlp plg*, "a chiliarch of a *plg*." This indicates that the *plg* designates a larger unit, consisting of more than a thousand men. The Semitic root means "divide" and the noun thus indicates "a division." In Syriac usage *palgāʾ* is used for "a phalanx" or "a battalion."[21]

Herodotus, in describing the great army of Xerxes, mentions captains over a thousand (χιλιάρχος) and captains over ten thousand (μυριάρχος) as well as leaders of ten men (δεκάρχος) or of a hundred (ἑκατοντάρχος).[22] Under the commander-in-chief of the Persian army there were general officers, heads of corps or divisions, of which, in one instance, there were as many as nine.[23] Below them in rank were the chiefs of the ethnic contingents, generally the satraps of the provinces.[24] Rawlinson says of the myriarch, "The officer over ten thousand was sometimes a divisional chief (as Hydarnes, the commander of the 'Immortals' in the army of Xerxes [Herod. vii. 83]); sometimes he was subject to the commander of the ethnic contingent, who was himself under the orders of the head of a division."[25]

Those bearing the title *plg* in these texts are doubtless "divisional commanders" with a title equivalent to that of the Greek myriarch and the Jewish *nśy hrbwʾ* of the Qumran War Scroll.[26] Again the vocalization of the title is uncertain, but in the light of the Arabic *ʿārîq*, "lieutenant," "centurion," one might conjecture something like *palîg > pelîg*.

---

[10] A *šmh* alone is found in No. 112:3. Compare the Biblical Aramaic in Ezra 5:14 and the Aramaic papyri (Cowley, *AP*, Nos. 28, 33, etc.).

[11] Meillet and Benveniste, *Grammaire*, p. 179, Sec. 312; Kent, *Old Persian*, p. 81, Sec 251c and p. 97, Sec. 312.

[12] Nos. 36, 90, 91, and 119.

[13] Behistun Inscription (Old Persian text), col. i, ll. 35 and 74, col. ii, ll. 5 and 79.

[14] Nos. 52 and 118.

[15] M. D. Cassuto and N. H. Torczyner, "*ʾallûf*," *Encyclopaedia Miqraʾith* I (Jerusalem, 1950), cols. 332–33.

[16] Schmidt, *Persepolis* I 168–69; F. Justi, "Der Chiliarch des Dareios," *ZDMG* L (1896) 659 ff.; E. Benveniste, *Titres et noms propres en iranien ancien* ("Travaux de l'Institut d'études iraniennes de l'Université de Paris" I [Paris, 1966]), pp. 67–71.

[17] Cowley, *AP*, p. 282 (glossary) and pp. xvi, 6; E. G. Kraeling, *The Brooklyn Museum Aramaic Papyri* (New Haven, 1953), p. 310 (glossary) and pp. 41–42. Kraeling (p. 42) thinks of a *degel* as 100 men, but Cowley (p. 6) regards the "hundred" as a subdivision of the *degel*.

[18] Tablets 12, 62, 236 (unpublished).   [20] Nos. 17, 19, 22, 31, 32, 47, 48, 63, 81, 83, 87, 88 *bis*, 130.

[19] Yadin, *Scroll*, pp. 49–50.   [21] J. Payne Smith, *A Compendious Syriac Dictionary* (Oxford, 1957), p. 447.

[22] Herodotus vii. 81; cf. Xenophon *Cyropaedia* III. iii. 11.

[23] Herodotus vii. 82–83, 88.   [24] Herodotus vii. 8, 19; cf. Arrian *Anabasis of Alexander* iii. 8.

[25] G. Rawlinson, *The Seven Great Monarchies of the Ancient Eastern World: The Fifth Monarchy* II (New York, 1885) 327–28.

[26] Yadin (*Scroll*, p. 50, col. iv, l. 16) denies that the "myriad" at Qumran can be regarded as a permanent tactical unit. He regards it as a "feeder unit" used to supply replacements in the losses of the *degel*, which he regards as the largest

It is perhaps significant that the celebrants with titles are only men of the very highest military rank. Presumably only the most distinguished personalities affixed their titles. One misses the lower officers, especially the Old Persian *satapati* (Greek *hekatontarchos*, Roman *centurion*), who commanded a hundred men.[27] It is likely that the lesser officers, possibly even the *dasapati*, who commanded ten men,[28] are among the many celebrants named without titles in the ritual objects.

Since it is extremely unlikely that the generals actually "made" the stone objects presented at the Treasury in Persepolis and it is improbable that the action described in the Aramaic texts is simply concerned with giving,[29] it is obvious that the Aramaic verb cannot be used in its most usual meaning. If, as seems likely, the verb should be translated as "worked," "operated," "used," with the implication that the officer named actually used the mortar and pestle in the haoma ceremony,[30] it is rather surprising to find someone who is not a priest performing this important act.

There is, however, some evidence that a military officer could attain the religious status of a Magian priest, an office originally hereditary in a special caste. In the bilingual Greek and Aramaic inscription from Farasha, Cappadocia, written during the Hellenistic period, it is stated that a "general" (Greek *strategos*, Aramaic probably *rb h̲[yl²]*) "became a Magus of Mithra" or "began to serve Mithra as a Magian" (Greek ἐμάγευσε Μίθρη; Aramaic *mgyš [lm]trh*).[31] Cumont suggested that the inscription was written on the occasion of an initiation, when a non-Magian could attain such status.[32]

The Aramaic ritual texts from Persepolis seem to indicate that already in Achaemenid times military men, at least in their own military cult, could assume priestly prerogatives and participate in the haoma ceremony.

But it is unlikely that the rite at Persepolis was one of initiation since, although the majority of celebrants seem to have served but once, according to the texts preserved, there is evidence that some celebrants participated in the haoma ceremony on several occasions. Thus, Rāman gave one pestle (No. 39) in the tenth year of Artaxerxes I, another (No. 40) in the same year, and a plate (No. 113) in a year that cannot be dated. Karabara presented a pestle (No. 11) in the sixteenth year of Xerxes and another (No. 12) in the following year. *Šwrty* gave a mortar (No. 36) in the seventh year of Artaxerxes I, and a plate (No. 119) and pestle (No. 120) in undateable years. In the latter case, although the years cannot be dated, they represent different occasions since the officers mentioned in the texts are different.[33]

---

permanent tactical organization. He finds that such usage "was almost the only current system in all armies (including the Roman army) until the present day." Benveniste (*Titres et noms*, pp. 70–71) cites the later use of the title "chef de dix mille" among the Mongols and, as *khri-dpon*, among the Tibetans.

[27] Such a military unit is mentioned in the Elamite Treasury tablets (Cameron, *PTT*, No. 1:7–8, No. 24:4; also, "New Tablets from the Persepolis Treasury," *JNES* XXIV [1965] 169), and its Aramaic equivalent (*m²h/m²t²*) is found in the Aramaic papyri (Cowley, *AP*, pp. xvi, 295a).

[28] Mentioned in the Elamite Treasury tablets (Cameron, *PTT*, Nos. 12, 15, and 84). Cameron (in *JNES* XXIV 169, 177) also finds in the Elamite texts a *caθru-pati*, who commands but four men.

[29] See pp. 38–39.   [30] See pp. 39–40.

[31] Henri Grégoire, "Note sur une inscription Gréco-Araméenne trouvé à Farasha (Ariaramnei-Rhodandros)," *Comptes rendus de l'Académie des inscriptions et belles-lettres*, 1908, pp. 434 ff.; M. Lidzbarski, *Ephemeris für semitische Epigraphik (1909–1915)* III (Giessen, 1915) 66–67.

[32] Franz Cumont, *Oriental Religions in Roman Paganism* (New York, 1956), p. 263, n. 16. Cumont also notes that Lucian mentions rites by which Mithro-barzanes made him (as Menippus) "a complete Magian"; Lucian *Menippus* 65, ll. 463 ff.

[33] Other multiple presentations involve *²dwst* (Nos. 3, 52, 133, representing a plate and two pestles), *Bhyyn* (Nos. 48 and 112, two plates), *Krpyš* (Nos. 25, 102, and 103, representing a mortar, plate, and a mortar and pestle set), and Draz-bāra (Nos. 34 and 38, two mortars).

Since such multiple presentations occur in separate years,[34] it seems likely that the haoma ceremonies were performed in conjunction with an annual festival held at Persepolis, perhaps the New Year's Festival or the one honoring Mithra.[35] Indeed, one text (No. 112) indicates that the action mentioned in the Aramaic text occurred during a festival.

At least one of the motives for the haoma ceremony may be found in a supplementary reference made in the text of some of the plates,[36] "a desire for good fortune" (r⁽yn bg).[37] The reason for the special interest of soldiers is not far to seek. In both India and Iran from ancient times the haoma rites were associated principally with the gods of war.[38] This persisted, too, in the Mithraism of Roman times, when initiates were under the particular patronage of Mars, the Roman god of war.[39] Vermaseren declares, "It is therefore little wonder that soldiers of all ranks in the Roman legions, orientals included, felt the lure of Mithras. Observance of the cult guaranteed assistance to all who pledged their lives to the Roman eagle. The assurance of divine aid on the battlefield, the military discipline and the taking of an oath as part of that discipline, were very important factors in the spread of the Mithras cult and its official recognition. Material evidence from the second century A.D. shows that wherever the Romans planted the standards, Mithras and his cult followed."[40]

Ancient Indians plied their gods with soma, not only to promote their immortality, but also to increase their strength for the struggle against their enemies. Indra, in particular, was offered great quantities of soma to fortify him for dealing with the various dragon figures that stood in the way of the advancing Aryans.[41] Among the Iranians Mithra was treated similarly. As a result the tenth Yasht is replete with references to Mithra's greatness and power and his readiness to fight. A worshiper declares, "I will worship Mithra, who is strong, supernatural, foremost, merciful, incomparable, high-dwelling, a mighty, strong warrior. Valiant, he is equipped with a well-fashioned weapon, he who watches in darkness, the undeceivable."[42]

The values attributed to haoma for the gods were also sought by men who drank the precious draught. For their continuing personal life men sought healing, vigorous health, nimbleness, strength throughout the body, prosperity, and wisdom in all things—the very things that the use of haoma had promised from the most ancient times.[43] The familiar epithet applied to haoma, "from whom death flees" (dūraoša),[44] attests its power of preserving life and granting immortality, supreme desires of all men but thoughts ever present to the soldier for whom battle is always imminent.

All men sought the values promised by haoma, but they were perhaps even more meaningful to the military man. Some expectations associated with the use of haoma, as declared in Persian scripture, seem to be more distinctly military in character. Thus, there are pleas to haoma for strength and ability to defend and a petition for "some of the victorious qualities by which Haoma is conqueror of those who attack."[45] Constantly there is urging for strength

---

[34] An apparent exception is Haoma-dāta's presentation of a mortar and pestle (Nos. 14 and 15) in the 19th year of Xerxes. However, these objects could have been given at the same time, as a set, as were several others that mention "mortar with pestle" (e.g., Nos. 1, 9, 10, 14, 16, 17, 46, 103, etc.). The only difference is that in such cases usually only one piece was inscribed.

[35] See pp. 15, 22; Frye, *Heritage*, p. 97.　　　　　　　　[36] See p. 50.

[37] It is natural that a god of health, prosperity, and immortality should be expected to bring "good fortune." When the Magus Tiridates I of Armenia sought coronation by the Emperor Nero, he is reputed to have said, "I come to you, my Lord, to worship you as it were Mithras; and I will be such as you grant me to be, because you are to me 'fate' (*moira*) and 'good fortune' (*tyche*)" (Dio Cassius lxii. 1–7).

[38] See p. 8.

[39] M. J. Vermaseren, *Mithras, the Secret God*, trans. F. and V. Megaw (New York, 1963), p. 144.

[40] *Ibid.*, p. 30.　　　　　　[42] Yasht 10:170.　　　　　　[44] Yasna 9:20–21, 27.

[41] Rig-Veda X, 119.　　　　　[43] Yasna 9:16–20, 10:9.　　　[45] Yasna 10:9.

from haoma to win the battle in overcoming those who are hostile and in vanquishing the Lie.[46] Once the request is for victory over the broad-fronted army that is drawn up deceptively.[47]

A prayer that in some respects is essentially that of a soldier, used during the ceremony of the pressing of haoma, exhorts, "O Haoma, . . . for aggressive strength I speak to thee, for that which smites with victory . . . and for manifold delights! Bear off from us the torment and malice of the hateful. Divert the angry foe's intent! . . . throw thou a veil of darkness o'er his mind; make his intellect (at once) a wreck!"[48] Thus, Mithra promises what haoma does. Cumont says, "As the god of armies, Mithra caused his protégés to triumph over the barbarous adversaries and likewise in the moral realm gave them victory over the instincts of evil inspired by the spirit of falsehood and he assured them of salvation, both in this world and the world to come."[49]

Thus, even the humblest member of the army could find solace and hope in the preparation and use of the precious religious intoxicant. But it is conceivable, too, that in the thought of Achaemenid Persians the haoma ceremony was of military value, as essential to victory as the "Prayer before Battle" was in the religio-military Jewish cultus at Qumran.[50]

From the "military" context of these Aramaic texts, it seems entirely probable that the inscribed green stone cult vessels from the Persepolis Treasury attest a military aspect of the cult of Mithraism which later strongly competed with Christianity in the West in Roman times.[51]

[46] Yasna 9:20.

[47] Yasna 9:18; F. Wolff (*Avesta* [Berlin, Leipzig, 1924], p. 33) translates it as "überwinde (die) . . . von dem breitfrontigen betrüglich ziehenden Feindsheer."

[48] Yasna 9:27–29 (*The Zend-Avesta*, trans. L. H. Mills ["Sacred Books of the East" XXXI, ed. F. Max Müller (Oxford, 1887)], Pt. III, pp. 238–39); cf. E. B. N. Dhabhar, "The Hôm Yasht and 'The Bacchae' of Euripides: A Contrast," *Essays on Iranian Subjects* (Bombay, 1955), p. 30; Wolff (*Avesta*, p. 34) renders the passage somewhat differently, "O Haoma . . . Her für meinen Leib rufe ich dich zu Kraft und Wehrhaftigkeit und zu viel Rettung bringender Stärkung. Schaff fort unserer Feinde Feindschaften, fort der ergrimmten Anschlag! Und jedweder Mensch, der an diesem Hause, der an diesem Dorfe, der an diesem Gau, der an diesem Lande Frevel übt, von dessen Füssen nimm die Stärke, seine Ohren reiss ab, zerstöre seinen Geist."

[49] Franz Cumont, *The Mysteries of Mithra*, trans. Thomas J. McCormack (2d ed.; New York, 1956), p. 143.

[50] See p. 23.

[51] Vermaseren, *Mithras, the Secret God*, pp. 27–36, 43–66.

VII

THE ACTION

T HE key word in the Aramaic texts on the ritual vessels from Persepolis, that which alone can lead to the proper interpretation of the texts, is the common Aramaic verb ꜥbd. The verb is certainly transitive, with the various stone objects on which it is written as its direct object. As will be contended below, the sphere of action is probably somewhere within the fortress of Persepolis or nearby.[1]

A normal translation of the verb ꜥbd in Aramaic should be "he made" or "he did." But in view of the relatively large number of persons who appear as subjects of the verb and because more than a dozen of them are identified as very high military officers who would not be expected to show the artistic talent and skilled craftsmanship necessary to shape the objects,[2] it is quite unlikely that such a translation is possible in these texts.

It has been proposed that the meaning should be "he had (someone) make." But the consonantal text does not permit the reading of a causative form of the verb (ꜣAfꜥel or Hafꜥel) nor can ꜥbd be a Paꜥel form used in a causative sense, for such a form of the verb is relatively rare in Aramaic and, as Syriac shows, when it does occur, the meaning is not "to make someone make (something)" but "to make someone serve."[3]

One might better appeal, if such a sense is desired, to the frequent use of the verbs "made," "built," and the like, in Semitic inscriptions which declare that a king had "made" a tomb or "built" a palace or even a city (for example, Moabite Stone, ll. 9–10, 18–19, 21–23, 25–26, 29) when he obviously did not do the work himself. Even more pertinent here would be King Kilamu's assertion that he "made" (qn klmw) the decorative golden shell or overlay for the handle of his "scepter" (or "whip"?).[4]

But such royal claims are quite understandable and of a different order from the use of the verb in these ritual texts. Moreover, it can scarcely be said that the objects were "made" in the prkn or srk, as the words are understood here. Nor would such an interpretation be suitable in the few instances wherein the action is said to have occurred "during a festival" (No. 112:5) or "during an important prk (great ceremony of crushing haoma?)" (No. 5:3). Moreover, such a translation does not construe well with the several prepositions that occur before the names of the officials mentioned in the texts. Furthermore, it would appear that the vessels presented in the Treasury were not always newly made for the celebrants since several of them show signs of having been broken and mended in antiquity.[5]

Because of the considerable number of ritual objects found in the Treasury, it is natural to assume that they were presented at the Treasury and that their Aramaic texts refer to their delivery at Persepolis. Such was the original premise of this writer and it is still the contention of Professor Cameron, who has translated the basic Aramaic text tentatively as follows:

---

[1] See pp. 20–22.   [2] See pp. 34–35.

[3] J. Payne Smith, *A Compendious Syriac Dictionary* (Oxford, 1957), p. 396b. In Talmudic Aramaic (Jastrow, *Dictionary* II 1035a) the *Paꜥel* form means "to prepare" and is used of dressing or tanning of hides, etc.

[4] F. von Luschan, *Die Kleinfunde von Sendschirli* ("Ausgrabungen in Sendschirli" V [Berlin, 1943]) p. 102, Pl. 47g; B. Landsberger, *Samꜣal* (Ankara, 1948), p. 42, n. 102.

[5] Nos. 5, 28, and 72.

In . . . the fortress, into the hand of *N* the *sgn*ᵓ, *X* made this mortar (*or* pestle *or* plate). To *Y* the treasurer, in the presence of *Z* the assistant treasurer (it is) a gift. Year. . . .[6]

In his translation of the Aramaic ᶜ*bd . . . lyd* as "into the hand of . . . *X* made," Cameron was doubtless influenced by a Persian idiom. In the Behistun Inscription of Darius I the king claims, "Afterwards Ahuramazda made them into my hand" (*pasāva diš auramazda manā dastayā akunauš*).[7]

But there are a number of reasons why Cameron's reading is unacceptable and these have led the writer to seek another meaning for the verb ᶜ*bd* and consequently another interpretation for the texts. The word that he translates as "a gift" (ᵓ*škr*) cannot have that meaning in these texts.[8] Without it in such a sense an awkward construction results—two widely separated prepositional phrases (*lyd*) dependent upon the same verb—a construction unlike the Persian idiom. It seems improbable that the presentation of the ritual objects was "made to the hand of the *segan*" and also "to the hand of the treasurer." Moreover, although the words ᶜ*bd . . . lyd*, literally "he made to the hand of," superficially resemble the Persian idiom "made into the hand of," it is not an exact rendition of the idiom. One should expect an Aramaic *byd* to render the dative case of the Persian noun "in the hand."[9]

The words "made to the hand of" are used nowhere else in Aramaic—not even in the Aramaic of Persepolis—as a circumlocution to express the idea "he gave." It is an awkward, distinctly non-Semitic expression that would be avoided in Aramaic, which has a good, short Semitic verb for "he gave." That verb is used elsewhere in the Aramaic fortification texts from Persepolis.

If the Persian idiom were used in the Aramaic texts for "he gave," the prepositional phrase *lyd* (or, preferably, *byd*) "to the hand" would be indispensable. But there are some texts in the cult vessels in which the verb ᶜ*bd*, "he made(?)," is used without the prepositional *lyd* and even without a reference to an official.[10] In a single, much abbreviated text (No. 127), only the verb ᶜ*bd* and a personal name are found. Obviously ᶜ*bd* alone cannot mean "he gave."[11]

While it is probably true that the ritual objects were presented in the Treasury at Persepolis where they were found, that is but an inference drawn from the fact that they were found there, presumably where they had been stored, rather than from any explicit statement of donation in the Aramaic texts. Both the verb ᶜ*bd* and the words *lyd* and *qdm*, which introduce the officials, must have some less usual meaning in the Aramaic texts.

Clarity is achieved only when the verb ᶜ*bd* is rendered as "worked," "operated," or "used." That the Semitic verb can have such meaning is seen from such Hebrew texts as "there was not a man *to work* the ground"[12] and "*you should work* the ground for him."[13] In post-Biblical Hebrew ᶜ*bd* can be employed in the sense of "to use (something, especially for idolatrous purposes)."[14] A possible Aramaic use of the verb ᶜ*bd* in the sense of "use" is found in the Peshitta text of Ezra 7:23, which can be read as "And everything in the tablet shall be given. And give to Him according to the law of the God of Heaven. He shall take (*nissab*) and he shall use (*wᵉneᶜbed*) and there shall not be anger against the kingdom of the king and his sons." The Akkadian verb *epēšu*, "to make," has had a similar development and was used similarly for "to use."[15]

---

[6] Cameron, in Schmidt, *Persepolis* II p. 55*b*.

[7] Behistun Inscription, col. iv, l. 35. [8] See p. 54.

[9] Henning ("Mitteliranisch," *Handbuch der Orientalistik*, ed. B. Spuler and H. Kees, IV: *Iranistik* [Leiden, 1958], Pt. 1, p. 27, n. 2) in translating words from a Nisā ostracon, which does not contain the Persian idiom, translates LYD PḤṬᵓ as "zu Händen des Satrapen" but in the footnote refers to "LYD im Sinne des sonstigen BYD" and refers to the usage in these mortars and pestles as though approving Cameron's translation. But he also mentions an alternative "unter der Autorität von," which Diakonoff and others use in rendering the *lyd* of the Nisā texts.

[10] Nos. 57, 59–63, 65, 66, 68–71, 126, 128, 129, 131, 133, 134.

[11] In a few texts (Nos. 54, 67, and 137) even the verb is purposely omitted.

[12] Gen. 2:5, cf. 3:23, 4:2 and 12, etc. [14] Jastrow, *Dictionary* II 1034, עבד, Qal 3) and *Nifᶜal*.

[13] II Sam. 9:10. [15] *CAD* IV 230, *epēšu*, 2f–6'.

Translation of ʿ*bd* as "he used," together with a permissible translation of the words *lyd* and *qdm* in the Aramaic texts,[16] makes possible a smooth, clear, and meaningful reading of the basic Aramaic text as follows:

In the ceremony[17] of the fortress, beside *W* the *segan*, *X* used this object[18] beside *Y* the treasurer, opposite *Z* the sub-treasurer. ʾ*skr* of year. . . .

Such a translation is usable even in the most abbreviated text, No. 127, where we can understand "*X* used (this)." Such usage is also appropriate for text No. 8, in which the verb ʿ*bd* is completed by the infinitive *lḥšl* to read "(he) used this mortar for pounding," and for those that suggest that the vessel was used "during a festival" (No. 112:5) and "in a great ceremony of crushing (haoma)" (No. 5:3).

In a few of these ritual texts there is a perplexing verbal phenomenon. Although there are examples of the plural form of the verb (ʿ*bdw*) when the subject is compound (Nos. 88 and 95), there are a few texts that use the same apparently plural form of the verb when the subject is unquestionably singular in number.[19] In these formulaic texts it is obvious that the forms ʿ*bd* and ʿ*bdw* have the same meaning and are used as equivalents, interchangeably, when the subject is singular.

Similar forms, apparently plural but used with singular subjects, are also found several hundred years later, in Middle Persian (Pahlavi).[20] They are encountered in the Nisā ostraca from Turkmenistan (100 to 29 B.C.),[21] in the third Avroman parchment from Kurdistān (A.D. 53),[22] and in the bilingual Armazi/Mtskheta inscription from Georgia (A.D. 30 to 60).[23]

In the Persian texts such forms (for example, זבנו, אכלו, and the like) are regarded as logograms composed of an Aramaic word with an additional letter affixed to indicate the tense of the Iranian word with which it is to be equated. Similarly constructed is such a form as זבנת, which is regarded by Nyberg as an Aramaic perfect verb form (*z*ᵉ*ban*) to which a letter -*t* is added as a "phonetic complement" to indicate the Iranian equivalent in the preterite tense, which ends with the phoneme -*t* (χ*rīt*).[24]

In Middle Persian the form *zbnw* is likewise explained as an Aramaic logogram to which an additional letter -*w* has been attached. While there is general agreement among Iranologists about the origin and significance of the final -*t* in such a word as *zbnt* and about its function as indicating the Iranian preterite tense, there are diverse views concerning the origin and significance of the -*w* in such forms as *zbnw*.[25]

Nyberg, who transcribed such a -*w* as -*u*, suggested that *zbnw* is the second person plural imperative Aramaic form, the "most common verbal form" used in the chancery of the Great King, that has been adopted for Iranian use.[26] He explains that in the development of Middle

---

[16] See p. 32.

[17] Here this word represents either the words "ritual" (*srk*), "ceremony of crushing (haoma)" (*prkn*), or the still untranslated *hst*.

[18] Mortar, pestle, or plate.

[19] Nos. 2:3, 13:2, 14:2, 15:3, and 20:3. Apart from No. 2 (478/77 B.C.) the verbs so written are found in texts dated within a few years at the end of the reign of Xerxes (468–466 B.C.) and in the first year of Artaxerxes I (464/63 B.C.).

[20] See p. 18.

[21] I. M. Diakonoff and V. A. Livshitz, *Dokumenty iz Nizy* (Moscow, 1960), pp. 55–56.

[22] H. S. Nyberg, "The Pahlavi Documents from Avromān," *Le monde oriental* XVII (1923) 182-230.

[23] B. M. Metzger, "A Greek and Aramaic Inscription Discovered at Armazi in Georgia," *JNES* XV (1956) 18–26; P. Grelot, "Remarque sur le bilingue Grec-Araméen d'Armazi," *Semitica* VIII (1958) 11–20; Frye (*Heritage*, p. 267, n. 37) says of the "notorious" Armazi inscriptions, "The question whether the Armazi inscriptions are written in ungrammatical Aramaic or in heterographic ancient Georgian, or in an Iranian tongue, is not resolved."

[24] Nyberg, in *Le monde oriental* XVII 208, 224.

[25] Henning, in *Handbuch der Orientalistik* IV, Pt. 1, p. 30.

[26] Nyberg, in *Le monde oriental* XVII 225.

Persian three forms of the present tense (second person plural imperative, second person plural indicative, and the third person singular indicative) ultimately coincided and that the form with the affixed -*w* could represent any one of them.[27] In fact, since the affix -*w* is also found on forms that appear to be the Aramaic participle used as a logogram (for example, *mbnw*), he conjectured that "the ending -*ū(n)*[28] is a mere affix with no authority in Aramaic but due chiefly to the practice of clerks who had got into the habit of regarding the Aramaic -*ū(n)* as the equivalent of every Iranian (ending) -*ēt.*"[29]

Henning agrees that forms like *ʿbdw*, as found in Middle Iranian texts, represent the Iranian present tense, but he notes the diversity of views among Iranologists regarding the ending -*w*.[30] However, because purely Iranian forms with quite similar -*w* endings are developed later,[31] he suggests that the ending -*w*, which serves as the sign of the present, is perhaps Iranian in origin.[32]

In the Nisā texts, as in these Achaemenid ritual texts, there are verbal forms both with and without the affix -*w* used with a singular subject. Diakonoff regards the troublesome -*w* as a non-phonemic, differentiating sign used to distinguish between the participial forms and the finite verb. The simpler form (*ʿbd*) he identifies as the participle and the affixed form (*ʿbdw*), when used as a singular verb, he considers to be the finite verb.[33]

Although the surprising occurrence of the form *ʿbdw* in these Achaemenid ritual texts may resemble heterographic writing and thus suggest that the texts in which it is found should be read as Persian rather than Aramaic, that seems quite unlikely. The time that elapsed between the ritual texts and those of the Middle Persian in which such heterographic forms are encountered is quite considerable, a matter of several centuries. On the basis of Persian material hitherto known, Henning has determined that it is certain that the Aramaic language was displaced by Iranian language using Aramaic logograms in its written expression about the middle of the second century B.C.[34] and that the earliest known example of such heterographic writing is found in a series of coins which began at about the end of the second century B.C.[35] Furthermore, there are no other examples of heterographic writing in the ritual texts of the Achaemenid period which are read otherwise quite readily as good Aramaic.[36]

As a homograph, the verbal form *ʿbd* could represent either the *Peʿal* or *Paʿel* perfect forms in Aramaic or the *Peʿal* masculine singular participle.[37]

---

[27] *Ibid.*

[28] The Arsacid ending was -*w* and it was -*wn* in Sassanian times. Nyberg (in *Le monde oriental* XVII 226) renders them as -*ū* and -*ūn*.

[29] Nyberg, in *Le monde oriental* XVII 226.

[30] Henning, in *Handbuch der Orientalistik* IV, Pt. 1, p. 30.

[31] *Ibid.*, p. 30. He cites as an example perhaps *kʾmyw*, "wish."

[32] *Ibid.*, p. 122 and n. 2. He regards it as the present sign of the -*a* class verb, corresponding to the -*yw* of the -*aya* class.

[33] Diakonoff and Livshitz, *Dokumenty iz Nizy*, pp. 55–56.

[34] Henning, in *Handbuch der Orientalistik* IV, Pt. 1, p. 30.   [35] *Ibid.*, p. 25.

[36] The influence of the Persian language on the Aramaic of these texts is quite apparent, as in the other Aramaic of the period. It is observable in such a hybrid combination as *lpty* (Nos. 43:4, 114:3) and in the reflection of Persian thought and syntax (see pp. 63–70), but aside from the strange *ʿbdw* there is nothing in the texts that resembles the logographic writing found in Pahlavi texts.

[37] If defective writing is possible, *ʿbd* might also represent the *Peʿîl* (passive) perfect and participle in the masculine singular form. Then *ʿbdw* would be identical with the form *ʿbydw* that Altheim (Altheim and Stiehl, *Aramäische Sprache* I 42–43) finds in line 4 of the Armazi text.

But in Biblical Aramaic and the papyri *Peʿîl* forms are always written with the letter *y* to represent the *i* vowel (*ʿbyd*). However, Nyberg (in *Le monde oriental* XVII 222) suggests that there was an archaic Aramaic dialect in Iranian territory wherein the use of *matres lectionis* must have been scarce, since the bulk of Aramaic ideograms are later taken over from Arsacid Pahlavi, which was founded on such an archaic Aramaic dialect.

Altheim and Stiehl attempt to explain such forms as ᶜ*bdw* as good Aramaic, a participle with an auxiliary finite verb. They consider the ᶜ*bydw* of the Armazi text to be a passive (*P*ᵉᶜ*îl*) participle with an enclitic auxiliary verb *h*ᵃ*wâ*, "he was," and they compare it to the Middle Persian *kart ēstēt*.[38]

The use of the participle with an auxiliary verb is already found in Biblical Aramaic, where the perfect form of the verb "he was" usually precedes the participle and only rarely follows it, as in ᵓ*âtê h*ᵃ*wâ* (Dan. 7:13). In such a construction the verb indicates a continuation of action in the past.[39]

Such usage is even more common later, in Syriac, where the auxiliary verb occasionally is placed before the participle but usually after it and, unlike Biblical Aramaic, it is written adjoined, with the initial letter *h* of the enclitic *h*ᵃ*wâ* written but unpronounced, making the form ᶜ*âḇēḏ(h)wâ*. In Syriac such a combination expresses continuance or repetition in past time. The form ܥ݁ܒ݂ܶܕ݂ ܗܘܳܐ is almost equivalent to the Latin "faciebat."[40]

In Syriac the use of an auxiliary verb in the perfect may be added to the perfect tense of the finite verb as well as to the participle. Then the past tense is brought into greater prominence and the construction of the perfect finite verb with an auxiliary perfect may often be translated as a pluperfect.[41] Such usage is still reflected in the neo-Aramaic dialect of Azerbaijan in which *past* time is indicated by "the unstressed past indicator -*wâ*" affixed to the forms of the "Aorist."[42]

In such constructions it is possible that there may be some relationship in syntax between Aramaic and Old Persian, wherein the copula *āha*, "was," appears virtually as an auxiliary verb.[43] Kent explains,[44] "The perfect tense is virtually lacking in Old Persian. . . . The meaning which in English is normally expressed by the perfect tense seems to be present in all instances where the participle is accompanied by the present copula. . . . Where the copula *āha* 'was' is expressed, the meaning seems to be that of the pluperfect: *parābartam āha* 'had been taken away';[45] *kartam āha* 'had been made.' "[46]

As the Persepolis ritual texts show by the identical placement of the verbs ᶜ*bd* and ᶜ*bdw* in the formula, the terms must be equivalent. If the interpretation proposed here is correct, both words must refer to past time. The action described in the ritual vessels was certainly completed, once and for all, with that particular vessel before it was inscribed. Each ceremony seems to have been regarded as a unit and not as an event in a continuing or repeated sequence of acts. This appears to be indicated by the fact that although some celebrants participated more than once in the ceremony, different objects were dedicated on the various dates.[47] On the basis of preserved texts it must be assumed that the majority of the celebrants participated but once.

---

[38] Altheim and Stiehl, *Aramäische Sprache* I 42–43, 274, ᶜ*bd*; also, *Supplementum aramaicum; Aramäisches aus Iran* (Baden-Baden, 1957), pp. 84–85. Altheim reads the word usually read as ᶜ*byd* (l. 4) as ᶜ*bydw*, parallel to the ποιήσαντος of the Greek text.

[39] *BLA*, pp. 292–93, Sec. 81 *p* and *q*; F. Rosenthal, *A Grammar of Biblical Aramaic* (Wiesbaden, 1961), p. 55, Sec. 177.

[40] T. Nöldeke, *Compendious Syriac Grammar*, trans. J. A. Crichton (2d ed.; London, 1904), p. 216.

[41] *Ibid.*, p. 206.

[42] I. Garbell, *The Neo-Aramaean Dialect of Persian Azerbaijan* (London, The Hague, Paris, 1965), pp. 66–68.

[43] E. L. Johnson, *Historical Grammar of the Ancient Persian Language* (New York, Cincinnati, Chicago, 1917), p. 217, Secs. 544–45.

[44] Kent, *Old Persian*, p. 91a, Sec. 288.   [45] Behistun Inscription, col. i, l. 62.

[46] Xerxes, Persepolis F. Inscription, l. 38; Kent, *Old Persian*, p. 150.

[47] Such multiple presentations include: a mortar (No. 25), a plate (No. 102), and another mortar (No. 103); two mortars (Nos. 34 and 38); a pestle (No. 3), a plate (No. 52), and another pestle (No. 133); a pestle (No. 39), another pestle (No. 40), and a plate (No. 113); and a complete set of a mortar (No. 36), pestle (No. 120), and plate (No. 119).

The simple form of the verb, ʿbd, must represent the *Pᵉʿal* perfect form, to be rendered as a present perfect, "he used," as the sense requires, and the variant ʿbdw must have had a similar or identical meaning, possibly "he has used."

Perhaps the answer to the problem of diversity of form here lies in the Old Persian manner of thinking about tense, wherein there was no precise distinction in forms in the representation of ideas normally expressed by the perfect tense in English. Kent says, "it is doubtful if such distinctions [in tense] would have been felt by the speaker of Old Persian, since all past ideas seem to have been merged into one set of forms, including imperfects, aorists, and perfects, and a passive periphrastic of the past participle, with or without the copula (usually without it)."[48]

[48] Kent, *Old Persian*, p. 91a, Sec. 288.

VIII

THE UTENSILS

THE nature of the ritual objects[1] at Persepolis is indicated not only by their familiar shapes but also by the names they bear in the Aramaic texts. Only a single severely abbreviated text on a pestle head (No. 127) lacks the name of the object. The word *hwn* identifies the mortar, *ᵓbšwn* the pestle, and *shr* the plate. The Aramaic name for the tray unfortunately is not preserved on the only specimen that bears an Aramaic text.

The ritual objects are made of a hard, flinty green stone that is usually more or less patterned with lighter and darker grayish-green bands, veins, or lines.[2] Petrological examination indicates that the stone is an impure chert which owes its green color to such impurities as clay and probably glauconite.[3] Herzfeld claimed, "There are plenty of stone vessels in Persepolis, mostly of green stone which protects against poison, *patizahr > bezoar*,"[4] but he does not specify which of the several types he means. Schmidt associated the word *patizahr* (> *pāzahr*) with the mottled black and green serpentine stone used for the royal tableware. But since all of the ritual vessels are made of the same green chert, one wonders whether it was believed to have some peculiar, perhaps apotropaic, value that made it suitable for religious purposes and apparently for nothing else.[5]

Frequently in the Aramaic texts the objects are described as being *zy gll*, "of *gll*." The word *gll* is identical with the *galâlu* or *ᵃᵇᵃⁿgalâla* of Akkadian[6] and the equivalent *ᵓeben gᵉlâl* of Biblical Aramaic (Ezra 5:8, 6:4). The use of the logogram *aban*, "stone," in Akkadian suggests that *galâla* was originally either a distinct kind of stone or one that had been treated in some special way. According to Herzfeld, the word indicated the manner by which the vessels were made, by "turning."[7] But the designation is used elsewhere for architectural elements which certainly were not "turned." Landsberger rejected Herzfeld's interpretation and agreed with Scheil[8] that *galâla* represented a property of the stone, perhaps "hard."[9] Since the Semitic root *gll* can mean "to move in a circle," the word originally might have referred to the natural circular movement of the arm in polishing, leading to the concept of "polished stone." At least the inscribed surfaces of many of the ritual vessels were polished before the texts were written. But whatever the original significance of *galâla*, by the Achaemenid period the word with or without the logogram for stone had come to mean simply "stone."[10] In bilingual texts the Old Persian equivalent for *galâla* is simply *aθaⁿgaina*, "of stone."[11]

---

[1] See Schmidt, *Persepolis* II 53–56.

[2] *Ibid.*, p. 53*b*; Cameron, *PTT*, p. 6*a*.

[3] Schmidt, *Persepolis* II 53, n. 55.

[4] E. Herzfeld, *Zoroaster and His World* (Princeton, 1947) II 788.

[5] Schmidt (*Persepolis* II 55*a*) properly suggests that an uninscribed green chert bowl with three lion legs, which he included in the category of tableware, and other uninscribed objects of the same material may have been for ritual use. See p. 51 and Pl. 1 below.

[6] *CAD* V 11, *galâlu*.

[7] E. Herzfeld, *Altpersischen Inschriften* (Berlin, 1938), p. 100.

[8] V. Scheil, *Inscriptions des Achéménides à Suse* ("Mémoires de la Mission archéologique de Perse" XXI [Paris, 1929]), p. 31.

[9] See Schmidt, *Persepolis* II 55, n. 68.

[10] R. A. Bowman, "גְלָל אֶבֶן—*aban galâlu* (Ezra 5:8; 6:4)," *Dōrōn: Hebraic Studies* (New York, 1965), pp. 64–74.

[11] Kent, *Old Persian*, p. 166*a*, *aθagaina*.

44

That *zy gll* means only "of stone" seems supported by the fact that sometimes writers attempt greater precision by expanding *zy gll* to indicate a particular kind of stone or some characteristic of it. These additions, almost all as yet unidentified, include *bz* (Nos. 91, 116), which is sometimes rendered as *bzy* (Nos. 92 and 112), *tzgbs* (No. 1) or *ggbs*(?), and *hmš*. . . (No. 105), which unfortunately may be incomplete. Another addition to *zy gll* is *ʾḥšynpyn* (No. 75), which is also spelled *ʾḥšynpn*, and an incomplete word (No. 74) ending with *-nḥwyn*, of which I assume the lost part likewise to be [*ʾḥšy*]*n-*. Since the element *ʾḥšyn-* is probably the Old Persian *axšaina*, "dark-colored,"[12] some of the terms above which include it as an element probably refer to the color of the stone.

A single text (No. 122:2) supplements *zy gll* with the word *kpwtk* which doubtless represents the Old Persian *kapautaka*, usually translated as lapis lazuli.[13] Since the stone is definitely not lapis lazuli and it is unlikely that anyone familiar with that blue stone would make such an identification, it is possible that the reference is to stone color, a reversion to or survival of *kapautaka* in the sense of pigeon-colored.[14] It is possible, however, that the term may refer to some quality or characteristic that the stones had in common, such as "veined" or "marbleized." R. C. Thompson, apparently on the basis of a rendering by Scheil rather than of any more specific evidence, has identified *galâla* as "marble."[15]

MORTAR

It is assumed that the green stone vessels recovered from the Persepolis Treasury are cultic because just such a mortar and pestle is portrayed beside a fire altar in a religious theme depicted on cylinder seal impressions from the time of Xerxes.[16] That seal motif appears to capture the moment during the haoma ceremony just before the haoma liquid was consumed. The content of the Aramaic texts, as conjectured here, supports the assumption that the vessels found had been used in the haoma ceremony before being presented in the Persepolis Treasury.

A surprising number of mortars was found in the Treasury. Of 97 recovered, 79 bore Aramaic texts. In the Aramaic texts the mortar is identified as the *hwn, havana*. The word, like haoma, the name of the sacred drink, is derived from a root meaning "to press."[17] The noun, meaning "the presser," "(wine) press,"[18] is used in a dual form to designate the two essential parts used for the crushing operation.

According to Bartholomae, the word *havana* describes both the mortar and pestle. Unless a careless error is involved, that is supported by a single text on a pestle (No. 24:4) which describes the object on which it is written as "this *havana*." Such usage would be appropriate when, in the earliest days, the mortar and "pestle" consisted of a pair of stones. In their pressing of soma (= haoma) the Brahmans in India "beat the stalks of the plant, which are placed on a large flat stone [*upara*], with a smaller stone [*grāvan*] till they formed a single mass."[19] On the basis of Yasht 10:2, Herzfeld contended that the Persians, too, used such a press, made of a "principal" (*frataram*) and an "upper" (*uparam*) *havana*.[20] Such usage doubt-

---

[12] *Ibid.*, p. 165*b*, *axšaina*; *BAiW*, col. 51, Avestan *a-xšaēna*, "dunkelfarbig." Cf. No. 11:3.

[13] Kent, *Old Persian*, p. 178*b*.

[14] Meillet and Benveniste, *Grammaire*, pp. 58, 159, Secs. 98, 273.

[15] R. C. Thompson, *A Dictionary of Assyrian Chemistry and Geology* (Oxford, 1936), p. 160.

[16] Schmidt, *Persepolis* II 6, 26, Seal 20; see Pl. 1 here.

[17] *BAiW*, col. 1781, ¹*hav* (Avestan *hav;* Sanskrit *su;* Old Persian *hu*). The noun survives in modern Persian *hāvan* and is borrowed in modern Arabic and Turkish (cf. W. Eilers, "Traubensyrup in Iran," *Orientalistische Literaturzeitung* XLIV [1941], col. 8, n. 1; Schmidt, *Persepolis* II 55*b*, n. 65).

[18] *BAiW*, col. 1786, *havana*.   [19] Haug, *Parsis*, p. 282.

[20] Herzfeld, *Zoroaster and His World* II 546.

less reflects the earlier stage in the development of the pressing process, a stage at which both stones formed a single object and bore the same name.

But it is certain from the Aramaic texts that as early as the Achaemenid period the Persians had begun to distinguish clearly between the mortar and pestle and at least tended to reserve *havana* for the mortar. Not only does each object usually bear its distinctive name, but a number of texts describe the set as "this mortar with a pestle" or "this pestle with a mortar."[21] Since the mortar and pestle was regarded as a unit, it is apparent that the donor usually had but one object inscribed.[22] That would account for the relatively large number of uninscribed objects of the same shapes and material.

According to ancient texts, the mortar could be made either of stone (*asmana hâvana*)[23] or of iron (*ayanghahena hâvana*).[24] Most of the mortars found at Persepolis were of green chert but an uninscribed one of creamy-white and orange limestone (PT5 911) was also found in the great Hall 38 of the Treasury, where most of the ritual objects were recovered. Even more interesting are the uninscribed mortar (PT6 195) and pestle (PT6 123) of bronze which are identical in shape with those of green chert.[25] Pavry explains that formerly two mortars were used at the same time in the haoma ceremony, a stone one for pounding haoma and an iron one for producing a ringing sound.[26] The Parsis today use mortars and pestles of bell metal (brass or copper) because the sonorous ringing of the mortar with the pestle is a conspicuous part of the haoma-crushing ceremony.[27]

Mortars now used by the Parsis are described as "generally shaped like a wine glass with a foot and stem, but much larger."[28] On the basis of one complete example[29] and a number of fragments, the excavator says of the mortars found at Persepolis, "The mortars as well as the pestles of green chert have stereotyped shapes. Almost all mortars have a roughly hemispherical top with squared rim. However, in a few cases the top part is oblong, with almost straight sides. The conoid base has squared edges, beveled in some instances with an inward slant. The bottom is frequently more or less convex. As the mortar would have greater stability if its bottom were flat, the purpose of the convexity may have been to facilitate rocking or revolving."[30]

Inscribed mortars, some of which were for cultic use (Akkadian *madaqqum, madākum, mazuktum*), are already known from Iraq.[31] But none are like the ritual objects from Persepolis, which bear more extensive and significant texts, written in ink and in the Aramaic alphabet and language. The inscribed mortars have their texts written across the bottom surfaces of their bases, some of which were polished before the texts were written.

From the Aramaic texts we learn that three sizes of mortars were recognized, although not all examples are so designated. Semitic words are used to designate the "large" (*rb*)[32] and "small" (*zᶜyr*)[33] sizes but, lacking a precise Semitic word for "medium-sized," the Iranian *mdm* (Avestan *maδəma*)[34] is used for mortars in that category.[35]

Because the vessels are fragmentary, it is impossible to make an over-all comparison for

[21] See Nos. 1:3, 46:4, 103:3, and also in Nos. 9, 10, 13, 14, 16, 17, and 79.

[22] Nos. 14 and 15 indicate that at times both objects could be inscribed.

[23] Vendidād 14:10.   [24] Yasna 22:2; Visparad 10:2.

[25] Schmidt, *Persepolis* II, Pl. 80: 7*a, b*. Found in the vestibule (50) at the northern exit of the Treasury.

[26] C. E. Pavry, *Iranian Studies* (Bombay, 1927), p. 198.

[27] Modi, *Religious Ceremonies*, pp. 291, 309; Pavry, *Iranian Studies*, p. 198.

[28] Haug, *Parsis*, p. 396.   [29] PT5 7 (No. 33).   [30] Schmidt, *Persepolis* II 55.

[31] F. Thureau-Dangin, *Die sumerischen und akkadischen Königsinschriften* (Leipzig, 1907), pp. 28 ff.; W. Eilers, "Die Ausgrabungen in Persepolis," *Zeitschrift für Assyriologie* N.F. XIX (1959) 259, n. 16*b*.

[32] Nos. 14, 16, and 88.   [34] *BAiW*, cols. 1114–15.

[33] Nos. 31, 33, 38, 108, 118, and 147.   [35] Nos. 41, 55, 56, 80, 97, 124.

size. But there is a rather constant relationship between the mortar and its base. Where even a part of the circumference of the base is preserved, the whole can be determined and its diameter computed for purposes of comparison.[36]

According to Nīrangistān 108, the smallest mortar permissible could accommodate only three haoma twigs.[37] The smallest in the Persepolis collection (Nos. 34 and 105) have a base diameter of 7.1 cm. Those designated as "small" in the text have base diameters of 7.6 cm. (No. 38), 7.7 cm. (No. 108), 8 cm. (No. 31), 8.2 cm. (Nos. 33 and 118), and 9.3 cm. (No. 147).[38]

The smallest mortar called "medium" (No. 80) has a base diameter of 11.2 cm., and the largest of that category (No. 124) measures 13 cm. Another called "medium" (No. 97) has a diameter of 12.5 cm.[39]

The smallest mortar called "large" (No. 14) measures 16.7 cm. and the largest so designated (No. 16) measures 18 cm. But the largest by measurement (No. 5) has a base diameter of 18.9 cm.[40]

A single mortar text (No. 8) furnishes the rather unnecessary information that it was used "for pounding" (*lḥšl*). More valuable are the additions to the text indicating that the mortar was used "during a festival" (No. 112:5) and "in a great (ceremony of) crushing" (No. 5:3).

PESTLE

Pestles used by the Parsis, described as "chisel-shaped at one end,"[41] are now called "handle" (*dasta*) or "tulip" (*lālā*).[42] Neither of these names are found for the pestle in the Persepolis texts, nor is the ancient pestle like the modern Parsi type in its shape. The Achaemenian Aramaic word used for the object is *ᵓbšwn*.

Altheim and Stiehl transcribe the word as *ᵓbšwn* and propose an etymology **abi-sā-van*, "rings, sehr scharfend, sehr spitzend," relating it to Old Indic *śiśāti*, "he sharpened," modern Persian *sūdan* and Avestan *saēnay*, "sharp," "point," "top."[43] More likely is the suggestion of Eilers, who sees in it the prefix *ᵓb* (*abi-*), "against,"[44] and a form of the verb *su*, "press out,"[45] with the *s* properly becoming *š* after the preceding *i*-class vowel.[46] Eilers suggests that the use of the sibilant *s* instead of *h* indicates a borrowing of the word from the East. The concluding -*n* Eilers sees as an affix encountered elsewhere in the names of implements (for example, *safkon*, "strainer"). Thus, the word *ᵓbšwn* means "an instrument pressed against something" or "an instrument used for pressing out something."[47]

---

[36] Checking measurements shows that the figures for "diameters" in the excavator's Field Register are the measurement of the base, usually reconstructed from a fragment and that the figures are accurate and trustworthy.

[37] *BAiW*, col. 1786.

[38] Other small mortars are Nos. 34 and 105 (7.1 cm.); 46 and 116 (7.2 cm.); 32 (7.3 cm.); 121 and 125 (7.5 cm.); 83 and 143 (7.6 cm., also No. 38); 160 (7.7 cm., also No. 108); 8 and 30 (7.8 cm.); 130 (7.9 cm.); 1, 84, 99, 138 (8 cm., also No. 31); 146 (9.7 cm.); and possibly No. 74 (*ca.* 10 cm.).

[39] Other medium-sized mortars are Nos. 139 (11.2 cm., also No. 80); 96 (11.4 cm.); 159 (11.5 cm.); 79 (11.6 cm.); 162 (11.9 cm.); 9, 25, 101, 103, 135, 145 (12 cm.); 13 and 144 (12.2 cm.); 93 (12.5 cm., also No. 97); 76 and 82 (13 cm.); and 106 (13.1 cm., also No. 124).

[40] Large mortars include Nos. 149 (15.8 cm.); 86 (16 cm.); 94 and 122 (16.5 cm.); 91 (16.7 cm., also No. 14); 36 (17.7 cm.); and 75, 85, 89, 90, 136 (18 cm., also No. 16).

[41] Haug, *Parsis*, p. 396.

[42] Modi, *Religious Ceremonies*, p. 259; F. Steingass, *A Comprehensive Persian-English Dictionary* (London, 1892), p. 525a دسته, *dasta*.

[43] Altheim and Stiehl, *Aramäische Sprache* I 19, 101.

[44] As a verbal prefix *abiy-* appears as *abi-*; Meillet and Benveniste, *Grammaire*, p. 143, Sec. 246.

[45] The form *su* is the Sanskrit equivalent of the Persian *hu* (e.g., *soma/haoma*).

[46] Kent, *Old Persian*, p. 40a, Sec. 115 (1), p. 40b, Sec. 117, p. 48a, Sec. 140, VI.

[47] Bartholomae (*BAiW*, col. 1781, ¹*hav*) indicates that when *hav* is used with *aiwi/abiy* the meaning is "auskeltern," "to press out."

At least four times the word *pyrk* is used as an adjective to characterize the pestle.[48] Although such a form is unusual for Aramaic, it has parallels in other Semitic languages.[49] The word is doubtless derived from the Semitic root *prk* meaning "rubbing," "smashing," "crushing" and is thus related to the *prkn* and *prk* (No. 5:3) used in the ritual texts.

Of the pestles recovered at Persepolis Schmidt says, "All pestles have a discoid head, usually somewhat convex on top, and a shaft with rather straight sides which are in some cases slightly convex or, rarely, somewhat concave. The shaft expands toward the round grinding end. Two pestles in our collection consist only of a shaft with two wrought ends.[50] It may be that the heads of these specimens were accidentally broken and that the fractured ends were carefully reground."[51]

Most of the pestles found are badly broken. Only two may be regarded as complete. A small one (PT5 8), which belongs with mortar No. 33, is now illegible and may not have been inscribed.[52] The larger one (No. 54), which perhaps would be classified as "medium-large," is only slightly damaged on the edges of its head.

Noteworthy is the uninscribed bronze pestle (PT6 123) that was found with the bronze mortar (PT6 195) to which it belongs. It is shaped exactly like the ritual pestles of green chert.

Because mortars and pestles formed sets to be used together,[53] it should be expected that pestles, like mortars, would come in three sizes, and they do. Here, too, some are called "large" (*rb*),[54] others "medium-sized" (*mdm*),[55] and "small" (*zᶜyr*).[56]

The smaller pestle called "small" (No. 123) has a head diameter of 3 cm., but there are even smaller ones (Nos. 60 and 131 of 2.7 cm. diameter and No. 78 of 2.9 cm. diameter). The larger pestle called "small" (No. 87) has a head diameter of 3.3 cm., exactly the size of another (No. 57) which is called "medium."[57] Others called "medium" measure 3.4 cm. (No. 2), 3.5 cm. (No. 17), 3.6 cm. (No. 100), and 3.7 cm. (No. 21). The largest called "medium" has a head diameter of 4.3 cm.[58] Since the smallest pestle designated as "large" (No. 10) measures 5.8 cm., it is difficult to determine whether those that measure 5 cm. or over[59] should be regarded as medium-sized or large. The largest pestle so designated (No. 64) measures 6.5 cm., almost the diameter of the base of a small mortar. Another (No. 39) called "large" has a head diameter of 6 cm.[60]

Of the 80 green chert pestles found, 68 were inscribed with an Aramaic text written in ink. The normal place for the text is on the discoid top of the pestle, but the small space sometimes imposed severe restrictions in the formulae. In order to gain more writing space, scribes wrote texts lengthwise along the shaft of a few pestles (Nos. 17, 81, and 124).

Just as the texts of mortars occasionally refer to their pestles, a few pestle texts mention

---

[48] Nos. 9, 13, 14, and 17.

[49] *Fayᶜal* and *fayᶜâl* forms are found in Arabic in such words as *ḥayðar*, "rambling," or *hayṣār*, "tearing"; cf. Henri Fleisch *Traité de philologie arabe* I ("Recherches de l'Institut de lettres orientale de Beyrouth" XVI [Beyrouth, 1961]) 353*h* and n. 1; Carl Brockelmann, *Grundriss der vergleichenden Grammatik der semitischen Sprachen* I (Berlin, 1908) 344, Sec. 129.

[50] Neither of these are of green chert nor are they inscribed. One (PT4 991), of tan limestone, was found in Room 34 of the Treasury and the other (PT3 300), also of tan limestone, was recovered in Yard 21.

[51] Schmidt, *Persepolis* II 55, see Pl. 24: 7, 8, 9, and Pl. 1 here.

[52] The Field Register calls for one line of Aramaic but nothing is now visible on the pestle head.

[53] No. 39 is designated as "this mortar" using the term *havan* for the set; see p. 45.

[54] Nos. 7, 10, 39, and 64.   [55] Nos. 2, 17, 21, 23, 57, and 100.   [56] Nos. 87 and 123.

[57] Other "small" pestles are Nos. 60 and 131 (2.7 cm.); 78 (2.9 cm.); 134 (3 cm., also No. 123); 59, 63, and 137 (3.1 cm.); and 29 and 66 (3.2 cm.).

[58] Medium pestles include also Nos. 27, 67, 70, 77, and 127 (3.5 cm., also No. 17); 69 (3.6 cm., also No. 100); 4 and 71 (3.7 cm., also No. 21); 6, 20, 62, and 126 (3.8 cm.); 65 and 81 (3.9 cm.); 68 (4 cm.); 58 (4.1 cm.); 117 and 161 (4.3 cm., also No. 23); and probably 37 (4.6 cm.) and 54 (4.8 cm.).

[59] Nos. 11 (5.3 cm.), 40 (5.4 cm.), and 128 (5.5 cm.).

[60] Large pestles are Nos. 26 (5.8 cm., also No. 10); 12 and 120 (5.9 cm., also No. 7); 3, 15, 22, 115 (6.1 cm.); 24 (6.2 cm.); 28 (6.3 cm.); and 61 (6.5 cm., also No. 64).

their companion mortars.[61] One text (No. 10) mentions "this large pestle of stone with a large mortar" and another (No. 17) has the text "a mortar of stone with a medium-sized crushing pestle."

One text (No. 39) calls the pestle "this large mortar." Unless this is an error, it could be a reminiscence of the earlier period when the mortar and pestle together were considered to be one implement that could be called *havana*, "mortar."[62]

Most interesting are the two pestles on which the texts offer further description of the object. One (No. 29) describes it as *ʾbšwn zy bʾt*, "pestle of wine." The other (No. 62), according to Cameron's copy, is called *ʾbšwn zy ʾškr*, "pestle of *ʾškr*," which holds some promise of defining the obscure term *ʾškr*.[63] If *ʾškr* is similar to *bʾt* in meaning, the words *ʾbšwn zy ʾškr* may signify "pestle of the intoxicant (haoma?)."

PLATE

The third largest class of green chert ritual objects found at Persepolis has been called "plates" by the excavator but he recognized that "certain . . . vessels which we classify as plates could actually be termed bowl as well."[64]

The modern Parsi name, *tašta*,[65] is not used in the Achaemenid ritual texts. The vessel is invariably called *šḥr*. Altheim read the word as *šḥr* and equated it with the *šḥr* of Hebrew (Cant. 7:3; English vers. 7:2), the *ʾaggan hassahar*.[66] Because Semitic *ḥ* or *ẖ* may sometimes be represented by Aramaic *h* in the Aramaic of Persepolis but Semitic *ḥ* seems never to be rendered by the letter *ḥ* there,[67] Altheim's etymology seems suspect. The explanation of *šḥr* is still uncertain.

On the basis of many fragments of plates recovered in the Persepolis Treasury the excavator reports, "Three of the eighty-five plates have a rounded, laterally projecting lip. Where preserved, the lips of all others are squared. On one plate a groove encircles the exterior just below the rim. Otherwise, there are only minor variations in size, thickness, and depth. The bases of all plates project somewhat and form a flat disk, at times slightly convex at the bottom. . . . Except for their usually thinner walls, many serpentine plates which we classify as royal tableware are identical in shape with the green chert plates with squared lips."[68] A beautiful, complete specimen of such a plate was found by the Archaeological Institute of Persepolis in 1949.[69]

Professor Schmidt recognized "minor variations" in the size of the plates. As with the mortars, the diameters of the plates, when they can be determined, can furnish some basis for indicating relative size.[70] Unlike the mortars and pestles, only the "large" (*rb*) plates are so designated in the Aramaic texts.[71]

---

[61] Nos. 10 and 17.

[62] *BAiW*, col. 1786.

[63] See pp. 54–55.

[64] Schmidt, *Persepolis* II 89*b*.

[65] The word *tašta*, used as early as the Vendidād for the plates of the haoma ceremony (Vendidād 19:8), is cognate with the French and German "tasse" and English "dish."

[66] Altheim and Stiehl, *Aramäische Sprache* I 19. He compares the Syriac *sahrāʾ*, "moon," and other words derived from the Semitic root *šhr*, "be round," but also refers to the root *šḥr*, "to go in a circle," "to surround," "to enclose."

[67] See p. 64. But in Iranian words an Iranian *h* may be represented by an Aramaic *ḥ*; cf. No. 24, pp. 96–97, Āraya(t)-vahuš and Āraya(t)-vaḥuš for the same person.

[68] Schmidt, *Persepolis* II 53, Pl. 24:1, 2, 3, 5.

[69] No. 43. Ali-Sami, *Persepolis (Takht-i-Jamshid)*, trans. R. N. Sharp (4th ed.; Shiraz, 1966), pp. 67–68; also portrayed on an unnumbered plate at the end of the booklet, pp. 95–96, No. 10. There are also several complete but uninscribed plates; see Pl. 1 here.

[70] More fragile than the mortars, the plates are often broken into shapes that almost defy the reconstruction of their base measurement. Moreover, when the over-all diameter of the plate can be ascertained, the Field Register sometimes gives that figure rather than the diameter of the base.

[71] Nos. 18 (13.5 cm.) and 43 (9.3 cm.).

Although the plates are made of the same material as the other ritual objects, it is a peculiar fact that only a few plates (Nos. 109, 111, and 113) include in their description of the objects the words *zy gll*, "of stone," which are used rather constantly on the other implements. The usual formula in the plates is *ᶜbd sḥr znh*, "used this plate."

In addition to the usual formula of the Aramaic text several plates have some modifying words not encountered elsewhere. Because the words are often badly preserved and the writing of many of the letters at times is ambiguous, little can be learned from some of such additions that occur only once.[72]

An expression found on two plates is *rᶜyn bg*,[73] which appears to be a mixture of Aramaic and Iranian words. As the letter *ᶜaiyn* was used in Persian only in Aramaic logograms, the first word must be Semitic. It appears to be the Aramaic *raᶜyân*, which appears in Biblical Aramaic and later Jewish Aramaic, as well as in late Hebrew, in the form *raᶜyôn*.[74] Its Semitic root, *rᶜy* (Arabic رَضِي), signifies "to take pleasure in (something)" or "to desire."[75] From Biblical contexts in which it is found it is clear that the word involves "striving" or "longing" (in Ecclesiastes) and "desire" (in Daniel), as well as "ambition" and "greed" in later Aramaic.[76]

The word *bg*, however, is doubtless the Persian *baga*, which usually means "god" but can also mean "portion," "lot," "fortunate lot," "good fortune," and "luck."[77]

One would expect *rᶜyn bg*, which appears only on plates, to refer to the object and furnish some description of the vessel, but that appears not to be the case. It seems to be a parenthetic comment relating to the verb. As "the desire of god," it might indicate that the ceremony was performed to please the god. More probable, however, is the translation "a desire for good fortune," which would indicate that the purpose of the generals in participating in the haoma rite was to gain personal good fortune, military victory, immortality, health, and prosperity.

A few plates that are unfortunately very badly preserved have a textual insertion including a numeral after the description of the vessel.[78] The difficult passage was clarified with the discovery of a complete text which shows that the numeral indicates the value of the vessel being presented.[79] One such plate and a mortar were worth eight shekel coins and one "large" plate cost nine.

In any set of haoma vessels one would expect to find the cup from which the liquid was drunk. One would expect this vessel, above all others, to be the dedicated memorial of the occasion of participation in the haoma ceremony. At the present time the Parsis use a round-bottomed cup the size of a teacup in the ceremony,[80] but no such vessels were found at Persepolis, either among the ritual vessels or among the royal tableware. It is clear that cups were indeed known in ancient Iran,[81] but there are none of the green chert used for the ritual vessels. Perhaps the solution lies in the fact that in the Achaemenid period bowls were used for drinking purposes. This is suggested by the motif on a cylinder seal of the period which depicts a meal in which the eater is about to drink from a bowl.[82] While it may be that at least

---

[72] E.g., see No. 48:5.　　　　　　　　　　　　　[73] Nos. 47 and 52.

[74] Dan. 2:29–30, 4:16, 5:6 and 10; Eccles. 1:17, 2:22, 4:16.

[75] Professor J. Harmatta informs me that *rᶜyn* appears in Sogdian texts as an Aramaic logogram for the Iranian *kāma*, "desire," "wish."

[76] Jastrow, *Dictionary* II 1487.

[77] Kent, *Old Persian*, p. 199a, *baga;* *BAiW*, col. 921, *baga-*, "Herr," "Gott" or "Anteil," "Los," "günstiges Los," "Glück."

[78] Nos. 43, 73 and mortar No. 135.　　　[79] No. 43:4, see pp. 112–14.　　　[80] Haug, *Parsis*, p. 394.

[81] They are portrayed on reliefs at Persepolis as gifts being brought to the king and some were recovered among the foreign ware in the Treasury (Schmidt, *Persepolis* II 94–95).

[82] *Ibid.*, Pl. 16 (PT6 1) and p. 45b. Schmidt (p. 96a) suggests that some small bowls may have served as cups.

some of the smaller and lighter plates or bowls of green chert could represent the vessels from which the drinking was done, the weight of the larger ones and the relatively thick rims of all would seem to make drinking from them awkward and difficult. It might have been managed, however, if ceremonial requirements demanded it.

If the green chert vessels are indeed plates and not drinking bowls, of the five plates now essential for the Parsi haoma ceremony, those chosen for inscription and dedication at Persepolis probably correspond to those now called *hōm nō tašto* (*tašta haomya*), the plate used for holding the haoma twigs needed for the ceremony.[83]

TRAY

Many fewer "trays" were found at Persepolis than any other type of green chert vessels. Those found are represented by three curved fragments and four pieces with straight sides. Of two trays with curved outline one has an intermittent ledge such as is found on many plates and trays of royal tableware. One of the pieces with straight sides is the corner of an angular tray.[84]

Of seven trays recovered, only one (No. 142), a smooth, oblong vessel of green chert with grey veins, shows evidence of having been inscribed.[85] Only three letters, the beginnings of two incomplete words, remain of the Aramaic text that had been written on the flat bottom of the tray. The traces are too incomplete to preserve even the name of the object, as a clue to its use in the haoma ceremony.

No "tray" is listed among the paraphernalia now used by the Parsis in their haoma ceremony. It seems probable, however, that the "trays" functioned in ancient times as the slabs, later known as *hwān's*, "tables," in the modern ceremony.[86] Six such stone slabs or *hwān's*, cut of stone or marble, are used in the Parsi ceremonial room today. One such stone platform (*takht-i-âlāt*) now holds the cups and saucers, the *barsom* stand, and other apparatus necessary for the ceremony.

Only one of the slabs of the modern ceremony, however, has rounded ends to resemble the shape of the inscribed tray from Persepolis. That one, a slab about fifteen inches long, is now called the *kundi nō hwân*, the "table" for the *kundi*, the large vessel containing the ritually pure water in which the smaller implements, including the pestle, were kept when not in use.[87] It seems quite probable that the oblong-oval inscribed green chert "tray" at Persepolis is an earlier form of the "slab" for the *kundi*-vessel, just as the stone mortars and pestles antedated the bell metal ones now in use.

The *kundi* itself may be represented at Persepolis by the apparently uninscribed green chert bowl with lion legs, which has usually been included in the category of royal tableware, but which Schmidt suspected of being for ritual use.[88] This seems likely because all of the inscribed ritual vessels are of the same green chert stone. It would appear that such stone was reserved for ritual vessels and therefore that all objects of that stone served a ritual purpose. The green chert tripod vessel would thus have stood on the oblong-oval green chert tray.

Since most of the green chert ritual objects are identified by the demonstrative pronoun *znh*, "this," it seems probable that the objects inscribed are the very ones that were used by

---

[83] Vendidād 14:8; Modi, *Religious Ceremonies*, p. 260.

[84] Schmidt, *Persepolis* II 53*b*–55*a*, Pl. 24:4 and 6, Pl. 64:1, 3, and 5.   [85] *Ibid.*, Pl. 24:4.

[86] Modi (*Religious Ceremonies*, pp. 254 ff.) calls the object a "stone slab," which might well characterize a tray, but the vessel is now called by the Arabic name *hwân* (خوان), "table," "tray," because it now stands on four feet, like a table; cf. Steingass, *A Comprehensive Persian-English Dictionary*, p. 480*b*.

[87] Modi, *Religious Ceremonies*, pp. 254, 258.

[88] Schmidt, *Persepolis* II 55*a*, 89*a*, Pls. 55:3, 56:1.

the celebrant in the haoma ceremony. There are, however, a number of texts in which the demonstrative pronoun is not used.[89] Indeed, some texts have the unit stroke, which should be rendered as an indefinite pronoun rather than a demonstrative. A single text which mentions both a mortar and pestle (No. 14), written on a mortar, describes the mortar with the demonstrative "this" but uses the unit stroke "one" or "a" for the pestle.

Such texts might suggest that the vessels so inscribed were not the identical ones used in the ceremonial. Perhaps this should not be overstressed, however, since it would be most likely that the celebrants would have preferred to present the very ones they used, appropriately inscribed.

Since all of the vessels were not preserved intact as a collection, but were shattered and scattered, it cannot be decided whether each celebrant presented a complete set of the objects used. The relative scarcity of trays suggests that they were not normally regarded as part of a "set" and the tripod vessels are even more rare. The fact that many of the cultic vessels were not inscribed suggests that Aramaic texts, in some cases at least, may have been written on only one piece of a set. This seems particularly clear with the mortars and pestles, for they were regarded as a unit and either part could be called *havana*, "mortar."[90] It is possible that the pestle was an indispensable part of the mortar, for in a few instances the mortar and pestle are both mentioned on the same object.[91]

It is probable that the mortar and pestle was the usual dedication and that the mortar and pestle presented by Haoma-dāta in a single year (Nos. 14 and 15) represent such a presentation. Others show their intention to present a complete set, even though time elapsed between the presentations. Thus Rāman presented two pestles, and a plate (Nos. 39, 40, and 113) in different years, probably indicating participation in the haoma ceremony several times. *Šwrty*, too, gave three pieces, although the loss of dates prevents a decision as to whether they were all presented at the same time.

It may be that less than a set, even a single piece, was given as a token of the event. Thus, *Bhyyn* dedicated two plates (Nos. 48 and 112); *ʾdwst* and Rāman two pestles and a plate in different years (Nos. 3, 52, and 133; Nos. 39, 40, and 113); *Krpyš* two mortars and a plate (Nos. 25, 102, and 103); *Krbr*, two pestles in different years (Nos. 11 and 12); and Kālī, a mortar and a plate (Nos. 94 and 95).

Other celebrants seem to have presented only a single inscribed object each. As in the case of some mentioned above, there may have been an intention to complete a set over a period of years. Sometimes there was a considerable interval between the dedications. Forty years elapsed, for example, between the presentation of a pestle (No. 3) by *ʾdwst* in the tenth year of Xerxes and a plate (No. 52) in the twenty-ninth year of Artaxerxes I.

[89] E.g., Nos. 4, 11, 12, 17, 22, 29, 87, 116, 131.

[90] See pp. 45–46.

[91] Nos. 1, 9, 10, 13, 14, 16, 17, 46, 79, and 103.

IX

ˀŠkr

JUST before the date in the standard Aramaic text on the ritual vessels from Persepolis is a single, somewhat enigmatic word ˀškr. Except for a few pestles with extremely abbreviated formulae,[1] the word ˀškr, or some evidence of its presence, is found in the text of every inscribed mortar, pestle, or plate on which the end of the Aramaic text is still preserved.

The word might be either Semitic or Persian in origin. J. Duchesne-Guillemin has suggested that it might be the Persian āškār, meaning "clear," "open," "public," "evident," "manifest."[2] Such a meaning would be appropriate if the Aramaic texts recorded the presentation of the ritual vessels at Persepolis in a public ceremony, but the simple solution is not persuasive. Furthermore, as will be shown below, the word appears in these texts as a modifier of the word "pestle."

If the word is Iranian, the letters -kr at the end of the word might represent the Persian element -kara, which is found in two senses in combination. It can be a verbal noun expressing "agent," "maker," as in hamārakara, "accountant," or it can be used in a passive sense, "a thing made," as in patikara, "image," "reproduction."[3]

The initial element ˀš- might then be a substantive expressing the nature of the maker or of what is made. Gathic and Late Avestan aša signifies "law," "justice,"[4] but in some contexts it appears to have a more dynamic quality of cosmic power affecting the strength of life and healing damage caused by evil powers. Nyberg claims that in a certain sense the term comes close to the concept "health."[5] The term aša occurs in the Haoma Yasht (Yasna 10:8), where haoma, the beneficial drink, is contrasted with all others. As "health-producing" the term ˀškr would seem to be an appropriate epithet for haoma. But etymologically the word aša is related to the Sanskrit ṛtá, "cosmic order," which should be spelled arta in Old Persian, where it is found as an element in many personal names.

In Late Avestan a word aša, when used as an adjective referring to grain, signifies "crushed."[6] This meaning, too, would be suitable as a modifier of "pestle" and "maker of something crushed" would be an appropriate title for the hāvanān, who crushed the haoma, and "(something) crushed" would certainly characterize the haoma liquid itself. But, like that aša mentioned above, this aša, too, should be arta in Old Persian.

In Pahlavi āš means "meat," "pottage," "soup," "broth," "food"[7] and the same meaning

---

[1] Nos. 27, 54, 57, 65, 77, 126–29, 131, 133, 134. The only complete longer text in which the word is missing, according to Cameron's copy, is No. 30 (a mortar).

[2] F. Steingass, *A Comprehensive Persian-English Dictionary* (London, 1892), p. 65*b*, اشكار (ˀaškār).

[3] Meillet and Benveniste, *Grammaire*, pp. 166–67, Sec. 289; Kent, *Old Persian*, p. 179*b*, -*kara*.

[4] *BAiW*, cols. 229–38, [1]aša-; Kent, *Old Persian*, p. 170*b*, arta-.

[5] Nyberg, *Religionen*, p. 130.

[6] *BAiW*, col. 239, [4]aša-. Modern Persian ās-, "a grinding (of wheat, barley, etc.)," may be related and āśkardan (āś+kar) means "to crush," "to bruise," "to grind"; cf. Steingass, *A Comprehensive Persian-English Dictionary*, p. 46*b*.

[7] D. H. Jamasp and M. M. Gandevia, *Vendidād* II (Bombay, 1907) 31, āsh-.

is found in modern Persian, where the composite noun *aškāra* means "a maker of food, a cook."[8] While haoma is certainly a liquid, it hardly qualifies as a food.

Altheim's suggestion, that the word is *ᵓbzkr*, the **a-bāži-kara*, "who brings tribute," found in the Nisā ostraca,[9] should not be considered because it is based on a faulty reading of a single text. The word occurs often enough to certify its spelling as *ᵓškr*.

Cameron, regarding the ritual texts as being simply a statement of the presentation of the objects in the Treasury in the presence of officials, translated *ᵓškr* as "a gift" on the basis of the *ᵓeškār* found in the Bible (Ezek. 27:15; Ps. 72:10).[10] But the Biblical *ᵓeškār* is doubtless a borrowing of the Akkadian *iškaru*,[11] which probably ultimately derives from Sumerian. Among the several meanings of Akkadian *iškaru* are "assigned work" and, only in the Neo-Assyrian period, "(a kind of) tax."[12] In the Biblical passages in which the word occurs, the reference is certainly to "imposed tax" or "tribute" rather than to a free-will offering or "present," the sense in which Cameron assumes that the Aramaic texts on the ritual vessels have it.

Because of the intoxicating character of haoma, it is tempting to regard *ᵓškr* as a causative (*ᵓAf⁽el*) form of the Semitic root *škr*, "to fill," "to saturate," "to drink freely" and to translate *ᵓškr* as the verb, "he became intoxicated." But it is the *Pa⁽el* rather than *ᵓAf⁽el* or *Haf⁽el* form of the verb *škr* that is used in Aramaic to indicate intoxication. Moreover, although there may be traces of an *ᵓAf⁽el* form in Biblical Aramaic[13] and Egyptian Aramaic,[14] only *Haf⁽el* forms are attested hitherto in the Aramaic of Persepolis.

Most promising for a Semitic solution to the word *ᵓškr* is the Akkadian word *šikâru*, "drink," "beverage," "intoxicating drink."[15] It is found in Hebrew as *šēkār* with the meaning "intoxicating drink"[16] and in Aramaic as *š⁽kar*, which is used for "strong drink other than wine."[17] In Pahlavi the Aramaic *škr* is a logogram for Iranian *xᵛar*, "intoxicating drink." It can correspond to the Avestan *hurā*, "kumiss."[18] Such Aramaic forms with a double consonant at their beginning because they do not have a full vowel in their first syllable may take a prosthetic *ᵓaleph* in the Aramaic of Persepolis, as occasionally also in Biblical Aramaic. Thus, *š⁽kar* may become *ᵓiškar*, just as Aramaic *ṭ⁽ba⁽* becomes *ᵓiṭba⁽* in these texts.[19]

Such an explanation of *ᵓškr* makes sense in the only text in which there is a demonstrable syntactical relationship with an adjacent word. There (No. 62:3) the *ᵓškr* is associated with the word "pestle" as *ᵓbšwn zy ᵓškr*, "pestle of (the) *ᵓškr*." One might conjecture from this that the text should be read as "pestle of (the making of) the intoxicant" or "pestle of (the maker of) the intoxicant." Some such translation is supported by a seemingly parallel expression that

---

[8] Steingass, *A Comprehensive Persian-English Dictionary*, pp. 62a, 65b; D. D. Kapadia (*Glossary to the Pahlavi Vendidād* [Bombay, 1953], p. 231) cites a word *ās-* of uncertain origin, in the Pahlavi Vendidād, with the meaning "drinking" or "drinker" and, as a noun, "a drink," "beverage," "cordial," "wine." This, too, in its sense might be appropriate to indicate haoma; but we should then expect a spelling *ᵓskr* instead of *ᵓškr*.

[9] Altheim and Stiehl, *Aramäische Sprache* I 20–21.

[10] See Schmidt, *Persepolis* II 55.

[11] Koehler and Baumgartner, *Lexicon in Veteris Testamenti Libros* (Leiden, 1948), p. 94a.

[12] *CAD* VII 248, *iškaru* A, 4; C. Bezold, *Babylonisch-assyrisches Glossar* (Heidelberg, 1926), p. 73b, "regelmässige . . . Abgaben; Zuwendungen oder Lieferungen."

[13] *BLA*, p. 36, cf. p. 370, note concerning p. 62q–r.   [14] *Ibid.*, p. 49, Sec. 29a–b.

[15] Bezold, *Babylonisch-assyrisches Glossar*, p. 273b, *šikâru*, "getrank," "Rauschtrank."

[16] Koehler and Baumgartner, *Lexicon in Veteris Testamenti Libros*, p. 972; Jastrow, *Dictionary* II 1576.

[17] J. Payne Smith, *A Compendious Syriac Dictionary* (Oxford, 1957), p. 577b, ܫܟܪ.

[18] H. F. J. Junker, *Das Frahang i Pahlavīk* ("Iranische Texte und Hilfsbücher," I [Leipzig, 1955]), p. 7; *BAiW*, col. 1837, *hurā*; *BLA*, p. 44, Sec. 12b. Junker (*Das Frahang i Pahlavīk*, pp. 16–17) refers to the logograms ḤLYᵓ (cf. Syr. ܚܠܝܐ, "sweet") and DYTVF as indicating a Persian *šakar* with the meanings "Süssigkeit," "Most," and "Rauschtrank." These might indicate a Persian borrowing of *iškar* as *aškar*.

[19] See No. 43:4, *ᵓṭb⁽n*.

occurs in another text (No. 29:4), *ꜣbšwn zy bꜣt*, "pestle of wine." Thus, the *ꜣškr* must refer to the intoxicating drink, haoma.

It seems likely, then, that the *ꜣškr* should not be regarded as standing in isolation before the date but must be construed with it. Possibly it should be read as "the intoxicant of year x" and elsewhere as "the intoxicant in year x." But such a rendition is not entirely satisfactory, because the reference, it seems, should be to the ceremony of preparation rather than to the drink itself. Hence, the word is simply transliterated in the translations of the texts.

X

THE DATE

THE last item in the Aramaic formula on the Persepolis ritual objects is the date. Although many of the texts are incomplete at the end and therefore lack their date, the more complete texts usually have a date, even when their formulae are abbreviated, as on the smaller pestle tops. There is some evidence for its deliberate omission, however, on a few of the most severely reduced texts on pestles.[1]

Dates are recorded by the year but without reference to the reigning sovereign. The dates range from the first year to the twenty-ninth in the dated texts, but a comparison of the officials mentioned in them indicates that not all texts are from the same reign.

According to Professor Erich Schmidt, the Great Hall of the Hundred Columns (Room 38), in which most of the fragments of the ritual objects were recovered, belongs to the third building phase of the Treasury, which was constructed probably after the death of Darius I. Since its building was closely connected with the construction of Xerxes' Harem building, for which the western parts of the first two sections of the Treasury were razed, Schmidt is inclined to date the construction of the Hall of the Hundred Columns to the early years of Xerxes, between 486 and 480 B.C.[2]

Because the debris of Hall 41 and all other parts of the Treasury contained only a few specimens of the green chert ritual vessels, the excavator declares that he is tempted to conclude that the ritual objects of green chert were made and used only after Hall 38 had been added to the building.[3]

In seeking an even more precise date for the green chert objects, Schmidt depended principally on the preliminary work done on the objects by Cameron, who noted that in the Elamite Treasury tablets only one treasurer at a time was found at Persepolis in the texts that are securely dated to the time of Darius I and Xerxes.[4] Since he found that the treasurers mentioned in the Aramaic texts differed from those named in the Elamite texts in the tablets, Cameron contended that the Aramaic texts must be later than the time of Xerxes, dating possibly from the reigns of two consecutive later rulers, probably Artaxerxes I (464–424 B.C.) and Darius II (423–405 B.C.) or, less probably, Artaxerxes II (404–359 B.C.) and Artaxerxes III (358–338 B.C.).[5]

Cameron arrived at his dating by setting the texts in order, according to the officials mentioned in them. To the reign of Artaxerxes I he attributed the ritual objects that mentioned the treasurer Baga-pāta between the fifteenth and twenty-fourth regnal years (450–441 B.C.) and those remaining, which name Baga-pāta as treasurer presumably replaced by Dāta-Mithra, he assigned to the period 420–405 B.C., the fourth to the nineteenth years of the succeeding ruler, Darius II, providing the first group was correctly dated to the reign of Artaxerxes I.[6]

---

[1] Nos. 77, 126–29, 131, 133, 134.

[2] Schmidt, *Persepolis* I 200.

[3] *Ibid.*, p. 182b.

[4] Cameron, *PTT*, p. 10a.

[5] *Ibid.*, p. 34; Schmidt, *Persepolis* I 182b, II 55–56.

[6] Cameron, in Schmidt, *Persepolis* II 56. Schmidt (p. 26, n. 122) therefore contends that none of the inscribed ritual objects can be assigned to a date prior to the fifteenth year of Artaxerxes I.

Since Artaxerxes I ruled 41 years (464–424 B.C.) and Artaxerxes II ruled 46 (404–358 B.C.), such a distribution of texts as Cameron proposed would leave a huge unexplained gap between the reigns—seventeen years if the first ruler were Artaxerxes I and twenty-two years if he were Artaxerxes II.

But Cameron's distribution of texts is not the only one possible. An arrangement based on both dates and official names here proposed[7] produces more satisfactory results, with which Cameron now concurs. It is preferable to assume that the treasurer Dāta-Mithra preceded rather than followed Baga-pāta, since it is probable that the seal impressions depicting a scene from the haoma ceremony which date from the time of Xerxes[8] are in fact those of the treasurer Dāta-Mithra, who is named in many of the Aramaic texts on the ritual vessels.

If we assume for the moment that Dāta-Mithra served as treasurer during the reign of Xerxes, the first dated text comes from the seventh year of his reign (479/78 B.C.),[9] approximately the date posited by the excavator on archeological grounds for the building of the Hall of the Hundred Columns (Room 38), in which most of the cult objects were found. Thereafter, Dāta-Mithra served as treasurer for some years while Mithra-pāta served as the *segan*.

The nineteenth year of Xerxes (467/66 B.C.) appears to have been a critical one at Persepolis for the officers mentioned in the ritual vessels. It was a time of complete change, when all offices were passed to others. During that year there were two treasurers and two *segan*'s as well as two sub-treasurers. They appear to have served contemporaneously and in various combinations during that year of transition.[10] The in-coming officers, the treasurer Baga-pāta and the *segan* Mithraka are found together in the nineteenth year[11] and serve alone in the twentieth year and thereafter.

Dāta-Mithra and Mithra-pāta are no longer encountered as officers after the nineteenth year. There are no inscribed ritual vessels dateable to a twenty-first year[12] but in a new series of dated texts, beginning with year one, the new officials, Baga-pāta the treasurer and Mithraka the *segan*, are named.[13] Thus, the dated texts indicate a change of personnel in the nineteenth year and a change of reign after the twentieth. The only Achaemenid reign that qualifies for the first series of texts is that of Xerxes, who ruled exactly that long.

Therefore, the texts in which Dāta-Mithra is mentioned belong to the first nineteen years of the reign of Xerxes and those in which Baga-pāta appears as treasurer come from the last two years of that reign and for at least the first twenty-nine years of Artaxerxes I.[14] That some of the undateable texts probably go beyond the twenty-ninth year of Artaxerxes I is suggested by a text (No. 122) that names an Arta-čanah as treasurer instead of Baga-pāta, as though he were a successor.

Historically, the period covered by the dated ritual texts, which refer to many high military officials, was a most momentous one for Persia, politically and militarily. It encompasses the time of conflict between Persia and the Greeks and the subsequent withdrawal of the Persians to Asia.

The year 480 B.C., just before the dated ritual texts began, was the apex of Persian military

---

[7] See Table 1.   [8] See p. 6.   [9] No. 1.

[10] See Nos. 14–18 inclusive; Dāta-Mithra and Mithra-pāta (Nos. 14, 15); Baga-pāta and Mithra-pāta (No. 16); and Dāta-Mithra and *Tmrk* (= Mithraka) (No. 17); and the completely new corps of Baga-pāta, Mithraka, and Mazda-data (No. 18).

[11] No. 18.

[12] An Egyptian papyrus (Cowley, *AP*, No. 6) extends the reign of Xerxes to a 21st year, which it calls "when King Artaxerxes sat on his throne" (i.e., the accession year of Artaxerxes I). But the sequence of dated texts at Persepolis agrees with the situation in Babylonia, where there are no known dated cuneiform texts for a 21st year of Xerxes (see R. A. Parker and W. H. Dubberstein, *Babylonian Chronology 626 B.C.–A.D. 45* ["Brown University Studies" XIX (Providence, 1956)], p. 15).

[13] Nos. 20–38.   [14] No. 52 (29th year) is the last dated text.

TABLE 1. DATING OF RITUAL OBJECTS

	Year	Date	Object	Treasurer	Sub-Treasurer	*Sogan*	Celebrant	Text
					REIGN OF XERXES			
	7	479/78	Mortar	Dāta-Mithra		Ama-dāta	... *mbwš*	1
	8	478/77	Pestle			Mithra-pāta	*Snpk*	2
	10?	476/75	Pestle			Mithra-pāta	ꜣ*dwst*	3
	10?	476/75	Pestle			Mithra-pāta	Arta-dāta	4
	10?	476/75	Mortar		Māh(a)-dāta	Mithra-pāta	Gāθā-vahya(?)	5
	11	475/74	Pestle	Dāta-Mithra		Arta-dāta	Vahu-farnah	6
	11	475/74	Pestle	[Dāta-Mithra]	[Māh(a)-dāta]	Mithra-pāta	Mithra-pāta	7
*	12	474/73	Mortar	Dāta-Mithra		Mithra-pāta	Draya-vāna	8
*	13	473/72	Mortar	Dāta-Mithra		Mithra-pāta	*Sbgyš*	9
	13?	473/72	Pestle	Dāta-Mithra		Mithra-pāta	Vahu-farnah	10
	16?	470/69	Pestle	Dāta-Mithra		Ama-dāta	*Krbr*	11
	17	469/68	Pestle	Dāta-Mithra		Ama-dāta	*Krbr*	12
*	18	468/67	Mortar	Dāta-Mithra	Māh(a)-dāta	Mithra-pāta	ꜣ*twn*	13
†	19	467/66	Mortar	Dāta-Mithra	Māh(a)-dāta	Mithra-pāta	Haoma-dāta	14
	19	467/66	Pestle	Dāta-Mithra		Mithra-pāta	Haoma-dāta	15
		467/66	Mortar	Baga-pāta		Mithra-pāta		16
		467/66	Pestle	Dāta-Mithra		*Tmrk* = Mithraka	... *štn*	17
	19	467/66	Plate	Baga-pāta	Mazda-dāta	Mithraka	Bago-paušta	18
*	20	466/65	Plate	[Baga-pāta]		Mithraka	*Krwt*	19
					REIGN OF ARTAXERXES I			
	1	464/63	Pestle	Baga-pāta				20
	2	463/62	Pestle	Baga-pāta		Mazza-farnah	Frāda	21
	2	463/62	Pestle	Baga-pāta			Baga-farnah	22
	3	462/61	Pestle	Baga-pāta	[Mazda-dā]ta	Mithraka	Arbazaki	23
	3	462/61	Pestle	Baga-pāta		Āraya(t)-vahuš	Adrāθa	24
	3	462/61	Mortar	Baga-pāta			*Krpyš*	25
	4	461/60	Pestle		Mazda-dāta	Mithraka	*Dsptrwk*	26
	4	461/60	Pestle			Mithraka	*Trsph*	27
	4	461/60	Pestle		Mazda-dāta	Mithraka	Tīri-dāta	28
	5	460/59	Pestle			Mithraka	Arta-bar-wāna	29
	5	460/59	Mortar	Baga-pāta	Mazda-dāta	[Mithraka]		30
	6	459/58	Mortar	Baga-pāta	Mazda-dāta	Mithraka	Aspa-bāra	31
	6	459/58	Mortar	Baga-pāta	Mazda-dāta	Mithraka	Māh(a)-čārā	32
	6	459/58	Mortar	*Mbm*		Mithraka	Arta-...	33
	6	459/58	Mortar	Baga-pāta		Mithraka	Draz-bāra	34
	6	459/58	Mortar		Mazda-dāta			35
	7	458/57	Mortar	Baga-pāta	Mazda-čiθra	Vinda(t)-farnah	*Šwrty*	36
	7	458/57	Pestle			Mithraka	Hvaršya-pāta	37
	7	458/57	Mortar		*Mbm*	Mithraka	Draz-bāra	38
	10	455/54	Pestle	Baga-pāta	Mazda-dāta	Ama-dāta	Rāman	39
	10	455/54	Pestle		Mazda-dāta	Ari-bānu	Rāman	40
	11	454/53	Mortar	Baga-pāta	Mazda-dāta		ꜣ*mdsm*	41
	11	454/53	Plate	Baga-pāta		Āraya(t)-vahuš		42
*	13	452/51	Plate	Baga-pāta		Āraya(t)-vahuš	Artama	43
*	13	452/51	Plate	Baga-pāta		Suxra-raθa		44
*	14	451/50	Plate	Baga-pāta				45
	14(?)	451/50	Mortar	Baga-pāta		Āraya(t)-vahuš	*Rtbr*(?)	46
*	15	450/49	Plate	Baga-pāta	Artamaka	Āraya(t)-vahuš	*Byšꜣzꜣ*(?)	47
*	19	446/45	Plate	Baga-pāta		Āraya(t)-vahuš	*Bhyyn*	48
	20	445/44	Plate			Āraya(t)-vahuš	*Vntšk*	49
	21	444/43	Plate	Baga-pāta	Čiθra-farnah	Āraya(t)-vahuš	*Kqyz*	50
*	24	441/40	Plate	Baga-pāta		Āraya(t)-vahuš		51
*	29	436/35	Plate	Baga-pāta		Āraya(t)-vahuš	ꜣ*dwst*	52
	20+		Plate	Baga-pāta	Čiθra-farnah	Āraya(t)-vahuš	Arta-yāna	53
					UNASSIGNABLE			
	1		Pestle			Mazda-farnah(?)	*Gyt*	54
	2		Mortar				*Pr* ...	55
	3		Mortar				... *mꜣ*	56
	3		Pestle				*Šyqmnt*	57
	4?		Pestle			Arta-m ...	Ātar-b ...	58
	4?		Pestle					59
	5		Pestle				*Kš*	60
	6		Pestle				Dāraya-farnah	61
	6		Pestle					62
	7		Pestle				Pāpā	63

TABLE 1—*Continued*

	Year	Date	Object	Treasurer	Sub-Treasurer	*Segan*	Celebrant	Text
	1+		Pestle		Mazda-dāta	Mithraka	Rao-raθa	64
	2+		Pestle			Ama-dāta	Arta-vāna	65
	10		Pestle				*Šyr*	66
	10		Pestle				*Šyqmnt*	67
	10+?		Pestle				Pouru-bātu	68
	10		Pestle				Gaubaruva	69
	12		Pestle				Š . . .	70
	13		Pestle				Baga-farnah	71
	+1		Plate		Mazda-dāta	Mithraka	Manda(t)-farnah	72
[*]	+3		Plate			Āraya(t)-vahuš	Arta-dāta	73

No Date Preserved

		Object	Treasurer	Sub-Treasurer	*Segan*	Celebrant	Text
		Mortar	Dāta-Mithra	*ʿrzrtyn*		. . . *brtn*	74
		Mortar	Dāta-Mithra		Mithra-pāta	Arəgiš	75
		Mortar	Dāta-Mithra				76
		Pestle			Mithra-pāta	Arta-*wrm*	77
		Pestle			Mithra-pāta	*ʾbrš*	78
	*	Mortar			[Mithra-pāta]		79
		Mortar		Māh(a)-dāta			80
		Pestle	Baga-pāta	Mazda-dāta	Mithraka	. . . *mbyk*	81
		Mortar	Baga-[pāta]		Mith[raka]		82
		Mortar			Mithraka		83
		Mortar			Mithraka		84
		Mortar			*Mrtk* = Mithraka	*Rm* . . .	85
		Mortar			Mithraka		86
		Pestle		Mazda-dāta	Mithraka	*Kbrrmštr*	87
		Mortar	[Baga-pā]ta		Mithraka		88
		Mortar			Mithraka	Xšaθra	89
		Mortar			Mithraka	. . . *pāhr*	90
		Mortar	Ba[ga-pāta]	Maz[da-dāta]	Mithraka	*Dmwš*	91
		Plate			Mithraka	*Tʾpmrkd*	92
		Mortar			[Mith]raka		93
		Mortar	Baga-pāta	Mazda-dāta		Kālī	94
[*]		Plate	Baga-pāta			*Hrwn* and Kālī	95
		Mortar	Baga-pāta				96
		Mortar	Baga-pāta	Mazda-dāta			97
		Plate	Baga-pāta			Husadaka(?)	98
		Mortar	Baga-pāta				99
		Pestle	Baga-pāta			B . . . t-pāta	100
		Mortar			Ama-dāta		101
		Plate			Āraya(t)-vahu(š)	*Krpyš*	102
		Mortar			Āraya(t)-[vahu(š)]	*Krpyš*	103
		Plate	Baga-pāta		Āraya(t)-va[hu(š)]		104
		Mortar			Āraya(t)-[vahuš]		105
		Mortar			Āraya(t)-vahuš		106
		Pestle			[Āra]ya(t)-vahuš		107
		Mortar			Āraya(t)-vahuš	Mithra-farnah	108
		Plate	Baga-pāta		[Āraya(t)-va]huš		109
	*	Plate			Āraya(t)-vahu	Bāta-rātā(?)	110
		Plate			Āraya(t)-vahuš	Baga- . . .	111
		Plate			Āraya(t)-vahuš	*Bhyyn*	112
		Plate			Āraya(t)-vahuš	Rāman	113
		Mortar			Āraya(t)-vahuš		114
		Pestle			[Āraya(t)-vahu]š		115
		Mortar	Ba[ga-pāta]	Āraya(t)-vahuš		Pāhra-barana	116
		Pestle	Baga-pāta			Baga-čiθra	117
		Mortar			Mazza-farnah	*Šbr*	118
[*]		Plate	[Ba]ga-pāta	*Šrwn*	Vahu-farnah	*Šwrty*	119
		Pestle			*Šwrty*(?)	*Šwrty*	120
		Mortar			*Bhprt*		121
		Mortar	Arta-čanah		*Srby*	*Ryb* . . .	122
		Pestle				*ʾp* . . .	123
		Mortar					124
		Mortar	[Čiθra-fa]rnah			Visa-farnah	125
		Pestle				Aspa-stāna	126
		Pestle				Ātar-barzana	127
		Pestle				*Nrys*	128
		Pestle				*ʾrdm*	129
		Mortar				*Drgs*	130
		Pestle				Fraza(?)	131
	*	Plate					132
		Pestle				*ʾdwst*	133

TABLE 1—*Continued*

	Object	Treasurer	Sub-Treasurer	*Segan*	Celebrant	Text
			No Date Preserved—*Continued*			
[*]	Pestle				[Ba]ga-pāta	134
	Mortar					135
	Mortar					136
	Pestle					137
	Mortar					138
	Mortar					139
	Mortar					140
	Mortar					141
	Tray					142
	Mortar					143
	Mortar				*Th* . . .	144
	Mortar	[Dāta-Mi]thra		A[ma-dāta]		145
	Mortar					146
	Mortar				*Rgpt*	147
	Plate				Vinda(t)-farnah	148
	Mortar				*Kp* . . .	149
	Mortar			Mith[ra-pāta]		150
	Plate					151
	Plate				. . . *byzt*	152
	Plate					153
	Plate					154
*	Plate					155
	Plate					156
	Plate					157
	Plate					158
	Mortar				*Nš* . . .	159
	Mortar					160
	Pestle					161
	Mortar					162
	Plate					163

* Object bears the phrase "who is in Arachosia."
† Object bears the phrase "who is in *Ghštk*."

and political fortunes. Despite naval disasters at Artemisium and Salamis, the massive armies of Xerxes in that year penetrated Europe at the expense of the disorganized and competing Greek states. They crossed the Hellespont at Abydos, secured the pass at Thermopylae, entered Athens without opposition by mid-August, and burned most of the city, including the temples on the Acropolis. Victoriously the Persians returned to Asia to winter at Sardis in Lydia under the command of General Mardonius.

The first year of the dated ritual texts, 479/78 B.C., began well for the Persians but ended in irretrievable disaster for them when the Greek states began a defensive war to drive the Persians from Europe and to recover Asiatic cities that had been settled earlier by the Greeks. When diplomatic overtures by the Persian general, Mardonius, who sought to avert further military conflict, were repulsed by the Greeks, the Persians again marched against an abandoned Athens, where they destroyed whatever remained of the city and desolated Attica before retiring to a stockaded camp near Plataea.

From August of 479 B.C. to the end of the reign of Xerxes, the Persians knew nothing but disaster. The Greeks under Pausanius soundly defeated them at Plataea, capturing their camp, routing the armies, and slaughtering Persians without mercy. On August 27, 479 B.C., they were utterly defeated in a decisive battle at Mycale in which their fleet was burned and native Persians died almost to a man.

During the year, two of the six Persian armies in Europe were completely destroyed and a third had to leave Europe to guard the centers in western Asia that were under Persian control. But the Greeks followed up their successes, driving the Persians eastward. In the spring of 478 B.C. a small Athenian fleet under Pausanius snatched from Persian authority the Greek islands off the Carian coast, Cyprus, and Byzantium.

By the end of 478 B.C. the Delian League was formed by the Greeks to consolidate the activities of the maritime Greek states around the Aegean to revenge Persian attacks in Europe and to press the Persians back until all cities of Asia inhabited by Greeks would be freed from Persian rule. In 475 B.C. Cimon led the Greek fleet of the Delian League against Eion on the Strymon, one of the last points in the West still held by the Persians. Then only Doriscus remained as a Persian stronghold in Europe.

In 466 B.C., under the leadership of Cimon, the war against Persia was resumed. By persuasion or force revolt was stirred in the cities of Caria and Greek garrisons were set in them. When Xerxes sent a large fleet and army under Ariomandes against Cimon, another decisive battle was fought at the mouth of the Eurymedon River during which the Persians were soundly defeated. So helpless had the Persians become that in 465 B.C. Cimon with only four ships drove thirteen Persian vessels from the Chersonese.

By 465 B.C. the die was cast. Europe was lost to Persia and even the Asiatic Greeks turned westward, with large numbers of them, including Carians and Lycians, joining the Delian League against Persia. Before the end of the year the disaster became personal for Xerxes, and he lost his life in a palace revolt, bequeathing a world of problems to his successor.

The early years of Artaxerxes I were busy with personal problems arising from harem intrigue and from competition for the throne. But the West, at that time, was in the midst of a conflict between Athenians and Spartans and was no better prepared to prosecute the war. The Athenian Cimon was ostracized in 461 B.C. and a new leader, Ephialtes, at once sent the Athenian fleet eastward, looking in vain for the grand fleet of Persia. When Pericles came to power, he, too, prepared to confront the Persians. He equipped two hundred ships to invade Cyprus, which had returned to Persian control.

In 462 B.C. Prince Hystaspes, the satrap of Bactria, rebelled against central authority and sought independent rule. Artaxerxes ordered his destruction, and after two bloody battles royal authority was restored in Bactria. Meanwhile, in Egypt, too, there was rebellion, for the native Inaros challenged Persia and sought Athenian support. Pericles diverted to Egypt the vessels he had prepared for the Cyprus invasion, and the rebels and their Greek allies captured Memphis and besieged the Persian garrison within the White Wall.

Artaxerxes sent another large army led by Megabyzos from Cilicia to relieve the Memphis garrison in 456 B.C. The tide turned in Persia's favor; the allies, decisively defeated, fled to an island in the swamps of the Egyptian delta where they were besieged for eighteen months before they surrendered. Fifty Greek triremes that had been sent to relieve the embattled Greeks and Egyptian rebels were sunk by the Phoenician allies of the Persians. The Egyptian revolt was ended and Megabyzos returned to Susa in triumph in 454 B.C. with Inaros and the Greek generals.

In 451 B.C., anti-Persian Cimon returned to Athens after ten years in exile and began at once to stimulate an anti-Persian policy in the West. A renewal of the war was voted in 450 B.C., and a fleet was sent to assist an Egyptian rebel, Amyrtaeus. Another fleet invaded the Persian territory of Cyprus, where Marium was captured and Citium was besieged until provisions failed and Cimon died.

After the death of Cimon the Greeks realized the futility of expecting a total victory over wealthy Persia and its seemingly unlimited manpower. An embassy, headed by Callias, was sent to Susa in 449 B.C. to discuss peace. Since both sides realized that a stalemate had been reached, two spheres of influence in the West were determined, separated by a demilitarized zone.

But the Peace of Callias was not a lasting one. By 445 B.C. Pericles had become as anti-Persian as his predecessor Cimon had been. After a thirty-year peace had been concluded with Sparta, Athens was free to renew the war against Persia. A bribe from the Libyan rebel Psammeticus again involved the Greeks in an Egyptian revolt against Persia, breaking the Peace of Callias. Pericles broke another point in the agreement by pushing Athenian control eastward to include in Athenian tribute districts the states that Athens had left to the Persian satrapies—Caria, Ionia, Hellespont, and the islands. He took advantage of a quarrel between Samos and Miletus in 441 B.C. to invade the island of Samos and reorganize it as a democracy. But appeals from Samos to the Persian satrap at Sardis produced funds for mercenaries who then recovered the island and turned its Athenian garrison over to the Persians.

In retaliation the Persians again moved into Lycia and by the end of 440 B.C. they had won back Gargara, Scepsis, Cebren, the Western Zeleia, and Astacus. They next secured the whole interior of Caria and so much of the coast that between 440 B.C. and 438 B.C. twelve cities were dropped from the Athenian list of tributaries.[15]

In the spring of 439 B.C. Pericles again regained Samos and began to exert the authority of the Greeks in the Black Sea area, where Amisus was colonized as a second Piraeus and in 438 B.C. Sinope became a Greek colony.[16]

In 431 B.C. plague struck Ethiopia, Egypt, Athens, and large parts of the Persian empire. In that year, too, the Peloponnesian War (431–404 B.C.) broke out, and Artaxerxes I spent his last years watching his enemies destroy one another.

Thus, the period covered by the dated ritual objects (479–435 B.C.) was a critical one for Persia and a trying one for its armies. The threat of the West was a real one. The reign of Xerxes was a disaster after 480 B.C., with one critical loss after another by the Persian armies. Troops were constantly being marshalled for service, grappling with the foe, and being reconstituted as a military unit after disaster. Only limited success marked the reign of Artaxerxes I.

Persian commanders learned the bitterness of defeat. They led great armies into battle only to see them decimated or utterly destroyed. Desperately they sought support and victory. They needed the wise guidance and support of Mithra, their god of war, as well as that of Ahuramazda. In such a context the haoma ceremony became meaningful throughout the period and the participation of the chief military leaders of the Persian armies during that interval is understandable.

[15] Olmstead, *History of the Persian Empire* (Chicago, 1948), p. 343.

[16] *Ibid.*, p. 344.

XI

THE LINGUISTIC PHENOMENA

THE formulaic character of the ritual texts inevitably restricts the number of grammatical and syntactical phenomena to be considered. They are principally those already encountered in the Aramaic papyri and parchments of the Achaemenid period. Deviations from the structures and uses of standard "Reichsaramäische" are to be construed as evidence not that the texts are in the Persian language[1] but that Aramaic has been influenced by Old Persian. As might be expected, Aramaic and Persian in use side by side mutually influenced one another. Kent has suggested that the written style of Old Persian reflects that of Aramaic.[2] But, as will be seen below, in some respects the Aramaic texts here discussed have departures from normal Aramaic usage which are perhaps due to the influence of Old Persian syntax.

LOANWORDS

There is a surprising number of loanwords in these rather brief texts.[3] A few are words from Akkadian that have been Aramaized and have long been known from Biblical Aramaic and the papyri (for example, *byrtʾ*, Akkadian *bîrtu; sgnʾ*, Akkadian *šaknu/šakēnu*).

As might be expected, most of the loanwords are Iranian. These include:

ʾbšwn, "pestle" (Iranian *abi-su-ana?*)

ʾḫšynpyn/ʾḫšynpn, "dark . . . color" (?) (cf. Old Persian *axšaina*)

ʾpgnzbr, "sub-treasurer" (Old Persian *upa-ganzabara*)

bʾt, "wine" (Old Persian *bātu*)

bg, "god," "portion," "good fortune" (Old Persian *baga*)

bz/bzy, a kind(?) (or quality?) of stone

gnzbrʾ, "treasurer" (Old Persian *ganzabara*)

hwn, "mortar" (Old Persian *havana*)

kpwtk, "blue (pigeon color)," "lapis lazuli" (Old Persian *kapautaka*)

mdm, "medium-sized" (cf. Late Avestan *maδəma*)

pty, "value," "worth" (Old Persian *patiy*)

PHONETICS

SEMITIC

Although the Semitic dental spirant δ is usually represented by *z*, there is one instance (No. 44:3) in which the letter *d* is used (*dnh*), although in the same text it appears as *z* (*zy*).[4] The use of a prosthetic *ʾaleph* and vowel (probably *-i*) to break up a consonantal cluster at the beginning of a word[5] is attested by the words *ʾṭbʿ* (*ʾiṭbaʿ*), "(shekel) coin" (compare Talmudic Aramaic *ṭᵉbaʿ*), and presumably also in *ʾškr*, "intoxicant" (compare Aramaic *šᵉkar*).[6]

---

[1] See p. 41.   [2] Kent, *Old Persian*, p. 9, Sec. 12.

[3] A few words are still uncertain as to etymology and linguistic relationship. Some also are problematic as to their reading, for instance, *ggbs* or *.tzgbs* or *nzgbs* in No. 1:3, *wtpn* in No. 161:1, *..šnḫwyn* in No. 74:3. Perhaps here *srk/srwk*, *hst*, and *šḥr* also belong.

[4] Such a phenomenon is also found in the Aramaic papyri; cf. P. Leander, *Laut- und Formenlehre des Ägyptisch-Aramäischen* ("Göteborgs Högskolas Årsskrift," XXXIV [1928], No. 4), p. 8, Sec. 2f, and p. 33, Sec. 14b.

[5] *BLA*, p. 44, Sec. 12b.   [6] See Nos. 43:4, 1:4 and p. 54.

Iranian

All the implications of the use of Aramaic signs for rendering Iranian phonemes are not yet clear. But there are some Aramaic letters, especially those used to express non-Semitic sounds, that deserve special consideration here.[7]

In the transcription of Iranian words and names the Aramaic letters *ṭ*, *ʿaiyn*, and *ṣ* are not used in these ritual texts, although *ṭ* and *ṣ* are used in Middle-Iranian words found in the Talmud.[8] Since Aramaic *l* would not be expected in a Persian name, its single example, in the name *Kl* (Kālī?), in two texts (Nos. 94 and 95), must mark a foreigner. The Semitic letter *q* occurs rarely, once in a difficult combination, in the curious name *Kqyz* (No. 50:2).

As in the Talmud,[9] Iranian *h* is expressed in the Persian names here by either Aramaic *h* or *ḥ*. Thus, the Persian *vahu*, "good," can be spelled as either *vahu* (for example, *Whwprn*, Vahu-farnah, in No. 119:1) or *vaḥu* (as in Āraya(t)-vahuš in No. 48:2; compare Āraya(t)-vahuš in No. 49:2 and others) and *hu-* is written as a name element either as *h* (for example, *Hsdk*, Husadaka(?) in No. 98:2) or *ḥw-* (*Ḥwršypt*, Hvaršya-pāta, in No. 37:3).

But Aramaic *ḥ* is also used to indicate the Persian voiceless velar spirant *x*, just as in the later Talmudic transcriptions of Persian loanwords.[10] Thus, the element *suxra-* appears as *sḥr-* in the name *Sḥrrt*, Suxra-raθa (No. 44:2).

If the name *ʾdwst* (Nos. 3:3, 48:2, 120:2) is derived from **a-daušta* or **a-dušta*, there is manifest already in Persepolis the change *št* > *st* characteristic of Middle Persian (*daušta* > *dōst*) noted by Eilers.[11]

Aramaic *š* is used in the ritual texts to indicate both the Iranian alveolar sibilant *š* and the palatal affricate *č*, which Kent symbolizes by *c*. Such usage, too, is found in the Talmudic treatment of Middle-Persian loanwords.[12] Thus, we find in these texts the name elements *-čanah* (in *ʾrtšnʾ*, Arta-čanah in No. 122:3), *-čāra* (in *Mhšr*, Māh(a)-čāra, No. 32:2), and *-čiθra* (*Bgštr*, Baga-čiθra in No. 117:3 and *Mzdštr*, Mazda-čiθra in No. 36:2).

Aramaic *t* is used for both the Persian dental stop *t* and its voiceless spirant *θ*.[13]

The Iranian phoneme *θ^r* is a special problem for transcription into Aramaic letters. The sound *θ^r* persisted in Avestan and Median but became a sibilant (symbolized by *ç* by Kent) in Old Persian, where it "apparently was a sound intermediate between the pure dental *s* and the palatal *š*."[14]

In the Aramaic transcriptions of Persian names in the ritual texts the phoneme *θ^r* occurs often in the name Mithra, perhaps in the element *pāθra-* in the name *Dsptrwk* (No. 26:3), and quite frequently with the word *čiθra*.[15] It cannot be determined from the Aramaic spelling *mtr* whether the pronunciation was *Miʰtra* or *Miʰθra*, both of which are found in Old Persian inscriptions.[16] But the use of the double consonant *tr* regularly in *pāθra* and *čiθra* seems to favor the latter form.

[7] S. Telegdi, "Essai sur la phonétique des emprunts iraniens en araméen talmudique," *JA* CCXXVI (1935) 207–9.

[8] *Ibid.*, p. 237, No. 44, and p. 205. There the letter *ṭ* is used for *t* in the words *-pāta* (spelled *-pṭʾ*) and *tōzī* (as *ṭwzyg*) and *ṣ* is used for *č* in Parsik words.

[9] *Ibid.*, p. 207, Sec. 24.

[10] *Ibid.*, pp. 197 f., Sec. 17. The letter *ḥ* is characteristic for the earlier words in the Talmud. Later *x* is rendered by *k*.

[11] W. Eilers, "Iranische Beamtennamen in der keilschriftlichen Überlieferung," *Abhandlungen für die Kunde des Morgenlandes* XXV, No. 5 (1940), p. 99.

[12] Telegdi, in *JA* CCXXVI 205, Sec. 22.

[13] See *drāθa* (*adrt*, Adrāθa, No. 24:3), *friθa* (*Bḥprt*, Ba(n)ha-friθa(?), No. 121:2), *gāθā* (*Gtwhy*, Gāθā-vahya, No. 5:2), and *rāθā* (*Bʾtrt*, Bāta-rāθā in No. 110:3).

[14] Kent, *Old Persian*, p. 31a, Sec. 78.

[15] E.g., Mithra-pāta (*Mtrpt*), Mithraka (*Mtrk*), and Arta-Mithra (*ʾrtmtr*); and Baga-čiθra (*Bgštr*), Mazda-čiθra (*Mzdštr*), and others.

[16] Kent, *Old Persian*, p. 31b, p. 203b, *Miθra-*.

In one name, however, if it is correctly identified, the sibilant character of the phoneme (ç) is apparent. It appears that Čiθra-farnah is written as *Ššprn* (Nos. 50:3 and 53:5). It would seem that even after a sibilant the θr became ç and was then assimilated to the preceding sibilant.[17]

In Middle Persian the phoneme ç becomes *h* and it is often so spelled in Persian loanwords found in the Talmud.[18] There may be evidence for such a shift as early as Achaemenid times if the name *Phrbrn* (No. 116:2) is Pāhra-barana for an earlier Pāθra-barana and the element ...*phr* in a broken name (No. 90:2) represents earlier *pāθra*.

The familiar Persian consonantal cluster *xš* appears as *ḫš* in the name *Ḫštr*, Xšaθra (No. 89:2) and apparently also in the adjective *axšaina*, "dark," if that is indeed an element in the Persian word *ʾḫšyn-pyn/ʾḫšyn-pn* (for example, Nos. 11:3, 101:2, and others).

It has been noted above that there is a possible example of assimilation of consonants in the name *Ššprn* for Čiθra-farnah (for example, *čiθra > čiçra > čičra* [or *šišra*?]). Unless there is a simple error in spelling, another example of assimilation may be found in the spelling *snʾ* for *sgnʾ*, *segan* (No. 124:2). The *g* appears to be assimilated to the following *n* as *signāʾ* becomes *sinnāʾ*. Still another instance may exist in the name Mazda in which the letters *zd* seemed to trouble some writers. The name *Mzprn* (Nos. 21:2, 118:2) may represent Mazza-farnah for Mazda-farnah, just as Mazdaka is written Mazakes (Μαζάκης) in Greek.[19]

The awkward *Mdzprn* (No. 54:2) shows another treatment of the *zd* in Mazda involving metathesis. Other examples of metathesis found in the ritual texts include the spellings *tmrk* and *mrtk* for the *segan* Mithraka (Nos. 17:2, 85:2) and *ʿdb* for the verb *ʿbd* (No. 134:2).

VERBS

INFINITIVE

The single example of an infinitive in the ritual texts is *lḫšl* (No. 8:3) used to express purpose, "for crushing."

The form is rather unusual for the simple Aramaic infinitive, since such a form has been displaced usually by the *miqtal* nominal form.[20] One would have expected *lmḫšl*.

There is abundant evidence, however, for the survival of the older form of the infinitive as *lʾmr*, which is found as late as Assyrian times[21] and is used in the Aramaic papyri of the Achaemenid period far more often[22] than the expected forms לְמֵאמַר[23] and לְמֵמַר.[24] One might perhaps regard *lʾmr* as a stereotyped survival of the earlier form that has come to be used to indicate direct discourse. But such an early form also persists in the Biblical *lbnʾ* (Ezra 5:3, 13), which Rosenthal rightly recognizes as a survival of the older form.[25]

FINITE VERB

There is but scant evidence for the verb in these formulaic texts, but what is found is interesting and significant. The verb usually encountered is the homograph *ʿbd*, which could be

---

[17] *Ibid.*, p. 31*b*, Sec. 79. Perhaps a similar phonetic situation is encountered in the Elamite names Mauzišša (*Vahu-čissa) and Mauzittarra (*Vahu-čiθra) in which Benveniste (*Titres et noms propres en iranien ancien* ["Travaux de l'Institut d'études iraniennes de l'Université de Paris" I (Paris, 1966)], p. 88) sees the element *čiθra* behind both *zišša* and *zittarra*.

[18] Telegdi, in *JA* CCXXVI 196 ff., Sec. 16.

[19] F. Justi, *Iranisches Namenbuch* (Hildesheim, 1963), p. 201*b*.

[20] *BLA*, p. 105, Sec. 38; Leander, *Laut- und Formenlehre des Ägyptisch-Aramäischen*, p. 48, Sec. 26*a*.

[21] M. Lidzbarski, *Altaramäisch Urkunden aus Assur* ("Wissenschaftliche Veröffentlichung der Deutschen Orient-Gesellschaft" XXXVIII [Leipzig, 1921]), pp. 11–12, ll. 8, 10.

[22] Cowley, *AP*, p. 276*a* (index).

[23] Dan. 2:9; cf. Aramaic Ahiqar papyrus, l. 115 (Cowley, *AP*, p. 216).

[24] Ezra 5:11; Cowley, *AP*, No. 32:2.

[25] F. Rosenthal, *A Grammar of Biblical Aramaic* (Wiesbaden, 1961), p. 45, Sec. 111, p. 51, Sec. 149.

either the perfect verb or the participle. Since the form used where the subject is plural is ᶜ*bdw* (No. 95:3), it is apparent that the perfect form rather than a participle is intended. Thus, it is probably to be understood as the P*eᶜal* perfect form of the verb and translated as "he worked" or "he used" the object.[26]

What appears to be the masculine plural form ᶜ*bdw* is found not only in the few instances in which the subject is compound (Nos. 88 and 95) but also, surprisingly, in a number of examples in which the subject is singular (Nos. 2:3, 13:2, 14:2, 15:3 and probably 20:3). Such usage, what appears to be a plural verb for a singular subject, is also found in the ostraca from Nisā in Turkestan and in the controversial bilingual text found at Armazi.[27] Since the ritual texts are several hundred years earlier than the earliest recognized "heterographic" writing of Aramaic as Persian logograms and since there are so few examples in these many texts, it is probable that there is an Aramaic explanation of such forms.[28] The proposal of Altheim and Stiehl, that the additional -*w* is an enclitic form of an auxiliary verb, as found elsewhere in later Aramaic,[29] is worth consideration. Perhaps the past character of the action is stressed by such an addition and the form is to be translated as "he has used."

ADVERB

As the Aramaic text of the Behistun Inscription shows,[30] the Aramaic noun *šmh*, "his name," reflects syntactically a typical Old Persian phenomenon, the adverbial use of *nāma*, "by name," or "namely," after a personal name. In Persian it is used with the first reference to the name of any person or place, other than that of a governmental province or the ruling king.[31] In these texts the word is never used with the name of a place or with those of the *segan* or treasurers but only after the name of the celebrant.[32]

NOUNS AND ADJECTIVES

GENDER AND NUMBER

Most of the nouns encountered in the ritual texts are masculine and singular. The only feminine noun is *šnt*, "year," which appears in most texts, and the only plural form is the masculine absolute plural ᵓ*ṭbᶜn* (Nos. 43:4, 73:5). There are no examples of the determinate plural.

STATE

Absolute.—Absolute forms are found more frequently than those in the determinate state. The titles ᵓ*lp* and *plg* are regularly absolute in form, appositive to the names that precede them. The word *gll*, "stone," is absolute. So, too, is the Persian *bᵓt*, "wine," and ᵓ*škr*, where it is in the same construction as *bᵓt* (No. 62:4). The Aramaic *prk* (No. 5:3) is also absolute. Of the names of the objects, *hwn*, "mortar," is invariably in the absolute state and the words for "pestle" (ᵓ*bšwn*) and "plate" (*sḥr*) usually are. The few examples of *byrt*, "fortress," that seem to be in the absolute state where the determinate form is expected, are apparently incomplete words.[33]

The indefinite character of absolute nouns is frequently indicated in these texts by the use

---

[26] See pp. 39–40.   [27] See pp. 40–42.   [28] See pp. 42–43.

[29] See p. 42; Altheim and Stiehl, *Aramäische Sprache* I 43, 274, ᶜ*bd*.

[30] Behistun Inscription, col. ii, l. 49 (= Aramaic l. 7), col. iii, ll. 21 (= Aramaic l. 22), 30–31 (= Aramaic l. 25).

[31] Kent, *Old Persian*, p. 97*b*, Sec. 312.

[32] Such usage is found in the Bible (Ezra 5:14) and in the Aramaic papyri (Cowley, *AP*, No. 28:4, 5, 9, 13, No. 33:1–5, and No. 66 Frag. 1, Ahiqar, ll. 1, 5, 18) and often in the Aramaic text of the Behistun Inscription (see n. 30 above).

[33] See p. 20. Unless what seems to be *byrtn* (No. 77:2) is a misspelling or presents a unique form of ᵓ*aleph*, resembling letter *n*, the word may be a hybrid showing Persian influence (see p. 141).

of a single unit stroke, numeral one, used as an indefinite article (for example, ו אבשׁון [Nos. 26:4, 66:3] instead of simple אבשׁון [No. 131:3]).[34]

Construct.—At least one example of the construct state of a noun is found in almost every text. The only feminine form is *šnt*, "year of," which precedes the figure in every date that is preserved.

The words *srk/srwk*, *prkn*, and *hst* before the word *byrtꞋ* at the beginning of each text are invariably construct nouns.[35] Such, too, must be the syntax of *Ꞌlp plg*, "a chiliarch of a division" (No. 118:3), and of the collocation *rᶜyn bg* (Nos. 47:3, 52:3). It seems that a double construct occurs in the numerous instances in which the word *Ꞌškr* appears before the date.

Determinate.—The determinate state, "status emphaticus," is found in the ritual texts, as in the papyri and Biblical Aramaic, but it is not always found where expected. As in Biblical Aramaic,[36] foreign words are less likely than Semitic words to have the final *Ꞌaleph* of the determinate state. But the title of the *segan* is invariably in the determinate state and the word *byrtꞋ* is presumably always intended to be so. The names of the pestle (*Ꞌbšwn*) and plate (*sḥr*) may appear in the determinate state when used with the demonstrative pronoun *znh*.[37]

It is difficult to be sure of the state of the titles of the treasurers. They appear to be determinate because of their final *Ꞌaleph*, but that may only be an attempt to render the final -*a* of the Persian word *ganzabara*. The Persian word *hwn*, "mortar," is never in the determinate state, not even when the use of the demonstrative pronoun would call for a determinate noun to conform to correct Aramaic syntax. Such usage is also found in the majority of instances when the object is the pestle[38] and less often, apparently analogically, when it is a plate.[39] Those omissions are probably due to Persian influence, since there is no definite article in Old Persian.[40]

ADJECTIVES

Since the ritual objects are of various sizes, adjectives mentioning the fact are frequently encountered. Mortars, pestles, and plates are called "large" (*rb*); only mortars and pestles are called "small" (*zᶜyr*) or "medium-sized" (*mdm*, an Iranian word). The word "large," in the determinate state (*rbꞋ*) to agree with the noun *sgnꞋ*, is used to designate the "chief" official of the class (No. 2:2), and *rb* is also used to indicate a "great" or "important" ceremony in which the vessels were used to crush haoma (No. 5:3). In a few instances (Nos. 9:3, 13:3, 14:3, 17:5) the adjective *pyrk*, "crushing," is used to modify the noun "pestle." The difficult reading *nqwr*, which appears without context in a badly damaged text (No. 161:2), is also apparently adjectival since its root seems to be *nqr*, which is used in the sense of "to chisel," "to shape stones."[41]

Sometimes there is an attempt to indicate the color of the stone. It is probable that the Persian word *kpwtk*, *kapautaka*, must be an adjective of color, "pigeon color" (greenish-blue?)

---

[34] Biblical Aramaic uses the numeral *ḥd*, "one," as an indefinite article (Ezra 4:8, 6:2; Dan. 2:31). So also in the papyri (Cowley, *AP*, Nos. 26:12, 27:5). In the Behistun Inscription (col. iii, l. 57), where the Old Persian has 1 *martiyam*, the Aramaic version (l. 38) has *Ꞌyš ḥd*, "a man," which is the equivalent of *Ꞌyš 1* in these ritual texts. Cf. Kent, *Old Persian*, p. 85*b*, Sec. 262, II.

[35] The lack of the word "fortress" (No. 137:1) is the result of abbreviation and does not necessarily indicate that the *srk* is to be regarded as absolute.

[36] *BLA*, p. 308, Sec. 88*g*; Rosenthal, *A Grammar of Biblical Aramaic*, p. 24, Sec. 46.

[37] *ꞋbšwnꞋ znh* only in Nos. 13:3 and 15:4; *sḥrꞋ znh* often (e.g., Nos. 19:3, 43:3, 44:3, etc.).

[38] *Ꞌbšwn znh*, Nos. 2:3–4, 3:4, 10:3–4, etc.

[39] *sḥr znh*, Nos. 18:2, 48:4–5, 52:3, 92:4, etc. Likewise in the Aramaic inscription of Hellenistic Warka, a Semitic word is written ungrammatically in the absolute state when the Akkadian expression *ša sumišu šanû* is written *zy šmh Ꞌhrn* instead of *zy šmh ꞋhrnꞋ* (R. A. Bowman, "Anu-Uballiṭ–Kefalon," *AJSL* LVI [1939] 233).

[40] Kent, *Old Persian*, p. 85*a*, Sec. 262.

[41] Jastrow, *Dictionary* II 935*a*, נקר I. = "dig," "chisel," "bore," "perforate," "chisel (stones)."

since the usual translation of the word as "lapis lazuli" is inappropriate. It seems likely also, that *ʾḥšynpyn/ʾḥšynpn* represents a color, for the first part of the compound, *ʾḥšyn-*, is probably the Persian *axšaina-*, "dark." Other words, *tzgbs* (or *ggbs*) and *bz* (var. *bzy*), the meanings of which are not yet determined, also appear to be adjectives descriptive of the stone.

Noun Types

The following Aramaic noun types are found, *qal: yd*, "hand" (in the preposition *lyd*, "beside"); *qil: šm*, "name"; *qatl: plg*, "division" (Syriac *palgāʾ*), probably *prk*, "crushing (ceremony)" (as a "nomen vicis"), *ʿyd*, "festival" (Yadin would put *srk* [*serekh*] here also, but see below); *qall: rb*, "large," "chief," "important"; *qatîl: plg*, "myriarch" (compare Arabic *ʿārîq*, "lieutenant," "centurion"), possibly *ʾlp*, "chiliarch" (but Hebrew has *qattul: ʾlluf*), *zʿyr* (*zᵉʿîr*), "small"; *qatâl: gll*, "stone" (Akkadian *galâla*); *qatûl*(?): *nqwr*, "chiseled," and probably *srwk*, "ritual(?)"; *qaytâl: pyrk*, "crushing"; *qatlân: rʿyn*, "desire" (Biblical *raʿyôn*), and possibly *prkn*, "crushing(?)";[42] nouns with prosthetic *ʾaleph: ʾṭbʿ*, "(shekel) coin" (compare Aramaic *ṭᵉbaʿ*), and probably *ʾškr*, "intoxicant" (compare Aramaic *šᵉkar*).

It is probable that *sḥr*, "plate," is Semitic, but its etymology is not clear and its vocalization cannot yet be determined.

Numerals

The numerals used in the ritual texts are figures and are never written out. The usage is identical with that of the Aramaic papyri of the Achaemenid period: small vertical strokes in groups of three, up to nine, are used to indicate units. The number one is often used in the sense of an indefinite pronoun. A horizontal arc (¬) is used for ten, and a double arc, resembling a figure 3, stands for the figure twenty.

What appears to be a figure 5[43] in No. 4 is doubtless an unusually vertical figure 10.

PREPOSITIONS

Prepositions figure prominently and importantly in the ritual texts. The prefixed letter *b*, "in," begins most texts, introducing the construct nouns *srk*, *prkn*, and *hst*. It is also used with the absolute nouns *prk* as "in a crushing (ceremony)" (No. 5:3) and *ʿyd* as "in a festival" (No. 112:5). It occurs, too, with place names to indicate places associated with the *segan* (No. 94:2) and the treasurers (Nos. 9:4, 13:4, 14:4 and others).

The preposition *l*, "to," is used once with an infinitive form to express purpose (No. 8:3). Elsewhere it is used in these texts only in combination. It occurs with the noun "hand" (*lyd*) to express the positional idea of "at the hand of" or "beside" to indicate the relative positions of the celebrant, the *segan*, and the treasurer during the haoma ceremony.[44] As "to" or "for" the preposition *l* is combined in rather unusual fashion with the Persian preposition *patiy*, used in the sense of "value" or "equivalence" (No. 43:4).

In the sense of "before" or "opposite" the preposition *qdm*, "in front of," is used in the ritual texts to indicate the relative positions of the celebrant and sub-treasurer during the haoma ceremony.

The preposition *ʿm*, "with," or "together with," occurs on mortars (Nos. 1:3, 46:4, 103:3; compare Nos. 14:3, 16:3) when their related pestles are also mentioned in the texts and on pestles (Nos. 10:4, 17:4) when the accompanying mortars are also named.

[42] Unless the word is a hybrid with the Persian affix *-ana* to indicate "*place* of crushing"; cf. p. 22.

[43] Such a figure is found in the Samaritan ostraca, Palmyrene, and elsewhere but not in the Aramaic papyri. It would be unique in the ritual texts and definitely not part of the numerical system.

[44] See p. 32.

PRONOUNS

PRONOMINAL SUFFIX

The only example of a pronominal suffix in these texts is the affixed *h* used with *šm*, "name," as *šmh*, "his name," when used for the Old Persian *nāma*, "namely" (see above).

DEMONSTRATIVE PRONOUN

The demonstrative pronoun *znh*, "this," (once *dnh* in No. 44:3) is used only adjectivally in these Aramaic texts, following the noun as in the majority of instances in Biblical Aramaic and the papyri.

Sometimes the noun so designated is in the determinate state, as it should be in Aramaic (for example *ʾbšwnʾ znh* in Nos. 13:3, 15:4 and *šrʾ znh* in No. 19:3). But quite often the noun is in the absolute state (*ʾbšwn znh* in No. 27:5 and *šr znh* in No. 18:2). That phenomenon may reflect the influence of Old Persian, which lacks an article.[45]

RELATIVE PARTICLE *zy*

The indeclinable particle *zy* is used, as elsewhere in Aramaic, to introduce a relative clause. Thus, there is found sometimes *gnzbrʾ zy bhrḥwty*, "the treasurer who is in Arachosia" (Nos. 9:4, 43:5–6, and others) and "the treasurer who is in *Ghštk*" (No. 14:4).

As in Biblical Aramaic and the papyri, the particle *zy* is also used to express a relationship between nouns. Most frequently it is found in such a construction as *hwn zy gll*, "a mortar of stone" (literally, "a mortar, that which is stone"). It may also be used as a modifier of *gll*, "stone," as in the example *hwn zy gll zy bz*, "a mortar of *bz* stone" (No. 116:2–3).

Two texts which show its use in establishing relationship between nouns deserve special consideration. One (No. 29:4) describes a pestle as *ʾbšwn zy bʾt*, "pestle of wine," which must signify "a pestle used for making wine." The other (No. 62:3) has *ʾbšwn zy ʾškr*, "pestle of *ʾškr*," which must have a similar meaning. It must indicate "the pestle used for making the intoxicant," in these texts, "the pestle used for pressing haoma."

WORD ORDER

SUBJECT–VERB

Normally in the ritual texts the subject precedes the verb, following an order sometimes also encountered in Biblical Aramaic,[46] even when there is no special emphasis on the subject to warrant such deviation from the more normal Semitic order. The phenomenon is probably due to the influence of Old Persian, in which it is normal for the subject to precede.[47]

ADJECTIVE AND DEMONSTRATIVE

As indicated above, the demonstrative pronoun is used in adjectival position after the noun that it modifies. Except in the case of the Persian noun, which is always in the absolute state, the noun with the demonstrative pronoun may be in the determinate state (Nos. 15, 19, 49, 73) or, more usually, in the absolute state (Nos. 52, 54, 58, 59 and others).

When an adjective of size is added, the scribe could write *ʾbšwn mdm* (No. 57) or *ʾbšwn mdm* 1 (No. 21) for "a medium-sized pestle" or *hwn rb znh* for "this large mortar" (No. 14; compare

---

[45] Kent, *Old Persian*, p. 85a, Sec. 262.

[46] *BLA*, p. 332, Sec. 99, pp. 342 ff., Sec. 101, and p. 372.

[47] Kent, *Old Persian*, p. 96, Sec. 310. Bauer and Leander (*BLA*, p. 332, Sec. 99a) attribute such order to the influence of Akkadian, but the order in Old Aramaic, which might be expected to show such influence, places the verb first. It would be better to assume Persian influence. The statistics on order in Biblical Aramaic presented by W. Baumgartner ("Das Aramäischen im Buche Daniel," *ZATW* XLV [1927] 128 ff.) show that the proportion of subject–verb to verb–subject is in the Aramaic of Daniel 120 to 80 and of Ezra 30 to 15.

Nos. 38, 55, 64). But the latter can be written also with the adjective after the demonstrative pronoun as *shr² znh rb* (No. 43; compare No. 41:2–3) or even as the unusual *shr znh rb* 1 (No. 18), which perhaps must be read as "this one large plate" or "this, a large plate."

Similarly, when the descriptive *zy gll*, "of stone," is used with the demonstrative pronoun, the writer had the option of writing it as *hwn zy gll znh*, "this mortar of stone" (Nos. 24, 33), or as *hwn znh zy gll* (No. 5; compare Nos. 20, 72, 109, 112, 113). When an adjective of size is involved, it is usually written as *hwn zy gll zʿyr znh*, "this small mortar of stone" (Nos. 31, 118; compare No. 88:3), with the demonstrative pronoun at the very end. But there is one example (No. 33) where the text probably has *hwn zy gll znh zʿyr* with the adjective "small" after the demonstrative pronoun.

Where both the mortar and pestle are mentioned in the same text, a demonstrative pronoun at the end perhaps refers to both objects, whether used in such a simple form as *hwn ʿm ²bšwn znh*, "this mortar with (this) pestle" (No. 46), or in such a complex statement as *hwn zy gll (ʿm) ²bšwn pyrk znh*, "this mortar of stone (with) (this) crushing pestle" (No. 13), or *hwn zy gll tzgbs ʿm ²bšwn znh*, "this mortar of *tzgbs* stone with (this) mortar" (No. 1). But a scribe could also write *hwn znh [zy gll ²m] ²bšwn pyrk*, "this mortar [of stone with] a crushing pestle" (No. 9).

XII

TEXTS

1. Mortar (PT5 427A[1])   T (18);[2] Pl. 2

[בסר]ך בירתא ליד אמדת סֹגֹנֹא	1) [In the ritu]al of the fortress, beside Ama-dāta the *segan*,
.מֹבוש [עֹבֹד]³ הון זֹ֗ גלל֗	2) .*mbwš* used this mortar of . . . stone
תֹֹזֹגבס עֹם [א]בשון זנֹה	3) with pestle
[ל]יד דתמתר גנזברֹא אֹשכרֹ	4) beside Dāta-Mithra the treasurer. ʾškr of
שֹ[נֹ]ת *iii iii i*	5) year 7.

DESCRIPTION

A fragment of a green chert mortar, consisting of most of the inscribed base (base dia. 8 cm., present max. height 4.8 cm.). Part of the right side of the base is broken away, damaging the first letters of each line of the text.

Five lines of Aramaic are on the bottom of the base. A deep circular depression in the stone mars the beginning of the last line.

FIND SPOT

Because of confusion in field numbers the find spot of this object cannot be determined. It certainly came from the Treasury, perhaps from Room 38, where so many others were found.

DATE[4]

Seventh year of Xerxes (479/78 B.C.).[5]

LINE 1

The restoration of the first word is certain, for *srk* is often found in this context. Usually it is spelled *srk*, but in one text (No. 54:1) it is written *srwk*. Altheim, expecting a place name, read it faultily as *prs*, "Parsa" (Persepolis), on the basis of a photograph of a single text[6] and drew invalid conclusions from his error.

The exact meaning of the term is still somewhat uncertain. A word spelled similarly is found in a much later literary work of the Jewish community at Qumran in Palestine, where it has both military and religious significance, as it also seems to have here. Since it has com-

---

[1] Two objects bear the number PT5 427. PT5 427B (No. 153), a section of a plate (T [35]), is the article listed in the Field Register under that number.

[2] The fragments recovered at Persepolis in 1966 do not yet bear accession numbers of the museum. When sent to Teheran from Persepolis, they were given sequential white numbers which are here given in parentheses preceded by the letter *T*.

[3] In transcription, letters supplied conjecturally are placed within brackets; where there is some trace of letters, however slight, they are dotted within brackets; those that are broken but highly probable are simply dotted but without brackets.

[4] Dates used in this work are drawn from the carefully compiled tables of R. A. Parker and W. H. Dubberstein, *Babylonian Chronology 626 B.C.–A.D. 45* ("Brown University Studies" XIX [Providence, 1956]).

[5] See Table 1.

[6] No. 39 (PT5 492). Schmidt, *Persepolis* II, Pl. 23:3; Altheim and Stiehl, *Aramäische Sprache* I 18.

71

plex ritual values at Qumran, for the moment, at least, it is translated in these texts by "ritual."[7]

The word *byrt*, "fortress," often appears after city names, but it seems that in these Aramaic texts the words preceding it stand in construct relationship with it and the word *byrt* represents fortified Persepolis itself.[8] As the title of the treasurer Vahush in the Elamite Treasury tablets shows, "the fortress" was an alternate term for Parsa.

The *lyd* that normally occurs before the names of the *segan* and the treasurer in the Aramaic texts is here rendered as "beside" because it indicates the relative positions of the celebrant and the officers as participants in the haoma ceremony. Such use of *lyd* is attested in Akkadian and the Bible and also in the Aramaic fortification tablets of the time of Darius I.[9]

The name *ꜣmdt* is doubtless the same as the [m]*am-ma-da-a-tu* mentioned in a cuneiform text of the time of Darius I.[10] It may also be concealed in the name Madatas mentioned by Xenophon[11] and the Medāthā and Ἀμαδάθης by which Josephus (*Antiq.* XI. vi. 5) and the Septuagint respectively render the Persian name Hammedatha of the Bible (Esther 3:1).[12] While the present *ꜣmdt* might be a graphic variant of the Biblical name, it is preferable to regard the first element of the name as the Persian *ama-*, "strength," "might," which sometimes is used to indicate a divine manifestation.[13]

The title *segan*, an Aramaized form of Akkadian *šaknu*, which originally meant a royal appointee, still indicates a relatively important official in these Aramaic texts.[14] As in the Bible (Dan. 2:48) there appears to have been a "chief *segan*" who, at this time, was Mithrapāta.[15]

Ama-dāta was apparently a subordinate *segan*. He is found sporadically in the reigns of both Xerxes and Artaxerxes I, as well as in some undateable texts.[16]

LINE 2

The name of the celebrant, the subject of the verb *ꜥbd*, is uncertain. It is probably damaged at the beginning, where the edge of the inscribed surface is broken away. One, or possibly even two letters could have stood there. The first visible traces, at the very edge of the break, suggest the lower part of a letter *m*. The final letter of the name is certainly *š*, which may be added optionally to noun stems ending in the vowels -*i* and -*u*, as in the names Dāraya(t)-vahu(š) and Āraya(t)-vahu(š).[17] Before the -*š* are two letters that appear to be identical and most closely resemble the letter -*s*. But the combination -*ssš* is impossible and the reading must be . . *mbwš*, which could represent either Iranian . . *mbwš* or . . *mbwč*.

The verb *ꜥbd* regularly describes the action in the Aramaic texts. None of the usual meanings ("make," "prepare," "serve") suit the context of the Aramaic texts. Only a meaning "worked" or "used" gives an acceptable translation.[18] The subject here invariably precedes the verb in Persian rather than Aramaic fashion.[19]

[7] See pp. 22–24.   [8] See pp. 20–22.   [9] See p. 32 n. 55.

[10] Cf. W. Eilers, "Iranische Beamtennamen in der keilschriftlichen Überlieferung," *Abhandlungen für die Kunde des Morgenlandes* XXV, No. 5 (1940), p. 113, n. 3.

[11] Xenophon *Cyropaedia* V. iii. 41.

[12] Justi (*Iranisches Namenbuch* [Hildesheim, 1963], p. 125, Hamdāthā), like Jensen, regarded the first element of the Biblical name as an Elamite divine name Humman or Umman and called the name "Susian" (i.e., Elamite); Benveniste (*Titres et noms propres en iranien ancien* ["Travaux de l'Institut d'études iraniennes de l'Université de Paris" I (Paris, 1966)], p. 77) sees Elamite Ammadadda as representing either *Ama-dāta or Hama-dāta.

[13] *BAiW*, col. 140 ²*ama-*, 2A; Nyberg (*Religionen*, pp. 70, 74) recognizes a goddess Ama, "Kraft," in Mithra circles.

[14] See pp. 25–27, 32.   [16] See p. 27 and Table 1.   [18] See pp. 38–40.

[15] No. 2, between lines 2 and 3.   [17] See pp. 81, 96–97.   [19] See p. 69.

The noun *hwn*, found on the mortars, is the Persian word *havana*,[20] which is still used by the Parsis to designate the mortar in the modern haoma ceremony.[21]

The word *gll*, already known from Biblical Aramaic (Ezra 5:8, 6:4) corresponds to the Akkadian *abangalâla*, which in the Achaemenid period meant simply "stone."[22] Such a meaning is supported in these texts by an occasional addition of a modifier to indicate more precisely the character of the stone.[23]

LINE 3

Except for its first word, which is difficult, this line is illegible, with isolated, badly faded letters. But, as in the lines that follow, the text can be restored with great probability on the basis of well-recognized formulae.

The first word, the clearest in the line, is nevertheless difficult and uncertain. To judge from its position, it must modify *gll*, indicating the kind or quality of the stone. The last three letters are clearly *gbs*, but it is uncertain what is before them. A letter may be missing at the beginning of the word, where the margin is broken. Close inspection suggests that the most likely reading is *.tzgbs* or less probably *ɔnzgbs*. Its etymology and meaning are still uncertain.

Since several mortar texts mention the pestle used with them (for example, Nos. 46:4, 103:3), this line doubtless makes such a reference, introduced by a somewhat smudged *ᶜm*, "with," near the middle of the line. Traces of the word *ɔbšwn*, "pestle," follow it. The word is apparently Indo-Iranian, formed from the elements **abi-su-ana*.[24]

LINE 4

Although the first trace of a letter in the line is somewhat obscure, it is a combination of the letters *l* and *y*, which are followed by the head of a *d* for the preposition *lyd*, which normally precedes the name of the treasurer.

The name of the treasurer is *Dtmtr*, which Eilers suggests might represent either Dāta-Mithra ("To whom friendship [Mithra] has been given") or Dāta-Mathra ("To whom the holy word [Mathra] has been given").[25] Elsewhere the name Mithra-dāta appears.[26]

In these texts Dāta-Mithra is found as treasurer from the seventh through the nineteenth years of Xerxes (479–466 B.C.) and is thereafter supplanted by Baga-pāta. In the thirteenth and eighteenth years he is called "the treasurer who is in Arachosia."[27] It is likely that the seal impression portraying a scene from the haoma ceremony found on labels in the Persepolis Treasury from the time of Xerxes[28] are the marks of his seal. The name, written in Aramaic on the seal, was formerly read as "Datames,"[29] but it is incompletely impressed and should be read as *Dtm[tr]*, "Dāta-Mithra."

The title of Dāta-Mithra is always *gnzbrɔ* (Old Persian *ganzabara*), "treasurer."[30] Although the spelling of "treasure" elsewhere as *gnz*[31] suggested such a spelling for the title, the word is found in these texts for the first time spelled in this fashion.[32] In these texts the title "treas-

---

[20] *BAiW*, col. 1786, *havana*.   [21] See p. 46.

[22] See pp. 44–45. R. A. Bowman, "וְאֶבֶן גְּלָל-*aban galālu* (Ezra 5:8; 6:4)," *Dōrōn: Hebraic Studies* (New York, 1965), pp. 64–74.

[23] See p. 45.   [24] See p. 47.

[25] Justi (*Iranisches Namenbuch*, p. 81, Δατάμης) suggests that the name Datames may abbreviate Dāta-Mithra.

[26] Ezra 4:7; Cowley, *AP*, No. 26:2, 7 (412 B.C.) and No. 80:7; E. G. Kraeling, *The Brooklyn Museum Aramaic Papyri* (New Haven, 1953), No. 3:23; cf. Justi, *Iranisches Namenbuch*, pp. 209–13.

[27] See pp. 28–30.   [29] See pp. 6–7.

[28] See Pl. 1.   [30] See pp. 28–29.

[31] Cowley, *AP*, No. 26:4, 13, No. 69*b*; G. R. Driver, *Aramaic Documents of the Fifth Century B.C.* (Oxford, 1954), No. X, l. 5; see p. 28, n. 27 here.

[32] Eilers, in *Abhandlungen für die Kunde des Morgenlandes* XXV, No. 5, pp. 123–24.

urer" may perhaps indicate a priest, possibly connected with the army, who participated in the haoma ceremony.[33]

At the end of the line is the word *ʾškr*, which normally appears just before the date. The only passage in which *ʾškr* appears in syntactical relationship (No. 62:4) links the word to the "pestle" as "pestle of *ʾškr*," which seems parallel to "pestle of wine" (No. 29:4) and suggests that *ʾškr* means something to drink. The most probable etymology suggests that it is the word *šᵉkar*, "intoxicant," with a prosthetic *ʾaleph*.[34] Because "ceremony of making the intoxicant" rather than "intoxicant" itself would be expected before the date, the word is merely transliterated in these translations of the ritual texts.

2. Pestle (PT5 789) Pl. 2

[בפרׄכׄן בירׄ[תׄ]א]	1)	[In the (haoma-)crushing ceremony of the fortress,]
[לׄי̇]ד מתרפת סגנׄ]א] רׄבׄא	2)	beside Mithra-pāta the chief *segan*,
[סׄ]נפׄך̇ *i* עבדו אבשון	3)	1 *Snpk* has used this
[זׄי גׄלׄלׄ] מדם זנה	4)	medium-sized pestle of stone.
אשכר שנׄת̇	5)	*ʾškr* of year
ii [*iii iii*]	6)	8.

DESCRIPTION

A fragment of a green chert pestle (head dia. 3.4 cm., max. length 8.1 cm.) with a broken shaft.

Six lines of Aramaic are on the top of the pestle head. The letters of the first line are faint and almost illegible as are also those at the beginnings of lines and the figure in the last line.

FIND SPOT

The northeastern part (HF 47)[35] of Room 38.

DATE

Although the date line is extremely faint, the spacing of the unit groups as well as traces of the strokes indicate the figure 8, as Cameron also saw it. The first group is almost illegible and the second is quite faint. The text is from the eighth year of Xerxes (478/77 B.C.), when Mithra-pāta served as *segan*.[36]

LINE 1

The letters have almost disappeared in this line, but familiarity with the usual formulae facilitates the identification of the words in the shadowy traces of the letters that remain.

The word *prkn*, found quite often in these texts, is new to Aramaic. It probably derives from the Semitic root *prk* meaning "to rub," "to grind down," "to pulverize," "to pound," indicating the action of using a mortar and pestle. Elsewhere (No. 5) a word *prk* is apparently used of a ceremony of crushing or of the place in which such action occurred. The affixed *-n* of *prkn* probably represents the Aramaic affix *-ân*, which is frequently used to form abstract nouns. As such, the word means "crushing" and is here translated as "the (haoma-)crushing ceremony." Less likely, *prkn* could be a Persianized hybrid formation with a Persian affix *-ana*, used to indicate a place where the crushing was done.[37]

---

[33] See pp. 31–32.   [34] See p. 54.

[35] Such plot references are to the archeological grid, see Fig. 1.

[36] Justi, *Iranisches Namenbuch*, p. 209, Μιτροβάτης. See p. 27 and Table 1.

[37] See p. 20 n. 6.

LINE 2

Cameron copied a few signs between the second and third lines and correctly noted that there is apparently an insertion there. The photograph shows what seem to be the letters *rbᵓ*, "the chief." It is apparently a supplement to the title *segan* at the end of the second line. It suggests that Mithra-pāta, like Daniel (Dan. 2:48), was the "chief *segan*." As such, he is named with considerable regularity in the texts, while those who appear only sporadically must be his subordinates.

LINE 3

Because the letters at the beginning of the line are very faint and the word written between lines 2 and 3 interferes with the tops of the letters, the name of the celebrant is quite uncertain.

In the photograph the faint traces of the last three letters appear to be *-npk* or *-nwk*, which agrees with Cameron's copy. My independent reading was *-nrt* or *-npt*. The next to last letter appears to be the letter *r* but the hooklike stroke that makes it appear to be that letter may belong to the *ᵓaleph* written between the lines. It is possible that the last consonant is *k*, followed by a unit stroke which makes it appear to be a *t*. There is room for one or possibly two consonants before the *n*. Cameron shows no trace of a letter and I found none there, but the photograph shows what might be a faint trace of the head of a letter *s*. Thus, the name could be read 1 *Snpk*.

Although the subject of the verb is singular, the verb seems to be plural in form, as *ᶜbdw*. That it is not an error is indicated by other such examples in these texts[38] and by similar phenomena found elsewhere.[39] It is doubtless to be equated in tense with the simple *ᶜbd* that is normally found and it must indicate past action. Altheim has explained such forms as a Semitic verb with an enclitic auxiliary verb *hᵃwâ*.[40]

LINE 4

The first words are extremely faint, but remaining traces make the reading certain as the *zy gll*, "of stone," that often follows the name of the object.

The word *mdm* indicates that the pestle is of "medium size," but it is the smallest in that category.[41] Because there is no Aramaic word for "medium size," an Iranian word *maδəma* is used.[42]

3. Pestle (PT5 728) Pl. 2

[בֹּפֹּר]כֹן בִּירֹ[תֹא]	1)	In the (haoma-)crushing ceremony of the fortress,
לִיד מתר[פֹּתֹ] סגֹנֹא	2)	beside Mithra-pāta the *segan*,
אדוסת עבֹדֹ	3)	*ᵓdwst* used
אבשון זֹנה	4)	this pestle.
אשכר שנת ⟜	5)	*ᵓškr* of year 10.

DESCRIPTION

A green chert pestle fragment (head dia. 6.1 cm., max. length 8.4 cm.). Because of a wide band of deeper color, a little more than a third of the head is difficult to read.

Five lines of Aramaic, written in quite thick letters, are on the top of the pestle head. The beginnings and ends of lines are somewhat smudged and faint.

---

[38] Nos. 13:2, 14:2, 15:3, and probably 20:3.

[39] See pp. 40, 66.

[40] See pp. 42–43.

[41] See p. 48 and n. 57.

[42] *BAiW*, cols. 1114–15, *maδəma*.

FIND SPOT

Northwestern part (HF 48) of Room 38.

DATE

Mithra-pāta as *segan* indicates the reign of Xerxes, whose tenth year was 476/75 B.C.

LINE 3

The spelling of the celebrant's name is verified by several other texts (Nos. 52:2 and 133:2). In the twenty-ninth year of Artaxerxes I (436/35 B.C.) he is identified as a chiliarch (No. 52).

Justi cites an Adosthos,[43] but since that name is apparently derived from Old Iranian *A-dušta*, "blameless," and one would expect Old Persian *duš-*, the spelling expected here should then be *ᵓdwšt*. But Eilers shows that the phonetic change, -*št*- > -*st*-, characteristic of Middle Persian, is already encountered in Old Persian.[44] Frye privately suggested as other possibilities **A-daiva-stu*, "Non-worshipper of daiva," or **A-dvašt* (Avestan *A-zoaš-t*), "Finding taste in. . . ."

4. Pestle (PT5 419) Pl. 2

בפרכן בירת	1)	In the (haoma-)crushing ceremony of the fortress,
ליד מתרפת סגנ[אֹ]	2)	beside Mithra-pāta the *segan*,
[אֹ]רתדת עבד אבש[וֹ]	3)	Arta-dāta used a pestle
זי גלל אשכר	4)	of stone. *ᵓškr* of
שנת יֹ	5)	year 10(?).

DESCRIPTION

A green chert pestle fragment with a broken shaft (head dia. 3.7 cm., present max. length 10.1 cm.).

Five lines of Aramaic are inscribed on the top of the pestle head.

FIND SPOT

North of the center (HF 29) of Room 38.

DATE

Mithra-pāta as *segan* indicates the reign of Xerxes but the numeral is somewhat uncertain.

Since there are otherwise no well attested ritual texts dating before the seventh year of Xerxes, the rather vertical numeral can scarcely be the year 1 and nowhere else in these texts is there a figure 5.[45] Since Mithra-pāta was displaced by Mithraka in the nineteenth year of Xerxes[46] the figure cannot be 20. It closely resembles the vertical figure 10 of No. 9:5. The tenth year of Xerxes was 476/75 B.C.

LINE 1

The word "fortress" at the end of the line lacks the usual *ᵓaleph* of the determinate state. Its omission is apparently due to lack of space, since the line runs downward as the edge of the pestle top is approached.

---

[43] Justi, *Iranisches Namenbuch*, p. 5*b*.

[44] Eilers, in *Abhandlungen für die Kunde des Morgenlandes* XXV, No. 5, pp. 98–99; cf. Meillet and Benveniste, *Grammaire*, p. 72, n. 2.

[45] A figure 5 of similar shape is found in the Samaritan ostraca. Since such a numeral appears to be hieratic Egyptian (Y. Aharoni, "The Use of Hieratic Numerals in Hebrew Ostraca and the Shekel Weights," *Bulletin of the American Schools of Oriental Research* CLXXXIV [1966] 13–19) one would scarcely expect its use in these distinctly Iranian texts.

[46] See p. 57.

LINE 3

According to Cameron, the first visible letter at the beginning of the line is obscured by the discoloration of the stone. It seems to be the letter *r*. But there is a smudge in the space before it, where it seems reasonable to restore an *ᵓaleph* to form the name Arta as the first element of the celebrant's name. The personal religion of Xerxes stressed the holy Arta.[47] The name is thus Arta-dāta,[48] a name already found on an Aramaic seal.[49]

As in line 1, the letters are badly crowded at the end of this line. The first letters of the word *ᵓbšwn*, "pestle," are of normal size; the *š* is narrower and slightly smaller than usual; and the *w* is extremely small and faint, crowded against the *n*, which is at the very edge of the pestle top.

5. Mortar (PT5 768) Persepolis Museum 102; Pl. 2

בפרכן בירתא ליד מתר[פ]ת סנ[נא]	1)	In the (haoma-)crushing ceremony of the fortress, beside Mithra-pāta the *segan*,
[נ]תוהי עבד הון זנה [זי] גללי	2)	Gāθā-vahya(?) used this mortar of stone
בפרך רב / קדם מהדת אפנ[נוברא]	3)	in a great (ceremony of) crushing before Māh(a)-dāta the sub-treasurer.
אשכר שנת ÷	4)	*ᵓškr* of year 10(+?)

DESCRIPTION

A fragment of a large green chert mortar with a broken bowl (base dia. 18.9 cm., max. height 19.3 cm. [slightly reduced in illustration]). A large part of the lower right side of the base is lost and a very large chip has been struck from its left edge. A small, flat, rectangular metal piece is embedded in the stone base, apparently to strengthen and mend an ancient crack.[50]

Four lines of Aramaic are written on the bottom of the base. All of the text lies within the top third of the inscribed surface. The ends of the first three lines are lost in the damage to the left side of the base. The letters are very faint, especially toward the ends of lines, where they tend to become illegible. Reading is particularly difficult in the second and third lines, which are partly written over dark banding in the stone. The metal bit almost obliterates the letter *p* in the name of Mithra-pāta in the first line.

FIND SPOT

North of the center (HF 29) of Room 38.

DATE

Cameron copied the sign for 10, which is extremely faint in the photograph. It is impossible to tell how many unit strokes, if any, followed the sign for 10. According to clearly dated texts, Mithra-pāta served only until the nineteenth year of Xerxes. This text is thus probably from the tenth year (476/75 B.C.).

LINE 2

Cameron copied the first letter of the name of the celebrant as a *g*, but it has now disappeared completely. The letter following shows only the top of a *t*. Beyond it is the short horizontal stroke of the head of the letter *w*. The *h* that follows it is clear and certain and behind

[47] A. T. Olmstead, *History of the Persian Empire* (Chicago, 1948), p. 232.
[48] Justi, *Iranisches Namenbuch*, p. 33, Artadāt.
[49] A. H. Layard, *Nineveh and Babylon* (London, 1897), p. 606.
[50] Similar metal inlays are found in Nos. 28 and 72.

that is a semi-circular mark which Cameron properly recognized as the letter *y*. The name is thus *Gtwhy*.

The second element of the name is already familiar in Aramaic from the name *Bgwhy* in the papyri.[51] It has been regarded by some as the comparative adjective *-vahyah*, "the better,"[52] and by others as an element indicating an abbreviated name.[53] For the first element, *gt-*, Eilers has proposed *gāta* "going" or "coming" (from the verb *gam*), *gāθā*, "song," "hymn," or *gāθu* "throne," "place."[54]

LINE 3

Because the beginning of the line is written on a very dark band in the stone it is somewhat difficult to read. The traces of letters indicate *bprk*, followed by clearly written heads of letters and other traces of the word *rb*, as Cameron copied it. After a space a thick unit stroke completes the reading *bprk rb* 1. The unit stroke is used here not with a name, since that would only be found in these texts with the celebrant, who is named in the preceding line. The expression *bprk rb* 1 is related to the verb *ᶜbd* in the second line.

The *bprk*, reminiscent of the *bprkn* of the first line, is unique in this position. Since the Semitic root *prk* can signify the action of crushing, grinding, or pounding,[55] it is possible that *ᶜbd . . . . bprk rb* 1 could mean "used . . . in a large crushing room" or, more likely, "used . . . in a great (or 'important'?) ceremony of crushing (haoma)."

Justi reads the name Māh(a)-dāta as "Given by the moon god Māh." Benveniste finds this name in the Greek Μαιδάτης and the element *māh* in Greek names beginning with Μαι- or Μαϊ-.[56]

LINE 4

Between the first and second words of the fourth line there is a thick, heavy mark, resembling the top of the letter *n* as found in the word *prkn* in the first line. But the long, swinging stroke that would identify it as the letter *n* is missing. The mark is ignored in Cameron's copy, but it is clear in the photograph and on the mortar itself. Its presence leaves no space between the words and it raises the question whether or not it should be considered as a letter.

It is unlikely that the stroke represents a *b* for a reading *bšnt*, which is sometimes found,[57] for its shape is unlike that of the letter *b* found elsewhere in this text.

6. Pestle (PT5 116) T (82); Pl. 3

בסרך ביר[תֿ]אׁ ליׁד	1)	In the ritual of the fortress, beside
ארתדֿתֿ ס[גנׁ]א	2)	Arta-dāta the *segan*,
והוׁ[ו]פֿֿרֿן ﬠֿבֿוׁד אֿ[בׁ]שֿׁוׁן	3)	Vahu-farnah used (this?) pestle
. . . . גֿלֿלֿ [זׁי]	4)	of . . . stone
לׁיד דֿתֿ[מ]תֿ[ר גׁנׁזבׁ]רׁא	5)	beside Dāta-Mithra the treasurer.
[אשכר] שׁ[נׁת] ז̇ /	6)	[ᵓškr] of year 11.

DESCRIPTION

A pestle with a broken shaft (head dia. 3.8 cm., present max. length 6.8 cm.).

Six lines of Aramaic are written on the top of the pestle head. The letters are quite small and delicate. Many are incomplete and some are missing entirely. Only scant traces show in the fourth line.

---

[51] Cowley, *AP*, Nos. 30:1 and 32:1.   [52] *BAiW*, cols. 1405–6, *vahyah*.

[53] H. H. Schaeder, *Iranische Beiträge* I (Halle [Saale], 1930) 67–68, בנוהי; Justi, *Iranisches Namenbuch*, pp. 60a, 525, -oas.

[54] *BAiW*, cols. 493 ff., 519, *gāθā*; Kent, *Old Persian*, p. 183a, *gāθu*, p. 79b, Sec. 244.

[55] See p. 22.

[56] Justi, *Iranisches Namenbuch*, pp. 185b, 186; Benveniste, *Titres et Noms*, p. 105.

[57] Nos. 65:5, 69:4, 97:5.

FIND SPOT

The Persepolis Treasury.[58]

DATE

Dāta-Mithra was treasurer only during the reign of Xerxes, whose eleventh year was 475/74 B.C.

LINE 2

The name Arta-dāta appears as that of the celebrant in Nos. 4 and 73. The name is that of a *segan* only here, where the official is possibly a subordinate *segan*.

LINE 3

The name of the celebrant is difficult to read. The first two letters are certain. They are followed by two short lines which could be the remains of the letters *wp*, which precede a sign that seems to be the vertical stroke of a letter *r*. There is ample room for the final *-n* before the next word. Another *Whwprn*, Vahu-farnah, occurs as a celebrant in another text, dated a few years later in the reign of Xerxes (No. 10; see also No. 119).

LINE 4

The line is almost gone. Faint traces remain of the beginning. The remainder doubtless had modifiers descriptive of the quality of either the stone or the pestle.

7. Pestle (PT5 671) Persepolis Museum 213; Pl. 3

בירתא [. . . .]	1)	[In the . . . of] the fortress,
[ליד] מתרפת סגנא	2)	[beside] Mithra-pāta the *segan*,
מתרפת / עב[ד אבשון]	3)	1 Mithra-pāta used
זנה רב ליד [דתמתר]	4)	this large [pestle] beside [Dāta-Mithra]
גנ[ז]ברא [קדם מהדת]	5)	the treasurer (and) [before Māh(a)-data]
אפגנ[ז]ברא א[שכר]	6)	the sub-treasur[er. ᵓ]*škr* of
[ש]נת ⊢ /	7)	year 11.

DESCRIPTION

A pestle fragment of green chert (head dia. 5.9 cm., present max. length 10.4 cm.).[59] Almost a third of the upper right part of the head is lost, destroying the beginnings of the first two lines.

Of the seven lines of Aramaic on the polished pestle head, parts of the text are so faint as to be illegible.

FIND SPOT

Southwestern part (HF 38) of Room 38.

DATE

Eleventh year of Xerxes (475/74 B.C.).

LINE 3

Unless there is a scribal error, the *segan* and the celebrant both bear the same name, Mithra-pāta.

---

[58] The exact find spot cannot be determined since the Field Register lists a "pin" rather than "pestle" as PT5 116.

[59] Schmidt, *Persepolis* I 170*b*, II, Pl. 24: 7.

LINE 4

Cameron's copy shows the name of the treasurer in thin, faint lines in an area well shaded to indicate the obscurity of the text. His traces show something like *mhrmt* but he offered no transliteration. He noted that the traces do not look like Dāta-Mithra or Baga-pāta but that "it might conceivably be the former." Dāta-Mithra is the name expected before the nineteenth year of Xerxes for the treasurer.[60] Personal collation at Persepolis convinces me that although the reading is indeed difficult, the name is the expected Dāta-Mithra.

LINE 5

The missing name of the sub-treasurer should probably be Māh(a)-dāta, that of the only sub-treasurer found in dated texts before the nineteenth year of Xerxes (see Nos. 5, 13, and 14).[61]

LINE 6

It was Eilers who first recognized that the *ᵓp-* of *ᵓpgnzbrᵓ* was the Indo-European **upo-* (Old Persian *upa-*) and that the title was "sub-treasurer."[62]

8. Mortar (PT5 681) Pl. 3

בֹּ[סֹ]רֹךְ בירתֹ[א] ליד [מתרפ]תֹ	1)	In [the ritual of the fortress,] beside [Mithra-pā]ta
[סֹגֹנֹא] דריואן / עבד הֹוֹן	2)	the *segan*, 1 Draya-vāna used
זֹנֹה לֹחֹשֹל ליד דתמתֹר	3)	this mortar for pounding beside Dāta-Mithra
גנזב[רא] אֹשכֹר שנת יᗡ //	4)	the treasurer. *ᵓškr* of year 12.

DESCRIPTION

A fragment of a green chert mortar (base dia. 7.8 cm., present max. height 2.3 cm.).

Four lines of Aramaic are written on the bottom of the mortar base. A deep chip and a wide crack in the base destroy parts of the first two lines of the text.

FIND SPOT

South of the center (HF 38) of Room 38.

DATE

Twelfth year of Xerxes (474/73 B.C.).

LINE 2

The name of the celebrant, *Drywᵓn* may be formed of the element *dry-*, *drayah-*, "sea,"[63] and *-wᵓn*, *-vāna*, "conqueror."[64]

The practice of writing a unit stroke after a name in lists is of great antiquity, as can be seen in the Bible (Josh. 12:9–24) where an earlier figure has been spelled out. It is also used in lists in the papyri[65] and parchments.[66] At Persepolis, however, it is at times used even when the name is not in a list. The practice in these texts seems to reflect the use of the *ištên* sign with masculine names in Akkadian and of such Persian usage as the expression 1 *martiya* . . . *nāma*, "one man . . . by name."[67] In the ritual texts it is used only with the name of the celebrant.

[60] See p. 57.
[61] See p. 30.
[62] Cameron, *PTT*, p. 10, n. 64; Schmidt, *Persepolis* II 55, n. 69.
[63] *BAiW*, col. 1701, *zrayah;* Kent, *Old Persian*, p. 192b, *drayah.*
[64] Kent, *Old Persian*, p. 208b, under Vivāna.
[65] Cowley, *AP*, No. 33.
[66] Driver, *Aramaic Documents of the Fifth Century B.C.*, No. III, ll. 3–4, No. V, ll. 3–5.
[67] Behistun Inscription, col. i, ll. 36, 74, col. ii, ll. 8, 14, 79, etc.

LINE 3

There is a badly deteriorated patch in the surface before the word *lyd*, but traces of letters there mark a unique intrusion in the text. The reading is probably *lḥšl* modifying the verb *ᶜbd*, "used." The form is an unusual, archaic infinitive[68] from the root *ḥšl*, which in Jewish Aramaic means "to hammer," "to pound (grits)."[69] The infinitive presumably indicates purpose, "for pounding."

9. Mortar (PT5 674) Pl. 3

בפֿרכן בירתא ליד מֹ[תֹרֹפֹתֹ]	1)	In the (haoma-)crushing ceremony of the fortress, beside Mi[thra-pāta]
[סגנאֹ] סֹבנישׁ עֹ[ב]רֹ הון זֹ[נֹהֹ]	2)	[the *segan*,] *Sbgyš* used this mortar
[זי גלל עם] אבֹשון פיֹ[רֹ]ך ליד	3)	[of stone with] a crushing pestle beside
[דתֹ]מתר גנז[ברא] זי בהרחותֹי	4)	[Dāta]-Mithra the treasurer who is in Arachosia.
אשכר שנת ◄ ///	5)	*ᵓškr* of year 13.

DESCRIPTION

A mortar fragment (base dia. 12 cm., present max. height 12.4 cm. [slightly reduced in illustration]) of which three-quarters is missing. The right edge of the inscribed base has been badly chipped away by a heavy blow, damaging the beginnings of some of the lines of the Aramaic text.

Of the five lines of Aramaic written on the bottom of the base, all but the last line are so faint that they can be read only with difficulty.

FIND SPOT

Near the center (HF 39) of Room 38.

DATE

Thirteenth year of Xerxes (473/72 B.C.).

LINE 2

The name of the celebrant is quite faint and difficult to read. It seems to be *Sbgyš*, *ᵓbgyš*, or, less likely, *ᵓrgyš*, as in No. 75. The letter *y* could represent either a consonant or the long vowel *ī*. The *š* could be part of the name element or the *š* sometimes added to nominative forms of nouns of *-i*, *-u*, or *-î* stems, as in the name Āraya(t)-vahuš (see No. 24:2). If the reading is *ᵓbgyš*, Frye suggests as another possibility *abi*-GYŠ and compares the name *Sbgyš* of the Nisā texts.

LINE 3

Following the word "pestle" are traces of the word *pyrk*, which is found elsewhere as a modifier of "pestle."[70] It is an adjective from the root *prk* meaning "pound," "crush," "press."[71] Its form is unusual for Aramaic, but it is found quite often in Arabic,[72] where it appears as the type *fayᶜal* or *fayᶜâl* for such adjectives as *hayðar*, "rambling," or *hayṣâr*, "tearing."[73] Here it means "crushing" or "pounding."

---

[68] See p. 65.

[69] Jastrow, *Dictionary* I 511*a*.

[70] Nos. 13:3, 14:3, 17:5.

[71] See p. 22, n. 24.

[72] Henri Fleisch (*Traité de philologie arabe* I ["Recherches de l'Institut de Lettres Orientales de Beyrouth" XVI (Beyrouth, 1961)], § 77, pp. 352*f*, 353*h* and n. 1, 391, No. 2) indicates that the *Muzhir* of As-Suyūṭī (II 139–41) lists 116 words of such a form.

[73] C. Brockelmann, *Grundriss der vergleichenden Grammatik der semitischen Sprachen* I (Berlin, 1908) 344, Sec. 129.

LINE 4

Sometimes the treasurer is identified as the one "who is in *Hrḥwty*."[74] The spelling of the name, which is often damaged and incomplete in these texts, is clear in Nos. 43, 48, and 79. The name is already known from the Aramaic copy of the Behistun Inscription,[75] where it is spelled *Hrwḥty*, presumably following the Akkadian vocalization *ma*ʿ*a-ru-ḫa-at-ti*, "Arachosia." The spelling here corresponds more closely to the locative Old Persian form, *Harahuvatiyā*.[76]

The reference to Arachosia presumably signifies that the treasurers were normally stationed in Arachosia. Cameron sees here evidence that the vessels originated in Arachosia or at least in the East.[77] But it seems unnecessary to draw such a conclusion from these texts.[78]

Arachosia lay along the western border of India, and it has always had a mixed population, Indians and Iranians. It was constantly subject to Indianization and easily fell into the sphere of Indian influence. The soma/haoma rites seem to have had greater popularity and more prominence in that area than in the western part of the Persian empire. It seems likely that officials from Arachosia were regarded as adepts in the preparation and use of the sacred intoxicant and were welcomed at Persepolis to participate in the haoma rites celebrated there during festal times.

10. Pestle (PT5 801) Pl. 4

בסרך [ביר]ת[א]	1)	In the ritual of the fortress,
ליד מתר[פת ס]גנא	2)	beside Mithra-[pāta the *se]gan*,
והפֿרן עבד א[ב]שון ז[י]	3)	Vahu-farnah used this
גלל רב זנה [עם הון] ר[ב /]	4)	large pestle of stone [with a] large [mortar]
ליד דתמתר [גנזברא]	5)	beside Dāta-Mithra [the treasurer].
אשכר [שֹׁנֹת ـﻟ ///	6)	*ʾškr* of [year 1]3(?).

DESCRIPTION

A large green chert pestle fragment (head dia. 5.8 cm., present length 4.3 cm.).

Six lines of Aramaic cover approximately the upper two-thirds of the top of the head. A large spall at one edge of the head has struck away some of the Aramaic text and a dark horizontal band in the stone obscures a line of the Aramaic. The chip has removed the central parts of the first two lines. The fourth line is written on top of the dark band, rendering the end of the line almost illegible. The end of line five is completely gone and fading has almost obliterated the date in the last line, except for the three clear unit strokes at the end.

FIND SPOT

Near the center (HF 38) of Room 38.

DATE

The figure in line six is very faint. There are traces that suggest the *šn* of the expected *šnt*, "year," and the unit 3 is certain at the end of the line. Cameron's copy and reading indicate year 13 and the space available would seem to suit that figure, although it might be possible to insert another compact set of three strokes for the figure 16. Cameron indicates faint traces of the sign for 10.

The officers named indicate the reign of Xerxes, whose thirteenth year was 473/72 B.C. and whose sixteenth year was 470/69 B.C.

---

[74] Nos. 13:4, 19:4, 43:6, 44:5, 47:4, 48:7, 51:5, 52:5, 79:3, 95:5, 110:5, 123:4, 132:3, 155:4.

[75] Cowley, *AP*, p. 253, col. iii, l. 39.

[76] Kent, *Old Persian*, pp. 213–14; Sanskrit *sarasvatī*, "rich in waters"; Elamite *har-ra-u-ma-ti-iš*; Greek Ἀραχωσία.

[77] See pp. 28–29.　　　　　　　　　　　[78] See pp. 29–30.

LINE 3

The name of the celebrant is *Whprn*, Vahu-farnah,[79] which is spelled *Whwprn* in No. 119:1, where it is used of a *segan*. There is some slight damage to the letters in the name. Only the top of the *p* remains and the end of the horizontal stroke of the *h* touches it. The hook at the head of the *r* is preserved, but the rest of the letter is gone.

The name is compounded of *vahu*, "good,"[80] and *farnah*, which originally meant "a thing obtained or desired" and thence "good thing(s), welfare, fortune."[81]

LINE 4

The text is clear to the middle of the line but after the *znh* there is additional material. Because the letters are written on the dark band that crosses the stone, only traces of the tops of some of the letters are clearly visible. The line ends with *rb* 1, "1 large," but it is unlikely that the addition is all intended to modify the word "pestle." Since several mortars refer to the pestles used with them and at least one pestle (No. 39) refers to its mortar, it is probable that *ᶜm hwn*, "with a mortar," should be supplied before the modifiers *rb* 1.

11. Pestle (PT5 755 + 802) Pl. 4

בסרך בן‏י‏[ר‏]ת‏א ליד אמד[ת]	1)	In the ritual of the fortress, beside Ama-dā[ta]
סֿגֿנא כרבר עָֿבד אֿ[בשון]	2)	the *segan*, *Krbr* used a pestle
[ז‏י] גלל אחשינפין	3)	of dark . . . stone
[ליד‏] דתמתר גנז[ברא אשכר]	4)	[beside] Dāta-Mithra the [treasurer. ᵓškr of]
i [*// /*]*//* ‏- [שנ]ת	5)	year 16(?).

DESCRIPTION

Two fragments of green chert which join to form most of a pestle top. The smaller piece (PT5 802) forms the upper part of the head (2.5 cm. long and 2.1 cm. wide) and the larger (PT5 755) constitutes the major part of the head and shaft (head dia. about 5.3 cm., present max. length 10.3 cm.). Except for a very small part of the original circumference of the pestle head, all of the edges are broken away and the surface of the top is damaged by chipping from below.

The remains of five lines of Aramaic are on the top of the head. Letters on the smaller fragment are quite faint but legible while those on the larger piece appear fresh and black.

FIND SPOT

Both pieces were recovered just southwest of the center (HF 38) of Room 38.

DATE

The names of officials indicate the reign of Xerxes, but the exact year is uncertain, because of a break in the figure. Spacing seems to indicate year sixteen but the figure originally might have been as much as nineteen.

LINE 2

The name of the celebrant could be read as either *Krbr*, *Ksbr*, or even *Rsbr*, but the name of the celebrant in No. 12:2 supports a reading *Krbr*. The second element of the name is certainly *-br*, *-bāra* from the root *bar*, meaning "to bear," "to lift up," "to esteem," which is frequently the last element of Old Persian names.

---

[79] Eilers proposed Vahī'farnah here, but the spelling *Whwprn* in No. 119:1 suggests Vahu-farnah; Benveniste (*Titres et noms*, p. 87) sees the name Vahu-farnah in the Elamite Mauparna (var. -pirna).

[80] Kent, *Old Persian*, p. 206a, *vaʰu*.

[81] *Ibid.*, p. 208a, under Viⁿdafarnah; cf. H. W. Bailey, *Zoroastrian Problems in the Ninth Century Books* (Oxford, 1943), pp. 1–77, especially 1–3, 73–77.

The first element is more doubtful, both in reading and in interpretation. It could represent -kāra, signifying "people" or "army."[82]

LINE 3

The word ʾḥšynpyn, which appears again in No. 76:2 and possibly in No. 75:2 and, as ʾḥšynpn, in No. 101:2, modifies gll, "stone." The word seems to be a compound of which the first element is doubtless the Old Persian axšaina-. Meillet and Benveniste regard it as a dark blue stone[83] and Bleichsteiner considered it to be turquoise, a greenish-blue or greenish-gray semi-precious stone.[84] The color would be suitable but the substance is certainly not turquoise. Kent translates axšaina as "dark colored,"[85] a literal rendering of the word, and that is likely to be its use here.

The second element, -pyn or -pn, which seems to imply some such reading as -payn/-pēn/-pīn or possibly -fayn/-fēn/-fīn, perhaps indicates the basic color. From the nature of the stone one expects "green" or "grayish green." In No. 74:3 the word ʾḥšyn appears to be in combination with another basic color, ḥwyn.

12. Pestle (PT5 132) Pl. 4

בסרך בירתא ליד אמדֿת	1)	In the ritual of the fortress, beside Ama-dāta
סגנא כֿרֿבֿרֿ עֿבד אבשׁון	2)	the *segan*, *Krbr* used a pestle
ליד דֿתֿמתֿר גנזברא	3)	beside Dāta-Mithra the treasurer.
אשכֿר שׁ[נ]תֿ ⇀ /// /// /	4)	ʾškr of year 17.

DESCRIPTION

A fragment of a green chert pestle (head dia. 5.9 cm., present max. length 10.1 cm.).
Four lines of Aramaic, in rather thick letters, are written on the top of the pestle head.

FIND SPOT

At the center of the south wall (HF 49) of Room 38.

DATE

Seventeenth year of Xerxes (469/68 B.C.).

LINE 1

The last letter of the word "fortress," usually an ʾaleph, seems to be a letter m in the photograph and it was so copied clearly by Cameron, although he transliterated the usual byrtʾ. Since the ʾaleph is made in a peculiar fashion in the words sgnʾ and gnzbrʾ in this text, similar to the ʾaleph in the word "fortress," the letter in question should be read as an ʾaleph rather than as an m.

Ama-dāta again appears as a subordinate *segan*, as in text No. 1.

LINE 2

The celebrant is apparently the same as the one in No. 11 (another pestle) of the preceding year.

---

[82] Kent, *Old Persian*, p. 179b; Kāra-bāra could mean "Esteeming the army (or 'the people')."

[83] Meillet and Benveniste, *Grammaire*, p. 56.

[84] R. Bleichsteiner, "Altpersische Edelsteinnamen," *Wiener Zeitschrift für die Kunde des Morgenlandes* XXXVII (1930) 103–4; W. Hinz ("Zu den altpersischen Inschriften von Susa," *ZDMG* XCV [1941] 222–57) denies that axšaina is turquoise.

[85] Kent, *Old Persian*, p. 165b, axšaina; *BAiW*, col. 51, Avestan a-xšaēna, "dunkelfarbig."

LINE 3

At first glance, the name of the treasurer appears to be *Bgpt*, Baga-pāta, but closer study proves that it is the expected *Dtmtr*, Dāta-Mithra. The initial *d* has the swing of a *b* and, although the second letter seems to be a *g*, it is a *t*, of which the top and bottom of the long vertical stroke have faded away almost completely. The third letter is blurred but its almost rectangular shape suggests a letter *m* rather than a *p*. After the *t* that follows, a dark stroke represents the expected final *-r*.

The presence of Ama-dāta as the *segan* certifies the reign as that of Xerxes and the treasurer's name must be Dāta-Mithra, since Baga-pāta does not appear before the nineteenth year of Xerxes.

13. Mortar (PT5 333) Pl. 4

בפרכן בירתא ליד מתרפֿ[ת]	1)	In the (haoma-)crushing ceremony of the fortress, beside Mithra-pāta
סגנא אתון [ע]בדו הון זי גלל	2)	the *segan*, Arta(?)-wān has used this mortar of stone (with)
אב[ש]ונא [פ]ירך זנה ל[י]ד דתמתר גנזב[ר]א	3)	the crushing pestle beside Dāta-Mithra the treasurer
זי בה[רחותי]ן קדם מהדת אפגנזברא	4)	who is in Arachosia (and) before Māh(a)-dāta the sub-treasurer.
אש[כֿר] שנת ⟶ /// /// //	5)	ᵓš[kr] of year 18.

DESCRIPTION

A fragment of a green chert mortar (base dia. 12.2 cm., present max. height 7.4 cm.).

Five lines of Aramaic are written on the upper half of the base of the mortar in letters that are faint and sometimes almost illegible.

FIND SPOT

In the sherd yard among fragments from near the center of the south wall (HF 39) of Room 38 of the Persepolis Treasury.

DATE

Eighteenth year of Xerxes (468/67 B.C.).

LINE 2

Although the last two letters of the name of the celebrant are quite faint, the last is clear and certain. The other could be either *y* or *w*, but probably the latter. The name resembles one found in the Aramaic fortification tablets from Persepolis which similarly has a doubtful third consonant.[86] A more concise form, *ᵓtn*, is also found in the Aramaic tablets (49, line 4). If a *w* is to be read, the name suggests the *Ātūn* cited by Justi.[87] But Eilers, perhaps correctly, regards it as a scribal error for *ᵓrtwn*, Arta-wān (cf. No. 65:3).[88]

As in No. 2:3 and elsewhere,[89] what appears to be a plural form of the verb is found where a singular is expected.

---

[86] Tablet 151, l. 1 (unpublished).

[87] Justi, *Iranisches Namenbuch*, p. 51, Ātūn. He suggests that the name is a scribal fashion for abbreviating Ātūn-ōhanmazd.

[88] A Middle-Iranian form of Avestan *ašǎvan*, "belonging to Aša" (Middle Persian *ašavan*); so *BAiW*, cols. 246 ff. The spelling *ᵓrtyn*, Arta-yāna(?), also appears in these texts (No. 53:3).

[89] See n. 38 above.

Reference to the pestle in line 3 calls for either a conjunctive *w* or the preposition *ᶜm*, "with," at the end of the second line. If the demonstrative pronoun is intended to indicate both objects mentioned, there should be a conjunction before the word "pestle." Although there is room for *m* after the word *gll*, there is no trace of writing there.

Line 3

The line is extremely faint and almost illegible as far as the demonstrative pronoun *znh* in the middle of the line which is quite clear. The context calls for something like the *ᵓbšwn pyrk*, "crushing pestle," found in text No. 9:3 and elsewhere. Although the first two letters of the line seem to be *ᵓd-* in the photograph, the bottom of the second letter curves somewhat and the reading *ᵓb-* is not improbable. The faint traces of the following word suit *pyrk*, which elsewhere follows only the word "pestle" and the reading *ᵓbšwnᵓ pyrk* seems assured. The determinate form of the "pestle," appropriate with the demonstrative pronoun, is also found in No. 15:4. Here the adjective is written ungrammatically in the absolute state after the noun that it modifies.

Line 4

After the title "the treasurer" the letters *zy bh-* are clear, but a blank space follows them. The text here should be restored to *zy bhrḥwty*, "who is in Arachosia," as found elsewhere.[90]

The sub-treasurer Māh(a)-dāta is found serving in the eighteenth (No. 13) and nineteenth (No. 14) years of Xerxes (468–466 B.C.) and in another text (No. 5) dateable sometime between the tenth and nineteenth years of Xerxes. He is perhaps also to be supplied in No. 7 of year 11 and he is also found in an undateable text (No. 80).

14. Mortar (PT6 41) Pl. 5

בפרכן בירתא ל[יד] [מת]רפת סגנא	1) In the (haoma-)crushing ceremony of the fortress, beside Mithra-pāta the *segan*,
הומדת / עבדו הון רב זנה	2) 1 Haoma-dāta has used this large mortar
[עם אב]שון פירך / [ל'יד] דת̇מ̇תר גנזברא	3) [with] a crushing pestle beside Dāta-Mithra the treasurer
[זי] בנ̇השתך̇ קדם מה̇ד̇ת אפגנזברא	4) [who] is in *Ghštk*, before Māh(a)-dāta the sub-treasurer.
[אשכר] שנת ⟶ /// /// ///	5) [*ᵓškr* of] year 19.

Description

A fragment of a large green chert mortar (base dia. 16.7 cm., present max. height 19.3 cm. [slightly reduced in illustration]) with a semi-oval bowl and a disk base.

Five lines of Aramaic are written on the upper half of the bottom of the base. The letters of the third and fourth lines are blurred and faint.

Find Spot

The eastern part (HF 26) of Room 45 of the Treasury, which is a subsidiary room to the northwest of Room 38.

Date

The names of the officials indicate the reign of Xerxes, whose nineteenth year was 467/66 B.C.

Line 2

The name of the celebrant, Haoma-dāta, is already attested in the Aramaic papyri of the time of Xerxes.[91] Since there is little or no difference between the letters *d* and *r* in the Aramaic

---

[90] See n. 74 above.

[91] Cowley, *AP*, Nos. 8:2, 9:2 (460 B.C.).

writing of the Achaemenid period, the name might also be read as *Hwmrt*, Haoma-rātā, "He whose sacrificial gift is haoma."[92] In either case the first element is *haoma* (Old Persian *hauma*), the intoxicant prepared in the mortars at Persepolis.

Again, as in Nos. 2:3 and 13:2, what appears to be a plural form of the verb is used where a singular is expected.[93]

LINE 4

The officials named in this text are those found up to and including the nineteenth year of Xerxes, when the officers were completely changed.

After the treasurer's title, at the beginning of the fourth line there is additional text. The faint traces preserved do not fit the reading *zy bhrḥwty*, "who is in Arachosia," which is found elsewhere (for example, Nos. 43:6, 79:3 and others) in this position. What is visible appears to be *bghŝtk*, and it is almost certain that the word *zy*, "who (is)," should be restored at the beginning of the line.

Since Dāta-Mithra is usually described as "the treasurer who is in Arachosia," the new designation is surprising. It might be tempting to consider *Ghŝtk* as a district or city of Arachosia. The names of many places there are preserved, but no *Ghŝtk* is identifiable among them. In the Behistun Inscription Darius mentions the Gañdutava district, the fortress Kāpiśakāni, and the city Arśādā. Isidore of Charax names cities lying along the Arachotos River[94] and Ptolemy, too, lists a number of cities.[95] But there were many more settled communities in that fertile land of which the names have not been preserved. The Arab geographer Muqaddasī claimed that in his day (10th century A.D.) there were eleven hundred villages and hamlets in the district of Bust alone.[96]

However, since this text is from the last year of Dāta-Mithra, according to the dated texts, and his successor Baga-pāta is also described as "the treasurer who is in Arachosia" (Nos. 43, 44, 45, 47, 48, 51 and others), it is probable that *Ghŝtk* was the place to which Dāta-Mithra was transferred and it may not have been in Arachosia.

15. Pestle (PT5 416) Pl. 5

בפרכן בירתא	1)	In the (haoma-)crushing ceremony of the fortress,
ליד מתרפת סגנא	2)	beside Mithra-pāta the *segan*,
הומדת / עבדו	3)	1 Haoma-dāta has used
אבשונא זנה ליד	4)	this pestle beside
דתמתר גנזברא	5)	Dāta-Mithra the treasurer.
אשכר שנת	6)	*ᵓŝkr* of year
⸱ː ⫶ ⫶ ⫶	7)	19.

DESCRIPTION

A green chert pestle with a broken shaft (head dia. 6.1 cm., present max. length 12.3 cm.). Seven lines of Aramaic are written in rather thick letters on the pestle top.

FIND SPOT

West of the center (HF 29) of Room 38.

---

[92] *BAiW*, cols. 1732–34, *haoma*, col. 1519, *-rātā*, "Gabe," "Geschenk."

[93] See pp. 40–43.

[94] W. H. Schoff, *Parthian Stations by Isadore of Charax* (Philadelphia, 1914), p. 9, Sec. 19.

[95] Ptolemy *Geography* iv. 20.

[96] Ibn Aḥmad al-Muqaddasī, *Kitab . . . al-Aqalim*, ed. M. J. de Goeje ("Bibliotheca Geographorum Arabicorum" III [Lugduni-Batavorum, 1877/1906]), p. 297.

DATE

Although the figure 10 is blurred, there is a trace of it. The number is at least 18 but probably 19, with the final unit stroke merged with the bottom of the *n* of the word *šnt* of the line just above. It is probable that this pestle and the mortar No. 14 formed a set presented at the same time, the nineteenth year of Xerxes (467/66 B.C.), by the same celebrant.

LINE 3

The celebrant Haoma-dāta is the same one as in No. 14.

Again the verb appears to be plural in number (*ᶜbdw*) but is actually a singular as elsewhere (Nos. 2:3, 13:2, 14:2, and probably 20:3).

LINE 4

Only here and in No. 13:3 is the determinate state of *ᵓbšwn,* "pestle," used with the demonstrative pronoun, in correct Aramaic syntax.

16. Mortar (PT5 456) T (65); Pl. 5

[ב . . . . בירתא] ליד מתרפת סגנ[א]	1) [In the . . . of the fortress,] beside Mithra-pāta the *segan,*
זנה [. . . . . .] עבד הון זי גלל [רֹב]	2) . . . used this large(?) mortar of stone
[עם אבשֹוֹן] רֹב / ליד בֹגֹפֹתֹ	3) [with] a large pestle beside Baga-pāta
[גנזברא]	4) [the treasurer . . . .]

DESCRIPTION

A long, somewhat triangular piece of a very large green chert mortar base (base dia. 18 cm. [slightly reduced in illustration]).

Parts of three lines of Aramaic are all that remain on the bottom of the base. It is apparent that the lines were rather long and their beginnings have been lost. Only the very tops of the letters of the last line remain.

FIND SPOT

The center of the south wall (HF 49) of Room 38.

DATE

This fragment bears no date but can nevertheless be dated quite accurately on the basis of the personnel mentioned in the text.

Mithra-pāta served as *segan* with treasurer Dāta-Mithra until the nineteenth year of Xerxes (467/66 B.C.), when Baga-pāta became treasurer and Mithraka the *segan.* The *segan* Mithra-pāta and the treasurer Baga-pāta named here are not associated elsewhere. Similarly, in No. 17 the association of officers is unique.

Apparently Nos. 16 and 17 mark a transitional stage in which two sets of officers served simultaneously during the year and could be associated in any combination.[97] Since the change occurred in the nineteenth year of Xerxes (467/66 B.C.) Nos. 16 and 17 must come from that year. The former staff, Mithra-pāta the *segan* and Mithra-dāta the treasurer, are not encountered in the twentieth year of Xerxes or thereafter.

LINE 2

To judge from the end of the first line the name of the celebrant, which must have begun the second line, must have been followed by other text to fill out the line. It could have been a title and/or the word *šmh,* "his name (namely)."

[97] See p. 57.

Above the first two letters of the verb, written in smaller letters, is the demonstrative pronoun *znh*, as a later addition to the text. It is slightly mislocated, since it must modify the word "mortar." Perhaps it is intended to represent the order *znh hwn*, which is sometimes found also in Biblical Aramaic (Ezra 5:4, 15; Dan. 2:32, 4:15, 7:17) instead of the *hwn znh* usual in these texts.

After the word *gll* there is room for still another short word. There are traces of the head of a letter that could be *b*, *d*, or *r*. It might represent *zy gll bz*, "of *bz* stone," as in No. 91:3 or the adjective *rb*, "large," as in line 3, for that would be appropriate and expected on a mortar of such unusual size.

LINE 3

Only the tips of letters are preserved in this line but the reading is certain for all but the first word. The first traces of signs are so slight that they can only indicate the tips of letters and their spacing. If the preposition *ᶜm* was not at the end of the preceding line, it must have begun this one. It would be followed by a reference to the pestle. The first traces could represent the tips of the last three letters of the word *ᵓbšwn*.

At the end of the line there are traces of the name of Baga-pāta,[98] who is certainly the treasurer in this text. The name Baga-pāta is also found in cuneiform documents from the time of Darius I as ᵐ*Ba-ga-pa-a-tum*, ᵐ*Ba-ga-ᵓ-pa-a-tu*, ᵐᵈ*Ba-ga-pa-a-ta*, and other slight variations of such spellings.[99]

Baga-pāta appears here for the first time in the nineteenth year of Xerxes, as the successor of Dāta-Mithra. From the twentieth year of Xerxes all dated texts list him as the treasurer. An Arta-čanah, who is mentioned as treasurer in an undated text (No. 122), may have been his successor.

17. Pestle (PT5 729) T (51); Pl. 6

[בפרכֹן] בירתֹא ליד	1)	[In the (haoma-)crushing ceremony of] the fortress, beside
תמרֹך סגנא	2)	Mithraka(?) the *segan*,
[. . .]שתן פלג עבד	3)	. . . *štn*, a myriarch, used
ה[ו]ן זי גלל [עם]	4)	(this?) mortar of stone [with]
אבש[ו]ן פירך מדם	5)	a medium-sized crushing [pest]le
ל[י]ד דתמתר	6)	beside Dāta-Mithra
[גנזברא א]שכר	7)	[the treasurer. ᵓ]*škr* of
[שנת ⅄ /// /// ///]	8)	[year 19].

DESCRIPTION

A fragment of a green chert pestle (head dia. 3.5 cm., present max. length 5.8 cm.).

Seven lines of Aramaic are written lengthwise along the shaft of the pestle, just below its head.[100] Unusual spacing occurs between words and there is uneven spacing within words. The rather unusual shapes of letters, too, seem to indicate that the text was written by an

---

[98] Justi, *Iranisches Namenbuch*, p. 57b, Βαγαπάτης; some Greek texts have Μεγαβάτης; Benveniste (*Titres et noms*, p. 79) finds the name, like Greek Βαγαπάτης or Μεγαβατης in the Elamite Bakabada.

[99] A. T. Clay, *Business Documents of Murashû Sons of Nippur* (University of Pennsylvania Museum "Publications of the Babylonian Section" II, No. 1 [Philadelphia, 1912]), Nos. 4:17, 137:16; A. T. Clay, *Business Documents of Murashû Sons of Nippur* (University of Pennsylvania "Babylonian Expedition" X [Philadelphia, 1904]), Nos. 53:25, 70:7; *Texte und Materialen der Frau Professor Hilprecht-Sammlung . . . Universität Jena* (Berlin, 1932), II/III, Nos. 190:15 and rev., 191:17.

[100] See also pestles Nos. 81 and 123 for similar writing along the shaft.

inexperienced hand. Only the ends of lines remain. The beginnings of lines have been broken away with the bottom of the shaft. In the sixth line the last letter is written on the curve under the pestle head. Originally there must have been still another short line indicating the date.

FIND SPOT

At the base of the south wall (HF 48) of Room 38, where the great mass of fragments of the ritual vessels was found.

DATE

As in No. 16, the date line is missing but the text can be dated accurately on the basis of personnel. If, as is probable, the name of the *segan* represents Mithraka, the date must be the nineteenth year of Xerxes (467/66 B.C.), when two groups of officers were contemporary. The treasurer Dāta-Mithra does not occur in dated texts after the nineteenth year of Xerxes and Mithraka does not appear before that year. Only here are Mithraka the *segan* and Dāta-Mithra the treasurer associated.

LINE 2

The name of the *segan* is difficult. Cameron copied it as *tmrn* and later as *tmrp*. In his earlier copy the first two letters are written close together, but he later left space between them, as though they belonged to different words, possibly because he then thought that the remainder was *mdy*, "a Mede." There is no such space between the first two letters, and the last letter does resemble an *n*. It is possible that there was a letter or two before the letter *t*, but that is uncertain. If the name is read as .. *tmrn*, it is unique for an officer in these texts and might indicate another subordinate *segan*.

But the writer is inexperienced and the final letter might be a carelessly made *k*. In the light of the spelling *mrtk* for Mithraka (No. 85:2) it is probable that *tmrk*, too, is a misspelling of the name of the popular *segan* Mithraka. The error would be understandable since even in some experienced hands the letters *m* and *t* closely resemble one another, as indeed they do here in Cameron's earlier copy.

The name probably represents Mithraka,[101] an abbreviation of a longer name that began with the divine name Mithra. To Mithra is added the affix -*aka*, which is used for abbreviated or pet names.[102] The officer Mithraka is found as *segan* from the nineteenth year of Xerxes (467/66 B.C.) until the seventh year of Artaxerxes I (458/57 B.C.), while Baga-pāta was treasurer.

LINE 3

The name of the celebrant is broken at its beginning. Only the end -*štn* remains.

The title of the officer, *plg*, follows his name. It is a Semitic word derived from the root *plg*, "divide," indicating the commander of a division. In Syriac a *palgā*ʾ is "a phalanx" or "a battalion" and a *pᵉlāgā*ʾ is "a division."[103] From the title *ʾlp plg* (No. 118:3) it is clear that a *plg* had authority over more than a thousand men. Thus, he was the Persian military commander of ten thousand men corresponding to the myriarch of the Greeks and the *hnśyʾ hrbwʾ* of the Jews of Qumran.[104] Perhaps the title is to be vocalized as *pᵉlîg*.[105] Most of the military officers who serve as celebrants and bear titles are called *plg*.[106]

---

[101] Justi, *Iranisches Namenbuch*, p. 214, Mitnak.

[102] *Ibid.*, p. 521, -*aka* (2).

[103] J. Payne Smith, *A Compendious Syriac Dictionary* (Oxford, 1957), p. 4472, ܦܠܓܐ, ܦܠܓܐ.

[104] Yadin, *Scroll*, pp. 272–73, col. iii, l. 15, הנשיא הרבוא .

[105] Compare Arabic and Persian ʿarîf (عَرِيف) , "lieutenant," "centurion."

[106] See p. 34; Nos. 19, 22, 31, 32, 47, 48, 63, 81, 83, 87, 88 *bis*, 130.

18. Plate (PT6 258) Pl. 6

בסרך בירתא ליד מתרך סגנא	1)	In the ritual of the fortress, beside Mithraka the *segan*,
בגפֿשת / עבד סחר זנה רב /	2)	1 Bago-paušta used this plate, a large one,
[ליד בֿ]גֿפת גנזברא קדם מזדדת	3)	[beside Ba]ga-pāta the treasurer (and) before Mazda-dāta
אפגנזברא אֿשכר שנת ר ııı ııı ııı	4)	the sub-treasurer. ʾškr of year 19.

DESCRIPTION

A fragment of a large, green chert plate (base dia. 13.5 cm., present max. height 1.2 cm. [slightly reduced in illustration]), consisting principally of the inscribed part of the base. A small segment of the top of the inscribed surface of the base and almost half of its lower part are broken away and lost without damaging the inscribed text.

Four lines of Aramaic, written in neat, graceful letters, are on the bottom of the base.

FIND SPOT

Found during the sifting of material from the central part (HF 69) of Room 41 of the Treasury.[107] It lay near the third pillar from the north, in the fourth row in the room.

DATE

The nineteenth year of Xerxes (467/66 B.C.).

LINE 1

Here for the first time Mithraka the *segan* is found associated with Baga-pāta the treasurer. They remain together until the seventh year of Artaxerxes I (458/57 B.C.).

LINE 2

The name of the celebrant is *Bgpšt*. Eilers suggested that the second element of the name is derived from *upa-štā*, "helps." Parallel is the name Mithropastes,[108] which is constructed of the elements *Mithra* and *paustes* (Avestan and Old Persian *upa-štā*, "help," "aid").[109] Frye has proposed for the name **Baga-pušta*, "god-nourished."

The plate at Persepolis is called *sḥr* in these texts. Altheim relates it to the *sahar*, "round bowl," of the Bible (Cant. 7:3).[110] But the spelling is always with *ḥ*. While an Iranian *h* can be represented by Aramaic *ḥ* and Aramaic *ḥ* can sometimes be indicated by Aramaic *h*,[111] there are no examples at Persepolis of *ḥ* for *h* in Semitic words. Altheim also refers to the Jewish Aramaic root *sḥr* meaning "to go around," "to turn," "to trade," which, as סְחַר, can mean "enclosure." There is no vessel known to be derived from that root. Bezold lists a *saḫḫaru*, "kleiner Topf."[112]

---

[107] See Fig. 1.

[108] Justi, *Iranisches Namenbuch*, p. 216, Μιθροπαύστης, "Mithra anbetend."

[109] J. Marquart (*Die Assyriaka des Ktesias* ["Philologus Supplementband" VI (Göttingen, 1893)], p. 619) explains that the -*a* of Mithra- and the *u* of the -*upa* of upašta combine to form the *o* of the Greek Μιθροπαύστης; Eilers, in *Abhandlungen für die Kunde des Morgenlandes* XXV, No. 5, p. 125, cf. p. 65, n. 3; "Eine mittelpersischen Wortform aus frühachämenischer Zeit," *ZDMG* XC (1936) 173, n. 1.

[110] Altheim and Stiehl, *Aramäische Sprache* I 19.

[111] See No. 24:2 and p. 64. In the Aramaic fortification tablets we find *hmryn* for *ḥmryn* (Tablet 72, l. 2), *htm* for *ḥtm* (Tablet 48, l. 1), *qmh* for *qmḥ* (Tablet 84, l. 2), and *hmr* for *ḥmr* (Tablet 148, l. 1).

[112] *Babylonisch-assyrisches Glossar* (Heidelberg, 1926), p. 212a.

The word *šḥr* in the absolute rather than determinate state with the demonstrative pronoun *znh* often occurs in these ritual texts. It is also surprising to find the unit stroke, which should represent an indefinite pronoun, with a modifier of a noun made definite by the demonstrative pronoun *znh*.

LINE 3

The new sub-treasurer, displacing the earlier Māh(a)-dāta in the nineteenth year of Xerxes, is Mazda-dāta. He serves regularly in that office until at least the eleventh year of Artaxerxes I (454/53 B.C.), according to dated texts.

19. Plate (PT5 692) Pl. 7

ב . . . .]בירת[א ליד	1)	[In the . . . of the fortress,] beside
מתרך ס[גנא] כרות / פ]לג|	2)	Mithraka the *segan*, 1 *Krwt*, a myriarch,
עבד [ס]חרא זנה ליד	3)	used this plate beside
[בגפת] גנזברא זי בהרחו[ת]י	4)	[Baga-pāta] the treasurer who is in Arachosia.
[אשכר ש]נת 𐤂	5)	[*²škr* of] year 20.

DESCRIPTION

A fragment of the bottom of a green chert plate (base dia. 18 cm., present max. height 3.3 cm. [slightly reduced in illustration]), consisting of part of the base and some of the adjacent side of the bowl.

The remains of five lines of Aramaic text are preserved on the bottom of the base. Breakage and loss of part of the base have destroyed the beginnings of lines 1, 4, and 5. Some letters, especially in the first two lines, are extremely faint and difficult to read.

FIND SPOT

The floor near the middle of the south wall (HF 48) of Room 38.

DATE

The officials named would be appropriate for the reigns of either Xerxes or Artaxerxes I. But since the *segan* of the twentieth year of Artaxerxes I was Āraya(t)-vahuš rather than Mithraka[113] and Mithraka is not found after the seventh year (Nos. 37 and 38), this text must be from the twentieth year of Xerxes (466/65 B.C.).

LINE 2

The name of the celebrant could be read either *Kryt* or *Krwt*. Justi mentions a Median prince Karuti.[114] Eilers suggests, as a more Persian name, *Kāra-vat*.

After the unit stroke following the name there are traces of several letters, probably a title of the celebrant. The first mark seems to be the upper part of the letter *p* which at once suggests the title *plg* that is often found after the name of the celebrant.

LINE 4

The writer miscalculated and had to crowd his letters at the end of the line. The last two letters of the name *hrḥwty*, "Arachosia," are so compressed as to appear to be vertical lines.

Here the treasurer Baga-pāta is associated with Arachosia, as his predecessor Dāta-Mithra was. The designation occurs also in several other texts.[115]

---

[113] No. 49.

[114] Justi, *Iranisches Namenbuch*, p. 158*b*.

[115] Nos. 43:6, 44:5, 79:3, etc.

20. Pestle (PT5 660) Pl. 7

1)
2)
עב]דו אֹ[בשון זנה   3)   used this pestle
זי גלל ליד בגפת   4)   of stone beside Baga-pāta
גנזברא אש[כר]   5)   the treasurer. ᵓš[kr] of
שנת /   6)   year 1(?)

DESCRIPTION

A fragment of a green chert pestle (head dia. 3.8 cm., present max. length 8 cm.).

Four lines of what was perhaps originally six lines of Aramaic are preserved on top of the pestle head. The first two lines have disappeared completely and what remains is so faint as to be almost illegible. In a few places in lines 3 and 5 some letters are entirely gone.

FIND SPOT

West of the center (HF 38) of Room 38.

DATE

Baga-pāta served as treasurer during the reigns of both Xerxes and Artaxerxes I, beginning with the nineteenth year of Xerxes.

Of the numeral Cameron says, "The numeral is faint, most probably 1, although my earlier readings gave 1, 11, or 21 for it." Because Baga-pāta served as late as the twenty-ninth year of Artaxerxes I (436/35 B.C.), his name affords no help in arriving at a precise date. It is probably the first year of Artaxerxes I (464/63 B.C.) or, to judge from the spacing of Cameron's copy, one of the first few years of that reign.

LINE 3

While the spacing in Cameron's copy may be inexact, it would allow for four missing letters or spaces, too much for the expected verb ᶜbd alone before the word "pestle." Although it would help to read the verb as ᶜbdw, as in No. 2:3 and others, still too much space remains. If Cameron's spacing is even approximately right, one cannot conceive what might have intervened between the verb and its object.

In Cameron's copy the first letter of the word "pestle" appears to be a *k* but that is obviously incorrect. Numerous examples attest the spelling as ᵓbšwn and an ᵓaleph must somehow be involved in the sign that Cameron copied.

21. Pestle (PT5 403[116]) Persepolis Museum 188; Pl. 7

בסרך בי]רֹתֹ[א   1)   In the ritual of the fortress,
ליד מזפרן סגנ[א]   2)   beside Mazza-farnah the *segan*,
פרד עבד אבשון   3)   Frāda used
מדם / ליד בג]פֹֹ[ת   4)   a medium-sized pestle beside Baga-pāta
גנזברא אֹשֹֹכֹ[ר]   5)   the treasurer. ᵓškr of
שנת //   6)   year 2.

DESCRIPTION

A fragment of a green chert pestle (head dia. 3.7 cm., present max. length of shaft 7.7 cm.). Six lines of Aramaic are written on top of the pestle head. The last is very faint.

[116] At Persepolis the fragment bears the field number PT5 246, which the Field Register lists as a "tack." But close comparison with the photograph of PT5 403 proves the texts to be identical.

FIND SPOT

South of the center (HF 39) of Room 38 of the Persepolis Treasury.

DATE

A low year date with Baga-pāta listed as treasurer indicates the beginning of the reign of Artaxerxes I. The date line is extremely faint. Cameron read a single unit stroke but suggested there were possibly more. At Persepolis I found two strokes and no more. The first is clearly visible, but the second is rather indistinct. The second year of Artaxerxes I was 463/62 B.C.

LINE 2

The name of the segan is *Mzprn*. The name is written similarly but much more clearly in No. 118 and is probably identical with that of the *segan* named in No. 54 as *Mdzprn*. These are probably variant forms of the name Mazda-farnah. In *Mzprn* the phoneme *d* is assimilated to the preceding *z*[117] and in the latter the letters are inverted.[118] Frye offers as another possibility for the name *Mazāfarnah, "Having great *farnah*."

Since Mazza-farnah is found only twice and Mithraka much more frequently, it is probable that the latter was the "chief *segan*" and that Mazza-farnah was his subordinate.

LINE 3

Cameron first read the name of the celebrant as *nw-* and later as *td-/tr-* with an unidentified, blotlike third consonant. At Persepolis I copied it independently as *prd*, which I now believe to be correct.

The name thus appears to be Frāda,[119] that borne by a Margian rebel in the Behistun Inscription.[120] Kent regards the name as being probably "hypocoristic to a compound name of which the prior part was the participial stem to the same compound verb."[121] The compound name *Prdprn*, Frāda-farnah is now found in an Aramaic letter[122] and it appears to be written as ᵐ*Ip-ra-a-du-par-na-ᵓ* in a neo-Babylonian text.[123]

22. Pestle (PT5 718*A*[124]) Persepolis Museum 212; Pl. 7

בֹ[ס]רך ביר[תֹא]	1)	In the ritual of the fortress,
בגפ[רֹן] פל[ג] עב[ד]	2)	Baga-farnah, a myriarch, used
[אֹ]ב[שֹ]ו[ן] זי גלל	3)	(this?) pestle of stone
ליד בגפֿת גנזבר[א]	4)	beside Baga-pāta the treasurer.
ii אֹשֹבֹר שנת	5)	ᵓ*škr* of year 2.

[117] Eilers calls attention to the name Mazdaka (Justi, *Iranisches Namenbuch*, p. 201*b*) for which the Greek texts have Μαζάκης, with the ζ (*z*) representing *zd* of Mazda.

[118] Other examples of metathesis in these texts are *tmrk* for Mithraka (No. 17:2) and ᶜ*db* for the verb ᶜ*bd* (No. 134:2).

[119] Justi, *Iranisches Namenbuch*, p. 101, Frāda; Benveniste (*Titres et noms*, p. 90) finds the name in the Elamite Pirrada.

[120] Behistun Inscription, col. iii, l. 12, col. iv, l. 23; Darius' Behistun J, l. 1.

[121] Kent, *Old Persian*, p. 198*a*, Frāda. He compares the Avestan adjective *frādat-gaēθa*, "prospering the household," and would derive Frāda from *fra-+da*, with *vriddhi*, comparing the Avestan *frād-*, "further," "increase" (cf. *BAiW*, col. 1012).

[122] Driver, *Aramaic Documents of the Fifth Century B.C.*, No. VI, l. 2, and cf. p. 59.

[123] Clay, *Business Documents* ("Babylonian Expedition" X), No. 114:5–6; Eilers, in *ZDMG* XC 176, n. 1, and "Neue aramäische Urkunden aus Ägypten," *Archiv für Orientforschung* XVII (1956) 331; E. Benveniste, "Éléments perses en Araméen d'Égypte," *JA* CCXLII (1954) 300, n. 3.

[124] This object has a poorly written field number which appears to be PT5 7718, of which the first sign is peculiarly flag-like. That number is excessively large, but it cannot be PT5 718 since that is described in the Field Register as "a pestle with a chipped head, bearing 3 lines of Aramaic" (= No. 54).

DESCRIPTION

A fragment of a large, green chert pestle (head dia. 6.1 cm.) with five lines of Aramaic on the top of its head.

FIND SPOT

In the Persepolis Treasury but its exact site cannot be determined because of the faulty field number.

DATE

Second year of Artaxerxes I (463/62 B.C.).

LINE 2

The celebrant's name, *Bgprn*, Baga-farnah,[125] is found here and possibly also in No. 71:3 in these texts, but it is already known from the Aramaic papyri[126] and a parchment letter.[127]

LINE 4

This text is remarkable for its omission of the *segan*, a rare and unusual circumstance,[128] and its naming of the treasurer as its sole officer.

23. Pestle (PT5 493) Pl. 7

בסרך בי]ר[ת]א[	1)	In the ritual of the fortress,
ליד מתרך סגנ]א[	2)	beside Mithraka the *segan*,
ארבזך / עבד	3)	1 Arbazaki used
אב]שׁ[ון זי גל]ל[ל	4)	a medium-sized pestle
מדם / [קדם מזדדת]	5)	of stone [before Mazda-data]
אפגנ]ז[בר]א ליד	6)	the sub-treasurer (and) [beside]
בגפת גנזב]רא[	7)	Baga-pāta the treasurer.
א[שכר שנת ///	8)	*ᵓškr* of year 3.

DESCRIPTION

A green chert pestle with a broken shaft (head dia. 4.3 cm., present max. length 10.7 cm.).

Eight lines of Aramaic are written in ink on the top of the pestle head. Cameron notes that "melted iron," visible as large spots in the photograph, has ruined the legibility of this text.

FIND SPOT

The northeastern part of Room 38, at the north wall (HG 11) just east of the door of adjacent Room 48.

DATE

Third year of Artaxerxes I (462/61 B.C.).

LINES 1 AND 2

There are no final *ᵓaleph*'s where expected on the last words in these lines, presumably because they were crowded at the ends and there was no room. They may have been omitted or written as very small letters that have since disappeared. Cameron shows such a small, cramped letter in his copy of the second line, but it is no longer visible.

---

[125] Justi, *Iranisches Namenbuch*, p. 57a, Bagafarnah (Greek Megaphernes); Benveniste (*Titres et noms*, p. 79) finds the name in Elamite Bagaparna.

[126] Cowley, *AP*, No. 16:1, 6.

[127] Driver, *Aramaic Documents of the Fifth Century B.C.*, No. V, l. 4, No. VI, l. 1.

[128] See p. 25.

LINE 3

The name of the celebrant, *ʾrbzk*, resembles the Arbazakios cited by Justi.[129] It is possibly related to Aribazos[130] or Ariobazos[131] and seems to have the final affix *-ak* or *-ka*, as found in the name Mithraka. Frye has suggested as an alternative *Ara-bazū-ka*, "Having ready arms."

Presumably under the influence of the following letter, the writer began to write the verb *ʿbd* with the letter *b*. The head of the first *b* is dark and resembles the expected *ʿaiyn*. It may have been worked over a bit by the writer when he recognized his mistake.

LINE 4

Only the first two and the last letters of the word *ʾbšwn*, "pestle," are clear. The *š* resembles the usual form of the letter, but it is faint and shows some unusual characteristics. Where the *w* is expected there is a curved, almost oval line. It somewhat resembles a *p* but must be the expected *w*.

The remainder of the line, quite uncertain, must modify the noun "pestle." Traces preserved suggest the familiar *zy gll*, "of stone."

LINE 5

The last half of the line is too damaged to read. Since the next line begins with the title "the sub-treasurer," his name must be in the fifth line, preceded by the preposition *qdm*, "opposite," which is always used before the name of that officer. At the time, the regular sub-treasurer was Mazda-dāta and the restoration of that name here is most probable.

24. Pestle (PT5 454) Pl. 7

בפרכן ביר[תא]	1)	In the (haoma-)crushing ceremony of the fortress,
ליד אריוהש	2)	beside Āraya(t)-vahuš
סגנ[א] אדרת /	3)	the *segan*, 1 Adrāθa
עבד הון זי גלל [זנה]	4)	used [this] mortar of stone
ליד בגפת גנז[ברא]	5)	beside Baga-pāta the treasurer.
אשכר שנת ///	6)	*ʾškr* of year 3.

DESCRIPTION

A green chert pestle with a broken shaft (head dia. 6.2 cm., present max. length 10.6 cm.). Six lines of Aramaic are on the top of its head.

FIND SPOT

Near the center of the south wall (HF 49) of Room 38.

DATE

Third year of Artaxerxes I (462/61 B.C.).

LINE 2

Besides the reading *ʾrywhš* of this text, the same name is written as *ʾrywhw* (Nos. 42:2, 46:2, 51:2 and others), *ʾryhw* (No. 47:2), and *ʾrywhwš* (Nos. 49:2 and 73:2). Noticeable here is the alternation between the letters *h* and *ḥ*. The phenomenon has already been noted

---

[129] Justi, *Iranisches Namenbuch*, p. 21.

[130] *Ibid.*, p. 25a; see Greek Ἀριαβαζος of Dura-Europos. See Benveniste (*Titres et noms*, pp. 115–16) on -βαζος as an element in names.

[131] Justi, *Iranisches Namenbuch*, p. 26a.

in Talmudic Aramaic by Telegdi, who says, "In the Aramaean borrowings, Iranian *h* is reflected by *h*.or *ḥ*. The correspondence Iranian *h* ∽ Aramaic *ḥ* is not surprising. In all the systems of writing which were in use in occidental Iran during the course of the Arsacid and Sassanian periods (Pahlavik, Parsik, Manichean) which have been derived from the Aramaic writing, it is the *ḥ* that serves to render Iranian *h* [except for final *h* which, in Manichean writing, is recorded as *h*]."[132]

Eilers has suggested that the name might be *Arya-wahuš, "Good in the Aryan sense" or, more likely, Āraya(t)-wahuš, "He who sets good in motion,"[133] a name of the type of Dāraya(t)-wahuš. The final *š*, which may or may not be written with the name, is the -*š* that may be added to the nominative case of noun stems ending in -*i* or -*u*.[134]

Line 3

Since the letters *d* and *r* are usually indistinguishable in form in these texts, the name of the celebrant could be read with any possible combination of the letters *d* and *r*. As *ʾrdt* the name might represent the Arîdāthā or Arîdāta used of a Persian in the Bible (Esther 9:8).[135] Eilers, however, proposes reading *A-drātha. A name Drātha, possibly an abbreviation, is found in Late Avestan.[136] A neo-Babylonian text mentions an *ᵐAd-ra-ta-ʾ* as the father of a *ᵐBa-gi-nu*.[137] Frye has suggested that the name might be "a short form of a name with the element Ādratha, 'Protected by. . . .' "

Line 4

Here, as elsewhere (Nos. 17:4 and 39:3), it is the pestle that bears the designation "mortar," a reminiscence of the time when both parts of the set bore the same name.[138]

25. Mortar (PT5 673) Pl. 8

‏[ב . . . . . בירתא] ליד‏	1)	[In the . . . . . of the fortress], beside
‏[. . . . .]ס[גנא כרפיש /‏	2)	[. . .] the *segan*, 1 *Krpyš*
‏[עבד הון זנה] קדם בגפת‏	3)	[used this mortar] before Baga-pāta
‏[גנזברא אשכר] שנת ///‏	4)	[the treasurer. *ʾškr*] of year 3.

Description

A fragment of a badly broken green chert mortar (base dia. 12 cm., present max. height 2.8 cm.) of which only the upper left part of the base remains.

The ends of four lines of Aramaic are preserved on the bottom of the base.

Find Spot

Near the center (HF 38) of Room 38.

Date

Baga-pāta as treasurer, with a low year date, indicates the reign of Artaxerxes I, whose third year was 462/61 B.C.

---

[132] Telegdi, "Essai sur la phonétique des emprunts iraniens en Araméen talmudique," *JA* CCXXVI (1935) 207.

[133] *Ārayat*- from *ar*-, "to set in motion," cf. *BAiW*, col. 183, *ar*-.

[134] Meillet and Benveniste, *Grammaire*, p. 70, Sec. 122; cf. Dāraya-vaʰu/Dāraya-vauš.

[135] Justi, *Iranisches Namenbuch*, p. 25a.

[136] *BAiW*, col. 774, Drāθa.

[137] *Vorderasiatische Schriftdenkmäler der königlichen Museen zu Berlin* III (Leipzig, 1907), No. 138, ll. 13–14.

[138] See p. 45.

LINE 2

Damage to the base has resulted in the loss of the *segan's* name. Both Mithraka (No. 23) and Āraya(t)-vahuš (No. 24) are attested for the third year.

The spelling of the name of the celebrant found here is confirmed by the undated texts (Nos. 102 and 103) which presumably refer to the same individual. It could be read *Krpyš* or *Kdpyš*, but its etymology is uncertain. Eilers, assuming the former to be correct, has suggested either Kāra-paiša[139] or Kərpaiča.[140] If *Kdpyš* is read, one might compare it with the much later Kadphises of Roman times.[141]

LINE 3

The use of the preposition *qdm* before the name of the treasurer Baga-pāta is quite unusual. It is found only here and in No. 113:3. Usually *lyd* appears before the names of the *segan's* and the treasurers and *qdm* before those of the sub-treasurers.

26. Pestle (PT5 418) T (20); Pl. 8

[ב]סרך ב[י]ר[תא]	1)	In the ritual of the fortress,
ל[י]ד מתרך סגנא	2)	beside Mithraka the *segan*,
[ד]ס[פתרוך עבד	3)	*Dsptrwk* used
אבשון / קדם	4)	a pestle before
מזדדת אפגנזברא	5)	Mazda-dāta the sub-treasurer.
אשכר שנת	6)	*ʾškr* of year
/ ///	7)	4.

DESCRIPTION

A green chert pestle with a broken shaft (head dia. 5.8 cm., present max. length 8.5 cm.).

Seven lines of Aramaic are written on top of the pestle head. All but lines 5 and 6 are quite faint.

FIND SPOT

West of the center (HF 29) of Room 38.

DATE

Fourth year of Artaxerxes I (461/60 B.C.).

LINE 3

The name of the celebrant fills most of the third line. Although the letters are quite faint, only the first two present any difficulty. The first is probably *d* or *r* but might be a *b*. The second is doubtless the letter *s*.

It is unlikely that the first part of the word should be read alone as *dspt*, the title *dasa-pati*, "commander of ten men," since that title is not found elsewhere in these texts. Moreover, titles are always written after the name in these texts. Eilers proposes reading *Dasa-pāθra-auka*.[142] Frye has proposed as an alternative *Dasa-pāθrauka*, "Having ten (i.e. many) kinds of protection."

---

[139] Eilers compares the Us-paēšata in *BAiW*, col. 408.

[140] Comparing Avestan *kəhrp*, "external appearance," "visible form," and Middle Persian *karp*, "form"; cft. *BAiW*, col. 467.

[141] Henning, "Mitteliranisch," *Handbuch der Orientalistik*, ed. B. Spuler and H. Kees, IV: *Iranistik* (Leiden, 1958), Pt. 1, p. 26.

[142] *BAiW*, col. 700, *dasă*, "zehn"; *ibid.*, col. 887, *pāθra'vant*, **pāθra*, "Schutz" (from *pā[y]*, "hüten"). Justi (*Iranisches Namenbuch*, p. 526) regarded the affix *-auka* or *-uka* as originally identical with *-aka* and *-uka*. He cites (*ibid.*, p. 283a) the name of Darius' daughter Σανδαύκη/Σανδάκη/Σανδώκης as having such an affix.

27. Pestle (PT5 720) Pl. 8

בסרך	1)	In the ritual of
בי֗ר֗[ת֗]א ליד	2)	the fortress, beside
מתרך [ס֗]גנא	3)	Mithraka the *segan*,
תרֹס[פ֗ה] עבד֗	4)	*Trsph* used
א֗בשון זנה	5)	this pestle.
שנת ‡ ‡‡‡ ‡	6)	Year 4.

DESCRIPTION

A fragment of a green chert pestle (head dia. 3.5 cm., present max. length 7.5 cm.).

Six lines of Aramaic are written on the top of the pestle head. Pitting and other damage to the inscribed surface distorts some letters and others are quite faint. Cameron notes that some of the surface of the pestle head has "flecked off."

FIND SPOT

West of the center (HF 38) of Room 38.

DATE

Mithraka as *segan* indicates the reign of Artaxerxes I, whose fourth year was 461/60 B.C.

LINE 4

The name of the celebrant, *Trsph*, suggests the name Tarāsp, possibly for Tarr-aspa, "Possessing young steeds," cited by Justi.[143] Eilers proposes reading Tarāspahē, "With horses that cannot be broken."[144]

LINES 5 AND 6

This text is unusual for its omission of the word *ᵓškr* before the date, presumably because of lack of space.

28. Pestle (PT5 752) Pl. 8

בסרך בירתא	1)	In the ritual of the fortress,
ליד מתרך סגנא	2)	beside Mithraka the *segan*,
[ת֗ר֗]דֹת ‡ עבד אבשון	3)	1 Tīri-dāta used
[זנה] ק֗דם מזדדת	4)	this pestle before Mazda-dāta
אפגנזברא	5)	the sub-treasurer.
אשכר שנת	6)	*ᵓškr* of year
‡ ‡‡‡ ‡	7)	4.

DESCRIPTION

A fragment of green chert pestle (head dia. 6.3 cm., present max. length 6.8 cm.). A small rectangular bit of metal,[145] possibly an ancient repair, is inset in the third line, where it damages the name of the celebrant.

Seven lines of Aramaic are written on the top of the pestle head. The letters at the beginning of the third and fourth lines are badly smudged.

FIND SPOT

The center of the south wall (HF 38) of Room 38.

---

[143] Justi, *Iranisches Namenbuch*, p. 322b.

[144] He compares Avestan *tara-*, "overcoming"; cf. *BAiW*, col. 640, *tara-*, "überschreitend," "überwindend."

[145] Such metal inlays are also found in Nos. 5 and 72.

DATE

The officers Mithraka and Mazda-dāta indicate the reign of Artaxerxes I, whose fourth year was 461/60 B.C.

LINE 3

The name at the beginning of the line is most difficult to read because of blurring, fading, and the metal inlay. The first trace of writing is the upper tip of a *t*, extending above the line of letters. A trace of the top of a letter *r* shows above the inlay, but the metal setting has destroyed the remainder of the letter. Just to the left of the metal piece is a *d* followed by a blurred but certain *t*. A unit stroke follows the name. Thus, the reading is most probably [*Tr*]*dt* 1, "1 Tīri-dāta."[146]

The name is also found in the Aramaic fortification tablets from Persepolis as *Trydt* (No. 112:1) and *Trydt⁾* (No. 114:2). Eilers cites a cuneiform example ᵐ*Ti-ri-ịa-da-a-*[*tu*],[147] but it is also found as ᵐ*Ti-ri-da-a-ta*.[148]

29. Pestle (PT5 764) Persepolis Museum 189; Pl. 8

בסרך בירת[א]	1)	In the ritual of the fortress,
ליד מתרך ס[גנא]	2)	beside Mithraka the *segan*,
ארתברון עבד	3)	Arta-bar-vāna used
אבשון זי בא[ת]	4)	a wine(?) pestle.
אשכר ש[נת]	5)	⁾*škr* of year
[// /]//	6)	5.

DESCRIPTION

A fragment of a green chert pestle (head dia. 3.2 cm., present max. length 7 cm.).

Six lines of Aramaic are written on top of the pestle head. At the ends of lines the letters become crowded and minute. It is possible that the writing continued on the side of the pestle head. At the end of the second line only half of the letter *g* is preserved. Cameron commented, "There seems to be nothing on the outer edge of the pestle head, but there once must have been, when the writing continued beyond the top of the pestle head."

FIND SPOT

The west-central part (HF 38) of Room 38.

DATE

Only the tops of two unit strokes now appear in the photograph but Cameron's copy clearly shows five. Mithraka as *segan* indicates the reign of Artaxerxes I, whose fifth year was 460/59 B.C.

LINE 3

For the name of the celebrant, ⁾*rtbrwn*, Eilers proposes the name Arta-bar-wāna. The first element is *Arta*, "law," "justice," the name of an archangel attending Ahuramazda.[149] The second part is the familiar *bar*, "to bear," "to bring,"[150] and the final one, *-vāna*, is from the root *van-*, meaning "excel," "overcome," "conquer," signifying "victory."[151] Frye has suggested, as an alternative, *Arta-bauda-van, "One having discrimination through Arta."

---

[146] Justi, *Iranisches Namenbuch*, p. 326*b*, Tiridates. Benveniste (*Titres et noms*, p. 94) finds the name in the Elamite Teriyadada. On names with the element Tiri- see Benveniste, *ibid.*, p. 116, n. 3.

[147] Eilers, in *Abhandlungen für die Kunde des Morgenlandes* XXV, No. 5, pp. 111–12, note on l. 7.

[148] Clay, *Business Documents* ("Babylonian Expedition" X), No. 74:4, 7, 11, and 12.

[149] Kent, *Old Persian*, p. 170*b*, Arta-.

[150] *Ibid.*, p. 200, bar-, bara; *BAiW*, cols. 933 ff.

[151] *BAiW*, cols. 1350–53; Kent, *Old Persian*, p. 208*b*, under Vivāna.

LINE 4

The final word in the line is crowded and written in very small letters. The reading is certainly not the expected *zy gll* found elsewhere. At first glance it seems to be *zy pʾt* but, since the first letter is similar to the *b* in the *byrtʾ* of the first line, the reading is probably *zy bʾt*.

The word could be the Persian *bāta*, "wine,"[152] as Eilers has suggested. It is probably also an element in the personal name *Bʾtdt* or *Bʾtrt* in No. 110:3.

The designation seems to indicate that the pestle was used for making wine.[153] Herzfeld once argued that the ancient haoma was actually wine.[154] The reading *zy bʾt* used with "pestle" seems parallel to the *zy ʾškr* of No. 62:3, especially if the *ʾškr* signifies "intoxicant."[155]

LINE 6

The date is difficult because it is faint and written on top of a dark band in the stone of about the same density as the unit strokes in the photograph. Cameron copied five clear strokes and so translated the date. The text must have deteriorated in the meantime for in my own collation, made at a much later date, I found only the two strokes now visible in the photograph.

30. Mortar (PT5 710) T (118); Pl. 8

[ב . . . . בירתא ליד]	1) [In the . . . of the fortress, beside]
[מתרך סגנא . . . . . עבד הון]	2) [Mithraka the *segan*, . . . used this mortar]
זי גלל [. . . . . קדם]	3) of . . . stone [before]
מזדדת אפגנ[זברא ליד]	4) Mazda-dāta the sub-treasurer, [beside]
בגפת גנז[ב]רא שנת	5) Baga-pāta the treasurer. Year
// ///	6) 5.

DESCRIPTION

A fragment of a green chert mortar (base dia. 7.8 cm., present max. height 1.8 cm.), consisting of only part of the base.

Originally there were six lines of Aramaic on the bottom of the mortar base. Now only the beginning of the third line and most of lines 4 through 6 remain. There is a slightly larger space than usual between the third and fourth lines but scarcely enough for another line of text. Only the fifth line can be used to estimate the approximate length of the lines.

FIND SPOT

The central part (HF 29) of Room 38.

DATE

The fifth year of Artaxerxes I (460/59 B.C.).

LINES 3-5

The preposition *qdm* must be restored at the end of line 3 before the name of the sub-treasurer and the preposition *lyd* at the end of the fourth line before the name of the treasurer.

---

[152] Kent, *Old Persian*, p. 199b, *bātugara;* cf. H. W. Bailey, "Indo-Iranian Studies II," *Transactions of the Philological Society*, 1954, p. 154; H. H. Schaeder, "Über einige altpersischen Inschriften," *Sitzungsberichte der Preussischen Akademie der Wissenschaften* (Philos.-hist. Kl.), 1935, pp. 489-90.

[153] Eilers notes that if *bʾt*, "wine," is certified here, it again raises the question whether or not the mortar was used in ancient times for crushing grapes for wine, contrary to prevailing practices ("Traubensyrup in Iran," *Orientalistische Literaturzeitung* XLIV (1941), cols. 7-9 and n. 1).

[154] See p. 13.

[155] See p. 54-55.

It is uncertain what should be supplied after the *zy gll* in the third line. In that position one expects some word characterizing the stone. It might have been something like the *ʾḥšynpyn* found elsewhere under similar circumstances (for example, Nos. 11:3, 75:2, 76:2, and 101:2).

There is not enough room in the fifth line for the *ʾškr* usually found before the word *šnt*, "year." Such an omission is unusual. It might be dropped on a pestle top, where space is limited (for example, No. 27), but hardly on a mortar or plate, where ample room is available.

31. Mortar (PT5 760) Pl. 8

בסרך בירתא ליד מתֿ]רֿךֿ[	1) In the ritual of the fortress, beside Mithraka
סגנא אס]פֿ[בר **/** פֿלֿג ע]בֿ[דֿ	2) the *segan*, 1 Aspa-bāra, a myriarch, used
הֿ]וֿ[ן זי גלל זעירֿ זנֿהֿ]לֿֿיֿד[	3) this small mortar of stone [beside]
בגפת גנזברא קדם	4) Baga-pāta the treasurer, (and) before
מֿזֿ]דדֿ[ת[אפגנזברא אשֿ]כֿר[	5) Mazda-dāta the sub-treasurer. *ʾškr* of
שֿנֿ]ת *iii iii*	6) year 6.

DESCRIPTION

A fragment of a green chert mortar (base dia. 8 cm., present max. height 4.8 cm.).

The remains of six lines of Aramaic are preserved on the bottom of the mortar base. A deep chip at the top of the inscribed surface damages the tops of the letters of the first word, but they are still identifiable. Elsewhere in the text some of the letters are extremely faint, and sometimes they have disappeared entirely.

FIND SPOT

The south-central part (HF 38) of Room 38.

DATE

The officials Mazda-dāta and Baga-pāta indicate the reign of Artaxerxes I. The figure in the last line is quite faint but Cameron's copy shows six distinct unit strokes and two sets of three strokes each are still discernible in the photograph. The sixth year of Artaxerxes I was 459/58 B.C.

LINE 1

Only the first two letters of the *segan*'s name are clear in the photograph, but Cameron's copy shows all four. Once the name is known, it is possible to see the last two letters in the faint, gray, vertical strokes at the end of the line.

LINE 2

The name of the celebrant is rather difficult to read. Cameron copied *ʾs* and *d* or *r* as clear, and he shows traces of the curving top of the *p* and the vertical stroke of the *t*. All of these are visible in the photograph except the *p*, but there is even some indication of the curving stroke of that letter. Thus, the reading *ʾspbr* is quite probable.

Justi lists an Ašpabara (with an Assyrian *š* instead of *s*) as well as an Aspabara.[156] Eilers, however, prefers the reading Aspa-bāri and compares the Old Persian Asa-bāra.[157]

The first two letters of the title *plg*, "myriarch," cannot be seen in the photograph because they are written over a broad, dark, vertical band in the stone. Cameron shows the letters to be quite visible on the stone by drawing them clearly in his copy and by transliterating them.

[156] Justi, *Iranisches Namenbuch*, p. 45*b*.

[157] Kent, *Old Persian*, p. 173*b*, *asabāra*.

LINE 3

The faint word after *gll* is copied by Cameron with traces of *y*, *d*, *z*, and *r*, but he does not transliterate. The word is *z͑yr*, "small," which is encountered elsewhere in these texts in a similar situation, and in Nos. 108:4 and 123:3 the reading is quite clear.

LINE 5

Cameron indicates that the name of the sub-treasurer is "not at all clear," but he copied a faint . . *ddt* and correctly restored [*Mz*]*ddt*. Traces in the photograph show the letters *zdd*, but the *t*, shown clearly by Cameron, is written on the dark band in the stone.

32. Mortar (PT5 380) Pl. 9

בסרך בֹ[י]רתֹ[א לידֹ]	1)	In the ritual of the fortress, [beside]
מתרך סגנא מֹהשֹ[ֹר] i	2)	Mithraka the *segan*, 1 Māh(a)-čārā,
פלג עבד הון זי גלל זנה	3)	a myriarch, used this mortar of stone
ליד בגפת גנזברא קדם	4)	beside Baga-pāta the treasurer (and) before
מזדדתֹ אפגנזברא אשכר	5)	Mazda-dāta the sub-treasurer. ᵓškr of
שנת /// ///	6)	year 6.

DESCRIPTION

A green chert mortar with a broken rim (base dia. 7.3 cm., present height 9.3 cm.).

Six lines of Aramaic are written in ink on the bottom of the base. Except for the ends of the first two lines, where the letters have disappeared completely, the writing is clear, regular, and carefully done.

FIND SPOT

Near the center of the south wall of Room 38.

DATE

The officials indicate the reign of Artaxerxes I, whose sixth year was 459/58 B.C.

LINE 2

The name of the celebrant is incomplete and therefore uncertain. Cameron copied *Rmsn* but transliterated *d/rm* . . . However, the photograph shows the last letter to be shorter than *n* and it is probably a *d* or *r*. It appears to be *n* only because its bottom is joined to the top of the *l* of the line below. The name is thus either *Mhšd* or *Mhšr*.

Justi lists a Māh-šad,[158] but its formation is too late for the Achaemenid period since its second element -*šad*, "joy" (Late Avestan *šāti*), should appear as *šiyāti* in Old Persian.

Eilers prefers reading *Mhšr* as Māh(a)-čārā, "He whose help is the moon god, Māh." The second element of the name is probably -*šr* for -*čārā*.[159] The use of Semitic *š* to represent the Iranian phoneme *č* is well attested. It is found in Biblical Aramaic, where *paršegen* (Ezra 4:11, 23, 5:6, 7:11) probably represents the Persian *para-čayan* or *pari-čayan*,[160] and also in Iranian loanwords in Talmudic Aramaic.[161]

---

[158] Justi, *Iranisches Namenbuch*, p. 187b.

[159] *BAiW*, col. 584, Late Avestan *čārā*, "Mittel" "Hilfsmittel"; Kent, *Old Persian*, p. 175a, *ucāra*, "well done," "successful," "good deed."

[160] P. de Lagarde, *Gesammelte Abhandlungen* (Leipzig, 1866), p. 79, No. 198; Eilers, in *ZDMG* XC 162, n. 4.

[161] Telegdi, in *JA* CCXXVI 204.

33. Mortar (PT5 7) Teheran Museum 2209; Pl. 9

בֹּסֹרֹך בֹּירתא	1)	In the ritual of the fortress,
לֹיֹד [מתרֹ]ךֹ סגנא	2)	beside [Mithra]ka the *segan*,
אֹרֹ[תֹמתר בר מֹתֹ]רֹפרן	3)	Ar[ta-Mithra, the son of Mith]ra-farnah,
[עֹבֹד] הֹ]ון זי גלֹלֹ] זֹנֹהֹ [זעיר]	4)	used this [small mortar of stone]
[קֹ]דם [מֹב]ם אפגנזברא	5)	before *Mbm* the sub-treasurer.
אֹ]שֹכר שֹ[נת *III III*	6)	*ᵓškr* of year 6.

DESCRIPTION

A complete green chert mortar with a globular body and a disk base (base dia. 8.2 cm., top dia. 6.7 cm., height 9 cm.). Its stone has concentric rings of light and dark green.[162]

Six lines of Aramaic are written in ink on the bottom of the base. A few letters remain clear and dark as they were originally, but most of them are extremely faint and shadowy and can be traced only with careful and intensive examination. A good bit of text, especially in lines 3 and 4, has disappeared almost entirely. The situation is not hopeless, however, since isolated words and sometimes even single letters remain as clues to the presence of expected formulae.

FIND SPOT

Recovered with a complete, uninscribed pestle (PT5 8, Teheran Museum 2208 [head dia. 3.2 cm., length 13.5 cm.]) with which it apparently belonged. They were recovered within Room 37 of the Persepolis Treasury, at the opening to the long passage/storage room (40) running northward (HG 33).

Since Rooms 37 and 40 were part of the long passageway leading to the northern exit of the Treasury, the objects must have been dropped or discarded by the plunderer as he was about to leave the building.

DATE

If, as seems probable, the *segan* is Mithraka, the text is from the time of Artaxerxes I, whose sixth year was 459/58 B.C.

LINE 2

Only the last letter of the name of the *segan* is clear, but there is a shadowy *r* before it. The space is right for the expected name Mithraka and only his name among those of the known *segan*'s fits the traces that remain.

LINE 3

The line is almost illegible. Normally the name of the celebrant occurs after the title of the *segan*. At the beginning of the line there are blurred traces which later collation certified as an *ᵓaleph*. It is followed by the tops of the letters *r* and *t*. Thus, the first element of the name is Arta-. Careful examination of the faint traces on the stone itself suggest that the second element is Mithra for a name Arta-Mithra.

There are a few dark letters at the end of the line which, in the photograph, seem to be -*n/zrn* but which collation shows to be -*r*(?)*prn*, which appears to include the familiar name element -*prn*, -farnah. The line is much too long to represent a single name. It could be that the traces represent the name of a second celebrant,[163] but they could also be an example of a patronymic, familiar elsewhere in Aramaic but unique in these texts. Collation seemed to indicate that the faint traces of the first name element is *Mtr*-, Mithra, and it appears that traces of such an element are faintly visible in the photograph.

---

[162] Schmidt, *Persepolis* II, Pl. 23:1*a, b*.

[163] Nos. 88 and 95.

LINE 4

The celebrant's name normally is followed by the verb and a description of its object. Such must be the case in this difficult line, which is the most defaced of all. Its center is completely gone and only faint traces of letters remain elsewhere. The first discernible traces of letters in the line are a faint *-bd*, which doubtless represents the verb *ᶜbd* (or *ᶜbdw?*), "used." Near the end of the line is the rather clear demonstrative pronoun *znh*, "this." In between the verb and the pronoun must lie the words "mortar of stone" and there are faint traces of some letters in the words *hwn zy gll*.

There is room after the *znh* for another word before the end of the line. There are possible traces of the word *zᶜyr*, "small," which would be appropriate for such a small mortar. One would expect the adjective to precede the demonstrative pronoun, but similar placement of the adjective after it is found elsewhere in these texts (Nos. 7, 18, 41, 43).

LINE 5

There is room for only three letters between the preposition *qdm* and the title of the sub-treasurer. Only the last letter of the name is clear and certain. Two shadowy traces appear before it. The name is probably that of the sub-treasurer mentioned in No. 38:4 which also has but three letters and concludes with a letter *m*. In that text the next to last letter is probably a *b*, or less likely *p*, while the very faint first letter seems to be another *m*.

34. Mortar (PT5 897) Persepolis Museum 32; Pl. 9

בֹּסֹרֹך בירתא ליד	1)	In the ritual of the fortress, beside
מתרך סגנא דרוֹזֹבֹר ⁄	2)	Mithraka the *segan*, 1 Draz-bāra
עבד הון זי גל[ל] זנה [לֹ]יד	3)	used this mortar of stone beside
[ב]גפת גזבֹר[אֹ] אש[כֹ]ר	4)	Baga-pāta the treasurer. *ᵓškr* of
III III שנת	5)	year 6.

DESCRIPTION

A fragment of a green chert mortar (base dia. 7.1 cm., present max. height 8.7 cm.[164]). Five lines of Aramaic are written on the bottom of the base of the vessel.

FIND SPOT

Near the center of the south wall (HF 38, 47, 48) of Room 38.

DATE

Mithraka and Baga-pāta indicate the reign of Artaxerxes I, whose sixth year was 459/58 B.C.

LINE 2

In my original reading it seemed that the name of the celebrant could be read *Drypr* or *Drypd*. The first element of the name, *dāraya*, "holding,"[165] is found elsewhere in these texts (for example, Dāraya-farnah in No. 61:2). The second element could be read as either *-pd* or *-pr*. As *pd*, *-pada*, it might be "post," "station."[166] If *pr*, it might represent *-pāra*, "border," "frontier."[167] The reading presumes that the stroke at the end is the unit stroke that sometimes accompanies the name of the celebrant, rather than a remnant of the vertical letter *-n*.

---

[164] These measurements, made at Persepolis, do not agree with those given for this item in the Field Register, which are diameter .161 m., height .178 m.

[165] Kent, *Old Persian*, p. 189b, Dāraya-vaʰu; Benveniste (*Titres et noms*, p. 82) cites an abbreviated Elamite name Dariya.

[166] Kent, *Old Persian*, p. 195a, pada-.

[167] *BAiW*, col. 889 ³*pāra*, "Ufer," "Grenze." Benveniste (*Titres et noms*, p. 90) mentions an Elamite Paradada or Pardadda for Para-dāta.

The name now appears to be *Drzbr*, who is found again in year seven as one who dedicated another mortar (No. 38). In each case the name is followed by a unit stroke.

For the name Eilers tentatively proposes *Draz-bāra for *Zraz-bāra, "Bringing along faith and confidence."[168] Possibly *dərəz* or *dərəzā*, "bond," "fetter,"[169] should be considered for the first element of the name "He who bears the fetters," as in the Late Avestan Dərəz-van, "He who bears the fetters" (that is, "He who is fettered").[170]

35. Mortar (PT5 424) Pl. 9

מזדדת [אפגנזברא אשכר]   Mazda-dāta [the sub-treasurer. *škr* of]
שנת *III III*   year 6.

Description

Fragment of the base of a green chert mortar (max. length 6.2 cm.).

The beginnings of the last two lines of a longer text in Aramaic, written in ink, are preserved on the bottom of the mortar base.

Find Spot

Recovered from a place north of the center (HF 29) of the great storeroom, Room 38, of the Persepolis Treasury.

Date

The name Mazda-dāta as sub-treasurer indicates the reign of Artaxerxes I, whose sixth year was 459/58 B.C.

36. Mortar (PT6 86) Persepolis Museum 1593; Pl. 9

בהסת [ביר]תא ליד ונדפרן סגנא שורתי שמה   1) In the *hst* of the fortress, beside Vinda(t)-
i עבד הון זנה   farnah the *segan*, 1 *Šwrty* by name used this mortar

ליד בגפת גנזבֿ[ר]א קֿ[דם מזדשתר אפגנזברא   2) beside Baga-pāta the treasurer (and) before
אשכֿר שנת *III III I*   Mazda-čiθra the sub-treasurer. *škr* of year 7.

Description

A fragment of a large green chert mortar (base dia. 17.7 cm., present max. height 7.6 cm. [slightly reduced in illustration]) of which the bowl is missing.

Two long lines of Aramaic are written in clear, easily legible letters on the bottom of the base.

Find Spot

At the eastern wall (HF 27) of Room 45 of the Persepolis Treasury. The room, a subsidiary of Room 38, seems to have been a minor depository for the ritual objects.

Date

Baga-pāta as treasurer, with a low year date, indicates the reign of Artaxerxes I, whose seventh year was 458/57 B.C. The treasurer in the seventh year of Xerxes (cf. No. 1) was Dāta-Mithra.

---

[168] *BAiW*, col. 1702, *zraz-dā*, "gläubig," "gläubig ergeben." Eilers suggests that in southwestern Persian dialect *zrz* would be *drz*.

[169] *BAiW*, col. 742.   [170] *Ibid.*, col. 745.

LINE 1

Three texts (Nos. 36, 119, and 120) form a separate group among the ritual vessels, for all are presented by the same celebrant and all mention *hst* of the fortress. Apart from the treasurer Baga-pāta, the officers named in them are unique and do not fit well into the general pattern of officials at Persepolis, as known from the other ritual texts. The word *hst*, found only in the three texts, is still somewhat obscure.[171]

The first letter of the name of the *segan* lies close to a crack in the stone and has a scratch running through it. Cameron copied it correctly as a *w*, and it can be verified by close scrutiny of the photograph. The name is *Wndprn*, Vinda(t)-farnah.[172] The spelling of the name of the celebrant, *Šwrty*, is attested in the related texts (Nos. 119 and 120). Unless there is a scribal error, a person with the same name also appears as *segan* in No. 120.

The use of *šmh*, "his name," with proper names, as found also in Biblical Aramaic (Ezra 5:14) and the Aramaic papyri, is a phenomenon of Persian syntax, corresponding to the Persian *nāma*, "namely." It is not found consistently in these texts, but where encountered it is always with the name of the celebrant and never with the names of the officials.[173]

LINE 2

The name of the sub-treasurer, *Mzdštr*, is found only here in these texts. Its first element is certainly Mazda, "The wise," "All-knowing," the highest Persian god.[174] The second element, -*štr*, which is found with other names,[175] as well as alone (for example, שֵׁתָר, Esther 1:14), has been interpreted as the Persian -*xšathra*, "kingship," "kingdom," "rule."[176] Bartholomae notes a Mazda-xšathra, "He who has his might from Mazda."[177]

But since the word *xšathra* elsewhere in these texts (No. 89:2) is transcribed as *hštr*,[178] it is probable that the -*štr* here is to be read otherwise as *čiθra* (Kent *ciça*), which has several meanings: (*a*) "seed," "lineage," "family" and (*b*) "visible, external, appearance," "countenance."[179] Thus, Mazda-čiθra signifies "Having an appearance (countenance) like Mazda," parallel to the Mithra-čiθra noted by Justi.[180]

37. Pestle (PT5 762) T (52); Pl. 10

בסרך בירתא	1)	In the ritual of the fortress,
ליד מתרך סגנא	2)	beside Mithraka the *segan*,
חורשיפת עבד	3)	Hvaršya-pāta used
אבשון זנה	4)	this pestle.
אשכר שנת	5)	*ʾškr* of year
I III III	6)	7.

[171] See p. 24. Could the word be related to the Akkadian *isittu/esittu* meaning "treasury," "storehouse," or "part of a temple"? Cf. *CAD* VII 243–44; Bezold, *Babylonisch-assyrisches Glossar*, p. 52*b*. The ceremony might have been held in Room 38, the very room in which the vessels had been stored.

[172] Justi, *Iranisches Namenbuch*, pp. 368–69, Windafarna(h); Kent, *Old Persian*, p. 208*a*, Viⁿdafarnah (Greek Intafernes).

[173] See pp. 34, 66.

[174] *BAiW*, cols. 1161–64; Kent, *Old Persian*, p. 203, *mazdāh*.

[175] *Kbrrmštr* (No. 87:3); *Bgštr* (No. 117:3); cf. also the *štr bwzny* of Ezra 5:3, 6, and 6:6.

[176] Justi, *Iranisches Namenbuch*, p. 292*a*, under Sathrabouzanes; *BAiW*, cols. 542–46; Kent, *Old Persian*, p. 181*a*, xšaça.

[177] *BAiW*, col. 1159.

[178] See also the use of Semitic *ḥ* with the *š* in the second element of the name of Artaxerxes in Aramaic, -*ḥššt* (Ezra 4:8, 11, 23, and 6:14); -*ḥšst* (Ezra 7:12, 21); and -*ḥšštʾ* (Ezra 4:7).

[179] *BAiW*, cols. 586–87.

[180] Justi, *Iranisches Namenbuch*, p. 216*a*. The name is found spelled *Mtrstr* on an Aramaic seal (O. Blau, "Ueber einem aramäisch-persischen Siegelstein," *ZDMG* XVIII [1864] 299–300).

DESCRIPTION

A fragment of a green chert pestle (head dia. 4.6 cm., present max. length 7.6 cm.[181]).
Six lines of Aramaic are written in rather thick letters on the top of the pestle head.

FIND SPOT

West of the center (HF 38) of Room 38.

DATE

Mithraka served as *segan* in the seventh year of Artaxerxes I, 458/57 B.C.

LINE 3

For the name of the celebrant, *Ḥwršypt*, Eilers has proposed the name Hu-aršya-pāta, "Well
protected by righteous men." Since Aramaic *ḥ* can be used for Iranian *h*,[182] the first element
could be *ḥu-* for *hu-*, "well," "good."[183] The second element could be *aršya*, "righteousness,"
"right-dealing."[184] The final element is *-pāta*, "protected."[185] To judge from such a word as
-uvaspa (for *ʰu-aspa* / Avestan *hvaspo*) this name should be Hvaršya-pāta.[186]

38. Mortar (PT5 169) Pl. 10

בסֹרֹך בּירתא ליד	1)	In the ritual of the fortress, beside
מֹ[תֹר]ך סגנא דרזבֹרֹ /	2)	Mithraka the *segan*, 1 Draz-bāra
עבד הון זֹעירֹ זנֹה [קֹ]דֹם	3)	used this small mortar before
[מֹ]בֹם [אֹ]פֹנֹ[זֹבר]א [אֹ]שֹכֹר	4)	*Mbm* the sub-treasurer. *ʾškr* of
שנת / /// /// /	5)	year 7.

DESCRIPTION

A polished green chert mortar with a semi-globular bowl, a conical stem, and a disk base
(base dia. 7.6 cm., present height 8.5 cm.).

Five lines of Aramaic are written on the bottom of the base in letters so badly faded that
they are sometimes illegible.

FIND SPOT

At the south wall (HF 48) of Room 38 of the Persepolis Treasury.

DATE

The officer Mithraka served during the reign of Artaxerxes I, whose seventh year was
458/57 B.C.

LINE 2

Although the last two letters of the celebrant's name are faint and shadowy, their reading
seems certain. They could be *bd* or *br* but, because of the frequency of the element *-br*, *-bāra*,
as a concluding element in Persian names, it seems preferable to read *-br* as the final element.
The *z* before the *br* is clear and dark. The first two letters of the word are almost identical
and could represent either combination, *dr* or *rd*. Because the staff of the former letter is

---

[181] The dimensions are reversed in the Field Register.

[182] See pp. 64, 96–97, *ʾrywḥš/ʾrywḥwš* (Nos. 24:2 and 49:2).

[183] *BAiW*, col. 1817, *hu-*, "wohl," "gut," "schön"; Kent, *Old Persian*, p. 175a, *ʰu*, "good," "well."

[184] *BAiW*, col. 356, *arašya*, "recht handelnd," "gerecht"; Justi, *Iranisches Namenbuch*, p. 485, *aršya-*, "mannhaft"; see Aršya as a Late Avestan personal name in *BAiW*, col. 206.

[185] The nominative singular masculine passive participle of *pā*, "protect"; Kent, *Old Persian*, p. 194a, *pā*; Justi, *Iranisches Namenbuch*, p. 505, *pāta*, "beschützt."

[186] Kent, *Old Persian*, p. 48a, Sec. 140, IV.

slightly shorter (by no means a sure criterion!), the reading should apparently be *dr*, a combination that frequently appears in Persian names. The most likely reading appears to be *Drzbr*, followed by the unit stroke. The celebrant is quite likely the same as that in No. 34.

LINE 3

As a modifier of *ḥwn*, "mortar," Cameron copied and transliterated *šš* and I did so independently, translating it as "marble" (cf. Cant. 5:15; Esther 1:6), regarding it, like *kpwtk* (No. 122:2), as an attempt to indicate the banding or marbling of the stone.[187] Greater familiarity with the texts and a subsequent close examination of the passage proves that the word is a carelessly written *zᶜyr*, "small," which is appropriate for a mortar of such size.

LINE 4

The name of the sub-treasurer is quite faint. It is a short one, consisting of probably just three letters. The last two seem to be *-bm*, or less likely *-pm*. The faint and rather blurred letter before them appears to be another *m*, for a name *Mbm* or *Mpm*. It seems to be identical with that of the sub-treasurer mentioned in No. 33:5, where the reading is equally difficult. Its etymology and vocalization remain uncertain.

39. Pestle (PT5 492) Pl. 10

בסֹרֹךְ בירתא	1)	In the ritual of the fortress,
ליד אֹמדת סגנא	2)	beside Ama-dāta the *segan*,
רמן / עבד הון	3)	1 Rāman used this
זנה רב ליד בגפת	4)	large mortar beside Baga-pāta
גנזברא קדם	5)	the treasurer (and) before
מזדדת אפגנזבר[א]	6)	Mazda-dāta the sub-treasurer.
אשכֹר שנת ⌐	7)	ᵓškr of year 10.

DESCRIPTION

A fragment of a polished green chert pestle banded in green shades of stone (head dia. 6 cm., present max. length 10.1 cm.).[188]

Seven lines of Aramaic are written in dark, clear, well preserved letters on the top of the pestle head.

FIND SPOT

The north wall (HG 11) of Room 38, at the doorway leading to the subsidiary storeroom (48) in the northeastern corner of the room.

DATE

Baga-pāta as treasurer indicates the reign of Artaxerxes I, whose tenth year was 455/54 B.C.

LINE 2

Ama-dāta served as *segan* both in the time of Xerxes (Nos. 1, 11, 12) and in the reign of Artaxerxes I. He was presumably a subordinate who could serve when the chief *segan* was unavailable.

LINE 3

The same celebrant, *Rmn*, Rāman(?) presented other vessels, another pestle (No. 40) and a plate (No. 113:2). The name occurs also on an Aramaic fortification tablet from Persepo-

---

[187] Bowman, in *Dōrōn*, pp. 68–69.

[188] Schmidt, *Persepolis* II 55, Pl. 23:3. The object unfortunately was lost at sea (*ibid.*, p. 151). It is the text misread by Altheim and Stiehl, *Aramäische Sprache* I 17–21.

lis.[189] Eilers suggests that the name might be Rāman, "Peace,"[190] abbreviated from such a longer name as Ariyā-rāmna.[191]

It is noteworthy that although the object is a very large pestle it is called "this mortar," apparently a reference to the set of mortar and pestle which could be regarded as a unit.[192] Since another pestle is presented in the same year (No. 40), with a different *segan* serving, it is apparent that participation in the haoma ceremony could occur more than once a year and that the service was apparently not linked to a single festival.

40. Pestle (PT5 659) Pl. 10

בס[ר]ך [בירתא]	1)	In the ritual of the fortress,
[לי[ד ארבן [סגנא]	2)	beside Ari-bānu [the *segan*],
רמן / עב[ד] אבשון ז[נה]	3)	1 Rāman used this pestle
קדם מזדדת	4)	before Mazda-dāta
אפונזבר[א א[שכר	5)	the sub-treasurer. *ᵓškr* of
שנ[ת ←	6)	[year] 10.

DESCRIPTION

A fragment of a green chert pestle (head dia. 5.4 cm., present max. length 8.6 cm.). Part of the upper left edge of its head is chipped away, destroying the last words of the first two lines of the text.

Six lines of Aramaic are on the top of the pestle. Many letters, especially in the fifth and sixth lines, are faint and almost illegible.

FIND SPOT

Just west of the center (HF 38) of Room 38 of the Persepolis Treasury.

DATE

Because the *segan* is unique, only the sub-treasurer gives a clue to the date. Mazda-dāta is found in the nineteenth year of Xerxes (No. 18), but he served principally during the reign of Artaxerxes I, whose tenth year was 455/54 B.C.

In Cameron's copy the last two lines are shaded, as though obscure, but in the last line he shows clear traces of the letter *t* and the figure 10 and he translates "year 10" without question.

Text No. 39, by the same celebrant, is clearly dated in the same year. The difference in *segan*'s, however, indicates that Rāman participated in the ceremony at least twice in the same year but on different occasions.

LINE 2

Cameron's copy shows the marginal chipping of the pestle top extending as far as the letter *-n* of the name. If complete, the spelling of the name is either *ᵓdbn* or *ᵓrbn*. Justi lists an Arbūn,[193] but Eilers prefers to read *Araya-bānu* or *Ari-bānu*.[194] Frye has proposed *Aryā-bānu*, "Glory of Aryans."

---

[189] Tablet 114, l. 4; cf. *rmyn* in Tablet 55, l. 1. Could this be related to the Elamite Ramaniš = *rāma-nī-* noted by Benveniste (*Titres et noms*, p. 91)?

[190] *BAiW*, col. 1524, *rāman*.

[191] *Ibid.*, col. 199, Ariyārāmna (*Ariyā-raman*). But Kent (*Old Persian*, p. 170a) derives the name from *Ariyā-* with the passive participle of *ā-ram*. Benveniste (*Titres et noms*, p. 91) recognizes Elamite Ramnakka also as a possible abbreviation of the name.

[192] See p. 45.

[193] Justi, *Iranisches Namenbuch*, p. 21a.

[194] *BAiW*, col. 198, *airya-*. For the initial element *ari-*, Eilers cites the discussion on *èri-/αρι* by P. Thieme, "Der Fremdling im Rig Veda," *Abhandlungen für die Kunde des Morgenlandes* XXIII, No. 2 (1938), 159 ff.

41. Mortar (PT5 488) Pl. 10

בסרך בירתא [ליד אריוהוש] 1) In the ritual of the fortress, [beside Āraya(t)-vahuš]

סֹגֹנא אמדסם [עבד הון זנה] 2) the *segan*, *ʾmdsm* [used this] medium-sized [mortar]

מדם ליד בגפת גֹ[נזברא קדם] 3) beside Baga-pāta [the treasurer (and) before]

מזדדת אפֹגֹנזברֹא [אשכר שנת] 4) Mazda-dāta the sub-treasurer. [*ʾškr* of year]

𐊠 ר/ 5) 11.

DESCRIPTION

A fragment of a green chert mortar with gray veins (base dia. 11.3 cm., present height 12.4 cm.). Its base, badly cracked and broken, was slightly polished on its bottom before being inscribed.[195]

The beginnings of five lines of Aramaic text are preserved on the bottom of the base. The writing is faint and blurred.

FIND SPOT

Among a small group of green chert fragments at the north wall in the northeastern part (HG 11) of Room 38, at the door leading to subsidiary Room 48.

DATE

The officials mentioned indicate a date during the reign of Artaxerxes I, whose eleventh year was 454/53 B.C.

LINE 1

The name of the *segan* has been lost. It might have been one of those who served in the tenth year, Ama-dāta or Ari-bānu, but it is probably Āraya(t)-vahuš, who then begins to serve as the chief *segan* (cf. Nos. 42, 43, and others).

LINE 2

Cameron transliterated the name of the celebrant as *ʾmst* but his copy and the photograph show *ʾmdsm*. The name is perhaps composed of the elements *ama-*, "strength," "might," "power," or even the divinity Ama,[196] and *-dasma*, "offering."[197]

42. Plate (PT5 170) Pl. 11

בפרכן בירתא 1) In the (haoma-)crushing ceremony of the fortress,

ליד אֹ[ריו]חו 2) beside Ā[raya(t)-va]hu(š)

סגנא . . . . 3) the *segan*, . . .

עבד ס[חר . . . . ליד] 4) used (this?) plate [beside]

[בגפֹ]ת גנזֹברֹא 5) [Baga-pā]ta the treasurer.

[אשכר] שנת ר/ 6) [*ʾškr* of] year 11.

DESCRIPTION

A fragment of a polished, green chert plate with a low, convex side and a flat-topped rim (base dia. 17 cm., present height 2.9 cm. [reduced in illustration]).

[195] Schmidt, *Persepolis* II 55, Pl. 24:11.

[196] *BAiW*, cols. 140–41, ²*ama-*; Kent, *Old Persian*, p. 169a, *ama*, "offensive power." In Mithraism *ama* was deified (cf. n. 13 above).

[197] Justi (*Iranisches Namenbuch*, p. 491) renders *dasma* as "Satzung" (cft. Parō-dasma). But Bartholomae (*BAiW*, col. 702) regards such a rendering as erroneous and translates it as "Darbringung."

Six lines of Aramaic are written on the bottom of the base. The text is in poor shape with many faint letters and some that are entirely gone.

FIND SPOT

Near the base of the south wall (HF 48) of Room 38 of the Persepolis Treasury.

DATE

Āraya(t)-vahuš served as *segan* during the reign of Artaxerxes I, whose eleventh year was 454/53 B.C.

LINE 2

The name of the *segan* is spelled ʾrywḥw elsewhere,[198] as it is here. Sometimes, however, a final *š* is added to the name, as is usual with the nominative case of nouns ending in -*i* or -*u* in Old Persian.[199] It is difficult to determine whether this name had the final *š* or whether it is one of the letters that has disappeared.

43. Plate, Teheran Museum 2974; Pl. 11

בפרכן בירתא ליד	1)	In the (haoma-)crushing ceremony of the fortress, beside
אריוהש סגנא	2)	Āraya(t)-vahuš the *segan*,
[אֹרֹתֹ]ם / עבד סחרא זנה	3)	1 [Arta]ma used this large plate
רֹבֹ לפתי אטבען ‏*III III III III*	4)	worth 9 (shekel?) coins
ליד בגפת גנזברֹאֹ זי	5)	beside Baga-pāta the treasurer who is
בהרחותי אשכר שנת	6)	in Arachosia. ʾškr of year
‏ר *III*	7)	13(?).

DESCRIPTION

A large, complete, beautiful plate of green chert with rather soft banding of a darker color. A wide, dark band covers about a third of the vessel, running diagonally across its base, dividing it into two areas. The diameter across the top is 19.8 cm. with a side thickness at its squared flat top of 1.2 cm. Its standing height is 4 cm. The diameter of the base is 9.3 cm.

Seven lines of Aramaic are carefully written on the bottom of the base. Except for the name of the celebrant, and possibly the end of the seventh line, the text is beautifully written and excellently preserved.

FIND SPOT

This beautiful vessel was found in 1949 by the Archaeological Institute of Persepolis while clearing the broad street along Mount Kuh-i-Raḥmat, east of the Hall of the Hundred Columns (Room 38 of the Persepolis Treasury).[200] It was doubtless lost or discarded in the street by a plunderer who left the Treasury by its eastern exit and proceeded northward along "Garrison Street."

DATE

The officials mentioned indicate the reign of Artaxerxes I, but there is some question about the actual year date.

The figure in line 7 is clearly 13, which is probably the correct date. But in a somewhat smudged place beyond, on the dark band in the stone, it sometimes appears that there are

---

[198] Nos. 46:2, 51:2, 102:2, 110:2; cf. also ʾryḥw in No. 47:2.

[199] See pp. 81, 96–97.

[200] Ali-Sami, *Persepolis* (*Takht-i-Jamshid*), trans. R. N. Sharp (4th ed.; Shiraz, 1966), pp. 67–68.

faint traces of still another group of three unit strokes and there could be as many as nine strokes in the line. It is probable, therefore, that the date is year 13 (452/51 B.C.), but it could be 16 (449/48 B.C.) or, less likely, 19 (446/45 B.C.).

LINE 3

The name of the celebrant is the only damaged word in the Aramaic text. To judge from the otherwise excellent state of preservation of the text, the name may have been erased deliberately. The final letter of the name and the unit stroke following it are all that remain certain. If the usual margin is followed, there is room for four letters in the name. The last letter is certainly *m*. The letter before it is smudged. It could be an *r* or *k*, but it seems more likely to be a *t*. Its long, vertical staff is nearly gone, but there seems to be a trace of its upper extension just to the left of the second letter in the name of the *segan* in line 2, and a dot of faded ink just above and to the left of the letter *y* of the word *lpty* in line 4 may mark the lower limit of the staff.

It is difficult to see anything of the first two letters on the bowl today, but the photograph shows smudged traces which may be identifiable. All that remains of the first letter is what seems to be the short, curving line that forms the upper right-hand stroke of the letter *ʾaleph*, as seen in the word *ʾškr* in line 6. The second letter shows only a smudge that resembles the head of a *d* or *r*. Thus, the name is probably to be read as [ʾr]*tm*, to be identified perhaps with the name Artames.[201] For a reading *ʾrkm* Frye has suggested *Arakāma, "One who has due desire" and he compares the Μασκαμης of Herodotus vii. 105.

LINE 4

In the margin to the right of the completed text, before and between lines 4 and 5, there appear to be two badly smudged, dark letters. When closely examined, they appear to be traces of the word *rb*, "large," which appropriately describes the size of the plate. The word was doubtless an afterthought added to the completed text. It is presumably to be read after the demonstrative pronoun *znh* at the end of the third line, a peculiar form of syntax encountered elsewhere in these texts.[202] It could not have been added to the third line, which runs to the very edge of the base.

The word *lpty* is difficult. It must further the description of the vessel, and from its position and context must describe the cost or value of the object.[203]

The use of the letter *l* suggests that the word is Semitic, but no Aramaic word seems to fit the present context. The word is probably Persian, related to the Avestan *paiti-*, Old Persian *patiy-*, which is used in the sense of "equivalence" and "for" when price or payment is involved.[204] In its context *lpty* must signify "for the value of," since what follows precludes an idea of the vessel's content. As is often the case, the Aramaic preposition *l*, "to" or "for," is prefixed to a word to form a compound preposition,[205] unless the word *pty* itself has come to be recognized as a substantive, "value," in Aramaic.

The word *ʾṭbʿn* preceding the numeral is the masculine plural form of *ʾṭbʿ* (*ʾiṭbaʿ*). The Semitic

---

[201] Justi, *Iranisches Namenbuch*, p. 37*a*, Ἀρτάμης; Benveniste (*Titres et noms*, p. 85) cites an Elamite Irtam for Irtambama, of which the first element represents *ṛtam*.

[202] Nos. 7, 18, 33, etc.; cf. pp. 69–70.

[203] See also Nos. 73 and 135.

[204] *BAiW*, col. 824 *paiti/patiy* II, 3, "zum Ausdruck des Gleichkommens Aufwiegens . . . bes zur Angabe dessen was als Preis oder Lohn geboten oder verlangt wird, 'gegen, um, für.'"

One might think of Akkadian *pūtu* or *pūt*, "instead of" or "in place of" (Bezold, *Babylonisch-assyrisches Glossar*, p. 218*b*), or its Syriac equivalent ܦܘܬ, "in proportion to" (Payne Smith, *A Compendious Syriac Dictionary*, p. 244*a*), but the spelling *pty* with a final *-y* rather suggests that the Iranian word was intended.

[205] The union of Semitic *l* with an Iranian word is unusual, but it sometimes occurred in later Persian as in the form *lḥwyš* for (*l*)*ḥawič* (cf. Henning, in *Handbuch der Orientalistik* IV, Pt. 1, p. 32).

root from which it derives means basically "to sink in,"[206] but its meaning is extended to "to impress (a seal or stamp)"[207] and the "coining (of money)."[208] Phoenician *ṭbᶜ*,[209] like Talmudic *ṭebaᶜ* and *ṭᵉbaᶜ*, means "a coin."[210] Obviously the Aramaic *ṭᵉbaᶜ* is here written with a prosthetic *ᵓaleph*.

The Hebrew and Aramaic *ṭᵉbaᶜ* was a coin equivalent to half a *selaᶜ*,[211] a coin equal to one sacred or two common shekels.[212] An Aramaic papyrus indicates that in Egypt, at least, a shekel was equivalent to a half-stater.[213] Thus, the *ṭbᶜ* was equal to a Babylonian shekel, a half of a Jewish *selaᶜ*, or a half of a Greek stater. Presumably the *ᵓṭbᶜ* of our text has the same value.

The coinage of Darius I, among the earliest known, consisted of the daric, a gold coin of very pure quality and a silver shekel (Greek *siglos*) of silver ninety per cent fine. These coins, roughly oval, were struck from egg-shaped globules of metal. Their types were the same. The obverse depicted the Persian king kneeling with a bow in his left hand and a spear in his right. The reverse had only a rough, irregular incuse caused by the striking. They bore no inscription. Darius I and his successors preferred the silver shekel, which was equal to one-twentieth of the gold daric and to the Greek half-stater.[214]

Plutarch preserves rumors of tremendous stores of coined money (νομίσματος) at both Susa and Persepolis when they were conquered by Alexander the Great. He reports that 40,000 talents of coined money was taken from the palace at Susa[215] and claims, ". . . they say that as much coined money was found there (that is, Persis/Persepolis) as at Susa and that it took 10,000 pairs of mules and 5000 camels to carry away the other furniture and wealth there."[216] Claudius Aelianus states that each ambassador to the court of Artaxerxes II received a Babylonian talent in coined silver in addition to other gifts.[217]

Despite such rumors of a huge deposit of coins at Persepolis, only thirty-nine coins were recovered there, only twenty-three from the Treasury. Most of them antedate the foundation of Persepolis. Surprisingly, there was not found among them a single Persian daric or shekel.[218]

In the Achaemenid period the Semitic shekel is well attested, not only in the cuneiform business documents of Babylonia but also, as a loanword, among the Jews of Palestine[219] and in Egypt.[220] The word has not yet been found at Persepolis. To judge from this text, the Aramaic word used for the shekel in Achaemenid Persia was *ᵓiṭbaᶜ*, which is also used in Talmudic circles of later times. Thus, this beautiful plate was valued at nine shekels and another (No. 73) was worth eight.

[206] Akkadian *ṭebû*, "sink in," Hebrew *ṭbᶜ*, "sink," "sink down."

[207] Arabic طبع "seal," "stamp," "imprint."

[208] E.g. Syriac *kispāᵓ ṭabīᶜāᵓ*, "coined silver" (Payne Smith, *A Compendious Syriac Dictionary*, pp. 166–67).

[209] C. Clermont-Ganneau, "Une inscription phénicienne de Tyr," *Revue archéologique*, Ser. III, Vol. VII (1886), pp. 1–9, l. 2; "Deux inscriptions phéniciennes inédits de la Phénice propre," *Annales du Musée Guimet* X (1887), No. II, pp. 509–16.

[210] Jastrow, *Dictionary* I 116–17.

[211] *Ibid.*, p. 519a, מֶבַע .

[212] B. Zuckermann, *Talmudische Münzen und Gewichte* (Breslau, 1862), pp. 9, 24.

[213] Cowley, *AP*, No. 35:3–4 (*ca.* 400 B.C.); cf. pp. xxxi–xxxii, 129–31.

[214] Olmstead, *History of the Persian Empire*, p. 188.

[215] Plutarch *Alexander* xxxvi. 1.

[216] *Ibid.* xxxvii. 2.

[217] Claudius Aelianus *Varia historia* i. 22 (G. L. F. Tafel, C. R. von Osiander, and G. Schwab, eds., *Griechische Prosaiker in neuen Übersetzungen* I [Stuttgart, 1839], clxxxii).

[218] Schmidt, *Persepolis* II 110a.

[219] Neh. 5:15.

[220] Cowley, *AP*, pp. xxx–xxxi, 314b, שקל; Kraeling, *The Brooklyn Museum Aramaic Papyri*, p. 318b. In Aramaic, *shekel* is found only a few times in the expected Aramaic form, *tql* (Cowley, No. 10:5, Kraeling, No. 2:8). Elsewhere it is spelled in Akkadian fashion as *šql*.

44. Plate (PT5 195) Pl. 12

בסרך בירתא	1)	In the ritual of the fortress,
[ליד] סחררת סׄגׄנׄא	2)	[beside] Suxra-raθa(?) the *segan*,
עבד סחרא דנה	3)	. . . used this plate
[ליד ב]גפת גנזברא זי	4)	[beside Ba]ga-pāta the treasurer who is
[בהרחות]יׄ אשכרׄ שנת ר ///	5)	[in Arachosia]. ᵓškr of year 13.

DESCRIPTION

A fragment of a green chert plate (base dia. 7.6 cm., present max. height 1.4 cm.) consisting of only part of the base and just a bit of the adjacent sides.

The remains of five lines of Aramaic are preserved on the bottom of the base. Because of breakage, the beginnings of all lines, except the first, are lost.

FIND SPOT

Among the many fragments of ritual vessels shattered against the south wall (HF 48) of Room 38 of the Treasury.

DATE

Baga-pāta functioned as treasurer principally during the reign of Artaxerxes I, whose thirteenth year was 452/51 B.C.

LINE 2

The name of the *segan* is somewhat uncertain since the third letter could be *w*, *d*, or *r* and the next might be *d* or *r*. The most likely reading is *Sḥr-rt*, which Eilers suggests might be composed of the elements *sḥr-*, *suxra*, "red,"[221] and *-rt*, *-raθa*, "wagon," "chariot,"[222] for a name "(He who has) a red chariot." The name is unique in these texts for a *segan*.

LINE 3

The demonstrative spelled *dnh* is unique here in these texts. The form is normal for Biblical Aramaic, but it is written elsewhere at Persepolis as *znh*. The situation is somewhat similar to that in the Aramaic papyri wherein there are rare examples of *dnh*[223] alongside the more usual *znh*. In the papyri as here the same initial phoneme appears as *z* in the word *zy* (line 4).

45. Plate (PT5 320) T (55); Pl. 12

	1)	
	2)	
	3)	
[וזי] בהרחוותׄיׄ ליד בגפת גנזברא אשכר	4)	beside Baga-pāta the treasurer who is in Arachosia. ᵓškr of
שנת ר /// /	5)	year 14.

DESCRIPTION

A fragment of a green chert plate (base dia. 12 cm., present max. height 1.9 cm.) consisting of little more than the lower half of the base and broken parts of the adjacent sides.

Originally the text must have had about five lines of Aramaic written on the bottom of the base. Only the last two lines and traces of the bottoms of a few letters of the line above remain.

---

[221] *BAiW*, col. 1582, *suxra*. [222] *Ibid.*, col. 1506, *raθa*.

[223] Cowley, *AP*, No. 16:9; Kraeling, *The Brooklyn Museum Aramaic Papyri*, Nos. 5:3, 10:3; Leander, *Laut- und Formenlehre des Ägyptisch-Aramäischen*, p. 8, Sec. 2f.

FIND SPOT

The northeastern corner (HG 40) of the large, square Room 41 of the Persepolis Treasury wherein the most precious royal tableware was stored.[224] It lay in a corner with fragments of royal tableware that had been shattered against the walls.[225]

DATE

Baga-pāta as treasurer indicates the reign of Artaxerxes I, whose fourteenth year was 451/50 B.C.

LINE 4

Above the line there is an added supplementary note, "who is in Arachosia." The use of that expression elsewhere shows that it should follow the title of the treasurer (Nos. 9:4, 43:6). It was apparently added to the completed text as something essential, to distinguish the special treasurer from those normally active at Persepolis.[226]

46. Mortar (PT5 824) Pl. 12

בסר]ך בירת[	1)	[In the ritual] of the fortress,
ליד] אריוחו[	2)	[beside] Āraya(t)-vahu
סגנא] רתבֿר / עבד[	3)	[the *segan*], 1 *Rtbr* used
הוֹן] עם אבשון זנה[	4)	this [mortar] with pestle
ליד] בֿגֿפת גֿנ[ז]ברא[	5)	[beside] Baga-pāta the treasurer.
אשכר שנת בֿ] [//] / [	6)	[*'škr* of year] 14(?).

DESCRIPTION

A fragment of a green chert mortar with a broken bowl (base dia. 7.2 cm., present max. height 8.4 cm.). A large piece of the upper right part of the base is broken away, damaging the beginnings of the lines.

Six lines of Aramaic are on the bottom of the base. The beginnings of the lines have been carried away by the loss of the right edge of the base. The final line is now so faint that it is almost illegible.

FIND SPOT

West of the center (HF 38) of the south wall of Room 38.

DATE

The officials mentioned indicate the reign of Artaxerxes I, but the actual date is difficult to read. Judging from the spacing of the single unit found in Cameron's copy and the extremely faint traces of strokes in the photograph, the date seems to be the fourteenth year (451/50 B.C.).

LINE 1

There is now no trace of the final *'aleph* of the determinate state expected on the word "fortress" at the end of the line, although there is room for it. The letter may have been omitted under the influence of Old Persian, which used no definite article,[227] or it may have simply faded away.

LINE 2

The spelling of the *segan*'s name without the final letter -*š* (as in No. 42:2) is but one form of the name as found in these texts (see No. 24:2).

---

[224] See pp. 3–4.   [225] See p. 3.   [226] See p. 29.   [227] See p. 67.

LINE 3

The name of the celebrant could be read as either *Dtbr* or *Rtbr* and the final letter could be *-d* as well, although that is less likely. The last element of the name is probably *-br*, which could be read as the familiar *-bara*, "bearer" or "bearing," from the root *bar*, which also means "lift up" and "esteem,"[228] or it could be *-bāri*, "borne by" or "rider of," as in the names Asa-bāri and Usa-bāri.[229]

The first element, if read *dt-* could indicate *dāta-*, "right," "law."[230] As *rt-* it could be either *rātā-*, "gift,"[231] or *raθa-*, "wagon," "chariot."[232]

It is unlikely that the name would be Dāta-bara, "lawyer,"[233] but the same spelling could mean "He who esteems the right." As *Rtbr* the name could signify Rātā-bara, "He who brings a gift," or Raθa-bāri, "Charioteer."

LINE 6

The line is almost invisible in the photograph. Cameron's copy shows the letters *-kr* of the first word to be faint and the *šn-* of the next word as clear. He also shows a single, clear unit stroke of the date figure.

47. Plate (PT5 73 + 724) Pl. 13

בפרכן בי[ר]ת[א ליד	1)	In the (haoma-)crushing ceremony of the fortress, beside
אריחו סגנ[א] ב[יש[א]ז[א]	2)	Āraya(t)-vahu the *segan*, By*š*²*z*²,
פלג עבד סח[ר]א ר[ע]ין בג]	3)	a myriarch, used (this) plate, [a desire for good fortune(?)]
ליד בגפת גנזבר[א זי בה]רחותי	4)	beside Baga-pāta the treasurer who is in Arachosia (and)
קדם ארתמך אפ[גנ]זברא	5)	before Artamaka the sub-treasurer.
אשכר שנת ⟶ iii //	6)	²*škr* of year 15.

DESCRIPTION

Part of a green chert plate, consisting of the base and small pieces of the adjacent sides (base dia. 7.5 cm.). It is formed of two parts, each approximately half of the base. The fragment of the right side (PT5 73) and that of the left (PT5 724) join to form the complete base.[234]

Six lines of Aramaic were written on the bottom of the base. The beginnings of the lines (on PT5 73) are written in rather thick, clear, well-preserved letters while the ends of the lines (on PT5 724) are faded and rather indistinct.

FIND SPOT

Both fragments were found together in the south-central part (HF 39) of Room 38.

---

[228] *BAiW*, cols. 933 f.; Kent, *Old Persian*, p. 200, *bar-* and *bara*.

[229] Kent, *Old Persian*, p. 200*b*, *bara-*; Eilers, in *Abhandlungen für die Kunde des Morgenlandes* XXV, No. 5, p. 94, n. 2.

[230] *BAiW*, col. 726, *dāta;* Kent, *Old Persian*, p. 189*a*.

[231] *BAiW*, cols. 1519–20, *rātā*, "Gabe," "Geschenk."

[232] *Ibid.*, col. 1506, *raθa;* Kent, *Old Persian*, p. 205*b*.

[233] Eilers, in *Abhandlungen für die Kunde des Morgenlandes* XXV, No. 5, p. 5, n. 3, notes the title *lúda-ta-bar-ra/ri* in cuneiform texts.

[234] Schmidt, *Persepolis* II 55, Pl. 23:5 and chart.

DATE

The officers mentioned were active during the reign of Artaxerxes I. Cameron says of the date figure, "Probably 15, but it could be less." The space beyond the figure 10 leaves room for one of the usual groups of three unit strokes, which are clearly visible. The fifteenth year of Artaxerxes I was 450/49 B.C.

LINE 2

The spelling of the *segan's* name, *ʾryḥw*, which is unique, is probably an error for the *ʾrywḥw* found elsewhere (for example, No. 46:2).

The name of the celebrant is extremely faint and uncertain. It certainly begins with the letter *b*, as Cameron read it. It is faint but relatively clear in the photograph. It seems to be followed by a *y* and a difficult sign which most resembles a *š*. The next letter is an angular one that could be either *g* or *ḥ* but is probably an *ʾaleph*. The vertical stroke after it must be a *z*. The smudged sign at the end of the line could possibly be another *ʾaleph* or the unit stroke sometimes found after celebrants' names.

Such a collocation of consonants, *byšʾzʾ* suggests the Late Avestan *baēšaza*, "medicine," "healing"[235] and, as *byšʾz 1, 1 bišaz*, "physician."[236] As in No. 17:3 and elsewhere, the celebrant is called a *plg*, a divisional commander (myriarch) of 10,000 men.

LINE 3

After the verb *ʿbd* one expects the name of the vessel as the object of the verb. The first two letters, *sḥ*- are clear and the *r* is split by the fracture that divides the base. The remainder of the word, on the other fragment that holds the rest of the line, is very faint and uncertain.

The substance of the remainder of the line should be descriptive of the vessel or concerned with the action of the verb. The space available and the traces of letters that remain suggest the reading *rʿyn bg*, which is certified by its occurrence on another plate (No. 52:3–4).

The use of the letter *ʿaiyn* in the word *rʿyn* indicates that the word is Semitic. Suggested at once is the word *raʿyôn*, which is found in both Aramaic and Hebrew texts. The root from which it is formed (Arabic رضى, Aramaic רעה, Hebrew רצה) signifies "to take pleasure in (something)" and "to desire." From the contexts in which *raʿyôn* is found, it is clear that its meaning involves "striving" or "longing" (Eccles. 1:17, 2:22, 4:16) and "desire" (Dan. 2:29–30, 4:16, 5:6 and 10) as well as "ambition" and "greed."[237] It is related to the Biblical *rē(a)ʿ*, "purpose," "aim" (Ps. 139:2, 17). Professor J. Harmatta indicates that in Sogdian writing the form *rʿyn* occurs as an Aramaic logogram for the Persian word *kāma*, "desire."

The word *bg*, associated with the word *rʿyn*, is apparently the Persian *baga*, which often means "god" but can also signify "lot," "fortunate lot," or even "good fortune."[238]

But what is the significance of the *rʿyn bg* and how should it be read? From its position and the fact that it occurs only on plates, one would expect that it would refer to the vessel, but the two words form a context inappropriate as a characteristic of a plate. It might be read as "a desire of god" indicating that the gift had divine approval.

It seems preferable, however, to regard it as a parenthetic comment indicating the purpose of the military officer in participating in the haoma rite. Like the Biblical *raʿyôn rû(a)ḥ*, "a striving after wind" (Eccles. 1:17), this *rʿyn bg* is "a striving after good fortune" or "a desire for good fortune." Thus, the general claims to have sought good fortune through participation in the haoma ceremony and the presentation of the vessel as a token of his experience.[239]

---

[235] *BAiW*, col. 914, *baēšaza*.

[236] *Ibid.*, col. 967, *bišaz* (Aryan **bhišaž*, "physician").

[237] Jastrow, *Dictionary* II 1487, רַעְיוֹן, רַעְיָנָא.

[238] Kent, *Old Persian*, p. 199a, *baga*; *BAiW*, col. 921, *baga*, "Herr," "Gott," "Anteil," "Los," "günstiges Los," "Glück."

[239] See p. 50.

LINE 5

Although the first letter of the name of the sub-treasurer is obscure, it is probably an ʾ*aleph* for the name Arta-. The rest of the name is quite clear. It is probably an Arta name with the affix of abbreviation (-*aka*) added to the initial letter of the second element of the full name. Thus, Artamaka could represent such a name as Arta-Mithra, just as Sisimakes abbreviates Sisimithres[240] and Sauromaces does Sauromates.[241] Eilers proposes, as a possible alternative, Artamaka, from Arta- and *ama*, "strength," with the affix -*ka*.

48. Plate (PT5 381 + 448 + 453) T (115); Pl. 13

בפרכן ב׳ירתא	1)	In the (haoma-)crushing ceremony of the fortress,
ליד אריוהש	2)	beside Āraya(t)-vahuš
[ס]גנא בהיין	3)	the *segan*, *Bhyyn*,
פלג עבד סחר	4)	a myriarch, used
זנה חזיד בו .[	5)	this . . . plate
ליד בגפת ג[נ]זברא	6)	beside Baga-pāta the treasurer
זי בהרחותי [א]שכ[ר]	7)	who is in Arachosia. ʾ*škr* of
שנת ⟍ ‖‖ ‖‖ ‖‖	8)	year 19.

DESCRIPTION

A fragment of a green chert plate composed of three separate pieces. Fragment PT5 448 (max. length 7.4 cm.) forms the upper part of the base, the principal area preserved. Piece PT5 381 (7.3 cm. by 5.3 cm.) constitutes the lower left part of the base and PT5 453 (max. length 7.5 cm.) forms the lower right. The base diameter is about 8.1 cm. The stone is heavily marked with darker bands and lines that run almost at right angles to the Aramaic text on the base.

There were eight lines of Aramaic written on the bottom of the base in rather thick letters. Dark bands make the letters difficult to read where the density of the ink matches that of the bands in the photographs. Under such circumstances Cameron's copy is invaluable as a clue to the correct reading.

FIND SPOT

All three pieces were found in Room 38 of the Treasury. Fragments PT5 381 and 448 were just south of the center of the room (HF 38) and PT5 453 lay near its south wall (HF 49).

DATE

The officials indicate the reign of Artaxerxes I, whose nineteenth year was 446/45 B.C.

LINE 3

The name of the celebrant, clearly *Bhyyn*, is confirmed by No. 112:3, in which he also appears. Eilers has proposed *Bahayaina or *Bahya-yāna from *Baŋhya-yāna, "He whose favor lies in hemp."[242]

---

[240] Justi, *Iranisches Namenbuch*, p. 303*b*.

[241] *Ibid.*, p. 292*b*.

[242] *BAiW*, col. 925, *baŋha, baṅgha*. Compare Pouru-baŋha, "Possessing much hemp," as a name in the Zoroastrian community according to the Fravashi Yasht (Yasht 13:124). See Nyberg, *Religionen*, p. 188; Henning, *Zoroaster—Politician or Witch Doctor?* (London, 1951), pp. 31–34.

Line 5

After the demonstrative pronoun *znh* there is additional text, several words that apparently modify the word "plate." Cameron's copy shows *ḥzyd br.* . . . The photograph agrees with his reading of the first word which could be either *ḥzyd* or *ḥzyr*. Since Aramaean *ḥ* can also reproduce Iranian *h*, if the word is non-Semitic it might be read as *ḥzyd* or *ḥzyr* as well. The second and third consonants are difficult because they are written on a broad, dark band in the stone, but they seem to be *-zy-* on the vessel.

The second word definitely begins with the letter *b* which is followed by a sign that could be either *b*, *d*, or *w*. Another letter that follows is broken and illegible because of the fracture in the base and whatever may have followed that is completely lost.

49. Plate (PT5 766) Pl. 13

בפרכן בירת[א]	1)	In the (haoma-)crushing ceremony of the fortress,
ליד אריוחוש	2)	beside Āraya(t)-vahuš
סג[נא] ונתשך עבד	3)	the *segan*, *Vntšk* used
סחרא זנה אשכר	4)	this plate. *ʾškr* of
שׁנת כ	5)	year 20.

Description

A fragment of a green chert plate (base dia. *ca*. 8.5 cm., present height 3.7 cm.).

Five lines of rather heavy Aramaic letters are written on the bottom of the base. Some letters are badly faded and parts of others are entirely gone.

Find Spot

Near the center (HF 38) of Room 38.

Date

Āraya(t)-vahuš as *segan* indicates the reign of Artaxerxes I, whose twentieth year was 445/44 B.C.

Line 2

The spelling of the name of the *segan*, *ʾrywḥwš*, is an expansion of the form *ʾrywḥw* found in Nos. 42:2, 46:2 and others and a variant of the *ʾrywḥwš* found elsewhere.

Line 3

The spelling of the name of the celebrant is somewhat uncertain. Cameron copied the first two signs as a single letter and transliterated it as *h* for a name *Hnšk*. But the strokes are not joined and an *h* is improbable. The first letter is certainly *w*. The second and third are difficult. The second resembles the letter *p*, as made by some hands, but it is unlike that letter in the word *prkn* of line 1. It resembles the *n* of the word *šnt* in the last line. The third resembles a letter *n* but it is probably a *t* that has lost part of its staff. The correct reading is probably *Vntšk*.

The name, if Persian, is subject to several explanations. Eilers has proposed for the first element *vana(t)*[243] or *vanta*.[244] The second element, which could represent either *-šk* or *-čk*, is difficult. Perhaps it is *šā*, "cheerful," "happy," "joy," "pleasure,"[245] with the affix *-aka*.

---

[243] Derived from *van* meaning (1) "prevail," "overpower," (*BAiW*, cols. 1350–52); (2) "win" (*ibid.*, cols. 1352–53); or, more likely, (3) "desire," "wish" (*ibid.*, col. 1353); Kent, *Old Persian*, p. 206*b*, *van-*, "desire."

[244] Meaning "friend," "loved one" or "praise," "homage" (*BAiW*, col. 1355). Could this be the difficult first element of the Elamite name Mantaštura mentioned by Benveniste (*Titres et noms*, p. 86)?

[245] *BAiW*, col. 1707, *šā-*, "froh," "Freude," "Behagen."

50. Plate (PT5 167) Pl. 14

בפרכן בירתא ליד אר[יוהש סגנא]   1) In the (haoma-)crushing ceremony of the fortress, beside Āra[ya(t)-vahuš the *segan*,]

כקיז עבד סֿחרא זנֹה [ליד בגפת]   2) *Kqyz* used this plate [beside Baga-pāta]

גנזברא ק[ד]ֿם ששפֹר[ן] אפגנזברא]   3) the treasurer before Čiθra-far[nah the sub-
treasurer].

אשכר שנת ‏ ‏   4) ʾškr of year 21.

DESCRIPTION

A fragment of a green chert plate (base dia. 11.6 cm., present max. height 1 cm.). The bottom of the plate was polished before being inscribed. About a third of the upper part of the
base was once broken away and separated from the rest but is now rejoined.

Four lines of Aramaic are written on the bottom of the base. While the two parts of the
base were separated, what was written on one part almost disappeared, destroying the ends
of the first three lines. With knowledge of the expected formulae one can still discern traces
of many of the faded letters and restore the text with confidence.

FIND SPOT

Amid the fragments of many other such ritual vessels on the floor of Room 38, at the base
of the south wall (HF 48).

DATE

Only part of the *segan*'s name is preserved here, but it can be restored from No. 53 wherein
ʾrywhš and Ššprn are associated with Baga-pāta, the treasurer during the reign of Artaxerxes I,
whose twenty-first year was 444/43 B.C.

LINE 2

The name of the celebrant is clearly written and certain. But the combination *Kq*- is unusual and unexpected. In these texts *q* is rarely used to represent an Iranian phoneme. Its vocalization and meaning are still uncertain.

LINE 3

The name of the sub-treasurer, only partly preserved here, is fully attested in No. 53:5,
where it is completely and clearly written. Eilers identified it as *Čiθra-farnah.[246]

51. Plate (PT5 334) Pl. 14

בפרכן בירתא   1) In the (haoma-)crushing ceremony of the fortress,

ליד אר[יו]ח[ו] סגנא   2) beside Āraya(t)-vahu(š) the *segan*,

עב]ד סֿ[חרא] . . . . .   3) . . . used [this(?)] plate

זנה] ליד בגפת גנזבר[א]   4) beside Baga-pāta the treasurer

זי בהרח]ות[י אשכר]   5) [who is in Arach]os[ia. ʾškr of]

שנת ‏ ///   6) year 24.

DESCRIPTION

A fragment of a green chert plate (base dia. 18 cm., present height 3.4 cm. [reduced in illus-
tration]).

There are traces of six lines of Aramaic written on the bottom of the base. The inscribed
surface is cracked and the letters are often so faint that there are areas where nothing can
be read.

[246] Justi, *Iranisches Namenbuch*, p. 164, Čiθrafarnā. For the phonetic problem involved, see pp. 64–65.

FIND SPOT

In the sherd yard among fragments recovered from the area at the south wall (HF 39) of Room 38 of the Treasury.

DATE

Since Xerxes ruled only twenty years, this text with Baga-pāta as treasurer, comes from the reign of Artaxerxes I, whose twenty-fourth year was 441/40 B.C.

LINE 2

Only the beginning of the name of the *segan* is preserved but the restoration is probable. The space available seems to indicate the spelling *ᵓrywḥw*, as found elsewhere, for example, Nos. 42:2, 46:2 and others.

LINE 4

The spacing in Cameron's copy indicates a word before the first legible sign in the line. It is doubtless a modifier of the word "plate" in the line above, probably the demonstrative pronoun, as restored.

LINE 5

Cameron's copy shows only two letters in the line. While the traces might be read as *pt*, as part of a personal name with the element *-pāta*, such a name could only be that of the sub-treasurer and none is known with a name bearing such an element. Furthermore, there is scarcely room at the end of the line for the title "sub-treasurer" and for the expected word *ᵓškr*. Cameron's spacing favors the emendation made above, a supplement to the designation of the treasurer known from other examples in these texts.

52. Plate (PT5 664) T (9); Pl. 14

בפרכן בירתא ליד	1)	In the (haoma-)crushing ceremony of the fortress, beside
אריוהש סגנא אדוסת	2)	Āraya(t)-vahuš the *segan*, *ᵓdwst*,
אלף עבד סחר זנה [ר]עין	3)	a chiliarch, used this plate (in a desire for)
בג ליד בגפת גנזברא	4)	good fortune, beside Baga-pāta the treasurer
זי בהרהֹ[ו]תי אשכר	5)	who is in Arachosia. *ᵓškr* of
שנת ₂ /// /// ///	6)	year 29.

DESCRIPTION

A fragment of a green chert plate (base dia. 7.9 cm., present max. height 1.3 cm.) consisting principally of the base of the vessel.

Six lines of Aramaic are on the bottom of the base.

FIND SPOT

West of the center of the south wall (HF 48) of Room 38.

DATE

During the reign of Artaxerxes I. Although Cameron copied the figure of the date as 19, the photograph seems to show 29, which would be 436/35 B.C.

LINE 2

The same celebrant offered a pestle in 476/75 B.C. (No. 3:3) and still another pestle at a time that cannot be determined (No. 133).

Lines 3 and 4

Like *plg*, "myriarch" (cf. Nos. 17:3, 31:2, 32:3 and others), *ᵓlp* is a military title. The vocalization of the title in Persia is uncertain but the word is certainly related to the Aramaic *ᵓalaf*, "thousand." It may have been the same as the Biblical *ᵓallûf*.[247] It is clear from the title *ᵓlp plg* (No. 118:3) that the *ᵓlp* was subordinate to the *plg*, "myriarch." He was the officer over a thousand men, a major officer of the Persian army.[248] He corresponded to the Persian *hazarapat*,[249] the Greek chiliarch, and the *šar ᵓlp* of the Qumran community. Yadin has shown that the chiliarch was the commander of the army unit known as the *degel*.[250]

Here, as in No. 47:3, the words *rᵓyn bg* are a parenthetic remark indicating the purpose of the military officer in participating in the ceremony and offering the vessel.

Line 5

In the photograph and on the vessel the spelling of Arachosia seems to be *Hrḥwtg* rather than *Hrḥwty*, which would be unique in these texts. However, it is probably the remaining outline of an extraordinarily large delta-formed *y* from which most of the ink has disappeared.

53. Plate (PT5 810) T (49); Pl. 15

בפרכן בירתׄ[א]	1)	In the (haoma-)crushing ceremony of the fortress,
ליד אריוהש [סגנא]	2)	beside Āraya(t)-vahuš [the *segan*,]
ארתׄין עבד ס[חרא]	3)	Arta-yāna used this plate
זנֹה [ל[יד בנפת [גנזברא]	4)	beside Baga-pāta [the treasurer] (and)
קדם ששפרן אפ[גנזברא]	5)	before Čiθra-farnah the sub-[treasurer].
אׄשכר שנתׄ בׄ[. . . .]	6)	*ᵓškr* of year 20+.

Description

A fragment of a green chert plate (base dia. 6.3 cm.), consisting of little more than half of its base and portions of adjacent sides.

The beginnings of six lines of Aramaic are preserved on the bottom of the base.

Find Spot

West of the center (HF 38) of Room 38 of the Persepolis Treasury.

Date

The officials Āraya(t)-vahuš and Baga-pāta indicate a date during the reign of Artaxerxes I. The exact date is uncertain, but the year is at least 20. There is a trace of a sign for 20, but the base is broken immediately after it and no unit strokes remain. Since the same sub-treasurer is found in the year twenty-one (No. 50:3), it would seem that these texts might be from approximately the same date.

Line 3

For the name of the celebrant, *ᵓrtyn*, Eilers proposes reading either Artaina, as an hypocoristicon, or Arta-yāna, "He whose grace comes from Arta" or "Having the grace of Arta."[251]

[247] M. D. Cassuto and N. H. Torczyner, "*ᵓallûf*," *Encyclopaedia Miqraᵓîth* I (Jerusalem, 1950), cols. 332–33.

[248] Herodotus vii. 81.

[249] F. Justi, "Der Chiliarch des Dareios," *ZDMG* L (1896) 659–64; P. J. Junge, "Hazarapatiš," *Klio* XXXIII, 1/2 (1940) 13–38; J. Marquart, "Untersuchungen zur Geschichte von Eran," *Philologus* LV (1896) 228.

[250] Yadin, *Scroll*, col. iv, l. 2, pp. 49–52, 53 n. 1, 59, 156–57, 276.

[251] *BAiW*, cols. 1285–86; Avestan *-yāna*, "favor," "good will" (of God toward man); cf. Vasō-yāna, cited by Bartholomae (*ibid.*, col. 1384). Benveniste (*Titres et noms*, p. 84) mentions an Elamite name Irdaya/Irteya, which he equates with Avestan Ašaya- and the Vedic participle *r̥tā̆yán*.

54. Pestle (PT5 718*B*[252]) Teheran Museum 2322; Pl. 15

בסרוך	1)	In the ritual (of the fortress),
גית / מדזפרן	2)	1 *Gyt*, (beside) Mazda-farnah(?) (the *segan*),
אבשׁון ז[נה]	3)	(used) this(?) pestle
/	4)	(in year) 1.

Description

A large, complete, light green chert pestle (head dia. 4.8 cm., length 22.3 cm., max. shaft dia. 16.2 cm.). It is beautifully banded with somewhat diagonal bands and lines of darker color. The only damage is to the edge of the head.

Four extremely brief lines of Aramaic are written on the top of the head. Only the end of the third line was damaged by the breaking of the edge of the head. The writing was done rather hurriedly by an inexperienced hand. Some of the letters are faint and incomplete.

The brevity of the text here is unnecessary on a writing space so large. This unique text only hints at the expected formulae. Its terse expression, in single pregnant words, each of which represents a whole element in a complete, normal text, omits key words which must be supplied on the basis of familiarity with the pattern of the normal text.

Find Spot

Just west of the center (HF 38) of Room 38.

Date

Although the word "year" has been omitted in this overly abbreviated text, the single stroke of the last line is in the normal position of the date and therefore should be considered as such. It is unlikely that there were other unit strokes at the end of the preceding line, which is broken, since the figure would not be separated when all of the last line was available for it.

Since there is no dated text prior to the seventh year of Xerxes and all lower year dates are in the reign of Artaxerxes I, it is probable that this text is from the first year of Artaxerxes I (464/63 B.C.). If the *Mdzprn* of line 2 is the *segan Mzprn* of No. 21:2, the date would be confirmed, for *Mzprn* functioned as *segan* in the second year of Artaxerxes I.

Line 1

The spelling *srwk* instead of *srk* is unique and significant. It has its parallel in the Jewish War Scroll from Qumran wherein the usual *srk* was once written as *srwk* and then altered to *sdwr*.[253] Two witnesses to the spelling *srwk* thus suggest that the pronunciation was not "serekh," as Yadin supposes, but something with the vowel *o* or *u*.

The writing of *sdr* for *srwk/srk* may be instructive if, as seems likely, the words at Persepolis and Qumran are related. The Semitic root *sdr* has much in common with *srk*. It connotes order, both spatial and sequential, especially in such matters as the arrangement of cultic materials and the sequence of prayers and scriptural readings.[254]

Line 2

The first word might be read as *gytz*, but its spacing suggests that it is *gyt* followed by the unit stroke that sometimes follows the name of a celebrant. Possibly the name is hypocoristic,

---

[252] Two objects bear the same field number, PT5 718 (Nos. 22 and 54).

[253] Yadin, *Scroll*, p. 250, Fig. 19, Group F, No. 7.

[254] Jastrow, *Dictionary* II 958, "to arrange," "to order"; סֵדֶר, "arrangement," "order," "succession," and p. 959*a*, סִדְרָא, "order" or "section (of scripture)," "colonnade," "hall (of studies)."

involving the noun *gaēθā* (Persian *gaiθā*), "cattle," "property," "living being."[255] It is tempting to read the *-yt* of the name as *-yāta*, indicating "possession," "portion."[256]

Close scrutiny of the second word indicates that its first letter is *m-* with its left stroke partly gone. It is followed by a sign *d* or *r* and a vertical stroke to be read as *z*. The letters crowded behind it, with no indication of word separation, are not the expected verb *ᶜbd* but the familiar name element *-prn*, *-farnah*. The word is thus *Mdzprn*, evidently the proper name of an official. It is probably the name Mazda-farnah with the metathesis of the *z* and *d*, a phonetic phenomenon also found elsewhere in these texts.[257]

In their present position it would appear that *Gyt* would be the name of the *segan* and *Mdzprn* that of the celebrant, since that is the usual order of occurrence in the normal formula. But the unit stroke marks *Gyt* as the celebrant and *Mdzprn* must be the official. In the normal formula only the treasurers are mentioned after the celebrant, but the name *Mdzprn* resembles the name of the *segan Mzprn*, which also is a form of Mazda-farnah. Furthermore, the *segan* is seldom omitted from the text when officers are mentioned, even when abbreviation means the dropping of the names of the treasurers.[258] It is likely, therefore, that *Mdzprn* represents the *segan* in this text.

LINE 3

The essential verb *ᶜbd*, "used," is omitted in this text, as in No. 137, and it must be supplied to make sense.

The word "pestle," normally spelled *ᵓbšwn*, seems to be *ᵓbšyn* here. But what looks like the letter *y* in the word might be the expected *w* that has lost its vertical stroke. It is therefore transcribed here as *ᵓbšwn*, in normal fashion.

55. Mortar (PT5 730) T (154); Pl. 15

[ליד] בירת[א .... ב	1)	[In the . . . of] the [fortress, beside]
.... סגנא פר[.	2)	. . . the *segan*, Pr . . .
עבד ה[ון [מ]דם זנה .....]	3)	[a . . . used] this medium-sized mortar.
[אשכר] שׁ[נ]ת //	4)	[*ᵓškr* of] year 2.

DESCRIPTION

A fragment of a green chert mortar (base dia. 12.7 cm., present max. height 2.7 cm.), consisting of almost half of its base.

Parts of four lines of Aramaic are written on the bottom of the base. Most of the ends of lines are preserved but the text is faint and some letters are gone entirely.

FIND SPOT

Found on the floor near the south wall (HF 48) of Room 38.

DATE

No officials are named to confirm the dating, but since there are apparently no dated texts in the second year of Xerxes, this text is probably from the second year of Artaxerxes I (463/62 B.C.).

56. Mortar (PT5 457) T (73); Pl. 15

	1)	
[..... סגנא] . . . מ̇א /	2)	[. . . the *segan*], 1 . . . *mᵓ*
[עבד הון] מדם / קדם	3)	[used] a medium-sized [mortar] before
[..... אפגנזברא] אשכר שנת ///	4)	[. . . the sub-treasurer]. *ᵓškr* of year 3.

[255] Kent, *Old Persian*, p. 182*b*; *BAiW*, cols. 476 ff., *gaēθa*.
[256] *BAiW*, col. 1283.

[257] See p. 65.
[258] See p. 25.

DESCRIPTION

A fragment of a green chert mortar (base dia. 12.8 cm., present max. height 3.3 cm. [slightly reduced in illustration]), consisting of only a little more than a quarter of the base. Horizontal banding in the stone is quite prominent.

Originally there must have been four lines of Aramaic on the bottom of the base, but the first line is gone completely. The line of breakage runs diagonally across the Aramaic text, leaving only the ends of the last three lines. Many of the letters are very faded but still legible.

FIND SPOT

Near the center of the south wall (HF 49) of Room 38 of the Persepolis Treasury.

DATE

The year date is certainly three and since the earliest dated text of Xerxes' reign does not occur until his seventh year, this fragment is probably from the third year of Artaxerxes I (462/61 B.C.).

57. Pestle (PT5 763) T (60); Pl. 15

בפרכן	1)	In the (haoma-)crushing ceremony,
שיקמנת	2)	*Šyqmnt*
עָבֹד [אָ]בשון	3)	used a medium-sized
מדם שֹנֹת	4)	pestle. Year
III	5)	3.

DESCRIPTION

A fragment of a green chert pestle (head dia. 3.3 cm., present max. length 5.2 cm.).

Five lines of Aramaic are preserved on the top of the head.

FIND SPOT

Near the center of the south wall (HF 38) of Room 38.

DATE

The year date is certain, but there are no officials to aid in checking the reign. It is probably from the third year of Artaxerxes I (462/61 B.C.).

LINE 2

The word, immediately preceding the verb ʿbd, is certainly the name of the celebrant. It is similar to, if not identical with, the name of the celebrant in No. 67.

LINES 4 AND 5

The usual ʾškr is omitted here.

58. Pestle (PT5 168) T (5); Pl. 16

בסרך בירתֹא	1)	In the ritual of the fortress,
ליד ארתמֹ.[.]	2)	beside Arta-m . . .
סגנא אֹתרב]. . . .]	3)	the *segan*, Ātar-b . . .
עבד אֹבשֹ]ון זנֹה]	4)	used this pestle.
אֹשֹכֹר	5)	ʾškr of
[שֹנֹת *i iii*]	6)	[year 4].

DESCRIPTION

A fragment of a polished green chert pestle (head dia. 4.1 cm., present max. length 9.6 cm.).

Six lines of Aramaic are written on top of the pestle head in squat, thick letters that are badly faded, especially below line 3 and at the ends of the second and third lines; the last two lines are almost illegible.

FIND SPOT

At the base of the south wall (HF 48) of Room 38.

DATE

Cameron's copy shows faint traces of four strokes, but there may have been more. Such marks are not now discernible in the photograph or on the object.

The incomplete name of the *segan* is valueless as a clue to the reign because it is unique. If Cameron's figure is correct, the text is probably from the fourth year of Artaxerxes I (461/60 B.C.).

LINE 2

The end of the *segan*'s name has been destroyed. It has Arta- for its first element, and the *m* that follows it indicates that the second element began with that letter, like that of the sub-treasurer Artamaka (No. 47:5). Only here is such a name found for a *segan*, who must have been a subordinate.

LINE 3

The deep chip at the end of the line has also mutilated the end of the name of the celebrant. The first element is doubtless *ātar-*, "fire," which is often used for the holy fire of the Persian cult.[259] The use of the word with a second element that begins with a *b* suggests such a name as Ātar-barzana (No. 127:1).

59. Pestle (PT5 696) T (80); Pl. 16

[בפּ[רכ]ן]	1)	In the (haoma-)crushing ceremony of
[בירת[א]	2)	the [fortress],
[. . . . .] עֹ[בד	3)	. . . used
[אבשו[ן זנה	4)	this [pestle.]
[אשׁ[כר	5)	ʾškr of
[ש[נת *iii* /	6)	year 4(?).

DESCRIPTION

A small, green chert pestle (head dia. 3.1 cm., present length 8.6 cm.). Chipping has badly damaged the head of the implement.

Parts of six lines of Aramaic are on the top of the pestle head. The last line, for lack of space, was written on the edge of the pestle top.

FIND SPOT

Found on the floor near the center of the south wall (HF 48) of Room 38 of the Treasury.

DATE

The date, written on the edge of the pestle head, is uncertain. The figure appears to be four and probably is, but it is also possible that the first stroke, which is somewhat curved, should be read as the sign for ten, making the date thirteen.

The lack of officials makes it impossible to determine the reign during which it was written.

[259] *BAiW*, cols. 312 ff., *ātar-*; Kent, *Old Persian*, p. 166a.

60. Pestle (PT5 826) T (113); Pl. 16

בסרך	1)	In the ritual of
בירתא כש	2)	the fortress, Kōša
עבד אבשון	3)	used this pestle.
זנה אשכר	4)	ᵓškr of
שנת iii ii	5)	year 5.

DESCRIPTION

A fragment of a small green chert pestle (head dia. 2.7 cm., present max. length 4.7 cm.). Five brief lines of Aramaic are written on the top of the head.

FIND SPOT

Recovered in the sherd pile, among fragments found near the center (HG 38) of Room 38 of the Treasury.

DATE

Cameron at first read four strokes but later raised the number to six. Only four are clear in the photograph, but it is likely that the tip of a fifth stroke is present. There is no trace now of a sixth.

Lack of officers in the text makes it impossible to determine whether it was written during the reign of Xerxes or Artaxerxes I. It was probably written during the reign of the latter, whose fifth year was 460/59 B.C.

LINE 2

Cameron's earliest copy shows the letters *kš* for the name of the celebrant. He conservatively transcribed it as *d/r/k+š*. But his later copy has *rš*, which he rendered as *d/rš*. The signs, however, most closely resemble Cameron's original *kš*. One might think of such a name as Kōša, the Late Avestan Kaoša, from a Sanskrit form Košá.²⁶⁰

60. Pestle (PT5 466) T (19); Pl. 16

בסרך בירת[א]	1)	In the ritual of the fortress,
דריפֿרן עבֿד [אבשון]	2)	Dāraya-farnah used
זנה אשכֿ שנת	3)	this pestle. ᵓškr of year
iii ///	4)	6.

DESCRIPTION

A fragment of a green chert pestle (head dia. 6.5 cm., present max. length 10.1 cm.). Part of the side of the head is broken away, damaging the ends of the first two lines.

Four lines of Aramaic are written on the top of the head.

FIND SPOT

Just east of the center (HG 20) of Room 38.

DATE

Although only the tips of the first three unit strokes are preserved, the figure six seems certain. Lacking the name of an official, it is impossible to ascertain exactly when the text was written. The sixth year of Xerxes was 480/79 B.C. and that of Artaxerxes I was 459/58 B.C.

²⁶⁰ Justi, *Iranisches Namenbuch*, p. 155*b*, Kaoscha (Sanskrit Košá); cf. *BAiW*, col. 432, *kaoša-*.

LINE 2

Cameron copied and transliterated the name of the celebrant as *Drypbn*, but it is probably *Dryprn*. The first element of the name, *Dry*, is probably *Dāraya-*, "holder," "possessor of," as in the name of Darius (Dāraya-vauš).[261]

If the vertical stroke at the end of the name were a unit stroke, one might conjecture that the celebrant's name was *Drypr*. But there is no space between the letter *r* and the vertical stroke at the end, which must thus be recognized not as a unit stroke but as a remnant of the letter *-n*. The second element must be the familiar *-prn*, *farnah*, "glory," "splendor," "majesty."[262]

62. Pestle (PT5 465) Pl. 16

בפרכן בירת[א]	1)	In the (haoma-)crushing ceremony of the fortress,
עבד	2)	. . . used
אבשון זי אשכ[ר]	3)	a pestle of *ʾškr*.
שנת *III III*	4)	Year 6.

DESCRIPTION

A fragment of a green chert pestle (head dia. 3.8 cm., present max. length 8.1 cm.).

Four lines of Aramaic are written on the top of the head. In the second line, which is written on a dark, horizontal band in the stone, only the last word is legible.

FIND SPOT

West of the center (HF 38) of Room 38.

DATE

The year is certainly six but there is no official to give a clue to the reign. It could come from the time of Xerxes (480/79 B.C.), but it is more likely to be from the time of Artaxerxes I (458/57 B.C.).

LINE 3

This line, as copied by Cameron, gives the only clue to the meaning of the word *ʾškr*. Elsewhere its syntactical relationship to adjacent words is not so apparent.[263]

Here, as Cameron copied the text, the line is clear and full, with scarcely a space left between the words. The reading here seems parallel to that in another text (No. 29:4) on a pestle which has *ʾbšwn zy bʾt*, "pestle of wine." Here we must read "pestle of *ʾškr*."

Such usage makes it unlikely that *ʾškr* is to be read as the Persian *aškār*, "clear," "evident," "manifest"[264] and makes it more likely that *ʾškr* means "intoxicant."[265] Presumably the text here means "the pestle of the making (or 'maker'?) of the intoxicant." Although the word is possibly related to Aramaic *šᵉkar* (Akkadian *šikaru*), a meaning "ceremony of the intoxicant (haoma)" or "the making of the intoxicant (haoma)" would read more smoothly here and elsewhere in these texts.

---

[261] Kent, *Old Persian*, p. 54, Sec. 162.

[262] *BAiW*, cols. 1870–73, *xᵛarᵊnah*; Justi, *Iranisches Namenbuch*, p. 493, *-farnah*, "Glück," "Majestät"; Kent, *Old Persian*, p. 208a, under Viⁿdafarnah. Benveniste (*Titres et noms*, p. 82) sees the Persian *Dāraya-farnah in the Elamite name Dariparna.

[263] See pp. 53–55.

[264] F. Steingass, *A Comprehensive Persian-English Dictionary* (London, 1892), p. 65, اشکار, *āškār*.

[265] See p. 54.

63. Pestle (PT5 121) T (153); Pl. 16

בסרך בירתא֯	1)	In the ritual of the fortress,
פף פלנ עבד	2)	Pāpā, a myriarch, used
אבשון זנה	3)	this pestle.
א֯שכר שנת	4)	ʾškr of year
׀ ׀׀׀ [׀׀׀]	5)	7(?).

DESCRIPTION

A fragment of a small green chert pestle (head dia. 3.1 cm., present max. length 2.8 cm.). A small bit of the edge of the head is broken away, damaging the beginning of the last line.

Five lines of Aramaic are clearly written in rather thin, elongated, graceful letters, on the top of the pestle head. Only the beginning of the last line, where the head is broken, is lost.

FIND SPOT

Near the center (HG 20) of Room 38 of the Treasury.

DATE

Only the last four unit strokes remain, but there certainly was something before them, where the pestle head is now broken away. There is room for a sign for 10 or 20, but there is also room for at least another set of three unit strokes, for a figure 7. Thus, the year is probably seven, but it could possibly be as much as fourteen or even twenty-four.

The reign during which this abbreviated text was written cannot be determined. The seventh year of Xerxes was 479/78 B.C. and that of Artaxerxes I was 458/57 B.C.

LINE 2

The name of the celebrant, *Pp*, is perhaps Pāp or Pāpā, like the modern Persian Bābā.[266]

64. Pestle (PT5 765) Pl. 16

בסרך בירתא	1)	In the ritual of the fortress,
ליד מ֯ת֯[ר]֯ך סגנא	2)	beside Mithraka the *segan*,
ר֯ורת ׀ עבד אבשון	3)	1 Rao-raθa used
רב זנה קדם מזד֯ד֯[ת]	4)	this large pestle before Mazda-dāta
אפגנזברא א֯[שכר]	5)	the sub-treasurer. *škr* of
שנת ׀[.	6)	year 1+.

DESCRIPTION

A pestle head of green chert (head dia. 6.5 cm., present max. length .2 cm.). Part of the lower left side of the head is broken away.

Six lines of Aramaic are on the top of the pestle head. The last word in the fifth line and most of the figure in the sixth were carried away with the missing part of the head.

FIND SPOT

Near the center (HF 38) of Room 38 of the Persepolis Treasury.

DATE

Mithraka and Mazda-dāta served during the reign of Artaxerxes I. Since the figure is lost in the date line, all that can be determined is that the text comes from some time during the first nine years (464–455 B.C.) of that reign, since those years are always designated by unit strokes.

---

[266] Justi, *Iranisches Namenbuch*, p. 241, *Pāp, Pāpā*; J. P. Margoliouth, *Supplement to the Thesaurus of R. Payne-Smith S.T.P.* (Oxford, 1927), p. 271a, ܦܦ. Benveniste (*Titres et noms*, p. 17) finds *Pāp-* as the first element in the Middle-Iranian name Pāpakān. The element is attested both in Pahlavi and in Armenian.

LINE 2

The name of the *segan* Mithraka (see Nos. 17:2 and 18:1) is rather faint, but clear traces of the first and last letters are observable in the photograph and Cameron's copy records the others.

LINE 3

The celebrant's name is written clearly, but because of the ambiguity of the script, its spelling could be either *Rwrt*, *Rwdt*, *Dwdt*, or *Dwrt*. Eilers properly recognizes that there are many possibilities for such a collocation of consonants, and he proposes, as a possible reading, Dava(t)-raθa, "Having a speedy chariot."[267] A name of similar meaning is achieved if the reading is assumed to be *Rwrt*, since there is an adjective rao-raθa, "driving a quick chariot."[268]

65. Pestle (PT5 695) T (23); Pl. 16

בסרך בירתא	1)	In the ritual of the fortress,
אמדת סגנא	2)	(beside) Ama-dāta the *segan*,
ארתׄון עבד	3)	Arta-vāna used
[א[בׄשון זנ]ה]	4)	this pestle
בשנת //[.	5)	in year 2+.

DESCRIPTION

A fragment of a green chert pestle (head dia. 3.9 cm., present max. length 7.6 cm.). An extensive chip and some marginal breakage damage the inscribed surface of the head.

Five lines of Aramaic are written on its head. The fourth line is broken and quite faint at its end and the figure in the fifth line is broken away after the second unit stroke.

FIND SPOT

West of the center of the south wall (HF 48) of Room 38 of the Treasury.

DATE

Cameron copied two unit strokes in the figure and that seems probable from the photograph, but there may have been more in the area now chipped away.

Since Ama-dāta was *segan* in the seventh year of Xerxes (No. 1) and in his sixteenth and seventeenth years (Nos. 11 and 12) as well as in the tenth year of Artaxerxes I (No. 39), the reign during which it was written cannot be determined. All that is certain is that the text is dated at some time during the first nine years of the reign.

LINE 2

The expected preposition *lyd*, "beside," has been omitted before the name of the *segan*, perhaps because of lack of space.

LINE 3

For the celebrant *ᵓrtwn* one might compare the Artūnēs cited by Justi,[269] but Eilers proposes reading Arta-wān, or Arta-vāna.[270]

LINE 4

There is scarcely room for the usual *ᵓškr* before the date.

[267] Apparently from *ᵊdav-* (*BAiW*, col. 688, "fortführen," "fortreissen") and *¹raθa* (*ibid.*, col. 1506, "Wagen").

[268] *Ibid.*, col. 1496 (Late Avestan rao-raθa).

[269] Justi, *Iranisches Namenbuch*, p. 40*b*. Benveniste (*Titres et noms*, p. 107) contends that the Armenian Artawan represents Old Persian Artabānu. The name Arta-bânu is found written as *ᵓrtbnw* in two papyri of the fifth century B.C. (Cowley, *AP*, Nos. 6:3 and 51:6).

[270] H. Hubschmann (*Persische Studien* [Strassburg, 1895], p. 195) posits an Old Iranian Artaṿan. *BAiW*, col. 253, ašǎvan, n. 12, and cols. 246 ff., Avestan ašǎ-van.

66. Pestle (PT5 699) Pl. 16

בסרך	1)	In the ritual
שיר עבד	2)	*Šyr* used
אבשון /	3)	a pestle.
אשכר	4)	*ʾškr* of
שנת ←	5)	year 10.

Description

A fragment of a small green chert pestle (head dia. 3.2 cm., present max. length 5 cm.). The head is completely preserved.

Five lines of Aramaic, in relatively large letters, are written on the top of the pestle head.

Find Spot

On the floor, east of the inverted plinth in the north-center (HF 28) of Room 38 of the Persepolis Treasury.

Date

The date is the tenth year, but the reign cannot be determined without a reference to known officials. It could come from the reign either of Xerxes (476/75 B.C.) or of Artaxerxes I (455/54 B.C.).

Line 2

The name of the celebrant, *Šyr*, can be read *Šyr*, *Čyr*, *Šyd*, or *Čyd*. The name could be an abbreviation of a name with the element *šīrā*, "sweet,"[271] but the first element of such a name as Siromitrēs, mentioned by Herodotus (vii. 68, 79), might also be considered.[272]

67. Pestle (PT5 825) T (97); Pl. 17

בסרך	1)	In the ritual,
שיקמנת	2)	*Šyqmnt* (used this).
אש]כר[	3)	*ʾškr* of
שנת ←	4)	year 10.

Description

A fragment of a green chert pestle (head dia. 3.5 cm., present max. length 2.2 cm.). It consists principally of the inscribed head of the object.

Four words of Aramaic in four lines are written on its top in very faint letters.

Find Spot

Recovered from a sherd pile among materials found near the center (HF 38) of Room 38.

Date

The year is certainly ten, but it is impossible to determine whether it is from the reign of Xerxes (476/75 B.C.) or Artaxerxes I (455/54 B.C.).

Line 2

The word in this line, which must be the name of the celebrant, closely resembles the one in No. 57:2.

Line 3

The text is unusual for its omissions: the word "fortress" in the first line and a reference to the object itself and the fact of its use. The retention of *ʾškr* in the face of such abbreviation is indicative of the importance of the word in the mind of the writer.

[271] Justi, *Iranisches Namenbuch*, p. 511; cf. such names as Σιράκης, Širārīān, and Širā-šamuk (*ibid.*, p. 302b).

[272] *Ibid.*, p. 303a, Σιρομίτρης.

68. Pestle (PT5 434) Pl. 17

בסרך	1)	In the ritual,
פור[ב]ת עב[ו]ד	2)	Pouru-bātu used
אבשון ז[נה]	3)	this pestle.
אשכר שנ[ת]	4)	ᵓškr of year
↱	5)	10(+?).

DESCRIPTION

A fragment of a green chert pestle with a complete head (head dia. 4 cm., present max. length 9.2 cm.).

Five lines of Aramaic are written in relatively large, thick letters on the top of the pestle head. The letters are quite faint, especially toward the ends of the lines, where some of the letters are entirely gone.

FIND SPOT

Found in the northwestern part of Room 38, near the northern wall and between the entrances to subsidiary Rooms 45 and 46 (HF 27).

DATE

Both Cameron's copy and the photograph clearly show the figure 10. It is possible, but unlikely, that there were additional unit strokes in the area to the left of the visible figure. There is no clue to whether the text was written during the reign of Xerxes or that of Artaxerxes I.

LINE 2

For the name *Pwrbt* Eilers has suggested reading Pouru-bātu, "He who has much wine."[273]

69. Pestle (PT5 754) T (44); Pl. 17

גוברו	1)	Gaubaruva
עבד [אבשון]	2)	used this [pestle].
זנה א[ש̇כר]	3)	ᵓ[škr]
בשנ[ת] ⇀	4)	in year 10.

DESCRIPTION

A fragment of a small green chert pestle (dia. of head 3.6 cm., present max. length 8.5 cm.).

Four lines of Aramaic are on the top of the pestle head, written in large, thick letters. A dark band in the stone, which runs through the second line, makes the reading difficult. The text is now very faint, especially at the ends of the third and fourth lines, which are almost illegible.

FIND SPOT

West of the center (HF 38) of Room 38 of the Treasury.

DATE

Cameron copied a figure 10, which can be seen in the photograph as a rather horizontal blur. It is doubtful whether there were additional unit strokes. There is no clue to the reign to which this text should be attributed. It could be the tenth year of Xerxes (476/75 B.C.) or of Artaxerxes I (455/54 B.C.).

[273] *BAiW*, col. 899, *pouru-*; Kent, *Old Persian*, p. 196a, *paru-*; cf. such a name as Pouru-baŋha (Justi, *Iranisches Namenbuch*, p. 254b). For *bātu*, "wine," see No. 29:4 and the name *bᵓtdt/bᵓtrt* (No. 110:3).

LINE 1

The name of the celebrant, *Gwbrw*, Gaubaruva, "Possessor of cattle"[274] (Babylonian *gu-ba-ru-ᵓ*; Greek Γωβρύας), is found in the Behistun Inscription as that of an ally of Darius I against Gaumata the Magian.[275]

LINE 2

The dark, horizontal band that runs through this line obscures the reading. The text can be restored with certainty by positing what the context demands. After the name of the celebrant the verb *ᶜbd* is expected. Both Cameron's copy and the photograph support such a reading. Before the word *znh*, "this," in the next line, we expect the name of the object, *ᵓbšwn*, "pestle," which must have stood at the end of the second line.

70. Pestle (PT5 421) T (36); Pl. 17

ב]פֿרכן בירתא[	1)	In [the (haoma-)crushing ceremony of the fortress],
ש]אֿ . . . . . . עבד[	2)	[Š̌ᵓ . . . used]
א]בשון זנה[	3)	this pestle.
אשכר שנת ⇁ //	4)	*ᵓškr* of year 12.

DESCRIPTION

A fragment of a green chert pestle (head dia. 3.5 cm., present max. length 10.1 cm.). A large spall damages about a third of the pestle head.

Traces of four lines of Aramaic are on the top of the head. Most of the first two lines have been lost by the destruction of the inscribed surface.

FIND SPOT

North of the center (HF 29) of Room 38 of the Persepolis Treasury.

DATE

The year date is certainly twelve, but the reign is uncertain. It could be the twelfth year of either Xerxes (474/73 B.C.) or Artaxerxes I (453/52 B.C.).

LINE 2

Because of the damage to the pestle head, the name of the celebrant is incomplete. Cameron copied two letters, of which the first is clearly *š*. The second he copied and transcribed as *ṣ*. But the letter *ṣ* is used nowhere else in the Aramaic transcription of Iranian names or words at Persepolis.[276] Although the traces on the pestle do resemble the head of an Aramaic *ṣ*, the staff is not long enough to represent that letter. It is better to regard the sign as being the right half of a letter *ᵓaleph*.

71. Pestle (PT5 675) T (74); Pl. 17

בסרך	1)	In the ritual of
ב]יֿ]רתֿאֿ[	2)	[the fortress],
בֿ]גֿפֿרֿן[	3)	[Baga-farnah(?)]
עב]דֿ א]בש]ון[	4)	[used (this) pestle.]
שֿ]נת ⇁ ///	5)	Year 13.

[274] Justi, *Iranisches Namenbuch*, p. 111, Gaubaruwa; Kent, *Old Persian*, p. 182*b*, Gaubaruva. Benveniste (*Titres et noms*, p. 85) finds this name in the Elamite Kambarma.

[275] Behistun Inscription, col. iv, l. 84, col. v, ll. 7, 9, 11.

[276] Telegdi (in *J A* CCXXVI 204) indicates that the Aramaic letter *ṣ* was not used in the Talmud for the transcription of Pahlavīk words but that it was used otherwise to render the phonemes *ǰ* and *ž* in Iranian words. There is no example of Aramaic *ṣ* elsewhere in these texts.

Description

A fragment of a green chert pestle (head dia. 3.7 cm., present max. height 7.5 cm.).

Traces of five lines of Aramaic are on the head but only the first and last lines can be read with certainty because of the faintness of the letters.

Find Spot

Near the center (HF 39) of Room 38 of the Treasury.

Date

The figure is certain, but the reign cannot be determined. It could be the thirteenth year of either Xerxes (473/72 B.C.) or Artaxerxes I (452/51 B.C.).

72. Plate (PT5 392 + 383) Pl. 17

ב]סֹרֹךְ בִּירתא ליד	1)	[In] the ritual of the fortress, beside
מתר]ךְ סֹגֹֹא מנדפרן	2)	[Mithra]ka the *segan*, Manda(t)-farnah,
[. . .]עֹ]בד סחר זנה	3)	[a . . .], used this plate
זי גלל קֹ]דם מזדדת	4)	[of stone be]fore Mazda-dāta
אפגנזבר]א אשכר	5)	the [sub-treasurer]. ʾškr of
שנת [. . .] /	6)	year . . . +1(?).

Description

A fragment of a green chert plate (base dia. *ca.* 7 cm.) consisting of little more than half of its base and portions of its adjacent sides. It is formed of two fragments, the upper part of the base (PT5 383), which itself consists of two pieces (max. breadth 6 cm., max. height 3.6 cm.), and the bottom (PT5 392) of the base (length 9 cm., height 5.5 cm.). The base has an inset small rectangular metal rivet which presumably indicates an ancient repair along the fracture that now divides the two sections of the base.[277] Before being inscribed, the bottom of the base was polished.

Portions of six lines of Aramaic remain on the bottom of the base. The letters are quite faint and almost illegible on fragment PT5 383 while those on PT5 392 appear clear and fresh. Because the right side of the base has been lost, only the ends of lines are preserved.

Find Spot

Fragment PT5 383 was found south of the center (HF 39) of Room 38 of the Persepolis Treasury. Fragment PT5 392 was found a considerable distance away, in another room. It was recovered at the north wall, in the northeastern corner (HF 49) of Room 41 of the Treasury.[278]

Date

The officials Mithraka and Mazda-dāta served together from the nineteenth year of Xerxes to the seventh year of Artaxerxes I. This text must fall somewhere within such limits (467–457 B.C.).

Since only a single unit stroke is preserved, the year date is useless in arriving at an exact date.

Line 2

All that remains of the name of the *segan* is the final letter, which is somewhat faint but certain. The only known *segan* with a name ending with the letter *k* is Mithraka, who is frequently mentioned.

---

[277] Such metal inserts are also found in Nos. 5 and 28.   [278] See pp. 3–4.

The name of the celebrant, *Mndprn*, suggests the cuneiform Mindaparnaⁱ cited by Eilers[279] for Wiñdafarnah (Elamite Mintaparna and Greek Intaphernes),[280] but Eilers prefers Manda(t)-farnah, "He who keeps the glory in memory."[281]

LINE 3

There is space for another word at the beginning of the line. It was doubtless the title of the celebrant, either *plg*, "myriarch," or *ʾlp*, "chiliarch."[282]

LINE 4

The missing words must modify "this plate." The most probable restoration, based on the space available, is *zy gll*, "of stone."

73. Plate (PT5 18 + 405) Pl. 17

[בירת]א [. . . . ב]	1)	[In the . . . of] the fortress,
אר]י[וחוש ל]ד	2)	beside [Āraya(t)-]vahuš
סגנא ארתדת [ו]	3)	the *segan*, 1 Arta-dāta
[עבד] סחרא [זנה]	4)	[used this] plate
לפתי אטבע[ן /// /// // ליד	5)	[worth] 8 [shekels] beside
בגפת גנז[ברא זי	6)	[Baga-pāta] the treasurer who is
בהרחותי אש]כר שנת	7)	[in Arachosia. ʾš]kr of year
/// [. . . . .]	8)	. . . + 3.

DESCRIPTION

A fragment of a green chert plate composed of two pieces (PT5 18 and PT5 405) which join to form a complete base. The base thus formed is not quite round. The diameter varies between 8.6 cm. and 8.3 cm.

Traces of eight lines of Aramaic are on the bottom of the base. The stone is heavily marked with light and dark horizontal bands and lines which make the letters, already very faint, quite difficult to read. Many letters are illegible. The last three lines are written on dark bands which in the photograph appear to have the same density as the ink used. A sharp blow has left a deep circular depression on the left side of the base that damages the ends of the third and fourth lines.

In many places where the photograph is difficult to read, Cameron's copy, made from the object itself, shows the readings clearly.

FIND SPOT

Fragment PT5 18 was found at the south wall of Room 38, near the doorway leading to Room 39 (HG 30). The other (PT5 405) was recovered in the southern part of Room 38, just west of the same doorway (HF 39).[283]

DATE

The date is quite uncertain. Cameron copied only three strokes, at the very end of the last line. Because of the dark band on which the figure is written, it is difficult to determine what preceded.

Since it is probable that Āraya(t)-vahuš is the *segan*, the text was written during the reign of Artaxerxes I and well along in that reign, for Āraya(t)-vahuš served from the eleventh to at least the twenty-fourth year (454–440 B.C.).

[279] Eilers, in *Abhandlungen für die Kunde des Morgenlandes* XXV, No. 5, p. 97, n. 3, [ᵐmi]-*in*-[*da-par*]-*na*-ⁱ.

[280] Justi, *Iranisches Namenbuch*, pp. 368–69.

[281] *Manda(t)*-, from *man*-, "think"; *BAiW*, cols. 1121 ff.

[282] See p. 34.

[283] See p. 3.

LINE 5

After the reference to the plate in the fourth line and before the preposition *lyd*, at the end of the fifth line, there is additional text that includes a figure that is clearly visible. The beginning of the fifth line is illegible but just before the figure Cameron copied the bottom of a letter -*n*, which can be seen in the photograph. The letter is doubtless the plural termination of a masculine noun. From its position the extra text could indicate either the measurable content of the plate or its value.[284]

The solution of the problem of such extra text is found in a complete text (No. 43) in which the words are perfectly preserved. That text, appropriate for the location and space available here, is restored in the text above.

LINE 6

The restoration at the beginning of the line is based on the fact that after the *lyd* of the fifth line the name of the treasurer normally appears. Baga-pāta was the treasurer through at least the first twenty-four years of Artaxerxes I.

LINE 7

The restoration here is suggested by the *zy* at the end of the preceding line which, when following the title of the treasurer, introduces in a number of texts the words "in Arachosia" (for example, No. 43). The word *ʾškr* normally occurs before the word "year."

74. Mortar (PT6 88) T (145); Pl. 18

[ב . . . . . בירתא ליד]	1)	[In the . . . of the fortress, beside]
[מתרפת סגנא . . . אַבְּרתן /	2)	[Mithra-pāta the *segan*], 1 . . . *brtn*
[עבד הון זי גלל אחשׁ[נֹחוֹין	3)	[used this mortar of dark
[. . . . . זנה] ליד דתמתר	4)	. . . stone . . .] beside Dāta-Mithra
[גנזברא קדם] ארזרתִין	5)	[the treasurer, before] *ʾrzrtyn*
[אפגנזברא] אשכֹר שנת	6)	[the sub-treasurer]. *ʾškr* of year
. . . . . .	7)	. . . .

DESCRIPTION

A fragment of the base of a green chert mortar (base dia. *ca.* 10 cm., present max. height .7 cm.). The piece of the base preserved (max. length 6 cm., max. breadth 4 cm.) comes from the left side of the base and thus preserves the ends of the lines of the text.

Five lines of Aramaic, of what was originally seven lines of text are preserved on the bottom of the base. Only the ends of the lines are preserved.

FIND SPOT

The northeastern corner of Room 45 (HF 27), a subsidiary chamber of Room 38 of the Persepolis Treasury.[285]

DATE

The year date is lost, but Dāta-Mithra served as treasurer from the seventh through the nineteenth year of Xerxes (479–466 B.C.).

LINE 2

The name of the *segan* has been lost, but contemporary with the treasurer Dāta-Mithra were the chief *segan* Mithra-pāta and his subordinate Māh(a)-dāta.

The unit stroke at the end of the line indicates that the name that preceded was that of the celebrant.

[284] See also No. 135:4.   [285] See p. 3.

LINE 3

Lack of spacing suggests that all of the letters that are preserved in the line are part of a single long word, broken at its beginning. Its position in the text shows that it is a modifier of the object.

Part of what remains suggests the ʾḥšynpyn that occurs elsewhere (Nos. 11:3, 101:2) presumably as an indication of the color of the stone. But the spelling is not identical. The damaged letter at the edge of the break is apparently a š but the y of the other form is missing here. What follows the š might be a w, but it is probably a relatively short n. Thus, the first element of the compound is perhaps ʾḥšn for ʾḥšyn, axšaina, "dark colored."[286] The second element, ḥwyn might be the objective xᵛaēna, "glowing,"[287] or, better, xᵛaini, "beautiful."[288]

Usually such an adjective modifies the noun "stone" in these texts. We thus expect zy gll before it. Since the name of the celebrant concludes line 2, the third line must also have included the verb ʿbd and the name of the object.

LINE 4

The beginning of this line, too, must have continued the description of the object or the stone. It is difficult to determine what stood there.

LINE 5

The position of the name in the text indicates that it is the name of the sub-treasurer. As such it is unique.

Except for the last two letters, the reading of the name is certain. After the t Cameron read a w, with which he concluded the name. But that letter need not be a w and can be a y, like the one near the end of the third line. The final sign is copied by Cameron as a smudged, diagonal line which he disregarded in his translation. But the stroke must not be ignored. Since it runs at a sharp angle to the prominent bands in that area of the stone and completely crosses a wide, light-colored band, it cannot be regarded as a natural line in the stone. It is too straight to be accidental and its width and density are identical with those of the strokes used to form most of the other letters. It seems to be a purposeful stroke, the letter n, as at the end of the third line.

The first element of the name seems to be ʾrz, which suggests the Avestan arəza, "slaughter."[289] The second element, -rty, could represent -rātay, "offering."[290] The terminal -n could indicate the affix -na expressing adjectival actor.[291] Like Vidarna it is possibly hypocoristic to a compound.[292] Could the name be "He who makes a slaughter offering"? Frye has proposed *Arjaraθina (or -raθaina), "Having precious chariots," as another possibility.

---

75. Mortar (PT5 812) Pl. 18

בפרכן בירתא ליד מתר[פ]ת סֻגנא	1)	In the (haoma-)crushing ceremony of the fortress, beside Mithra-pāta the *segan*,
ארגיש / עב[ד] הון זי גלל אֹח[שִׁי]נפ[י]ן	2)	1 Arəgiš used (this) mortar of dark . . . stone
[. . . . .] ליד דתמ[תר גנז[ברא] קֹד[ֹם]	3)	[. . . beside Dāta-Mi]thra the treasurer (and) before
[. . . . .] אפגנזברא אשכר שנת [. . . . .]	4)	[. . . the sub-treasurer. ʾškr of year . . . .]

---

[286] *BAiW*, col. 51, a-xšaēna; Kent, *Old Persian*, p. 165, axšaina.

[287] *BAiW*, col. 1861, xᵛaēna, "glühend," "lohend."

[288] *Ibid.*, col. 1864, xᵛaini, "schön," "wohlgefällig."

[289] *Ibid.*, col. 201, arəza-, "Schlacht."

[290] *Ibid.*, col. 1519, ²rātay, "Opfergabe."

[291] Kent, *Old Persian*, p. 51, Sec. 147 I; cft. Vi-dar-na.

[292] *Ibid.*, p. 208, under Vidarna.

DESCRIPTION

A fragment of a large green chert mortar (base dia. 18 cm., present max. height 3.9 cm. [slightly reduced in illustration]) of which less than half of the base is preserved.

The first three long lines of Aramaic text are preserved on the bottom of the mortar base. Originally there were one or possibly even two more lines. Almost all of the letters are faint, and some, especially at the end of the line, are now entirely illegible.

FIND SPOT

Just west of the center (HF 38) of Room 38 of the Persepolis Treasury.

DATE

The year date has been lost, but Mithra-pāta was the *segan* from the eighth to the nineteenth year of Xerxes (478–466 B.C.) according to dated texts.

LINE 2

Cameron copied and read the name of the celebrant as *ᵓrgyš*, and that seems likely from the photograph. It appears to be an abbreviation of a name from the root *arəg*, "be valuable," "have worth."[293] The *-š* at the end of the name is probably the *š* that may be affixed to the nominative and genitive cases of nouns with an *-i* or *-u* stem.[294]

After the *hwn*, "mortar," the line has some data about the vessel, introduced by the word *zy*. Cameron commented "not *gll*," presumably because the traces of letters running to the end of the line are too extensive for that simple reading. The line is difficult to read, not only because the letters are sometimes faint to the state of illegibility, but also because of the dark bands and lines in the stone and because the inscribed surface is scratched, pitted, and marred in various other ways. Nevertheless, through careful inspection of the photograph the reading *zy gll*, "of stone," is certified. Beyond it are many faint traces of letters that suggest the *ᵓhšynpyn* of Nos. 11:3 and 101:2. The first element of the compound is probably *axšaina*, "dark colored," and the second, *-pyn*, must indicate the basic color of the stone (green or gray?).

LINE 3

Further description of the mortar or the quality of its stone must have stood at the beginning of the third line, but there is no clue to what it was.

The word *qdm*, of which there are definite traces at the end of the line, is normally followed by the name of the sub-treasurer who, at this time, could be either Māh(a)-dāta or Mazda-dāta.

76. Mortar (PT4 887) T (56); Pl. 18

1) [ב .... ב . בירתא ליד .....]	1) [In the . . . of the fortress, beside . . .]
2) סג[נא ..... עבד הון ....]	2) [the] *segan*, [. . . used this mortar . . of]
3) אחשינ[פין .... ליד]	3) dark . . . [stone . . . beside]
4) דת[מת]ר גנ[נ]זבר[א ......]	4) Dāta-Mithra, the treasurer . . .
5) [...........]	5) . . .

DESCRIPTION

A green chert mortar that has been split almost exactly in half vertically. The diameter of the top was 11.6 cm., and it stands 13.4 cm. high. The diameter below the bowl is 7.2 cm. and that of the base is 13 cm.

---

[293] *BAiW*, col. 191, *arəg-*, "Wert haben"; adj. *arəǰa-*, "wertvoll."

[294] Meillet and Benveniste, *Grammaire*, p. 70, Sec. 122.

Because of the splitting of the vessel the relatively small cavity, 4.3 cm. deep at its center, is observable. The thickness of the side at the top is 1.5 cm. and its inside diameter at the top is about 7.9 cm.

Parts of three lines of Aramaic are preserved on the bottom of the base. The letters are faint, and some have disappeared entirely. Another line preceded in the original text, and at least one more followed it.

FIND SPOT

On the floor of Room 33,[295] in the long aisle, between the pillars, almost equidistant from the last four pillars on the east (HG 42).

DATE

If the treasurer's name is correctly read as Dāta-Mithra, the vessel comes from the reign of Xerxes, when Data-Mithra served in that office.

LINE 3

The first word is apparently the word *ʾḥšynpyn* found in No. 11:3, where it is descriptive of the dark color of the stone. The words *zy gll* must have preceded it at the end of the line above.

LINE 4

There is a relatively large space before the first word but it appears to be uninscribed, representing a wide margin.

The reading at first glance seems to be *dtsḥy*, but the title "the treasurer" follows it, and there is no other occurrence of that name. Closer examination shows that what looks like the letter *ḥ* is actually a *t* that has lost its vertical stroke; what seemed to be a letter *s* has some of the characteristics of a now incomplete *m;* and the final traces could as well be the head of an *r* as a letter *y*. The word is the name Dāta-Mithra.

In the title that follows the name the letter *z* is prolonged, but it is unlike the letter *n* as made by this hand. The letter *r* at the break on the left is a bit distorted but clear, and the customary *ʾaleph* at the end is broken away.

77. Pestle (PT4 303) Oriental Institute A23201; Pl. 18

בפרכן	1)	In the (haoma-)crushing ceremony of
בירתן ליד	2)	the fortress, beside
מתרפת סגנא	3)	Mithra-pāta the *segan*,
ארתורם עבד	4)	Arta-*wrm* used
אבשון זנה	5)	this pestle.

DESCRIPTION

Part of a green chert pestle (head dia. 3.5 cm., present max. length 4.5 cm.).
Five lines of dark, well-preserved Aramaic are written on top of its head.

FIND SPOT

Northwestern corner (HG 61) of Room 20.

DATE

There is no exact year date, but Mithra-pāta served as chief *segan* from the eighth to the nineteenth year of Xerxes (478–466 B.C.), according to the dated texts.

[295] See p. 4.

LINE 2

Instead of the expected *byrt*ʾ, the spelling is *byrtn*. The final letter is not the expected ʾ*aleph* of the determinate state but clearly and definitely the letter *-n*. It might be a simple error, but it could possibly be an attempt to form a Persianized hybrid by affixing the Persian element *-na* which indicates place, as in such words as *aydna: āyadanā*, "sanctuaries," and *vardanam*, "citadel."[296]

LINE 4

The first element of the name of the celebrant is ʾ*rt-*, probably for Arta. The second is somewhat ambiguous because its second consonant could be *r* or, less likely, *p*, for *-wrm* or *-wpm*.

78. Pestle (PT5 420) T (21); Pl. 18

בפרכן	1)	In the (haoma-)crushing ceremony of
בן[י]רתֿא לי]ד[	2)	the fortress, beside
מתֿרפֿתֿ סגנ]א[	3)	Mithra-pāta the *segan*,
]א[ברֿשֿ עבד	4)	ʾ*brš* used
אבשון זנה	5)	this pestle.

DESCRIPTION

A fragment of a green chert pestle (head dia. 2.9 cm., present max. length 7.2 cm.) with a complete head and broken shaft.

Five lines of Aramaic are written on its head in letters that are now very faint.

FIND SPOT

Just north of the center (HF 29) of Room 38.

DATE

Mithra-pāta as *segan* indicates a date between 478 and 466 B.C.

LINE 4

The name of the celebrant is difficult to read. Only a trace of the first letter remains. It seems to be a slight indication of the left side of an ʾ*aleph*. The third letter could be *d* or *r*. The final one looks like a *š*, which in these texts could represent either *š* or *č*.

79. Mortar (PT5 490) T (92); Pl. 19

ב . . . .] בירתא ליד מתרפֿת[סֿגנא	1)	In the . . . of the fortress, beside Mithra-pāta] the *segan*,
. . . . .] עבד הון זנה עם] אבשון	2)	[. . . used this mortar with] pestle
ליד . . . . .] גנזברא זי בֿ]הֿרֿחותֿי	3)	[beside . . . the treasurer who is in] Arachosia,
קדם . . . . . אפֿגנזברא] אֿשכר	4)	[before . . . the sub-treasurer]. ʾ*škr* of
שנת . . . . .]	5)	[year. . . .]

DESCRIPTION

A part of the left side of the base of a green chert mortar (base dia. 11.6 cm.).

Four words of Aramaic indicate the ends of four lines preserved on the bottom of the base. There was originally probably a short fifth line bearing the date.

FIND SPOT

At the north wall, just west of the door of Room 48, in the northeastern part (HG 11) of Room 38 of the Persepolis Treasury.

---

[296] Meillet and Benveniste, *Grammaire*, pp. 154–55, Sec. 265.

DATE

The name of the *segan* which, according to Cameron's copy, ended with the letter *t*, affords the only clue to a date, if it indicates the name of the chief *segan* Mithra-pāta, who served from the eighth to the nineteenth year of Xerxes (478–466 B.C.).

LINE 3

Cameron's copy shows an *ʾaleph* at the beginning of the word, and it appears to be so also on the base. But there is also a horizontal stroke before the word which must be considered. It seems clear now that the horizontal stroke, together with the small vertical stroke on the right of the *ʾaleph*, must be combined as the head of a prefixed letter *b*, and what appears to be the angular part of the *ʾaleph* is indeed the top of an incomplete letter *h*. The preserved word must be the familiar *bhrḥwty*, "in Arachosia," found in these texts.

80. Mortar (PT5 489) T (43); Pl. 19

ב[פֿרכן בירתא ליד . . . . .]	1)	In [the (haoma-)crushing ceremony of the fortress, beside . . .]
סגנא[. . . . . עבד הון]	2)	the *segan*, [. . . used]
מדם / [ליד . . . . גנזברא קדם]	3)	a medium-sized [mortar beside . . . the treasurer (and) before]
מהדת א[פגנזברא אשכר]	4)	Māh(a)-dāta [the sub-treasurer. *ʾškr* of year . . . .]

DESCRIPTION

A fragment of the base of a green chert mortar (base dia. *ca.* 11.2 cm., max. length of the piece 10 cm.). Only part of the right side of the base remains. The stone surface is variegated with wide bands, lines and marble-like swirls of darker and lighter colors.

The beginning words of four lines are preserved. The letters of the first three lines are particularly dark and clear.

FIND SPOT

At the north wall (HG 11) of Room 38 of the Treasury. It lay just east of the door leading to subsidiary Room 48.

DATE

There is no year date in this text. In dated texts, Māh(a)-dāta (l. 4) appears as sub-treasurer alongside Mazda-dāta from the tenth year of Xerxes until his nineteenth year (476–466 B.C.). Since there is no trace of a fifth line bearing a date, it must have been at the end of the fourth line. Although this would have made a very full line, it is located at the widest part of the base and, to judge from the beginning words, smaller letters were used in writing it.

81. Pestle (PT5 494A[297]) Pl. 19

בפֿרכן בירתא לי[ד] מתר[ך סגנא]	1)	In the (haoma-)crushing ceremony of the fortress, beside Mithra[ka the *segan*],
מֿביך פלג עבד אב[שון] . . .	2)	. . . *mbyk*, a myriarch, used (this) pestle
[ליד] בגפת גנזברא [קדם]	3)	[beside] Baga-pāta the treasurer (and) [before]
מֿ[ז]דדת [אפגנז]ברא א[שכר]	4)	Mazda-dāta the [sub-treasur]er. *ʾ[škr* of] . . . .

[297] This pestle and No. 133 both bear the same field number. The other object (PT5 494B) is also a pestle, but its inscription is on the top of the head and the Aramaic text is quite different. The number in the Field Register refers to this pestle (No. 81).

DESCRIPTION

Part of the shaft of a green chert pestle (max. dia. 3.9 cm., max. length 11.1 cm.).

The beginnings of four lines of Aramaic are preserved on the shaft of the pestle.[298] The lines begin just above the pounding surface and run toward the head, interrupted by the break, which destroys the ends of the lines. According to Cameron's copy, the letters at the beginning of the lines are very faint and often no longer legible.

FIND SPOT

At the north wall (HG 11) of Room 38 of the Treasury, just at the door to Room 48.

DATE

There was perhaps a year date at the end of the fourth line originally, but it is now lost. The officers named indicate that it was perhaps written sometime between the nineteenth year of Xerxes and the seventh year of Artaxerxes I (467–457 B.C.).

LINE 2

The name of the celebrant in line 2 is obscure. After slight and ambiguous traces of two letters, Cameron shows faint evidence of a sign that seems to be an *m* but might be a *t*. The last letters are definitely *-byk*.

82. Mortar (PT5 393) Pl. 19

‏[ב . . . . בירתא ליד]‏	1) [In the . . . of the fortress, beside]
‏מת]רך סגנא . . . . . עבד]‏	2) Mith[raka the *segan*, . . . used]
‏הון ז]י גלל . . . . . .]‏	3) (this) mortar of . . . [stone]
‏ליד בג]פת גנזברא קדם . . . . .]‏	4) beside Baga[-pāta the treasurer (and) before . . .]
‏אפגנז]ברא . . . .]‏	5) the sub-trea[surer . . . .]

DESCRIPTION

A fragment of a green chert mortar (base dia. *ca.* 13 cm.) consisting of a small piece from the right side of the base (max. width 3.5 cm., max. length 6.9 cm.).

The first words of four lines of Aramaic are preserved on the bottom of the base. If the text were complete, there would be a line above and two below those preserved.

FIND SPOT

At the north wall of Room 41 of the Persepolis Treasury.[299] It lay among many fragments of royal tableware in the northeastern corner (HF 49) of the room.

DATE

The names of Mithraka and Baga-pāta suggest a date for this piece sometime between the nineteenth year of Xerxes and the seventh year of Artaxerxes I (467–457 B.C.).

LINE 4

The name of the sub-treasurer, which ended this line, is now lost, but it was probably Mazda-dāta.

[298] Other pestles inscribed on the shaft are Nos. 17 and 123.

[299] See pp. 3–4.

83. Mortar (PT5 447) T (112); Pl. 19

בפרכן] בן]י]ר]תא[ליד מתרך	1)	[In the (haoma-)crushing ceremony of the fortress] beside Mithraka
סגנא] . . . .] פלג עב]ד]	2)	[the *segan* . . .], a myriarch, used
הון] . . . .]	3)	[(this) mortar . . . .]

DESCRIPTION

A fragment of the upper edge of the base of a small, green chert mortar (base dia. 7.6 cm.). The length of the fragment is 6.7 cm. and its width 2.5 cm.

Parts of three lines of Aramaic text are on the bottom of the base. In the first line most of the first word is broken away and the second has faded to illegibility. Only the very tops of two letters remain in the third line.

FIND SPOT

South of the center (HF 39) of Room 38 of the Treasury.

DATE

The name Mithraka indicates a date between the nineteenth year of Xerxes and the seventh year of Artaxerxes I (467–457 B.C.).

LINE 1

Only a trace of the top of the final letter of the first word remains. It is certainly not part of the word *srk*. It might be part of the vertical staff of *t* for *hst*, but that word is rarely used in these texts. It is more likely to be the top of the *-n* of the word *prkn*.

LINE 2

Only the final letter of the celebrant's name remains. It could be either *r*, *d*, or *k*.

84. Mortar (PT5 688) Pl. 20

ב]סרך בירתא	1)	[In] the ritual of the fortress,
ליד מת]רך סגנא .]	2)	[beside Mith]raka the *segan*,
עבד] הון ז]י גלל] . . . . .]	3)	[. . . used] (this) mortar [of stone]. . . .

DESCRIPTION

A fragment of a small green chert mortar (base originally *ca.* 8 cm.). It is now roughly a square (3.5 cm. × 3.2 cm., present max. height 1.5 cm.). The original curve of the base is preserved on one side but the other three sides show sharp, straight-edged breaks.

Traces of three lines of Aramaic are preserved on the bottom of the base.

FIND SPOT

Recovered in the refuse of plot HF 38, which came from the area before the south wall of Room 38 of the Treasury.

DATE

Mithraka as *segan* suggests, as possible limits for the date, 467 B.C. and 457 B.C.

85. Mortar (PT5 758) T (6); Pl. 20

בסרך בירת]א[ליד	1)	In the ritual of the fortress, beside
מרתך סגנא המ].] . .]	2)	Mithraka(?) the *segan*, *Hm* . . .
עבד הון ז]נה ליד]	3)	[used this mortar] beside. . . .

DESCRIPTION

A fragment of the base of a green chert mortar (base dia. 18 cm., present max. height 3.8 cm.).

Parts of three lines of a longer text remain on the bottom of the base. They are written in relatively large, thick letters.

FIND SPOT

Near the center (HF 38) of Room 38 among the many fragments of green chert vessels shattered against the south wall.

DATE

If the *segan* is Mithraka, as seems probable, the text must come from the period of his administration, 467–457 B.C., according to dated texts.

LINE 2

The spelling of the name of the *segan* is clearly *mrtk*, but there is no other example of such a *segan* in these texts. It seems likely that, as Cameron has suggested, the name is "an error for *mtrk*, Mithraka." Another example of metathesis with this name is the *tmrk* of No. 17:2.

Cameron copied the beginning of the name of the celebrant as a heavy, thick letter *r* superimposed on a lightly made letter *g*—possibly representing an ancient correction. Thus, it is possible that a letter *h* is intended. Hence, the name could begin with *hm-*, *rm-*, or *gm-*, but it is incomplete and unidentifiable.

86. Mortar (PT5 792) Pl. 20

ב[. . . . בירת[א ליד מתרך סגנא	1)	[In the . . . of the fortress] beside Mithraka the *segan*,
. . . . . (traces)	2)	. . . .

DESCRIPTION

A fragment of the base of a large green chert mortar (dia. of base 16 cm., present max. height 4.3 cm.). Only the upper left part of the base is preserved.

The end of a single line of Aramaic is preserved on the bottom of the base. There are also a few traces of the upper tips of the letters of a second line. The text originally was much larger.

FIND SPOT

The northwestern corner (HF 36) of Room 38 of the Treasury.

DATE

Mithraka as *segan* indicates that the limits for the date of this text are 467–457 B.C.

87. Pestle (PT5 196) Pl. 20

ב]סֹרך בירתא[	1)	[In] the ritual of the fortress,
ליד מתרֹך סגנֹא	2)	beside Mithraka the *segan*
כברֹרמֹשֹתֹר פֹלֹג	3)	*Kbrrmštr*, a myriarch,
עבֹד אבשון זעֹירֹ	4)	used (this) small pestle
קדֹם מֹזדדת	5)	before Mazda-dāta
אפגנזברֹא]	6)	[the sub-treasurer] . . . .

DESCRIPTION

A fragment of a small green chert pestle (head dia. 3.3 cm., present max. length 2.5 cm.), of which the lower margin of the head is broken away.

Five lines of Aramaic, written in very minute, delicate letters, are on the top of the pestle head. There is room for another line of text where the lower part of the pestle head is broken away, and there is some trace of the final letter in that line.

FIND SPOT

At the south wall (HF 48) of Room 38 of the Persepolis Treasury.

DATE

The line broken away must have held the title of the sub-treasurer rather than a year date. The officials Mithraka and Mazda-dāta served together from the nineteenth year of Xerxes to the seventh year of Artaxerxes I (467–457 B.C.).

LINE 3

Because the letters are very small and badly crowded, the name of the celebrant is difficult to read. Cameron copied *bprwsš* without transliterating and remarked, "The name and really the whole line is gone." But close inspection of the photograph makes a reading possible.

The last three letters of the name are faint but certainly *-štr*. The first letter is probably a *k* and it is followed by a certain *b*. The third letter is somewhat doubtful. It has a definite head, like a letter *b*, *d*, or *r*, and its vertical stroke bends somewhat, but not to the same degree as the certain *b* that precedes it. It could represent either a *k* or *r*. The following letter, more vertical, is a good *r* or *d*. Cameron copied the following letter as *s*, but that is unlikely before the letter *š* and it is probably a letter *m*. The most likely reading of the name is *Kbrrmštr*.

This long name must be constructed of several elements, the last doubtless the familiar *-štr*, *-čiθra*, "seed," "family," "lineage."[300] The remainder of the name is difficult and uncertain.

After the name there is a space followed by a *p* and what appears to be an *h*. The latter is not the letter *h* but the lower part of an *l* joined to a letter *g*. The word is the title *plg*, "myriarch."

LINE 4

The traces of a word in the middle of the line, written on a dark band in the stone, spell *ʾbšwn*, "pestle." After it, at the very end of the line, and written in most minute letters, is the word *zʿyr*, "small."[301]

LINE 6

After the name Mazda-dāta the title "sub-treasurer" is expected. That presumably stood in line 6, which is now missing. A small, dark, horizontal mark, below the *t* of the name in the fifth line, is apparently a trace of the final *ʾaleph* of the title *ʾpgnzbrʾ*, "the sub-treasurer." There is no room on this small pestle head for the word *ʾškr*, which regularly precedes the date, nor is there room for a year date which should conclude the text.

88. Mortar (PT6 38) T (67); Pl. 20

[ב . . . . ב]ירתא ליד מתרך	1)	[In the . . . of] the fortress, beside Mithraka
[סגנא . . . . .] פלג/[ג]זד מֹזד פלג	2)	[the *segan*, . . .] a myriarch [and . . .]-Mazda, a myriarch,
[עבדו הון זי גל]ל רב גל[ל זנה	3)	[used] this large [mortar of . . . stone]
[. . . . .] ליד בגפ[ת	4)	[beside Baga-pā]ta
[גזברא אשכר שנת . . . .]	5)	[the treasurer. *ʾškr* of year . . . .]

DESCRIPTION

A fragment of the base of a large green chert mortar (base dia. 16.9 cm., max. height 3.7 cm.), consisting of the upper left part of the base. The stone is marked by dark and light

---

[300] See No. 36:2, Mazda-čiθra.   [301] See No. 31:3.

bands, including some very dark, thin, wavy lines that run horizontally across the written text, passing directly through the second line.

The ends of four lines of Aramaic are written in well-made letters on the bottom of the mortar base. There were perhaps originally one or two more lines at the end, to complete a normal text.

FIND SPOT

The eastern part (HF 26) of Room 45, a subsidiary chamber entered from the northwestern part of Room 38.[302]

DATE

With the date line lost, only the name of the *segan* Mithraka furnishes a clue to the date. He served from the nineteenth year of Xerxes to the seventh year of Artaxerxes I (467–457 B.C.).

LINE 2

The double occurrence of the title *plg* in the second line indicates that two celebrants are mentioned in this unusual text.[303] Since the haoma was prepared twice during the ceremony,[304] the men may have participated in turn. Or, since the vessel is a large and more expensive one, they may have used the same vessel in separate ceremonies and shared its purchase and presentation.

The name of the first celebrant is lost entirely. A small diagonal stroke at the edge of the break seems to indicate that the name ended in a letter *š*. The reading of the second name is extremely difficult because the dark lines in the stone obliterate the faint letters at the beginning of the name. The second element, however, appears to be *-mzd*, -Mazda.

89. Mortar (PT5 290) T (13); Pl. 21

1) בסרך בירתא ליד מתרך	1) In the ritual of the fortress, beside Mithraka
2) סגנא חשתר / עבד הון זי	2) the *segan*, 1 Xšaθra used (this) mortar of
3) גלל] . . . . . (traces)	3) [stone . . . . . .]

DESCRIPTION

A fragment of a green chert mortar (base dia. 18 cm., present max. height 5.6 cm.).[305] It consists of approximately the upper third of the base, which is marked with dark banding. The bottom of the base was polished before being inscribed.

Two lines of Aramaic, the beginning of a longer text, are all that is preserved. They are written in dark, clear, well-formed letters on the polished bottom of the base. There are traces of the tops of a few letters of a third line along the broken lower edge of the base.

FIND SPOT

The northeastern part (HG 10) of Room 38 of the Treasury.

DATE

The presence of Mithraka as *segan* indicates a date sometime between 467 and 457 B.C.

LINE 2

The name of the celebrant, *Ḥštr, Xšaθra,* "lordship," "kingdom,"[306] is doubtless an hypocoristicon of such a longer name as Xšaθra-dāra.[307]

---

[302] See p. 3.

[303] Two celebrants also occur in No. 95.

[304] Modi, *Religious Ceremonies*, p. 296.

[305] Schmidt, *Persepolis* II 55, Pl. 24:10 and chart.

[306] *BAiW*, col. 542 ff., *xšaθra;* Kent, *Old Persian*, p. 181a, *xšaça.*

[307] Justi, *Iranisches Namenbuch*, pp. 174 ff., *xšaθra-dāra.*

90. Mortar (PT5 669) Pl. 21

בסרך בירתא ליד מת[רך סגנא]   1)   In the ritual of the fortress, beside Mith[raka the *segan*]

[סֹא]פהר שמה / עבד ה[וֹן]   2)   1 [Sᵓ]pāhr(?) by name used [this mortar].

DESCRIPTION

A fragment of the base of a green chert mortar (base dia. 18 cm., present max. height 3.8 cm.).

Parts of two lines of Aramaic, written in large letters, are preserved on the bottom of the base. The letters of the first line are rather dark and clear, but those in the second are grayer and somewhat faded. The ends of the lines are gone, and the lower part of the text has been broken away.

FIND SPOT

At the base of the south wall near its center (HF 38) in Room 38.

DATE

As in the preceding text, the *segan* Mithraka indicates a date within the years 467–457 B.C.

LINE 2

Cameron copied and transliterated the name of the celebrant as *phr*, which is legible in the photograph. It must represent the Persian *pāhr*[308] for *pāθra* or *puhr* for an earlier *puθra*,[309] which is characteristic of Middle-Persian phonetics.[310] Such a reading is based on the assumption that the name is complete and that the letter *p* is the beginning of the line, because it is exactly below the first letter in the line above.

But there are traces of letters that Cameron ignored before the letter *p*. Because of the circular shape of the base, there is more room in the second line, and there could be a few more letters to the right of the *p* in the name. The density and width of line in the traces before the *p* suggest that they were made with the same implement used for the rest of the text.

The first trace of a sign resembles the letter *s*, and there is still room between it and the *p* for such a narrow letter as *z*, *y*, or *n* but nothing is identifiable there. But directly above the space, as though a later addition to the word, there are definite traces of a free-standing ᵓaleph. Could the name represent *Sᵓphr*?

91. Mortar (PT5 679) T (91); Pl. 21

בסרך בירֹתֹא ליד מתרך   1)   In the ritual of the fortress, beside Mithraka

סגנֹא דמוֹשֹ שמֹה / עבד [הוֹן]   2)   the *segan*, 1 *Dmwš* by name used (this) mortar

זי גֹלֹל בז ליד בֹ[נפת גנזברא]   3)   of *bz* stone beside Ba[ga-pāta the treasurer]

[קֹ]דם מז[דֹדת אפגנזברא]   4)   (and) before Maz[da-dāta the sub-treasurer.]

DESCRIPTION

A fragment of a green chert mortar (base dia. 16.7 cm., present max. height 3.9 cm.), consisting of only a portion of the upper part of the base.

Parts of four lines of Aramaic are preserved on the bottom of the base. There must have been originally another line bearing the date.

FIND SPOT

At the center of the south wall (HF 48) of Room 38 of the Treasury.

---

[308] *Ibid.*, p. 237b; see also *Phrbrn* in No. 116:2 here.

[309] H. S. Nyberg, *Hilfsbuch des Pehlevi* II (Uppsala, 1928), 188, *pus;* northwest form *puhr;* cf. Šāhpuhr.

[310] See p. 65.

DATE

The name of Mithraka as *segan* dates the text within the years 467–457 B.C.

LINE 2

Cameron copied and transliterated the name of the celebrant as *rmš* or *dmš*, but there is difficulty in reading the end of the name. The photograph shows the bottom of a vertical stroke between the letters *m* and *š*. It could be read as *rmwš*, *dmwš*, or possibly even *rmnš*.

If *dmwš* be read, it could represent an Iranian *dmwč*. The first element of the name might then be the Avestan *dāmi*, "creation,"[311] and the second, *wš*, the Avestan *vačah*, "word," "whispered utterance," "prayer."[312] A name *Dāmi-vač*, "Conveying creative utterances," suggests such a name as the *Sawaṅha-wāč*, "Conveying useful utterances," about which Justi comments, "According to Avestan conception they were useful for the good creation."[313]

If the reading be *rmwš*, the first element could be *rāman*, "peace," "quiet," which appears in combination as *rāma-*.[314]

LINE 3

After *zy gll* there is an additional word *bz*, which is also found elsewhere under similar circumstances.[315] It appears to be a modifier of *gll*, "stone," but its etymology and meaning are as yet not determined.

92. Plate (PT5 461) T (1); Pl. 22

בפֿ]רכן בירתא	1)	[In] the (haoma-)crushing ceremony of the fortress
ליד] מתרך	2)	[beside] Mithraka
סגנא] תאפֿמרכד *i*	3)	[the *segan*] 1 *Tᵓpmrkd*
עבד] סחר זנה	4)	[used] this plate
זי גללֹ] בזי קד(ם)	5)	[of] *bzy* [stone] opposite
מזדדת אפגנז]בֿרא	6)	[Mazda-data the sub-treas]urer
ליד בגפת גנזב]רֿא	7)	[beside Baga-pata] the treasurer.

DESCRIPTION

A fragment of a green chert plate (base dia. 8.3 cm.), consisting of the left portion of the base and its adjacent side.

The ends of seven lines of text are preserved on the bottom of the base. Only a few letters of the last two lines remain. Originally there must have been another line for the date, but it is entirely gone.

FIND SPOT

Just south of the center (HF 39) of Room 38 of the Treasury.

DATE

Mithraka as *segan* indicates a date between 467 and 457 B.C.

LINE 3

The line is packed with the many letters of the long name of the celebrant. The vertical stroke at the end is probably a unit stroke rather than the letter *z*, which is made similarly. The reading is clear, but the last letter, here read as *d* because of its shorter vertical stroke, may, as usual, also represent a letter *r*.

---

[311] *BAiW*, col. 737, *dāmay*, which is *dāmi-* in combination.

[312] *Ibid.*, cols. 1340–42; Justi, *Iranisches Namenbuch*, p. 516, *wāč*.

[313] *Iranisches Namenbuch*, p. 293a.

[314] *BAiW*, col. 1525, *rāman-*.   [315] No. 116:3; cf. *bzy* in Nos. 76:2, 92:5, 112:5, and 163:3.

LINE 5

The trace of a letter before the word *bzy* is perhaps the bottom of the last *l* of the expression *zy gll* which must have been in this line.

There is no trace of the final letter of *qdm* at the end of the line. It was probably omitted for lack of space since it is unlikely that it would be dropped to the beginning of the next line.

LINES 6 AND 7

The few letters that remain at the ends of the lines are doubtless the last letters of the titles of the treasurers. Their names were at the beginnings of the lines and have been lost. Perhaps they can be restored from No. 18, wherein the colleagues of Mithraka are named.

93. Mortar (PT5 668) T (114); Pl. 22

ליד מת[רך סגנ(א) . . . .]	1)	[. . . beside Mith]raka (the) *segan*
עבד הון זי גלל זי [. . . . .]	2)	[. . . used (this) mortar of . . . stone]
ליד [. . . . .]	3)	[. . .] beside . . . .

DESCRIPTION

A fragment of a green chert mortar (base dia. 12.5 cm., present max. height 2.3 cm.). It is from the left margin of the base and preserves the ends of lines.

There are traces of three lines remaining on the bottom of the base, but only a few letters are left in each line.

FIND SPOT

Near the south wall and toward the center (HF 38) of Room 38 of the Treasury.

DATE

Traces of the name of Mithraka as *segan* indicate a date somewhere within the years 467–457 B.C.

LINE 1

There is not room at the end of the line for the *ᵓaleph* of the word *sgnᵓ*.

94. Mortar (PT5 770) T (54); Pl. 22

בסרך [בירתא ליד מתרך]	1)	In the ritual of [the fortress, beside Mithraka]
ס[ג]נא בר[ז]נֹמ [. . .]	2)	the *segan* in *Rgym* . . . ,
כל ⁄ עבד הו[ן] זי [גלל]	3)	1 Kālī used (this) mortar of [stone]
קדם מזד[ד]ת אפג[נ]זברא לי[ד] ב[גפת]	4)	before Mazda-[dāta] the sub-[treasurer] (and) beside Ba[ga-pāta]
גנזברא א[ש]כר שנ[ת] [. . . . .]	5)	the treasurer. *ᵓškr* of year . . . .

DESCRIPTION

A somewhat triangular fragment of the base of a green chert mortar (base dia. *ca.* 16.5 cm.). Its shortest dimension is part of the circumference of the right side of the base.

The beginnings of five lines of Aramaic, written in rather delicate letters, are preserved on the bottom of the base. Many of the letters are quite faint and some, especially in the fourth line, are gone entirely. The reading of the second line is made difficult not only by the faintness of the letters but also because it is written on a darker band in the stone. There are also some thin, horizontal lines in the stone that interfere with the letters. Part of the last line is destroyed by a deep crack with heavy chipping at its sides.

FIND SPOT

The northwestern corner (HF 36) of Room 38 of the Treasury.

DATE

If, as seems likely, the sub-treasurer is Mazda-dāta, it is possible that the text comes from sometime between the tenth year of Xerxes and the eleventh year of Artaxerxes I (476–453 B.C.) when he is found serving as sub-treasurer.

LINE 2

Normally the name of the celebrant occurs immediately after the title of the *segan*, but in this text it is not found until the beginning of the third line. The additional text must relate to the *segan*. The reading is difficult because of the faded letters and the dark background of the band in the stone on which the line was written. The fracture of the stone ends the line after the first few letters.

Cameron copied and transliterated a clear *b* and *r* after the title, but there are traces of several more letters before the break. The signs are difficult to read and uncertain, but they suggest a *g*, an obscure mark that might be a *y*, and a letter *m* for a reading *brgym*. . . . Since the length of the line cannot be determined, it is impossible to conjecture the length of the word or what, if anything, followed it in the line.

The letters *br* at first suggest a patronymic, for those letters can be read as "son of" and there is a probable example of such usage in these texts.[316] But there appears to be no space between the letter *r* and what follows. Perhaps it is to be read as a place name, "the *segan* in R. . . . ," denoting the place in which the *segan* normally officiated. We might have expected the word *zy* in the construction, as in the statement "who is in Arachosia," which sometimes follows the title of the treasurer.

LINE 3

The use of the letter *l* in the name of the celebrant indicates that it is not Persian. It could represent such a name as the Kālī listed by Justi.[317] That name is possibly found also in one of the Aramaic tablets from the fortification at Persepolis, from the time of Darius I.[318] The name is found also in the next text (No. 95:3).

LINE 4

Because the letters of the name of the sub-treasurer are faint and incomplete toward the end of the line, its reading is somewhat uncertain. Since carelessly written *zd* can look like the letter *h*, Māh(a)-dāta might be a possible reading, for he served as sub-treasurer in the tenth year of Xerxes (476/75 B.C.) and in his eighteenth and nineteenth years (468–466 B.C.). But because Māh(a)-dāta is not found elsewhere with Baga-pāta as treasurer, the name Mazda-dāta is restored here.

Only the *b* of the name of the treasurer remains, but the title at the beginning of the next line makes the restoration highly probable.

---

[316] See No. 33:3.

[317] Justi, *Iranisches Namenbuch*, p. 153, Kālī.   [318] Tablet 45, l. 2.

95. Plate (PT4 1077) Teheran Museum (unnumbered); Pl. 23

בּ]‏ . . . . בי‏[רתא ליד	1)	[In the . . . of] the fortress, beside
. . . . . .] סגנא הרّון *i*	2)	. . . the *segan*, 1 *Hrwn*
. . .] כל // עּבדו סחrּ	3)	[a . . . and] 1 Kālī used
זנה ליד] בגפת גנזברא	4)	[this] plate [beside] Baga-pāta the treasurer
זי בהרחֹ]‏ותי אש‏[כֹּרֹ	5)	[who is in Arachosia]. *ʾškr* of
. . . . שנת]	6)	[year . . . .]

DESCRIPTION

Part of a green chert plate (base dia. 21 cm.), consisting of less than a quarter of the base of the plate. Its straight sides measure 5.8 cm. and 7.3 cm. It is a relatively flat plate (height 4 cm.) with up-curved sides and a flat-top rim.

The ends of five lines of what was probably a six-line text are preserved on the bottom of the base.

FIND SPOT

Just north of the southeast door jamb (HG 33) in Room 37 of the Persepolis Treasury.[319]

DATE

Although the date line is lost, the official Baga-pāta as treasurer gives broad limits for the date. He served, according to dated texts, from the nineteenth year of Xerxes to at least the twenty-fourth year of Artaxerxes I (467–440 B.C.). The same celebrant, Kālī, is in No. 94, where the date is restricted between 476 and 453 B.C. by reference to the sub-treasurer Mazda-dāta.

LINE 2

The length of the second and third lines and the plural verb indicate that, as in No. 88, two celebrants are mentioned in this text.

After the *h* of the first name, the next two letters are blurred. The first is either *d* or *r* and the second is a *w* or, much less likely, a letter *p*. The name is thus *Hrwn* or *Hdwn*.

The second element of the name, -*wn*, is probably -*wāna*/-*vāna*, "prevailing,"[320] which is encountered in other names in these texts.[321] If the first element is *hd*, it suggests *hada*, "always,"[322] for Hada-vāna, "He who always prevails." If it be read as *hr*, it could possibly be *hār*-, "protector," "prince,"[323] for a name Hār-vāna, "Prevailing protector."

LINE 3

A title (*ʾlp* or *plg*) must have stood at the beginning of the line, following the name at the end of the line above and, since there were two celebrants, a conjunctive "and" must have preceded the second name.

At Teheran the text seemed to read *kl* 1, as in No. 94:3, but an enlarged photograph seems to show traces of two vertical strokes after the name. It is probable that the first is the remains of a *y* for the name *Kly*, Kālī. It is possible, however, that the name of another celebrant occurred earlier in the line, followed by a unit stroke, and that the legible text is *kl* 1 1 in the sense of "total 2" or "both."

---

[319] See pp. 4–5.

[320] *BAiW*, cols. 1350–53; Kent, *Old Persian*, p. 208*b*, under Vivāna.

[321] *ʾrtbrwn* (No. 29:3), *ʾrtwn* (No. 65:3), *Šrwn* (No. 119:4), and *Drywʾn* (No. 8:2).

[322] *BAiW*, col. 1755, *haδa*-.

[323] Justi, *Iranisches Namenbuch*, p. 126*b*, *hār*-, "Beschützer," "Fürst"; cf. *BAiW*, col. 1806, *hāra*, col. 1787, *hār*-.

LINE 5

Only the tops of letters remain in this line. Its reading would be quite uncertain without knowledge of the expected formula. The restoration here may be regarded as certain, establishing the length of line in the text. The traces that remain fit the reading *zy bhrḥwty*, "who is in Arachosia," that sometimes follows the title of the treasurer. The badly damaged final word is certainly the *ʾškr*, which normally precedes the date.

96. Mortar (PT5 682) Persepolis Museum 171; Pl. 24

ס]גנא[. . . . .] ליד[תא[חֹ]בירֹ כן בפר]כן	1)	In the (haoma-)crushing ceremony of the fortress [beside . . . the *segan*]
א[ֹברֹ]ז[נ]גֹ בגפֹ]ת ליד ה[וֹן עבד . . . .]	2)	[. . . used a mor]tar beside Baga-pāta the treasurer
לֹ].. כ ןֹשֹ	3)	(traces).

DESCRIPTION

A fragment of a green chert mortar (base dia. 11.4 cm., max. height 9.2 cm.). Most of the base is preserved.

Traces of three lines of Aramaic are found on the bottom of the base. There were originally, perhaps, one or two more lines to complete the text. Most of the letters are extremely faint and illegible. Distinct letters are found in only three lines which are widely spaced.

FIND SPOT

Amid the great mass of similar fragments to the west of the center of the south wall of Room 38 of the Treasury.

DATE

The only clue to the date is the name of Baga-pāta, the treasurer who served from 467 to 440 B.C.

97. Mortar (PT5 423) Persepolis Museum 173; Pl. 25

ב[. . . . . ב . . . . בירתא ליד]	1)	[In the . . . of the fortress, beside . . .]
סגנא[. . . . . עבד הון זי גללֹ]	2)	[the *segan*, . . . used (this)]
מדם ליד בגפת גֹ]נזברא קדם[	3)	medium-sized [mortar of stone] beside Baga-pāta the trea[surer (and) before]
מזדדת אפֹ]נזברא אשכר[	4)	Mazda-dāta the sub-[treasurer. *ʾškr*]
בֹ]שֹנֹת . . . . . [	5)	in [year . . . .]

DESCRIPTION

A complete green chert mortar (base dia. 12.5 cm., height 12.4 cm., top dia. 10.6 cm.).

Traces of the beginnings of three lines of what was probably a five-line text remain on the bottom of the base. Many letters are quite faint, and some have disappeared entirely.

FIND SPOT

North of the center (HF 29) of Room 38 of the Treasury.

DATE

The names of Baga-pāta and Mazda-dāta as officials indicate a date sometime between 467 and 443 B.C.

98. Plate (PT5 828) T (111); Pl. 26

[בסר]ךֿ בֿיֿרֿתֿ]א ליד . . . . . סנגא]   1)   [In the ritu]al of the fortress [beside . . . the segan,]

הסדֿך / עבד סֿ]חרא זנה]   2)   1 Husadaka(?) used [this plate]

[ליד ב]גֿפֿת גנזברא קדם [. . . .]   3)   [beside Ba]ga-pāta the treasurer (and) before . . .

[אפגנזבר]א אשכֿרֿ שנ]ת . . . .]   4)   the [sub-treasurer]. *ʾškr* of year . . . .

DESCRIPTION

A triangular piece of the base of a green chert plate (max. length 9.7 cm.).

Parts of four lines of Aramaic are written on the bottom of the base. Only the middle of the lines remain. All that is visible in the first line are the bottoms of the letters and the remainder of the text is extremely faint.

FIND SPOT

Recovered in the sherd yard from fragments found toward the western part of the north wall (HF 27) of Room 38.

DATE

Baga-pāta, who is the treasurer in this text, served at least from 467 to 440 B.C., according to dated texts.

LINE 2

The reading of the name of the celebrant is certain but, as usual, the third letter could be either *d* or *r* for *Hsdk* or *Hsrk*.

The *h* at the beginning of the name could be the inseparable prefix *hu-*, "good," "beautiful."[324] The final *-k* probably represents the affix *-aka* or *-ka*, indicating a pet name or abbreviation.[325] If the spelling *-sd-* is accepted, it might represent *saða*, "appearance,"[326] or, if taken as *sr*, it could mean *sar-*, "companionship," or "fellowship."[327] Thus, the name seems to be either Husadaka, "Good looking," or Husaraka, "Good fellowship."

99. Mortar (PT5 446) T (119); Pl. 26

סֿגנ]א]   1)   the *segan* . . .

ליד בגֿפֿת [גנזברא]   2)   before Baga-pāta [the treasurer].

א[שכר שנ]ת . . . .   3)   *ʾškr* of year . . . .

DESCRIPTION

Fragment of a green chert mortar (base dia. 8 cm.). The fragment comes from the lower right-hand part of the base.

The beginnings of the last three lines of the text are preserved in faint letters.[328]

FIND SPOT

The west-central part (HF 37) of Room 38 of the Persepolis Treasury.

DATE

The name Baga-pāta indicates a date after 467/66 B.C.

[324] *BAiW*, col. 1817, *hu-*; Kent, *Old Persian*, p. 175a, *ʰu*.

[325] Justi, *Iranisches Namenbuch*, p. 521, *-aka;* Kent, *Old Persian*, p. 51, Sec. 146.

[326] *BAiW*, col. 1557, *saða;* Justi, *Iranisches Namenbuch*, p. 508, *saða;* cft. the name Wīsaða.

[327] *BAiW*, col. 1564, *²sar-*, "Vereinigung," "Genossenschaft," "Gemeinschaft."

[328] The Field Register mentions four lines of Aramaic, but the text shows only three.

100. Pestle (PT5 723) T (11); Pl. 26

[ב . . . . ב‎[בירתא	1)	[In the . . . of the fortress,]
[ת‎ . . . . ליד]	2)	[beside . . . t]
סג‎[נ]א‎] ב . . תפת /	3)	[the *segan*,] 1 B . . t-pāta
ע‎[בד] אבשון	4)	[used] a medium-sized
מד‎[ם לי]ד	5)	pestle beside
[ב‎]גפת גנז‎[ברא]	6)	Baga-pāta the treasurer.

DESCRIPTION

A fragment of a green chert pestle (head dia. 3.6 cm., present max. length 5.6 cm.). Part of the head is broken and the fracture passes diagonally across the shaft of the pestle, of which the lower part is completely gone.

Traces of six lines of Aramaic, written in thin, casual strokes, remain on the pestle top. There are only scattered traces of letters in the first two visible lines, and the first has now disappeared entirely. Although a number of letters are gone in the last three lines, they can be reconstructed with certainty in the familiar text.

FIND SPOT

Amid the great mass of green chert fragments west of the center of Room 38.

DATE

The name Baga-pāta as treasurer indicates a date after 467/66 B.C.

LINE 2

Only a long vertical line remains of the name of the *segan*. It could be the remains of a *t* or *k* of the name Mithraka, who served with the treasurer Baga-pāta.

LINE 3

Only the letter *n* of the title *segan* remains. The name of the celebrant should follow. It begins with the letter *b* and concludes with *-pt*, presumably for the familiar *-pāta*. The fore part of the name concluded with the letter *t*, which can still be read. Perhaps two or three letters are missing between the initial *b* and the next visible sign. The reading of the name of the celebrant thus appears to be 1 B . . t-pāta.

101. Mortar (PT5 227) T (30); Pl. 26

[ב . . . . ב‎] בירתא ליד א‎[מדת סגנא	1)	[In the . . . of the fortress, beside A]ma-dāta the *segan*,
[. . . . .] עבד הון זי‎] גלל אחש‎ֹינפן	2)	[. . . used (this) mortar of] dark . . . stone,
ליד [. . . . .] גנזברא	3)	[beside . . .] the treasurer.
[. . . . אשכר שנת]	4)	[ʾškr of year . . . .]

DESCRIPTION

A fragment of the base of a green chert mortar (base dia. 12 cm., present max. height 3 cm. [slightly reduced in illustration]).

All that remain on the bottom of the base are the ends of three lines of Aramaic. There was originally probably a fourth, relatively short, line that bore the date.

FIND SPOT

Amid the mass of fragments at the south wall, just west of the center (HF 48) of Room 38 of the Treasury.

DATE

Only the name of Ama-dāta the *segan* gives a clue to the date. He served as *segan* in the seventh (479/78 B.C.) and the sixteenth and seventeenth years of Xerxes (470–468 B.C.) and in the tenth year of Artaxerxes I (455/54 B.C.), according to the dated texts.

LINE 2

The last word of the line has proven to be troublesome. Cameron copied and transliterated it as *ʾmᶜqnr*. It must be admitted that the photograph could possibly support such a reading, although the forms of some of the letters would then be rather unusual. The ᶜ*aiyn* would be too elongated and the vertical stroke of the supposed *qoph* would be much too long for such letters in these texts.

While the second letter does appear to be an *m*, the clear spelling of the word as proposed below, shows it to be a letter *ḥ* made with one stroke reclining against another. What has been called an elongated ᶜ*aiyn* is instead the letter *š* with its short internal stroke omitted or faded away. What looks like a *q* is really an extremely cursive, carelessly made *y*, written joined to an elongated *n*.

Since the word that precedes it is *gll*, "stone," the enigmatic word is apparently a modifier of "stone." It is probably to be read as *ʾḥšynpn*, a variant of the *ʾḥšynpyn* found in Nos. 11:3 and 75:2. The first element of the compound, *ʾḥšyn-*, is probably the Persian *axšaina*, "dark colored."

102. Plate (PT5 693) Pl. 26

בפרכן ב]ירתא	1)	In the (haoma-)crushing ceremony of [the for-tress,]
ליד אריוחו	2)	beside Āraya(t)-vahu(š)
ס]ג[נא כרפיש עבד	3)	the *segan*, *Krpyš* used
[. . . . סחרא זנה]	4)	[this plate]. . . .

DESCRIPTION

A fragment of a green chert plate (base dia. 18 cm., present max. height 3.8 cm. [reduced in illustration]) of which almost all of the upper half of the base is preserved.

Three short lines of Aramaic remain on the bottom of the base. A fourth line is needed to complete a simple text.

FIND SPOT

Just to the west of the center of the south wall (HF 48) of Room 38 of the Persepolis Treasury.

DATE

The name of the *segan* Āraya(t)-vahu(š) places the mortar in the time of Artaxerxes I. A closer date might be obtained if the celebrant is the same one named in No. 25:2, which is dated in the third year of that reign (462/61 B.C.).

LINE 2

Cameron's copy leaves blanks at the ends of the first two lines. It is impossible to tell whether the name here is complete (cf. Nos. 42:2, 46:2) or whether the optional final *š* has been lost. Since the title begins the next line nothing more than the *š* stood at the end of this line.

LINE 3

The same name is found for the celebrant in No. 25 (a mortar) and in No. 103:2 (another mortar). The use of two mortars by this celebrant indicates that he participated in the ceremony at least twice. Such multiple acts would exclude the idea that the ceremony was part of a rite of initiation.

103. Mortar (PT5 670) T (50); Pl. 27

בפרכן ב[י]רתא ליד אר[י]וחו]	1)	In the (haoma-)crushing ceremony of the fortress, beside Āraya(t)-[vahu(š)]
סגנא כרפיש עבד [הון זי]	2)	the *segan*, *Krpyš* used [(this) mortar of]
גלל עם אבֹ[שון . . . . . .]	3)	stone with a pestle . . . .

DESCRIPTION

A fragment of the base of a green chert mortar (base dia. 12 cm., present max. height 1.8 cm.).

Parts of three lines of an originally somewhat longer text are preserved on the bottom of the base.

FIND SPOT

Southwest of the center (HF 38) of Room 38 of the Treasury.

DATE

The *segan* Āraya(t)-vahu(š) indicates a date in the reign of Artaxerxes I. Nos. 25 (462/61 B.C.) and 102 name the same celebrant.

LINE 1

To judge from Cameron's copy, although the name of the *segan* is broken and incomplete, it must have been written (as in Nos. 42:2, 46:2) without the final -*š*, since there would not be room for the full form (as in No. 49:2).

104. Plate (PT5 431 + 463) T (88); Pl. 27

ב[פ]רכן בירתא ליד]	1)	In [the (haoma-)crushing ceremony of the fortress, beside]
אר[יו]חוש סגנא . . . . .]	2)	Āraya(t)-va[hu(š) the *segan*, . . .]
עבד סחרֹ[. . . . . ליד]	3)	used (this) plate [. . . beside]
בגפת גנז[ברא . . . . . .]	4)	Baga-pāta the treasu[rer . . . .]

DESCRIPTION

Two pieces, PT5 431 and PT5 463, which join to form a fragment of a green chert plate (base dia. 9.9 cm., present max. height 3.7 cm.). The fragments form part of the right side of the base of the plate and a portion of the adjacent side, including part of its flat-top rim.

The beginnings of four lines of Aramaic are preserved on the bottom of the base. Most of the text is found on fragment PT5 431 (marked T [88]). Only the first two letters in the fourth line and the lower half of the third letter in that line are on the other piece (PT5 463).

FIND SPOT

Both pieces were recovered in the south-central part (HF 39) of Room 38 of the Persepolis Treasury. PT5 431 was found in almost the center of the room and PT5 463 was a short distance away, closer to the southern wall.

DATE

There must have been originally one or two more lines, one of which must have included the date. The officers can give a clue to a general date. Baga-pāta was treasurer from the nineteenth year of Xerxes through at least the twenty-ninth year of Artaxerxes I (466–435 B.C.). But Āraya(t)-vahuš served as *segan* for a much shorter time, from the third year of Artaxerxes I (462/61 B.C.; cf. No. 24). However, he does not appear regularly until the eleventh year of that reign (454/53 B.C.), when he is found constantly until as late as perhaps the twenty-ninth year of Artaxerxes I (No. 52; 436/35 B.C.).

105. Mortar (PT5——[329])

בפרכן בירתא	1)	In the (haoma-)crushing ceremony of the fortress,
ליד ארי[וחוש]	2)	beside Āraya(t)-[vahuš]
סגנא [. . . . . עבד הון] זי גלל	3)	the *segan*, [. . . used (this) mortar] of *hmš* . . .
. . . . . המש	4)	stone . . . .
אש[כר שנת . . . .]	5)	ʾš[*kr* of year. . . .]

DESCRIPTION

A small green chert mortar (base dia. 7.1 cm., height 8.4. cm.).

There are traces of parts of five lines of Aramaic on the bottom of the base. The first line is complete and the third has both beginning and end, but the middle portion is lacking. Only the beginnings of the other lines remain. All of the letters are badly faded and almost illegible.

The face of the text has been made extremely difficult to read, not only through the fading of the ink but also through carelessness in the Persepolis Museum. There is now green paint on the Aramaic text, as though the mortar had been set on a freshly painted shelf, and the accession numbers of the Persepolis Museum have been scrawled over the inscribed surface in both ink and red crayon.

FIND SPOT

The Persepolis Treasury.[330]

DATE

The name Āraya(t)-vahuš suggests a date probably between years 462 and 435 B.C.

106. Mortar (PT5 806) T (42); Pl. 27

בפרכן ב[ירתא ליד]	1)	In the (haoma-)crushing ceremony of the for-[tress, beside]
אריוהש [סגנא . . . . .]	2)	Āraya(t)-vahuš [the *segan*], 1 [. . .]
/ עבד הון ז[נ]ה ליד בגפת	3)	used this mortar [beside Baga-pāta]
גנזברא אשכ[ר שנת . . . . .]	4)	the treasurer. ʾšk[*r* of year . . . .]

---

[329] The field number is uncertain, since it has been "corrected" on the vessel. The figure seems to be either 412 or 422. Since PT5 422 (No. 108), as copied by Cameron, is broken and this is whole, one would expect this to be PT5 412. But according to the Field Register that is a limestone fragment bearing Old Persian letters. Unfortunately, no hand copy or photograph of No. 105 can now be found.

[330] The piece is probably from Room 38, but its locus cannot be determined accurately because of uncertainty as to its field number.

DESCRIPTION

A fragment of the base of a green chert mortar (base dia. 13.1 cm., present max. height 3.3 cm.).

The beginnings of four lines of Aramaic are preserved on the bottom of the base.

FIND SPOT

The northwestern corner (HF 36) of Room 38 of the Persepolis Treasury.

DATE

The *segan* Āraya(t)-vahuš permits a general dating between the years 454 and 435 B.C., or, less likely, 462/61 B.C.

107. Pestle (PT5——[331]) Pl. 27

ב . . . . [ב]	1)	[In the . . . of the fortress, beside] בירתא ליד]
[אר]יוהש [סגנא]	2)	[Āra]ya(t)-vahuš [the *segan*]. . . .

DESCRIPTION

A very small fragment of a green chert pestle head.

Only part of a single word in Aramaic script is preserved on the top of the pestle head. Cameron's copy shows no trace of letters above the word, but there is sufficient space for a line there, and the normal text calls for an introductory line which has probably faded away to illegibility.

FIND SPOT

Somewhere in the Persepolis Treasury, probably in Room 38.

DATE

If, as seems likely, the fragmentary word preserved is to be restored as the name of the *segan* Āraya(t)-vahuš, this text probably comes from sometime between 462 and 435 B.C., when dated texts mention him as *segan*.

108. Mortar (PT5 422) T (103); Pl. 27

[ב]פרכן בירתא	1)	[In] the (haoma-)crushing ceremony of the fortress,
ליד אריוהש ס[גנא]	2)	beside Āraya(t)-vahuš the *segan*,
מ[תר]פרן עבד [הון זי]	3)	Mithra(?)-farnah used a small [mortar of]
גלל זעיר / [ליד בגפת]	4)	stone [beside Baga-pāta]
[ג]נ̇ז̇ב̇ר̇א	5)	the treasurer . . . .

DESCRIPTION

A fragment of the base of a green chert mortar (base dia. 7.7 cm., with present max. length of 6.9 cm.).

Parts of five lines of Aramaic, consisting of one complete line and the beginnings of four others are preserved on the bottom of the mortar base. There were perhaps one or more lines below the preserved text originally.

FIND SPOT

North of the center (HF 29) of Room 38 of the Persepolis Treasury.

---

[331] Although Cameron records the field number of this fragment as PT5 653, the Field Register lists a glass vial at that number. Lack of such a number prevents a measurement or a close identification of its find spot.

DATE

The name of the *segan* supplies as a general basis for dating sometime between the years 462 and 435 B.C.

LINE 3

Cameron read the name of the celebrant as Mithra-pāta, who also appears as a celebrant in No. 7:3. The name is difficult to read. The letter which Cameron read as an incomplete *t* at the end of the name I see as an *n*, with the last element of the name as -*prn*, -*farnah*. The first element seems incomplete. It begins with the letter *m*, but there is space for another letter before the next sign, which could be the vertical stroke of an *r* or *d*. Cameron presumably read it as the principal stroke of a *t*.

LINE 4

After the word *gll*, "stone," there is additional text, which Cameron's copy shows as obscure. Cameron's copy has letters that seem to be .*nryrz*, with an extra space before the first letter, but he does not transliterate. The word is doubtless the *zᶜyr*, which is found elsewhere (for example, No. 31:3).

109. Plate (PT5 382) Pl. 28

[בפר]כן בירתא ליד	1)	[In the (haoma-)crus]hing ceremony of the fortress, beside
[אריו]הש סג[נא . . א̇ת̇]	2)	[Āraya(t)-va]huš the *segan*, . . .
[עב]ד [ס]ח[ר] זנה [ז̇י̇ גלל]	3)	used this plate [of stone]
[ליד] בג̇פ̇[ת̇] ג̇ז̇נ̇ז̇[בר̇א]	4)	[beside] Baga-pā[ta the treasurer]. . . .

DESCRIPTION

A fragment of the base of a green chert plate (length 7.7 cm., present max. height 4.8 cm.).

Traces of the ends of four lines of badly preserved Aramaic are on the bottom of the base. Cameron's copy, especially shaded at the ends of all lines, indicates the faded character of the writing, which in many places has disappeared entirely.

FIND SPOT

The south-central part (HF 39) of Room 38 of the Persepolis Treasury.

DATE

Āraya(t)-vahuš as *segan* indicates a date in the reign of Artaxerxes I, sometime between the years 462 and 435 B.C.

LINE 4

Cameron's copy suggests that the reading here is *shrᵓ zy*, which would be out of place if the formula of the text is normal. The expected reference to the object is already found in line 3. While the reading might be such an unusual one as *shrᵓ zy* [ᵓškr], "plate of the intoxicant (haoma)," just as ᵓ*bšwn zy* ᵓ*škr*, "pestle of the intoxicant," is found (No. 62), it seems more likely that the reference is to the treasurer, which is expected after the reference to the vessel in line 3 and it has been so regarded in the transliteration and translation.

What Cameron copied as an *s* could be a *b* with an excessively curved line at its head. What he rendered as *ḥ* is unlike that letter in line 3 and is probably formed of two letters, *g* and *p*, which the angular strokes resemble. Then the *t* of the name *Bgpt*, Baga-pata, must be found in the vertical stroke that follows and the hooked horizontal stroke at the top must be extraneous. The word that follows could then be part of the expected title, *gnzbrᵓ*, "treasurer."

The *g* is perhaps concealed in the angular bottom of the letter *ʾaleph* that Cameron clearly shows, a letter in form unlike that in the first line. The vertical stroke for *n* must have stood in the space immediately after it and the *z* that would then follow is the letter next expected in the title. What Cameron shows as a *y* is perhaps a trace of the letter *b* and the expected *rʾ* has disappeared entirely.

110. Plate (PT5 406) T (4); Pl. 28

בפרכן ב[ירתא ליד]	1)	In the (haoma-)crushing ceremony of the for-[tress, beside]
אריוחו [סגנא]	2)	Āraya(t)-vahu(š) [the *segan*]
בֹאתרת / [עבד סחרא]	3)	1 Bāta-rātā(?) [used] this [plate]
זנה ליד [בגפת גנזברא]	4)	beside [Baga-pāta the treasurer]
זי בֹהֹרֹ[חותי . . . . . .]	5)	who is in Ara[chosia . . .]

DESCRIPTION

A fragment of a green chert plate (base dia. 13 cm., present height 3.8 cm.) consisting of approximately the upper right quarter of the vessel, from its base to rim.

The beginnings of five lines of Aramaic, written in rather thick letters, are on the bottom of the base.

FIND SPOT

Near the center of the south wall (HF 49) of Room 38 of the Persepolis Treasury.

DATE

The *segan* Āraya(t)-vahuš indicates a date between the years 462 and 435 B.C.

LINE 3

The name of the celebrant begins with an incomplete letter that has all the characteristics of the letter *b*. As usual, the fourth letter could be read as either *d* or *r*. Thus, the name could be read as *Bʾtdt* or *Bʾtrt*. Eilers has proposed reading the name as either Bāta-dāta, "One giving wine," or Bāta-rātā, "He whose (sacrificial) gift is wine." The first element *bʾt*, *bāta*, "wine,"[332] is found elsewhere in these texts (for example, No. 29:4). The second element in the compound could be either -*dāta*, "giving," which is often encountered in Old Persian names, or -*rātā*, "gift."[333]

LINES 4 AND 5

After the *lyd* in the fourth line, the text must have had the name of the treasurer, who is always Baga-pāta when Āraya(t)-vahuš is the *segan*. The restoration is supported by line 5, where the text must be completed as "who is in Arachosia," an expression associated with the treasurer Baga-pāta in a number of these texts.[334]

111. Plate (PT6 162) T (48); Pl. 28

בפרכן בירתא	1)	In the (haoma-)crushing ceremony of the for-tress,
לֹ[יֹ]רֹ אֹ[רֹ]יוהש	2)	beside Āraya(t)-vahuš

---

[332] R. G. Kent, "The Present Status of Old Persian Studies," *Journal of the American Oriental Society* LVI (1936) 215 and LVIII (1938) 327.

[333] *BAiW*, cols. 1519–20, *rātā*, "Gabe," "Geschenk."

[334] Nos. 43:6, 48:7, 79:3, etc.

. . . .‏בג[‏א‏]סגנ	3)	the *segan*, Baga- . . .
‏עבד ס[‏חר זי‏]	4)	used (this) pl[ate of] . . .
‏גלל‏	5)	stone . . .
‏ק[‏דם‏ . . . .]	6)	before . . .
‏אפגנזברא[‏. . . .]	7)	[the sub-treasurer . . . .]

DESCRIPTION

A fragment of a green chert plate (base dia. 8.3 cm., present max. height 1.9 cm.), consisting of top and part of the right edge of the base.

Two complete lines of Aramaic and the beginnings of four more are preserved on the bottom of the base. At least one more line would be necessary for a complete, dated text.

FIND SPOT

Just north of the center (HF 69) of Room 41 of the Persepolis Treasury, where most of the precious royal tableware was stored.[335]

DATE

Āraya(t)-vahuš served as *segan* in 462 B.C. and between 454 and 435 B.C.

LINE 6

The only sign visible in this line is obscure. Cameron's copy shows a combination of strokes that look like the tops of the letters *p* and *b* in contact. In combination they most resemble the top of the letter *q*, which might be expected as part of the preposition *qdm*, which introduces the sub-treasurer.

112. Plate (PT4 97) Pl. 28

‏בירתא‏ ‏כן[‏בפר]	1)	[In the (haoma-)crushing ceremony] of the fortress
‏אריוהש‏ [‏ליד]	2)	[beside] Āraya(t)-vahuš
‏מה[‏ש]‏בהיין‏ ‏סג[‏נא]	3)	the *segan*, *Bhyyn* by name
‏ז[‏י]‏זנה‏ ‏סחרא‏ [‏עבד]	4)	[used] this plate of
‏בזי‏ / ‏ב[‏עיד]‏גלל]	5)	[stone] in a festival . . . .

DESCRIPTION

A fragment of a green chert plate (base dia. 7.6 cm., present height 3 cm.), consisting of two-thirds of the base and a very small portion of the adjacent side.

The ends of five lines of Aramaic are preserved on the bottom of its base in letters that are badly faded and almost illegible.

FIND SPOT

Found in "Garrison Street," along the eastern side of the Treasury, just north of the eastern exit (HG 54) of the Treasury.

DATE

The *segan* Āraya(t)-vahuš indicates a date sometime within the years 462 to 435 B.C. The same celebrant dedicated another plate in the nineteenth year of Artaxerxes I (446/45 B.C.), presumably on another occasion.

LINE 3

The celebrant also occurs in No. 48:3, another plate, which identifies him as a *plg*, "myriarch."

[335] See p. 3.

LINES 4 AND 5

The fourth line has a faint letter *z* after the demonstrative *znh*. It is probably part of the word *zy*, which suggests that *gll*, "stone," was the first word in the fifth line.

One is inclined to read the first word in line five as *zᶜyr*, "small." But no other plate is designated as small and this one (base dia. 17.6 cm.) is certainly not small, for it belongs in the category of those called "large" (for example, No. 18, base dia. 13.5 cm.). Furthermore, the unit stroke after the word does not fit well syntactically with the *znh*, "this," of line 4.

The first sign at the edge of the break in line 5 has a blurred portion of the head of a letter and a faded, curved stroke that marks it as the letter *b*. The following letter is clearly an ᶜ*aiyn*, indicating a Semitic word. The next letter is a thick, heavy *y* and the last is either *d* or *r*, probably the former, to judge from the shortness of its vertical stroke. The reading, therefore, seems to be *bᶜyd*, which is followed by the unit stroke. The word is probably the Targumic Aramaic עֵיד, "appointed day," which is used in Hebrew for "anniversary" or "(idolatrous) festival."[336] It is the Arabic *ᶜīd* (عيد), "feast," "festival," which is also used in Modern Persian in the same sense, as in ᶜ*īdi nau-roz*, "Feast of the (Persian) New Year."[337]

The word ᶜ*yd* relates to the verb in the same way as in the ᶜ*bd . . . bprk rb* 1, "used (this vessel) in a great ceremony of crushing (haoma)" in No. 5:3.

After the *bᶜyd* 1 there appears the word *bzy*, which is used elsewhere as a modifier of the word "stone" (for example, Nos. 76:2, 92:5; cf. *bz* in No. 91:3). The meaning of the word is uncertain and, since the text is incomplete, its syntax and significance is unknown.

113. Plate (PT4 127) Teheran Museum 2225; Pl. 28

בֹּ[סֹ]רךֹ בִּירֹחֹא לִידֹ	1)	In the ritual of the fortress, beside
אריוהש סגנא רמן עֹבֹ[ד]	2)	Āraya(t)-vahuš the *segan*, Rāman used
סֹחֹר זנה [זִי] גלל קדם [בנפת]	3)	this plate of stone before [Baga-pāta]
גנזברא אֹ[שֹׁכֹר]	4)	the treasurer. ᵓ*škr*
[. . . . שֹׁנֹת]	5)	[of year. . . .]

DESCRIPTION

A fragment of a large green chert plate (base dia. 10.3 cm.), consisting of the upper part of the base and part of its adjacent side. Heavy banding and lines in the stone run diagonally through the inscribed text.

Traces of five lines of Aramaic are on the bottom of the base. The first line is very faint but still legible. Elsewhere the letters are faint and often illegible, especially those written on the dark bands. The letters of the last line are illegible.

FIND SPOT

The northeastern corner (HG 51) of Room 23 of the Treasury which, with Portico 19, formed a passage between the administrative compound (17) and Room 33.[338]

DATE

Āraya(t)-vahuš served as *segan* during the years 462–435 B.C. of the reign of Artaxerxes I. The date line of this text is lost. A celebrant with the same name, Rāman, is mentioned in No. 39:3 from the tenth year of Artaxerxes I (455/54 B.C.).

---

[336] Jastrow, *Dictionary* II 1067a. In Syriac (Payne Smith, *A Compendious Syriac Dictionary*, p. 400a, ܥܰܕ) the verbal root signifies "to fix a place or time of meeting," "to assemble," or "to celebrate," "to keep a feast."

[337] Steingass, *A Comprehensive Persian-English Dictionary*, p. 875b.

[338] See p. 4.

LINE 2

The same celebrant also has offered two pestles (Nos. 39 and 40), both in the tenth year of Artaxerxes I (455/54 B.C.) but on different occasions.

114. Mortar (PT5 711) Pl. 29

[ב . . . . בירתא ליד]	1)	[In the . . . of the fortress, beside]
ארי[והש סגנא . . . . . עבד הון זנה]	2)	Āraya(t)-[vahuš the *segan*, . . . used this mortar]
לפתי א[טבען . . . . . ליד בגפת]	3)	worth [. . . shekels, beside Baga-pāta]
. . . . גנזברא	4)	the treasurer . . . .

DESCRIPTION

A small, almost triangular fragment of the base of a green chert mortar (longest side 5.0 cm. and its base 3.9 cm.). The somewhat curved third side may be part of the original circumference of the base.

Parts of three lines of Aramaic, written in ink, are on the bottom of the base. In the proposed reconstruction it is assumed that the right-hand margin is original and that the words preserved represent the beginnings of lines. There was certainly at least one line above the preserved text and probably another below it, if the text were of normal size for a mortar.

FIND SPOT

Found near the center (HF 29) of Room 38 of the Persepolis Treasury.

DATE

The first three letters are probably the beginning of the name of the *segan* Āraya(t)-vahuš, who served from 462 to 435 B.C. according to dated texts.

LINE 3

The word *lpty* in the second preserved line introduces a statement regarding the cost of the vessel, as in No. 43:4 (and possibly in No. 73:5). Since the word elsewhere follows the description of the object, that should be restored in the preceding line.

The *ʾaleph* at the break must be the beginning of the word *ʾṭbᶜn*, "(shekel) coins," as in No. 43:4. It should be followed by the proper strokes of the numeral.

115. Pestle (PT5 76) Persepolis Museum 211; Pl. 29

[ב . . . .] בי[ר]תא	1)	[In the . . . of] the fortress,
[ליד אריוה]וש סגן	2)	[beside Araya(t)-vah]uš the *segan*
[. . . . .]תר	3)	. . . .

DESCRIPTION

A fragment of a green chert pestle (head dia. 6.1 cm., present max. length 10.8 cm.), consisting of the head and part of the shaft. The top of the head was polished before being inscribed.

There are faint traces of five lines of Aramaic text, but only the first two lines are legible. The letters are extremely faded and illegible, except at the ends of the first two lines. The Persepolis Museum accession number has been scrawled over the text on the top of the pestle head.

FIND SPOT

South of the center (HF 39) of the great Room 38 of the Persepolis Treasury.

DATE

The last two letters of the name of the *segan* are clearly *-wš*. The only suitable name is Āraya(t)-vahuš, who served during the years 462–435 B.C.

LINE 2

There is no room for the expected *ʾaleph* with *sgnʾ* at the end of the line.

116. Mortar (PT5 816) Pl. 29

בפרכן [בירתא]	1)	In the (haoma-)crushing ceremony of [the fortress,]
פהרברן עבד הון	2)	Pāhra-barana used (this) mortar
זי גלל זי בז קדם	3)	of *bz* stone before
אריוהש אפ[נ]זֹֹב[זֹב]רֹא	4)	Āraya(t)-vahuš the sub-treasurer (and)
ליד בֹ]גֹפֹת גנברא]	5)	beside Ba[ga-pāta the treasurer.]
[א]שֹ]כר שנת [. . . .]	6)	*ʾškr* of [year . . . .]

DESCRIPTION

A fragment of the base of a green chert mortar (base dia. 7.2 cm., present max. height 2 cm.). Six lines of Aramaic are preserved on the bottom of its base. Some of the letters have faded to illegibility.

FIND SPOT

North of the center (HF 29) of Room 38 of the Persepolis Treasury.

DATE

The year date is missing, but the name Āraya(t)-vahuš as an official furnishes some clue to the date. He served as *segan* possibly as late as the twenty-ninth year of Artaxerxes I (436/35 B.C.), the last dated text (No. 52). Only here, however, is Āraya(t)-vahuš called "sub-treasurer." He is doubtless the same person as *segan* and sub-treasurer. The date of this text is therefore probably after the twenty-ninth year of Artaxerxes I (436/35 B.C.), but before Baga-pāta was replaced by Arta-čanah as treasurer (No. 122).

LINE 2

The first element of the name of the celebrant, *phr* is perhaps the Middle Persian *pāhra* from an earlier *pāθra*, "protection."[339] It possibly occurs as an element in a name in No. 90. The second element is *-barana*, "bringing."[340] Thus, the name is Pāhra-barana, "He who brings protection."

LINE 3

Two short words follow the word *gll*, "stone." The first begins with a *z* followed by an angular *yodh*. The second word begins with the letter *b*, and it has after it what appears to be a blotlike *yodh*, which Cameron copied and transcribed, probably correctly, as a *z*. The word is doubtless the *bz* which elsewhere seems to designate a type or quality of stone (for example, No. 91:3).

The *qdm* at the end of the line normally introduces the sub-treasurer, further proof that Āraya(t)-vahuš is no longer a *segan*. It is difficult to determine whether the change in title indicates promotion or demotion.[341]

[339] *BAiW*, col. 887, Pāθraʾvant.

[340] *Ibid.*, col. 943, *barana*, "tragend."

[341] See pp. 27, 30.

LINE 4

The title is "sub-treasurer," as Cameron copied and read it and as the faint traces in the photograph indicate.

117. Pestle (PT6 59) Pl. 29

בסרך בּ[י]רתא 1) In the ritual of the fortress,

לִיד .....‏ [ס]גנ[א] 2) beside . . . the *segan,*

ב[ג]שׁתֹר / עֹבֹד אֹבֹ[שון] 3) 1 Baga-čiθra used (this) pestle

[ליד] בגפֹת גֹנ[ז]בֹּר[א] 4) [beside] Baga-pāta the treasurer.

[.... אֹשֹׁכֹר שנת] 5) [ᵓškr of year . . . .]

DESCRIPTION

A fragment of a green chert pestle (head dia. 4.3 cm., present max. length 11.6 cm.).

Traces of five lines of Aramaic, written in very small, delicate letters, are on top of the pestle head. Most of the letters are so faded that they are almost illegible. Except for an occasional trace of a letter, the surface almost seems to be uninscribed. The last line is written over a dark band in the stone. With knowledge of the general format of the texts and with long and diligent study of the text with a magnifying glass, it has been possible to recognize enough letters and words to construct a probable text.

FIND SPOT

At the east end (HG 11) of Room 48 of the Treasury. It was a subsidiary room entered from the northeastern part of Room 38.[342]

DATE

The date line is illegible because of the dark band on which it is written. Only the name Baga-pāta gives a clue. He served as treasurer from the nineteenth year of Xerxes to at least the twenty-ninth year of Artaxerxes I (467–435 B.C.).

LINE 3

The line, written across the center of the disk, is difficult to read. The letters are quite faint but structurally discernible. The first letter is a dark, blurred sign. It is followed by a somewhat "circular" mark which could be *g* for the first element *bg, baga-.*

The outside lines of the letter *š* are visible, as is most of the following *t*. The letter *r* that concludes the name is rather clear. The element *štr,* which also appears in other names,[343] suggests the Šethar of the Bible (Esther 1:14).[344] Since the word *xšaθra,* "kingdom," "rule," is elsewhere transcribed as *ḥštr* (No. 89:2), it is probable that *štr* here does not represent that word. It is likely that the name *bgštr* should be read as Baga-čiθra, "Of divine lineage." Justi conjectures that such a name lies behind the Greek *Megasidras* (Μεγασίδρας) mentioned by Herodotus (vii. 72).[345]

118. Mortar (PT5 749) Pl. 29

בסרך בירתא ליד 1) In the ritual of the fortress, beside

מזפרן סגנא שׁ[ב]ֹר 2) Mazza-farnah the *segan,* Šbr,

---

[342] See p. 3.   [343] Nos. 36:2, 87:3.

[344] Justi, *Iranisches Namenbuch,* p. 298*b,* Šēthār; I. Scheftelowitz ("Zur Kritik des griechischen und des massoretischen Buches Esther," *Monatsschrift für Geschichte und Wissenschaft des Judenthums,* XLVII [1903] 212) suggests that the Biblical name represents Old Iranian *šēθra,* "lord."

[345] Justi, *Iranisches Namenbuch,* p. 57*b,* *Baga-čiθra(?); Μεγασίδρας, "von göttlichem Geschlecht (Samen)"; Kent, *Old Persian,* p. 184*a, čiça-,* "seed," "lineage."

אלף פלג עבד הון זי 3) a chiliarch of a division, used

גלל זעיר זנֹה [לֹיֹדֹ] 4) this small mortar of stone [beside]

[. . . . אבֹּגֹפת גנזברא] 5) [Baga-pāta the treasurer. . . .]

DESCRIPTION

A small green chert mortar (base dia. 8.2 cm., present height 8.4 cm.), of which both the bowl and base are broken.

Four lines of Aramaic and the first two letters of a fifth are preserved on the bottom of the base. Another line would be necessary for a complete, dated text.

FIND SPOT

In the great mass of similar fragments in the west-central part (HF 38) of Room 38.

DATE

Mazza-farnah the *segan* is found elsewhere (No. 21) only in a text of the second year of Artaxerxes I (463/62 B.C.).

LINE 2

The *segan* *Mzprn*, who is also found in No. 21, has a name which may correspond to Mazda-farnah. It may also be the name that appears as *Mdzprn* for the *segan* in No. 54:2.

The name of the celebrant is somewhat difficult to read because the second letter is quite faint and the top of the third, also faint, is connected to the end of the *d* in the line above. The first letter is clearly a *š*. Cameron shows a trace of the curving bottom that marks the second letter as a *b*. The third letter is a *d* or *r*, as Cameron recognized. The name is short. Nothing is visible after the *r/d* in the photograph. The spelling could represent either an Iranian *šbr* or *čbr*, but the name is as yet unidentifiable.

LINE 3

The collocation *ʾlp plg* is significant for the light it casts on the titles given to the celebrants. They seem to be the titles *ʾlp*, "chiliarch" (cf. No. 52:3), and *plg*, "myriarch" (cf. No. 17:3), but both titles would not have been used at the same time. Only the first is the title. The second word is the noun used to designate the military unit of 10,000 men, the division.[346] Thus, in this text, "a chiliarch of a division" indicates that the *ʾlp*, "chiliarch," is a lesser office than the *plg*, "myriarch," the commander of a division. The *plg* here is the "division," a military organization composed of smaller units of a thousand, commanded by chiliarchs.

119. Plate (PT5 788) Pl. 29

בהֹסת בירתא ליד והופרן 1) In the *hst* of the fortress, beside Vahu-farnah

[סגנ[א שורתי שמה / עבד [ס[חֹר[אֹ] 2) the *segan*, 1 *Šwrty* by name used

[זנה ליד ב]גפת גנזברא זי 3) [this plate beside Ba]ga-pāta the treasurer who is

[בהרחותי ק]דם שרוֹן אפגנזברא 4) [in Arachosia, be]fore *Šrwn* the sub-treasurer.

[. . . . אשכר שנת] 5) [*ʾškr* of year . . . .]

DESCRIPTION

A fragment of the base of a green chert plate (base dia. 13.4 cm., present max. height 3.2 cm.). It consists of part of the top and left side of the inscribed base and part of the adjacent side, extending to the rim.

The remains of four lines of Aramaic are preserved on the bottom of its base. A last line is

[346] See p. 34.

needed to complete the text. The beginnings of the second, third, and fourth lines have been broken away and lost.

FIND SPOT

The southeastern corner (HF 47) of Room 38.

DATE

Loss of the date line precludes exact dating of the text, but the same celebrant is mentioned in a dated text (No. 36) of the seventh year of Artaxerxes I (458/57 B.C.).

LINE 1

The difficult word *hst* occurs only with vessels dedicated by the celebrant *Šwrty* (Nos. 36, 119, and 120).

The *segan* Vahu-farnah is unique in these texts, but the name appears as that of a celebrant on several texts (Nos. 6:3 and 10:3). Except for the treasurer Baga-pāta, the officers named on the vessels dedicated by *Šwrty* do not conform to those encountered regularly at Persepolis.

LINE 2

The celebrant *Šwrty* presented a mortar (No. 36) and a pestle (No. 120) in addition to this plate, thus giving a complete set of three pieces. Since the *segan* differs in each instance, the donations evidently mark different occasions.

LINE 4

The sub-treasurer *Šrwn* is found only here in the ritual vessels. Justi mentions a Šarwin,[347] but the last element of the name might represent the *-vāna*, "prevailing," "conqueror,"[348] found elsewhere in a number of names in these texts. The initial element *šr* could also be *čr* phonetically, possibly for *čāra*, "help(?)."[349]

120. Pestle (PT5 665) T (131); Pl. 30

בהסת בירת[א]	1)	In the *hst* of the fortress,
ליד שורתי סגנ[א]	2)	beside *Šwrty* the *segan*,
שורתי עבד אבש[ו]ן	3)	*Šwrty* used this pestle.
[ז]נה אשכר שנת	4)	*ʾškr* of year
. . . . .	5)	. . . .

DESCRIPTION

A fragment of the head of a green chert pestle (head dia. 5.9 cm.).

Four lines of Aramaic are written in rather large, thick letters on top of the pestle head. The figure of the date must have been in a short line below the preserved text, but that part of the head has been broken away.

FIND SPOT

Among the great mass of chert fragments just west of the center (HF 49) of the south wall of Room 38 of the Treasury.

DATE

Since the year date is lost, the problem of dating is identical with that of No. 119.

---

[347] Justi, *Iranisches Namenbuch*, p. 290.

[348] *BAiW*, cols. 1350–53; Kent, *Old Persian*, p. 208b under Vivāna.

[349] Kent, *Old Persian*, p. 175, under *učāra*; cft. Late Avestan *čārā*, "Hilfsmittel."

LINES 2 AND 3

The same celebrant is found in Nos. 36 and 119. Here (l. 2) the *segan* bears the same name as the celebrant. This is an unlikely coincidence, especially since no such *segan* is encountered elsewhere, and may be due to scribal error. It is probable that each of the vessels presented by *Šwrty* represents a different time and ceremony, for each of the *segan*'s mentioned (Vinda[t]-farnah [No. 36], Vahu-farnah [No. 119], and *Šwrty* [*sic*]) bears a different name.

121. Mortar (PT5 731) T (137); Pl. 30

ב[ס[ו]רך [ב]יר[ת]א	1)	In the ritual of the fortress,
[ל]יד בחפרת ס[ג]ג[נ]א	2)	beside *Bḥprt* the *segan*, . . .

DESCRIPTION

A fragment of a small, green chert mortar (base dia. 7.5 cm., max. height 7.35 cm.).

Traces of two lines of Aramaic are written in thin, fine letters on the bottom of the base. The text is incomplete. Some of the delicate letters are faded to illegibility and the banding and lines in the stone make the reading difficult.

FIND SPOT

Just west of the center of the south wall (HF 48) of Room 38 of the Treasury.

DATE

Since the date line is missing and the *segan* is unique, this text is undateable.

LINE 2

The name of the *segan*, *Bḥprt*, is found nowhere else in these texts. It suggests such a name as Baχtāfrīt, "Having the blessing of good fortune."[350] Because Aramaic *ḥ* may also represent Iranian *h*, Eilers has suggested that the name might represent *Bḥprt* for Baṇha-friθa, "Liking *hašīš*." This assumes that the first element *bh-* can represent *baṇha-*, "hemp," "*hašīš*."[351] The second element is *prt*, *-friθa*, "liking," "delighting in."[352]

122. Mortar (PT5 773) Pl. 30

בסרך בירתא ליד סרבי סגנא	1)	In the ritual of the fortress, beside *Srby* the *segan*,
ריב]. . עבד] הון זי גלל כפותך	2)	*Ryb* . . . [used] (this) mortar of pigeon-colored stone
[קדם . . . . . אפנגזברא לי[ד ארתשנ[א] גנ[ז]ובדא[	3)	[before . . . the sub-treasurer be]side Arta-čanah the treasurer.

DESCRIPTION

A fragment of the base of a large, green chert mortar (base dia. 16.5 cm., present max. height 4.6 cm.).

Parts of three lines are preserved on the bottom of the base, but the text is incomplete at the end. The text occupies only a small part of the surface of the base, even though the lines are rather widely spaced. Many of the letters are so faded as to be almost illegible. The last half of the first line is written over a dark band in the stone at the top of the base. Extensive

---

[350] Justi, *Iranisches Namenbuch*, p. 61, Baχtāfrīt.

[351] *BAiW*, col. 925, *baṇha, bangha-*, "Hanf" and "Narkotikum aus Hanf." Eilers suggests that the word "hemp" also may be an element in the name *Bḥyyn* (Baṇha-yāna?) in Nos. 48 and 112.

[352] *BAiW*, col. 1025, *friθa-*.

heavy chipping of the inscribed surface damages the second and third lines near their beginnings and the letters at the beginnings of the lines are so faint as to be almost illegible.

FIND SPOT

On the floor amid the columns in the northwestern part (HF 37) of Room 38 of the Persepolis Treasury.

DATE

Since the date line is lost and the officials are unique, the date of the text cannot be ascertained.

If the reading of the text is correct, its date must fall after Baga-pāta had been displaced by Arta-čanah as treasurer, sometime after the twenty-ninth year of Artaxerxes I (436/35 B.C.).

LINE 1

Because the letters are faint and written partly on a dark band in the stone, the name is very difficult to read. Cameron at first copied *rkby* and transliterated it as *r/dkbs* but later changed it to read only two letters, either of which could be either *d* or *r*, at the beginning of the word. In the photograph it appears to be *Srby* or *Sdby*. The name is unique for a *segan* in these texts.

LINE 2

The name of the celebrant is extremely faint and partly destroyed by the huge chip in the inscribed surface in the second and third lines. Cameron copied *brk* . . . or the like, but he transliterated only the first letter, *d* or *r*, and indicated that the text is obscure. The photograph seems to show *ryb* . . . or *dyb* . . . but the remainder of the name is gone.

The word *kpwtk*, which modifies *gll*, "stone," is doubtless the Old Persian *kapautaka*, which is normally used to indicate lapis lazuli.[353] But the green chert stone with dark, gray-green banding of which the ritual objects are made is obviously not lapis lazuli, "an opaque, dark blue stone which has spots, patches, or veins of white (calcite) and sometimes minute spangles of iron pyrites, looking like specks of gold. . . ."[354] The term may be used here in a specialized sense of "veined" or "marbled."[355] But the word *kapautaka*, derived from the word "pigeon" (Sanskrit *kapóta*), could mean "pigeon-colored," which might be appropriate for the grayish-green color of the chert vessels which often have bandings that resemble pigeon markings.

LINE 3

The spelling for the name of the treasurer could be either *ʾrtšnʾ* or *ʾrtčnʾ*, since there is a possibility of an *ʾaleph* in the very faint trace of a sign after the letter *n*. The name may also be found in the Aramaic fortification tablets from Persepolis from the time of Darius I.[356] It is found nowhere else in these texts as the name of a treasurer.

Justi lists an Iranian Artašin,[357] but Eilers prefers reading the name as Arta-čanah or Arta-činah, "He whose longing is for Arta."[358]

The two clear letters that follow the name and the trace of the preposition that precedes it indicate that the reference is to the treasurer. It is uncertain what stood at the beginning of the third line. It is conjectured that a reference to the sub-treasurer filled the space. Normally the name of the treasurer preceded that of sub-treasurer, but there are some examples of a reversal of that order (for example, No. 116).

---

[353] Meillet and Benveniste, *Grammaire*, p. 58, Sec. 98 and p. 159, Sec. 273; Kent, *Old Persian*, p. 178*b*.

[354] A. Lucas, *Ancient Egyptian Materials and Industries* (3d ed.; London, 1948), p. 455.

[355] Bowman, in *Dōrōn*, pp. 68–69. [356] Tablet 65, l. 2.

[357] Justi, *Iranisches Namenbuch*, p. 37, Artašin; Greek ᾿Αρτασίνης.

[358] Kent, *Old Persian*, pp. 183–84, canah, "desire"; cf. p. 173*b* under Aspacanah; Justi, *Iranisches Namenbuch*, p. 46, Aspačanah, p. 498, čanah; *BAiW*, col. 240, Avestan Aša-činah.

123. Pestle (PT6 92) T (22); Pl. 30

בפרכן בירת[א ליד . . . . .]	1)	In the (haoma-)crushing ceremony of the fortress, [beside . . .]
סגנא אפֹ[. . . עבד אבשון]	2)	the *segan*, Ap. . . [used]
זעיר / לי[ד . . . . .]	3)	a small [pestle] beside [. . .]
גנ[זֹבֹרא . . . .]	4)	the treasurer . . .
[אֹ[שֹכֹר] שנ]ת . . .]	5)	*ʾškr* of year . . . .

DESCRIPTION

The bottom of the shaft of a small green chert pestle (max. length 6 cm.; max. dia. 3 cm.).

The beginnings of five lines of Aramaic are preserved on the shaft of the pestle,[359] written from the tip toward the handle. The ends of all lines are broken away.

FIND SPOT

Recovered at the top of a flight of stairs (49) leading to the roof from a guardroom (50) at the northern exit of the Treasury (HG 01).[360]

DATE

The loss of the year date and the names of the officials makes dating impossible.

LINE 4

Although Cameron indicates that the fourth line is faint and obscure, he shows traces in his copy of letters that might be read *bḥk bk*, but he offers neither transliteration nor translation. The reading that his traces suggest might fit part of the expression [*zy*] *bhr*[*ḥwty*], "who is in Arachosia." But such a reading would presuppose the name and title of the treasurer at the end of the previous line, which would then be much too long.

The letters suggested by Cameron are not now visible on the pestle. The only complete structure might be taken as a *t* but it could equally well be *gn*, the first two letters of the treasurer's title and the few brief traces of letters beyond it would fit the reading *gnz*[*b*]*r*[*ʾ*], "the treasurer."

LINE 5

Cameron's copy shows only a letter *ʾaleph*. However, there appear to be some simple strokes that would suit the reading conjectured above.

124. Mortar (PT5 262) T (25); Pl. 30

בפרכֹן בירתא ליד . . . .]	1)	In the (haoma-)crushing ceremony of [the fortress, beside . . .]
ס⟨ג⟩⟨נ⟩א אֹ[. . . . . . עבד הון]	2)	the *segan*, A[. . . used] a
מדם / קֹ[דם . . . . . אפגנזברא]	3)	medium-sized [mortar before . . . the sub-treasurer].
[אֹשכר שנ]ת . . . . . .]	4)	*ʾškr* of year . . . .

DESCRIPTION

A fragment of a green chert mortar base (base dia. 13 cm., present max. height 3 cm.) from the right side of the vessel.

The beginnings of four lines of Aramaic are preserved on the polished bottom of the base. The large spall has carried away a good part of the fragment, but it damages only the first letter of the fourth line, which can be restored with certainty.

---

[359] Other pestles so inscribed are Nos. 17 and 81.

[360] See p. 5; Schmidt, *Persepolis* I 146, 186, and Fig. 73a.

FIND SPOT

In the street just outside of the northwestern corner of the Persepolis Treasury building (HF 24).

DATE

From the Achaemenid period and contemporary with the rest of the ritual objects but no closer date is possible.

LINE 2

Cameron's copy, supported by the photograph, spells the first word as *sn⁾* without the letter *g* for the expected title *sgn⁾*, "the *segan*." It is probably a scribal error rather than evidence of an assimilation of the *g* to the *n* for a pronunciation *sinnā⁾* for *signā⁾*.

125. Mortar (PT6 87) T (142); Pl. 31

בפרכן בירתא ליד . . . . . [סגנא]	1)	In the (haoma-)crushing ceremony of the fortress, beside [. . . the *segan*],
וספרן עבד ה[ון . . . .]	2)	Visa-farnah used (this) mortar [before(?)]
[ששפ]רן	3)	[Čiθra-fa]rnah(?) . . . .

DESCRIPTION

A fragment of the base of a small green chert mortar (base dia. 7.5 cm., present max. height 2.2 cm.). A wide dark band in the stone runs horizontally across the center of the base.

Parts of three lines of Aramaic, written in rather small letters on top of the dark band in the stone, are preserved on the bottom of the base.

FIND SPOT

At the east wall of Room 45 (HF 27), entered through a doorway in the western part of the north wall of Room 38 of the Persepolis Treasury.

DATE

Undateable unless the scant traces in the third line belong to the name *Ššprn*, Čiθra-farnah, who appears as a sub-treasurer (Nos. 50 and 53) in the twenty-fourth year of Artaxerxes I (444/43 B.C.).

LINE 2

The name of the celebrant, *Wsprn*, is regarded by Eilers as being Visa-farnah, "Having all glory."[361] According to Bailey's interpretation of the element *-farnah*, the name could mean "Everything desired."[362]

126. Pestle (PT5 440) Pl. 31

בפרכן בירת[א]	1)	In the (haoma-)crushing ceremony of the fortress,
א̇ספסתן עבד	2)	Aspa-stāna used
[א]בשון זנה̇	3)	this pestle.

---

[361] *BAiW*, cols. 1457–58, *visa-*, "all"; Kent, *Old Persian*, p. 208b, *visa-*. Benveniste (*Titres et noms*, p. 88) sees this name in the Elamite Mišparna.

[362] Bailey, *Zoroastrian Problems in the Ninth Century Books*, pp. 1–3, 73–77; cf. Kent, *Old Persian*, p. 208a, under Viⁿda-farnah.

DESCRIPTION

A fragment of a green chert pestle (head dia. 3.8 cm., present max. length 8.3 cm.).

Three lines of Aramaic are written in relatively large, thick letters on the top of the pestle head.

FIND SPOT

South of the center (HF 39) of Room 38 of the Persepolis Treasury.

DATE

Precise dating is impossible.

LINE 2

The first letter of the name of the celebrant is unique in form. It is a vertical stroke with a comma-like tail, somewhat like the basic stroke of a figure 5. It is certainly a cursive form of ʾ*aleph* peculiar to the hand of this text. The only discernible trace of the first letter in the word "pestle" in the third line is just such a vertical stroke and that seems to be true also with the almost illegible letter that concludes the first line. The name is ʾ*spstn*, of which the first element is *aspa-*, "horse," and the second *-stāna*, "place."[363] Eilers renders the name as "He whose place is with horses." As an alternative reading, Frye has proposed *Aspa-stana*, "Having a horse-like voice."

127. Pestle (PT5 439) Pl. 31

אתרברזן   1)   Ātar-barzana
עבד   2)   used (this).

DESCRIPTION

A fragment of the upper part of a green chert pestle (head dia. 3.5 cm., present max. length 4.8 cm.).

Two words, written in extra large, smudged letters, are on top of the pestle head. The first word is slightly above the middle of the disk and the other is just below it.

FIND SPOT

South of the center (HF 39) of Room 38 of the Treasury.

DATE

Precise dating is impossible.

LINE 1

The third letter in the name of the celebrant might be read as a *w*, but it is probably the letter *r*. The other letters in the name indicate that the writer was careless in making the heads of his letters.

The first element of the name is *ātar-*, "fire," which is used for both the hearth fire and the sacred fire.[364]

The second element, *-brzn*, is found in a number of Persian names.[365] It presents some diffi-

---

[363] *BAiW*, col. 1605, *-stāna*, "Stand," "Stelle," "Stall." The word is found in combination, as *aspōstāna* with the meaning "horse-stall" (*ibid.*, col. 219). Benveniste (*Titres et noms*, p. 78) sees in Elamite *Ašbašda* the Persian *aspastā-* in the sense of "He who has the bones (i.e., the breadth of shoulders) of a horse"; cft. Avestan *ast(a)*, "bone," "well-built bony structure," "corporeal strength." Could this, with the addition of a secondary affix *-na* (Kent, *Old Persian*, p. 51, Sec. 147, II) possibly be the name in question?

[364] *BAiW*, cols. 312–16; Kent, *Old Persian*, p. 166a.

[365] Justi, *Iranisches Namenbuch*, p. 517, *-warezāna*; cf. Ariobarzanes, Mithrobarzanes, Satibarzanes (Akkadian ᵐ*ša-ta-bar-za-na*).

culties in etymology and interpretation. Justi interpreted it as meaning "causing" (*warzana* or *warezana* from *warez/varəz/*.[366] Schaeder, while recognizing this possibility, suggests that it might be in origin from (*us-*)*barəz* in a causative sense of "to let grow up" or "to raise."[367] Eilers accepts the latter concept and renders the name as "He who cares for (that is, makes big) the Holy Fire." A name of a celebrant beginning *ᵓtrb . . .* is found in No. 58.

LINE 2

This is the briefest possible text. It is an incomplete sentence, a token of such a complete expression as "Ātar-barzana used this pestle" (cf. No. 129). It is significant for the meaning of the verb *ᶜbd* since without the preposition *lyd* it cannot possibly represent the Persian idiom "made into the hand of" for "gave."[368]

128. Pestle (PT5 727) Pl. 31

בפרכן בירת[א]	1)	In the (haoma-)crushing ceremony of the fortress,
נריס עבד [א]בשון	2)	*Nrys*(?) used
זנה	3)	this pestle.

DESCRIPTION

Part of a green chert pestle (head dia. 5.5 cm., present max. length 4.9 cm.).

Three lines of Aramaic are written on the upper half of the top of the pestle head. The remainder is blank. There are two full lines and a single word on the third. Damage to the left side of the pestle head does not affect the text.

FIND SPOT

At the foot of the west-central part (HF 48) of the south wall of Room 38 of the Persepolis Treasury.

DATE

Like the preceding text, it is too brief for precise dating.

LINE 2

Cameron copied the name accurately, as shown on the photograph, and transliterated it as *b/p r/d yw*. But the first letter appears to be a thick *n* and the last is certainly *s*. The second letter, as usual, could be either *d* or *r*, or even *b*, and the third either *w* or *y*, with the latter more likely. A reading *Nrys* seems most likely.

129. Pestle (PT5 719) T (106); Pl. 31

אׄרדׄם עבד	1)	*Ardm* used
[א]בשון זנה	2)	this pestle.

DESCRIPTION

A green chert pestle fragment (head dia. 3.6 cm., present max. length 4.9 cm.).

Two short lines of Aramaic are written on top of the pestle head.

FIND SPOT

Southwest of the center (HF 38) of Room 38 of the Persepolis Treasury.

---

[366] *Ibid.*, p. 291 under Σατιβαρξάνης, cf. pp. 488, 517.

[367] Schaeder, *Iranische Beiträge* I 271; cf. *BAiW*, col. 949, *barəz*; H. W. Bailey ("Armeno-Indoiranica," *Transactions of the Philological Society*, 1956, p. 117) points to an Indian *barz-*, "keep."

[368] See p. 39.

DATE

Doubtless from the same general period as the other ritual vessels, but it cannot be dated precisely.

LINE 1

At first glance the name of the celebrant appears to be the Hebraic Abram, which may also be found in the Aramaic fortification tablets. But the second letter is too erect and straight, unlike the *b* in the second line, which has a curved, swinging stroke. The second letter is thus probably the letter *r*, and it is followed by what appears to be a *d* or, less likely, a *w*. The name is probably to be read as *ʾrdm* or *ʾrwm*. Justi cites an Ardam written for Artames,[369] but that is unlikely here.

130. Mortar (PT5 460) T (148); Pl. 31

ב . . . . . ביר[תא ליד	1)	[In the . . . of] the fortress, beside
. . . . .] סגנא ד]רגס פלג	2)	[. . . the *segan*], Dāra-gēsa(?), a myriarch,
[עבד הון . . . . זנה] ליד	3)	[used this . . . mortar] beside
. . . . .] גנזברא]	4)	[. . . the treasurer] . . . .

DESCRIPTION

A fragment of the base of a small green chert mortar (base dia. 7.6 cm.). Several dark, wide, horizontal bands in the stone that cross the base make the reading of all but the second line difficult. Only a small portion of the upper left edge of the base is preserved.

The ends of three lines of Aramaic are on the bottom of the base.

FIND SPOT

Just south of the center (HF 39) of Room 38 of the Treasury.

DATE

Since the names of the officials and the date line are lost, the fragment is not closely dateable.

LINE 2

The name of the celebrant is broken at the beginning. The first visible trace seems to be part of the head of such a letter as *b*, *d*, or *r*. As usual in the writing of these texts, the next letter could be either *d* or *r*. If the name is complete as *Drgs*, the first element of the name could be *dāra-*, "possessing."[370] The second, more difficult, might possibly be a contracted form of *gaesa* (Modern Persian *ges*) meaning "curls," "curly hair."[371] Thus, *Drgs* might be Dāra-gēsa for Dara-gaēsa, "Having curly hair."

131. Pestle (PT5 756) Persepolis Museum 3; Pl. 32

בסרך	1)	In the ritual of
בירתא פרז	2)	the fortress, Frāza
[ע]בד אבשון	3)	used (this) pestle.

DESCRIPTION

A fragment of a small green chert pestle (head dia. 2.7 cm., present max. length 6.7 cm.). Three lines of Aramaic are written on top of the pestle head.

[369] Justi, *Iranisches Namenbuch*, p. 21*a*, cf. p. 37*a*.

[370] *Ibid.*, p. 491, *dāra-*; Kent, *Old Persian*, p. 189, *dar*, "hold," "possess."

[371] *BAiW*, col. 480; Late Avestan *gaēsa*.

FIND SPOT

Just southwest of the center (HF 38) of Room 38 of the Persepolis Treasury.

DATE

Close dating is impossible.

LINE 2

The reading of the name of the celebrant is doubtless *Prz*, although, as Cameron notes in his copy, there is a defect in the stone above the last letter. The name is also encountered in the Aramaic fortification tablets from Persepolis.[372]

Eilers suggests that the name may be an hypocoristicon of one with the first element Frāza.[373]

132. Plate (PT5 732) T (17); Pl. 32

[. . . . . בֹ[תֹ]ר עבד סחר	1)	[. . . used (this) plate . . .]
[. . . .].ךֹ קד[ם . . . . . אפגנוברא]	2)	. . . before [. . . the sub-treasurer]
[ליד . . . . . גנברא זי בהֹ]רחותֹי [אשכר שֹ]נֹת	3)	[(and) beside . . . the treasurer who is in] Ara-
[. . . .		chosia. ʾškr of year . . . .

DESCRIPTION

An irregularly shaped fragment of a large, green chert plate (base dia. *ca.* 21.4 cm.), consisting of a small bit of the circumference of the base having externally to it a small piece of the adjacent side and internally a long piece that extends irregularly into the base. The present maximum length of the piece is about 10.5 cm.

Traces of three lines of Aramaic text remain on the bottom of the base. These are the last lines of the text. Originally there were, perhaps, two more lines above them.

Discoloration of the stone makes the text difficult to read at the break at the right side in the first two preserved lines.

FIND SPOT

West of the center (HF 48) of the south wall of Room 38.

DATE

No precise date is possible.

LINE 1

Only the end of a word, possibly the end of the name of the celebrant appears. Discoloration of the stone makes its reading difficult and uncertain. At the edge of the break a slight bit of ink suggests the end of the tail of a letter *b*, but the identification is by no means certain. It is followed by a long vertical line that might be the principal stroke of a letter *t*. After it Cameron read a clear *r*.

Cameron next shows what seems to be the right side of an ʿ*aiyn* which is possibly part of the verb ʿ*bd* that usually follows the name of the celebrant, but it is not now visible in the photograph.

LINE 2

The dark discoloration of the stone makes the beginning of the line difficult to read. At the very edge of the break Cameron's copy suggests a long, somewhat curved stroke which could be a *k* or *p* and with such a suggestion the dense discoloration at that point seems to take on such a shape. It is followed by a smudged letter that looks somewhat like a *b*. Quite clear

---

[372] Tablet 126, l. 1.   [373] *BAiW*, col. 1688, *zā(y)*, cf. col. 1005, Late Avestan *frāza-baoδah*.

is the next letter, which could be a letter *r*, as Cameron saw it. But if its vertical stroke is as long as it appears to be in the photograph, it is probably a *k*. Whatever the reading, the place of the word in the formula of the text suggests that it is a modifier of the vessel or of the stone of which it is made.

The following word, *qdm*, introduces the sub-treasurer and his title and the remainder of the line might also have had the preposition introducing the treasurer named in the next line.

LINE 3

The letters here are clearer than the others. Only the first letter of the place name *ḥrḥwty*, "Arachosia," is missing. Since the expression "who is in Arachosia" in these texts is only associated with the treasurers, the name and title of the treasurer must have preceded it.

The word *ᵓškr* is clear and after it are traces of all three letters of the word *šnt*, "year," but the figure of the date that followed it is now gone.

133. Pestle (PT5 494*B*[374]) Persepolis Museum 187; Pl. 32

בפרכן	1)	In the (haoma-)crushing ceremony of
[בירתא] אדו[סֹ]ת	2)	[the fortress], *ᵓdwst*
ע[בֹֹ אבשון] זנה	3)	used this [pestle].

DESCRIPTION

A broken green chert pestle (head dia. 3.9 cm., length 9 cm.).

Traces of three lines of Aramaic are written on top of the pestle head in letters that have sometimes faded into illegibility.

FIND SPOT

Cannot be determined exactly, because of error in the field number.

DATE

If the celebrant is correctly identified as *ᵓdwst*, it may be associated with a presentation made by someone of the same name (No. 3) in the tenth year of Xerxes (476/75 B.C.) and again (No. 52) in the twenty-ninth year of Artaxerxes I (436/35 B.C.), when he is designated as a chiliarch. Lack of title in this text might suggest that this pestle should be dated sometime before he became chiliarch. But omission of the title here should not be stressed, for such details are frequently omitted on pestles where writing area is limited.

LINE 2

The reading of the name of the celebrant is probable, although the letter *s* is written simply, as a diagonal line.

134. Pestle (PT5 717) Pl. 32

בפרכן	1)	In the (haoma-)crushing ceremony,
[בֹ]גפת / עדב	2)	1 Baga-pāta used
אבשון זנ[ה]	3)	this pestle.

DESCRIPTION

The upper part of a green chert pestle (head dia. 3 cm., present max. length 8 cm.).

Three lines of Aramaic are written in crude letters on the top of the pestle head.

---

[374] In error, both this text and No. 81 bear the same field number, PT5 494, but only No. 81 meets the specifications of the number in the Field Register.

FIND SPOT

Just west of the center (HF 38) of Room 38 of the Persepolis Treasury.

DATE

No precise date is possible.

LINE 1

As in No. 133, the usual designation "the fortress" is missing, but it is probable that the word *prkn* is to be considered as definite. There are other examples of the omission of the ʾ*aleph* of the definite state of the noun in these texts.[375]

LINE 2

Cameron's copy shows but a slight trace of the first letter of the name of the celebrant. But he restores an ʾ*aleph* in his transcription and translation. Elsewhere in these texts Bagapāta occurs only as the name of the treasurer. Both by its position and the use of the unit stroke the name is shown to be that of the celebrant here.

As the forms of the letters show in Cameron's copy, there has been a transposition of the letters *b* and *d* in the spelling of the word ʿ*bd*. Such an error is in keeping with the crude letter forms in this text and indicates lack of experience in writing Aramaic.

LINE 3

After the first two letters, Cameron's copy shows an unusually large space between the letters *b* and *š* and again between the *š* and the following *w*. This, too, seems to indicate an inexperienced writer. It results in crowding the last word of the line. The short vertical stroke at the end of the line is the *z* of the word *znh*. Because of crowding the *n* of the word is written above the *z* as the last letter of the second line in such a way that it combines with the letter *b* of the verb to make that letter resemble a *t*. There is no room for the expected letter *h*.

135. Mortar (PT5 757) Pl. 32

[בירתא . . . . ב]	1) [In the . . . of the fortress,]
[ליד . . . . . סגנ]א	2) [beside . . . the *segan*]
[. . . . . עבד] הון	3) [. . . used (this)] mortar
[לפתי אטבען] ‖ ‖‖ ‖‖	4) [worth] 8 [(shekel) coins] . . . .

DESCRIPTION

A fragment of a green chert mortar (base dia. 12 cm., present max. height 2.6 cm.).

The traces of the ends of three lines of Aramaic are preserved on the bottom of the base. Originally there must have been another line above and two or three lines below the preserved text.

FIND SPOT

Southwest of the center (HF 38) of Room 38 of the Persepolis Treasury.

DATE

No precise date is possible.

LINE 4

The numeral occurring in the line after the word "mortar" must refer to the vessel's value, as in Nos. 43 and 73, rather than to the date.

---

[375] See p. 67. P. Grelot ("Remarque sur le bilingue Grec-Araméen d'Armazi," *Semitica* VIII [1958] 12–13) argues that the apparent lack of determinate endings may be due to defective writing and that the long vowels would be sounded after final consonants, where needed, without the final ʾ*aleph*.

136. Mortar (PT5 750) Pl. 32

[....ב ....] בירתא ל[יד ....]	1) [In the ... of] the fortress, be[side ...]
[סגנא .....].עבד הֹוֹן [זנה]	2) [the *segan*, ...] used [this] mortar
[ליד ....]גֹ[נזברא זי בהרחותי]	3) [beside ...] the treasurer [who is in Arachosia.]
[אשכֹ]ר שֹ[נת .....]	4) [ʾšk]r of ye[ar ....]

DESCRIPTION

A portion of the base of a green chert mortar (base dia. 18 cm., present max. height 4.3 cm.).
The middle parts of four lines of Aramaic are preserved on the bottom of the base. The beginnings of all lines are lost due to extensive spalling of the right side of the base and the ends of the lines are broken away.

FIND SPOT

Southwest of the center (HF 38) of Room 38 of the Persepolis Treasury.

DATE

No close dating is possible but the piece comes from the same period as the remainder of the dated ritual objects found with it.

137. Pestle (PT5 438) Pl. 33

בסרך	1) In the ritual (of the fortress)
אֹבשון	2) (this?) pestle (was used).

DESCRIPTION

The upper part of a green chert pestle (head dia. 3.1 cm., present max. length 5.7 cm.).
Cameron's copy shows only two words in two lines written on the top of the pestle head.

FIND SPOT

South of the center (HF 39) of Room 38 of the Treasury.

DATE

Dateable only by archeological context.

LINES 1 AND 2

If this text is complete, as Cameron's copy suggests, it is remarkable for what it omits. Most of the usual formula must be compacted in the two pregnant words. Not only are no officers named, but even the celebrant's name does not appear.

138. Mortar (PT5 715) T (149); Pl. 33

	1)
	2)
עבד [הון זנה ליד .....]	3) used [this mortar beside ...]
גנזברא [קדם .....]	4) the treasurer [before ...]
אפגנזב[רא ....]	5) the sub-treasurer ....

DESCRIPTION

A fragment of the base of a green chert mortar (base dia. 8 cm., present height 1.6 cm.).
The beginnings of three lines of Aramaic are written on the bottom of the base.

FIND SPOT

Southwest of the center (HF 38) of Room 38 of the Persepolis Treasury.

DATE

No precise date is possible.

139. Mortar (PT5 402) T (38); Pl. 33

בפרכן בׄירתא ליד . . . . .   1)   In the (haoma-)crushing ceremony of the fortress, beside . . .

אׄ[.ש̈].   2)   . . . .

DESCRIPTION

A fragment of the base of a green chert mortar (base dia. 11.2 cm., present max. height 2.9 cm.).

A full line of Aramaic and traces of the tops of the letters at the beginning of a second line remain on the bottom of the mortar base.

FIND SPOT

South of the center (HF 39) of Room 38 of the Persepolis Treasury.

DATE

No precise date is possible.

LINE 2

Only the tops of letters remain of the first word, which must be the name of the *segan*. The last letter appears to be an *ᵓaleph*. Before it is probably a letter *š* and at the beginning of the line is a letter with a head, probably a *b*, *r*, or *k*. There appears to be extra space between the letter *š* and the final letter. Possibly a *y* could have been there. But there is no *segan* in these texts whose name remotely resembles *Rš(y)ᵓ*. The reading is quite questionable and the line must be regarded as illegible.

140. Mortar (PT5 443) T (27); Pl. 33

בסרך [בׄירתא ליד . . . . סגנא   1)   In the ritual of [the fortress, beside . . . the *segan*],

[. . . . . גלל] זי הׄוׄן [עבד . . . . .]   2)   [. . . used (this)] mortar of [stone . . . .]

DESCRIPTION

Part of a large, green chert mortar (base dia. 18.2 cm.).

Traces of two lines of Aramaic remain on the bottom of the base.

FIND SPOT

South of the center (HF 39) of Room 38 of the Treasury.

DATE

No precise date is possible.

LINES 1 AND 2

According to Cameron's copy all that remains of the first line is the first word. Only the tops of letters appear in the second line but the *zy* is clear and the traces before it fit the word *ḥwn*, "mortar." The reading seems certain.

141. Mortar (PT5 761[376]) Pl. 33

בפרכן בירת[א] 1) In the (haoma-)crushing ceremony of the fortress. . . .

DESCRIPTION

A very small fragment of the base of a green chert mortar (max. width 5.5 cm.).

Two words of Aramaic are on the bottom of the base. They are the beginning of the first line of a much longer text.

FIND SPOT

Southwest of the center (HF 38) of Room 38 of the Treasury.

DATE

No precise date is possible.

142. Tray (PT5 736) Pl. 33

[. . . . . בי[רתא [. . . . .ב] 1) [In the . . . of the] for[tress . . .]
[. . . . . .]א . . . . 2) . . . .

DESCRIPTION

A piece of a smooth, oval, green chert tray with an intermittent ledge. The stone has gray veins.[377]

Only three letters, representing two words in two lines, remain on the bottom of the tray.

FIND SPOT

Near the north wall of Room 38 of the Persepolis Treasury, at the entrance to subsidiary Room 47 (HF 29).

DATE

No precise date is possible.

143. Mortar (PT5 75) T (83); Pl. 34

[. . . . . בירתא ליד . . . . .ב] 1) [In the . . . of the fortress, beside . . .]
[סגנא . . . . . עבד הון] 2) [the *segan* . . . used]
[זי] גלל [זֹעֹ]יר / ליד 3) a small [mortar of] stone beside
. . . . . גנזברא א[ש]כר 4) . . . the treasurer. ʾškr of
[שנת . . .] 5) [year. . . .]

DESCRIPTION

Approximately two-thirds of the base of a small mortar of polished green chert (base dia. 7.6 cm., present max. height 2.9 cm.).

Although the Field Register claims traces of three lines of text on this vessel, there were perhaps five, of which only two are now legible.

FIND SPOT

South of the center (HF 39) of Room 38 of the Persepolis Treasury, among the many fragments of ritual vessels near the base of the south wall of the room.

---

[376] The Field Register notes that three fragments were given the same number. Cameron reports that they did not belong together and that the other two fragments were not worth copying.

[377] See p. 51.

DATE

No precise date is possible.

LINE 3

The first legible word is certainly *gll*, "stone." The faint vertical stroke that follows is doubtless the first letter of the word *zᶜyr*, "small" and the last two letters of the word are clearly legible. The word is followed by a unit stroke. The *lyd* at the end of the line introduces the treasurer, whose name must have begun the fourth line.

The following texts have very little to contribute to this study since they consist largely of a few rather isolated words, usually familiar ones that may establish their place in the formula of the normal text. They are added here only for the sake of completeness.

For the most part they are fragments that were discarded at the Persepolis Museum shortly after the Oriental Institute had completed its work at Persepolis. Some were trodden there and so broken that their original field numbers and sometimes part of their inscribed surfaces have been lost.

When the fragments were prepared for shipment from the Persepolis Museum to the Teheran Museum for study, some texts that were already faint disappeared entirely and others were badly damaged.

144. Mortar (PT5 680) T (31); Pl. 34

בפרכן ב[י]ר[תא] . . . . . .   1)   In the (haoma-)crushing ceremony of the fortress . . .

סגנא תֿח . . . . . .   2)   the *segan*, Th. . . .

Base dia. 12.2 cm., present max. height 2.8 cm. Found west of the center of the south wall (HF 48) of Room 38.

145. Mortar (PT5 698) T (146); Pl. 34

ב . . . . . בירֿ[תא ליד אֿ]מדת סגנא]   1)   [In the . . . of the fortress] beside A[ma-dāta the *segan*,]

. . . . .] עבד] הון זי [גלל . . . . . .]   2)   [. . . used this] mortar of [. . . stone]

. . . . .] ליד דתמֿ[תר [גנזברא]   3)   [. . . beside Dāta-M]ithra [the treasurer] . . . .

Base dia. 12 cm., present max. height 2.9 cm.; parts of the center of the first three lines of a longer text are preserved on the bottom of the base. Recovered west of the center (HF 48) of the south wall of Room 38.

If the names of the officers are properly restored as Ama-dāta the *segan* and Dāta-Mithra the treasurer, the text must be dated between 479 B.C. and 466 B.C., while the latter was treasurer.

146. Mortar (PT5 713) T (150); Pl. 34

ב] . . . . . ביֿ[רֿ]תֿ[א]   1)   [In the . . . of the fortress]

. . . . . סֿ[גנא . . . . . ליֿ[ד   2)   [beside . . .] the *segan*, . . .

עבד הון זי גֿ[לל]   3)   [used this(?) mortar of] stone . . . .

Base dia. *ca.* 9.7 cm., max. length of fragment 4.6 cm. Found in the northern part of the west side (HF 35) of Room 42[378] of the Treasury, just opposite the door leading to Room 38.

[378] See p. 3.

147. Mortar (PT5 694) T (126); Pl. 34

[סגנא] רֹגֹפֹּתֹ עבד]   1)   [the *segan*], *Rgpt* [used]

[ה]ון [זי גלל ז]עֹיר / [ליד]   2)   a small mortar [of stone beside] . . .

[וגנז[בֹרֹ]א] . . . . .   3)   . . . the treasurer. . . .

Base dia. 9.3 cm., present max. height 2.9 cm. Traces of three lines from the middle of the text appear on the bottom of the base in widely scattered letters. Recovered west of the center of the south wall (HF 48) of Room 38.

The name in the first line is that of the celebrant. It appears to begin with the letter *r* or *d*, but the name may be Baga-pāta, as in No. 134.

148. Plate (PT5 683) T (140); Pl. 34

[. . . . . בירתא . . . .ב].   1)   In [the . . . of the fortress] . . .

[. . . . . . .ונד]פרן עבד   2)   Vinda(t)-[farnah used . . .]

. . . . [מֹ]תר]   3)   Mithra- . . .

. . . שֹ   4)   . . . .

Base dia. 9.8 cm.; found at the south wall (HF 48) of Room 38.

149. Mortar (PT5 491) T (15) and T (37); Pl. 35

. . . . . . .בפרכן בירתא ליֹד   1)   In the (haoma-)crushing ceremony of the fortress, beside [. . . the *segan*]

כפֹ].. . עבד הון זי גלל]   2)   *Kp* . . . [used this]

. . . . . .מֹד]ם   3)   medium-sized [mortar of stone] . . . .

A fragment composed of two pieces, T 15 and T 37, part of the base of a green chert mortar with a diameter of 15.8 cm.

Recovered in Room 38, just west of the door in the northeastern part of the room that led to subsidiary Room 48.

150. Mortar (field number lost) T (144); Pl. 35

[ליד] מת]רפת סגנא]   1)   [beside] Mith[ra-pāta the segan,]

[עבד] . . . . . הון זנֹהֹ]   2)   [. . . used] this mortar . . . .

A thick "slice" of green chert mortar base, 4.9 cm. × 2.2 cm. Parts of two lines of Aramaic are on the flat surface, the bottom of the base.

151. Plate (PT5 759) T (155); Pl. 35

בֹירתא[. . . . .]   1)   the fortress

ת[. . . . .]   2)   . . . *t* . . .

Base dia. 13.3 cm. The fragment measures 8.5 cm. exterior to the circumference of the base and 6.7 × 4.8 cm. as it projects from the circumference into the base. Found in Room 38.

152. Plate (PT5 462) T (8); Pl. 35

[. . .שֹ]מה . . . ביֹת   1)   . . . *byzt* by name,

[עבד סחרא] זנה . . . . .   2)   [used] this [plate] . . .

Base dia. 7 cm. Found south of the center (HF 39) of Room 38.

153. Plate (PT5 427*B*[379]) T (35); Pl. 35

. . . . . [סג]נ[א]	1)	the *segan* . . .
. . . . . [ס]חר	2)	plate . . .
. . . . ל[יד]	3)	beside . . .

Base dia. 6.5 cm. Found just north of the center (HF 29) of Room 38.

154. Plate (PT5 747) T (12); Pl. 35

. . . . . . ב	1)	In(?) . . .
. . . . . . סחר [עבד]	2)	[used (this)] plate
. . . . . ל[יד]	3)	. . . beside . . . .

Base dia. 9.3 cm. Recovered in the northwestern corner (HF 36) of Room 38.

155. Plate (PT5 677) T (39); Pl. 35

. . . . . סג[נא . . . . .]	1)	. . . the *segan* . . .
[. . . . . גלל] זי [ן . . . . . .]	2)	[. . . of] stone . . .
. . . . . . ליד	3)	. . . beside . . .
[גנזב[ר]א] [זי ב[הר]חותי]	4)	the treasurer [who is in] Arachosia . . . .

A segment 7.8 cm. × 7.3 cm. × 6.6 cm. of the base of a green chert plate (base dia. 10.8 cm.). Found west of the center of the south wall (HF 48) of Room 38 of the Treasury.

156. Plate (field number lost) T (81); Pl. 36

. . . . . . סחר [עבד . . . . .]	1)	[. . . used (this)] plate . . .
. . . . . ליד	2)	. . . beside . . .
. . . . . (traces)	3)	. . . .

Base dia. 9.2 cm.

157. Plate (PT5 738) T (128); Pl. 36

. . . . . ליד	1)	beside . . .
. . ב	2)	. . . .

Fragment 6 cm. × 5.4 cm. × 2.1 cm. Base dia. 12.5 cm. Found north of the center (HF 29) of Room 38. The Field Register indicates two lines of Aramaic, but only a single word is visible on the bottom of the base.

158. Plate (field number lost) T (122); Pl. 36

. . . . ב	1)	In . . .
. . . . ליד	2)	beside . . . .

Base dia. 13.1 cm.

[379] Same field number as No. 1.

159. Mortar (PT5 780) T (151); Pl. 36

[. . . . .**בירתא**[רכן **בֿ[פֿ**]   1)   In the (haoma-)crushing ceremony [of the fortress]

. . . .[**שׁ**]**נֿ**   2)   *Nš* . . .

[. . . . .**ד**[**י**]**לֿ**   3)   beside . . . .

A small fragment, 2.4 cm. × 3.8 cm., of a mortar base (base dia. 11.5 cm.). Found within Room 43 (HF 35),[380] a subsidiary room lying west of Room 38.

160. Mortar (PT5 445) T (116); Pl. 36

. . . . . .**ליד** . . . .   1)   . . . beside . . .

[. . . . **נֿקֿוֿרֿ** .] . . . . .   2)   . . . chiseled(?) . . . .

A fragment of a green chert mortar base (max. length 6.7 cm., base dia. 7.7 cm.). Found south of the center (HF 39) of Room 38. Only the tops of letters are visible in the second line and the reading is very uncertain.

The word *nqwr* may be from the root *nqr* meaning "to chisel," "to shape stones by chiseling," "to whet a millstone."[381]

161. Pestle (PT5 672) T (47); Pl. 36

. . . . . **ותפן** . . . . . . **בֿ**   1)   . . .

. . . . . . **בֿוֿ עם** . . . . . .   2)   . . . with (?) . . .

. . . . . (traces) . . . . .   3)   . . .

. . . . . **שנת** . . . .   4)   . . . year . . . .

Pestle fragment (head dia. 4.3 cm., present max. length 7.5 cm.) found southwest of the center (HF 38) of Room 38. The Field Register notes five lines of Aramaic, but there are now only traces of letters in four almost illegible lines.

162. Mortar (PT5 430) T (107); Pl. 36

ר הֿ[תֿ . . . .   1)   . . . .

A fragment of a mortar base (base dia. 11.9 cm., present max. length 9.5 cm.) found just south of the center (HF 39) of Room 38.

The Field Register calls for two lines of Aramaic, but only a few letters are now found.

163. Plate (PT5 229) T (2); Pl. 36

. . . . . . **ד**[**י**]**ל**   1)   beside . . .

. . . . **ר**[**חֿ**]**סחֿ עבד**   2)   used (this) plate . . .

. . . . . **בֿוֿ בי**   3)   *bzy* . . . .

An irregular fragmentary section of a green chert plate with a disk base, low convex side, and flat-top rim (base dia. 13.5 cm.).

---

[380] See p. 3.

[381] Jastrow, *Dictionary* II 935a.

Despite a long search, not all fragments have been recovered for study. To judge from those recovered in the Persepolis Museum in 1966, the missing texts would perhaps add little or nothing to what is known of the ritual texts, and it is not worth delaying publication until they are found.

The Field Register is somewhat misleading. For each inscribed fragment it notes a number of lines but in those recovered sometimes only a few letters or an isolated word remain to mark the line.

The following objects, noted in the Field Register, have not been copied or photographed and cannot now be found for study.

OBJECT	FIELD NUMBER	FIND SPOT	REMARKS
Mortar(?)	PT4 216	HG 61	2 lines of Aramaic across one corner (illegible)
Mortar	PT5 74	HF 39	parts of 2 lines
Pestle	PT5 131	HF 39	6 or 7 lines
Plate	PT5 171	HF 48	2 lines
Pestle	PT5 226	HF 48	4 lines
Plate	PT5 228	HF 48	1 line
Plate	PT5 240	HF 49 (Room 41)	2 lines
Plate	PT5 241	HF 49 (Room 41)	3 lines
Plate	PT5 321	HG 40 (Room 41)	4 lines
Plate	PT5 404	HF 39	3 lines
Pestle	PT5 420	HF 29(?) (Room 38)	5 lines (very faint)
Plate	PT5 425	HF 29(?) (Room 38)	5 lines
Plate	PT5 426	HF 29(?) (Room 38)	3 lines
Mortar	PT5 429	HF 39	5 lines
Pestle	PT5 441	HF 39	3 lines
Mortar	PT5 442	HF 39	5 lines
Mortar	PT5 444	HF 39	3 lines
Plate	PT5 449*	HF 39	4 lines
Plate	PT5 450*	HF 39	3 lines
Mortar	PT5 657	HF 38	4 lines
Pestle	PT5 658	HF 38	2 lines
Pestle	PT5 661	HF 38	faint traces
Pestle	PT5 684	HF 48	faint traces
Pestle	PT5 697	HF 48	4 lines (faint)
Mortar	PT5 705	HF 29	4 lines
Pestle	PT5 716	HF 38	6 lines
Pestle	PT5 722	HF 38	6 lines
Plate	PT5 737	HF 29	3 lines
Mortar	PT5 751	HF 38	3 lines
Pestle	PT5 753	HF 38	4 lines
Mortar	PT5 774	HF 37	6 lines
Pestle	PT5 827	HF 27	5 lines (faint)
Mortar	PT5 907	HG 28	3 lines
Mortar	PT6 85	HF 27	3 lines
Plate	PT6 510	HF 78	traces (illegible)
Plate	PT6 511	HF 38	faint traces

* Lost at sea.

GENERAL INDEX

Abel, F.-M., 26
aberetar, 11
ᵓbšwn, 73, 88; *see also* pestle
adhvaryu priest, 10
Aērpatastān, 31
Aharoni, Y., 76
Ahriman (Arimanius), 8
ahura, 8
Ahuramazda (Horomazes), 8
Aitchison, I. E., 12, 14
Ali-Sami, 4, 49, 112
Altheim, F., v, xiii, 20, 41, 42, 47, 49, 54, 66, 71, 75, 91, 109
Anquetil du Perron, A. H., 13
ᵓpgnzbrᵓ, 25, 30, 63, 80; *see also* sub-treasurer
Arachosia, 20–21, 28–30, 82, 87, 92
Aramaic, 16–19, 38–43, 54; phonetics of, 63; morphology and syntax of, 65–70; influence of, on Persian, 17, 63; influenced by Persian, 33, 41–43, 63
Aramaic ritual texts, 19, 32, 44; standard formula of, 19; Bowman translation of, 40; Cameron translation of, 38–39; abbreviated form of, 19, 44, 53, 56, 132, 174, 179
Aramaic writings, 17–20, 26, 28, 39, 57, 63, 68, 80
Archaeological Institute of Persepolis, 4, 49, 112
Armazi inscription, 40, 42, 66
Arrian, 34
Arvīs gāh/Dar-i-Meher, 8
asnātor, 11
ᵓškr, 53–55, 74, 129; omitted, 99, 102
ātarǝvaxša/agnīdhra, 6, 11, 12, 32
aθaⁿgaina, 44
Athenaeus, 6, 8
Aulus Gellius, 17
Avesta, 8, 12, 14
Avroman parchments, 40
axšaina, 45, 65, 68, 84, 156; ᵓḫšynpyn/ᵓḫšynpn, 45, 63, 65, 68, 84, 102, 139, 140, 156; [ᵓḫšy]nḥwyn, 45, 63, 84, 138

Bailey, H. W., 83, 101, 172, 174
Barbier de Meynard, C., 17, 21, 22
barsom, 6, 7, 11, 32, 51
Bartholomae, C., xiii, 45, 47, 107, 111, 113, 123
bātu, 49, 101; pestle of, 101; in Pouru-bātu, 13, 133; in Bᵓtdt/Bᵓtrt, 13, 161
Bauer, H., xiii, 33, 69
Baumgartner, W., 25, 32, 33, 54, 69
Behistun Inscription, 20, 39, 66, 87, 94, 134
Benveniste, E., xiii, 34, 35, 65, 72, 78, 83, 84, 94–96, 100, 105, 110, 113, 120, 122, 129–31, 134, 172, 173
Bezold, C., 54, 91, 107, 113
Bible, 17, 26, 27, 31, 33, 39, 72, 80, 97, 118, 166
Biblical Aramaic, 26, 28, 33, 34, 41, 42, 50, 54, 65–69, 73, 80, 89, 103, 104, 107, 114, 118, 166

Bīrūnī, 22
Blau, O., 107
Bleichsteiner, R., 84
Bowman, R. A., 16, 17, 44, 67, 73, 109, 170
Brahman(s), 9, 11, 12, 45
Brahman priests, 10, 11
Breasted, J. H., 16
Brockelmann, C., 48, 81
Bulsara, S. J., 31
Bundahišn, 13
byrtᵓ, 20; *see also* fortress

calendar (Zoroastrian), 9
Cameron, G. G., v, vi, vii, xiii, 6, 14, 15, 18, 21, 28, 29, 38–39, 54, 56, 57; passim in ch. xii
Cassuto, M. D., 34, 123
celebrant(s), 33–35, 179; titles of, 34–35; sharing one vessel, 33, 147, 152; with patronymic, 33, 104
ceremonial room (*Arvīs gāh/Dar-i-Meher*), 11, 22
ceremony of crushing (*prkn*), 20–22, 48, 67–68, 74, 78; *see also* ritual
chert, 44, 170
chiliarch (ᵓlp), 21–22, 34, 68, 76, 123, 167; see also *hazarapat*
Chopra, I. C., 12
Chopra, R. N., 12
Claudius Aelianus, 114
Clay, A. T., 26, 27, 89, 94, 100
Clermont-Ganneau, C., 114
coinage, 50, 113–14, 164
Courteille, Pavet de, 17, 22
Cowley, A. E., xiii, 26, 34
Crichton, J. A., 42
Ctesias, 8, 16, 17
Cumont, F., 13, 15, 35, 37

daēvas, 7–9, 11
Dar-i-Meher/Arvīs gāh, 22
dasta, 47
Dātastān-i-Dēnīk, 13
dating, 7, 56–57
Delaporte, L., 27, 33
Dhabhar, E. B. N., 9, 37
Diakonoff, I. M., 39, 40, 41
Dino, 6
Dio Cassius, 36
Diodorus, 1, 16, 17
Dioscurides, 13
Dougherty, R. P., 16
drinking vessels, 50–51
Driver, G. R., 17, 26, 73, 80, 94, 95
Dubberstein, W. H., 57, 71
Duchesne-Guillemin, J., 9, 53
dūraoša, 7, 36
Duris, 8

187

INDEX OF TEXTS

Restorations are indicated by brackets.

VOCABULARY

ᵓbšwn (pestle), Nos. 1:3, 2:3, 3:4, 4:3, 6:3, [7:3], 9:3, 10:3, 11:2, 12:2, 14:3, [16:3 (on mortar)], 17:5, 20:3, 21:3, 22:3, 23:4, 26:4, 27:5, 28:3, 29:4, 37:4, 40:3, 46:4, 54:3, 57:3, 58:4, 59:4, 60:3, [61:2], 62:3, 63:3, 64:3, 65:4, 66:3, 68:3, [69:2], 70:3, [71:4], 77:5, 78:5, 79:2, 81:2, 87:4, 100:4, 103:3, 117:3, 120:3, [123:2], 126:3, 128:2, 129:2, 131:3, [133:3], 134:3, 137:2; ᵓbšwnᵓ, Nos. 13:3, 15:4; ᵓbšwn zy bᵓt, No. 29:4; ᵓbšwn zy ᵓškr, No. 62:3

[ᵓḥšy]nḥwyn, No. 74:3

ᵓḥšynpyn, Nos. 11:3, 75:2, 76:3, 101:2

ᵓṭbᶜ ([shekel?] coin), Nos. 43:4, 73:5, 114:3, [135:4]

ᵓlp (chiliarch), Nos. 52:3, 118:3; ᵓlp plg, No. 118:3

ᵓnzgbs/.tzgbs/ggbs, No. 1:3

ᵓpgnzbrᵓ (sub-treasurer), Nos. 5:3, 7:6, 13:4, 14:4, 18:4, 23:6, 26:5, 28:5, 30:4, 31:5, 32:5, 33:5, [35:1], 36:2, 38:4, 39:6, 40:5, 41:4, 47:5, [50:3], 53:5, [56:4], 64:5, 72:5, 80:4, 81:4, 82:5, [87:6], [91:4], 92:6, 94:4, 97:4, 98:4, 116:4, 119:4, [122:3], 138:5

ᵓškr (intoxicant), Nos. 1:4, 2:5, 3:5, 4:4, 5:4, [6:6], 7:6, 8:4, 9:5, 10:6, [11:4], 12:4, 13:5, [14:5], 15:6, 17:7, 18:4, [19:5], 20:5, 21:5, 22:5, 23:8, 24:6, [25:4], 26:6, 28:6, 29:5, 31:5, 32:5, 33:6, 34:4, [35:1], 36:2, 37:5, 38:4, 39:7, 40:5, [41:4], [42:6], 43:6, 44:5, 45:4, [46:6], 47:6, 48:7, 49:4, 50:4, [51:5], 52:5, 53:6, 55:4, 56:4, 58:5, 59:5, 60:4, 61:3, 62:3, 63:4, 64:5, 66:4, 67:3, 68:4, 69:3, 70:4, 72:5, 73:7, 74:6, 79:4, 81:4, 94:5, 95:5, 98:4, 99:3, 105:5, 106:4, 113:4, 116:6, [117:5], 120:4, 123:5, 124:4, 132:3, 136:4, 143:4; omitted in Nos. 27, 30, 57, 65(?); ᵓbšwn zy ᵓškr, No. 62:3

b (in) see main entries: ḥst, ᶜyd, prk, prkn, rgym. . . , šnt, and hrḥwty under Geographical Names

bᵓt/bt (wine), No. 29:4; see also pwrbt and bᵓtrt under Personal Names

bg (god; good fortune), Nos. [47:3], 52:4

bz/bzy, Nos. 91:3, 92:5, 112:5, 116:3, 163:3

byrtᵓ (fortress), Nos. 1:1, 2:1, 3:1, 5:1, 6:1, 7:1, 8:1, 9:1, 10:1, 11:1, 12:1, 13:1, 14:1, 15:1, [16:1], 17:1, 18:1, 19:1, 21:1, 22:1, 23:1, 24:1, 26:1, 27:2, 28:1, 29:1, 31:1, 32:2, 33:1, 34:1, 36:1, 37:1, 38:1, 39:1, [40:1], 41:1, 42:1, 43:1, 44:1, 47:1, 48:1, 49:1, 50:1, 51:1, 52:1, 53:1, 55:1, 58:1, 60:2, 61:1, 62:1, 63:1, 64:1, 65:1, [70:1], [71:2], 72:1, 73:1, 75:2, 78:2, 81:1, 84:1, 85:1, 86:1, 87:1, 88:1, 89:1, 90:1, 91:1, 92:1, 95:1, 98:1, [100:1], 102:1, 103:1, 105:1, 106:1, 108:1, 110:1, 111:1, 112:1, 113:1, 115:1, [116:1], 117:1, 118:1, 119:1, 120:1, 121:1, 122:1, 123:1, 125:1, 126:1, 128:1, 130:1, 131:2, [133:2], 136:1, 139:1, 141:1, 142:1, 144:1, 145:1, 146:1, 149:1, 151:1, [159:1]; byrtn, No. 77:2; byrt, Nos. 4:1, 46:1

br (son), No. [33:3]

ggbs/. tzgbs/ᵓnzgbs, No. 1:3

gll (stone), Nos. 1:2, 2:4, 4:4, 5:2, 6:4, [9:3], 10:4, 11:3, 13:2, 16:2, 17:4, 20:4, 22:3, 23:4, 24:4, 30:3, 31:3, 32:3, [33:4], 34:3, [72:4], 75:2, [82:3], [84:3], [88:3], [89:3], 91:3, [92:5], [94:3], 101:2, 103:3, 105:3, 108:4, 111:5, [112:5], 113:3, 116:3, 118:4, 122:2, [140:2], 143:3, [145:2], 146:3, 155:2

gnzbrᵓ (treasurer), Nos. 1:4, 6:5, 7:5, 8:4, 9:4, [10:5], 11:4, 12:3, 13:3, 14:3, 15:5, [16:4], [17:7], 18:3, 19:4, 20:5, 21:5, 22:4, 23:7, 24:5, [25:4], 30:5, 31:4, 32:4, 34:4, 36:2, 39:5, 41:3, 42:5, 43:5, 44:4, 45:4, 46:5, 47:4, 48:6, 50:3, 51:4, 52:4, [53:4], 73:6, 75:3, 76:3, 81:3, [82:4], [91:3], 92:7, 94:5, 95:4, 96:2, 98:3, [99:2], 100:6, 101:3, 104:4, 106:4, 108:5, 113:4, 114:4, 117:4, 119:3, 122:3, 136:3, 138:4, 143:4, 147:3, 155:4

dnh (this), No. 44:3; see znh

hwn (mortar), Nos. 1:2, 5:2, 8:2, 9:2, [10:4], 13:2, 14:2, 16:2, 17:4 (on pestle), 24:4 (on pestle), 31:3, 32:3, 33:4, 34:3, 36:1, 38:3, 39:3 (on pestle), [41:2], [46:4], 55:3, 75:2, 82:3, [83:3], 84:3, [85:3], [88:3], 89:2, 90:2, [91:2], 94:3, [103:2], 106:3, [108:3], 116:2, 118:3, 122:2, 125:2, 135:3, 136:2, 140:2, 145:2, 147:2, 150:2

hmš. . . , No. 105:4

hst, Nos. 36:1, 119:1, 120:1

wtpn, No. 161:1

zy (which, who)
  zy gll, Nos. 1:2, 2:4, 4:4, 5:2, [6:4], [9:3], 10:3, 11:3, 13:2, 16:2, 17:4, 20:4, 22:3, 23:4, 24:4, 30:3, 31:3, 32:3, [33:4], 34:3, [72:4], 75:2, 82:3, 84:3, [88:3], 89:2, 91:3, [92:5], 94:3, [103:2], 105:3, [108:3], 111:4, 112:4, [113:3], 116:3, 118:3, 122:2, 140:2, [143:3], 145:2, [155:2]
  zy bhrḥwty, Nos. 9:4, 13:4, 19:4, 43:5, 44:4, [45:4], [47:4], 48:7, [51:5], 52:5, 73:6, [79:3], [95:5], 110:5, 119:3, 132:3, [136:3], [155:4]
  zy bghštk, No. [14:4]
  zy bᵓt, No. 29:4
  zy ᵓškr, No. 62:3

znh (this), Nos. 1:3, 2:4, 3:4, 5:2, 7:4, 8:3, 9:2, 10:4, 13:3, 14:2, 15:4, 16:2, 18:2, 19:3, 20:3, [24:4], 27:5, [28:4], 31:3, 32:3, 33:4, 34:3, 36:1, 37:4, 38:3, 39:4, 40:3, [41:2], 43:3, 46:4, 48:5, 49:4, 50:2, [51:4], 52:3, 53:4, 54:3, 55:3, [58:4], 59:4, 60:4, 61:3, 63:3, 64:4, 65:4, 69:3, 70:3, 72:3, 73:4, 77:5, 78:5, 85:3, 88:3, 92:4, [98:2], 106:3, 110:4, 112:4, 113:3, 118:4, [119:3], 120:4, 126:3, 128:3, 129:2, 133:3, 134:3, [136:2], 150:2, 152:2; see dnh

zᶜyr (small), Nos. 31:3, [33:4], 38:3, 87:4, 108:4, 118:4, 123:3, 147:2

ḥzyd, No. 48:5

ḥšl (pound), No. 8:3

191

BROKEN TEXTS

PLATES

PLATE 1

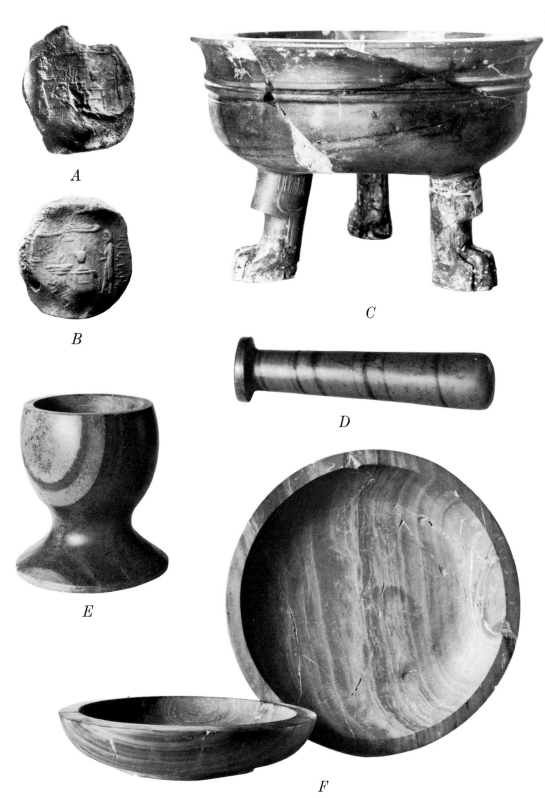

A

B

C

D

E

F

Impressions of Seal of Data-Mithra and Ritual Objects from the Treasury at Persepolis

A, B. Impressions of seal of Data-Mithra depicting a scene from the haoma ceremony. Data-Mithra is regularly mentioned as treasurer in Aramaic inscriptions on green stone ritual objects from Persepolis. Scale 1:1. (*B* is a plaster cast, from Erich F. Schmidt, *Persepolis* II, Pl. 7, Seal 20.) *C.* Uninscribed green chert bowl which may represent the *kundi*, the vessel for ritually pure water used in the haoma ceremony. Scale 1:2. *From* Schmidt, *Persepolis* II, Pl. 55. *D, E.* Green chert mortar (No. 33) and pestle. The mortar is inscribed on its base; the inscription on the head of the pestle is now illegible. Scale 1:2. *From* Schmidt, *Persepolis* II, Pl. 23. *F.* Bowls or plates of green chert which may have served either as drinking cups or as vessels for haoma twigs. Scale 1:3. *From* Schmidt, *Persepolis* II, Pl. 23.

PLATE 2

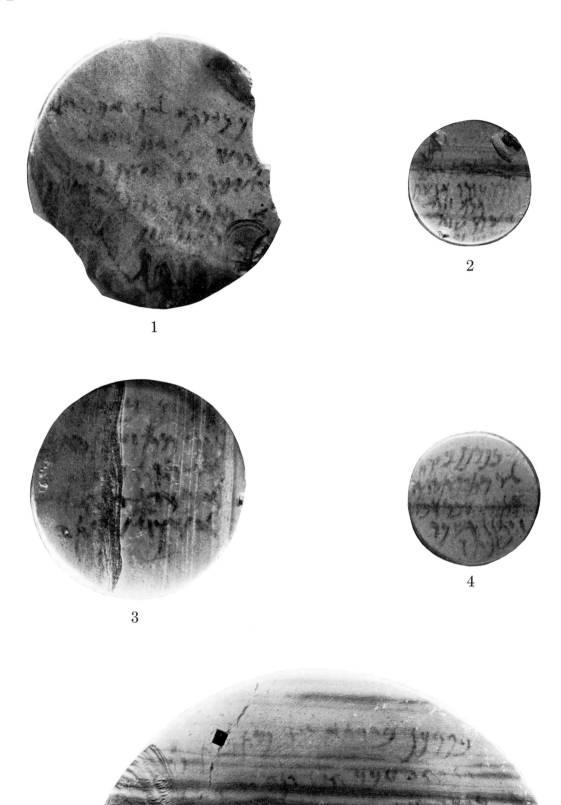

1

2

3

4

5

PLATE 3

6

7

8

9

PLATE 4

10   11

12

13

PLATE 5

14

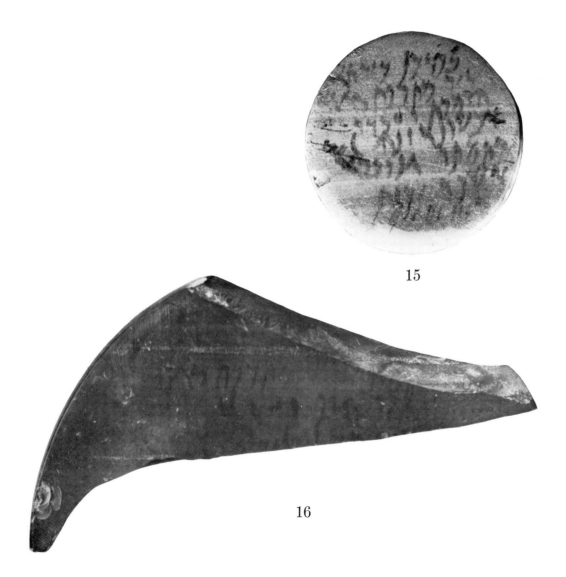

15

16

PLATE 6

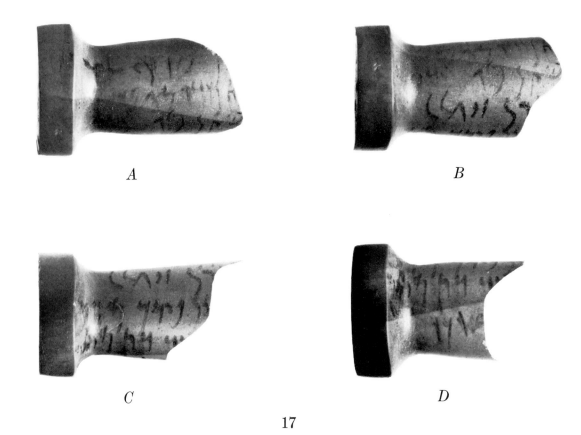

A

B

C

D

17

18

PLATE 7

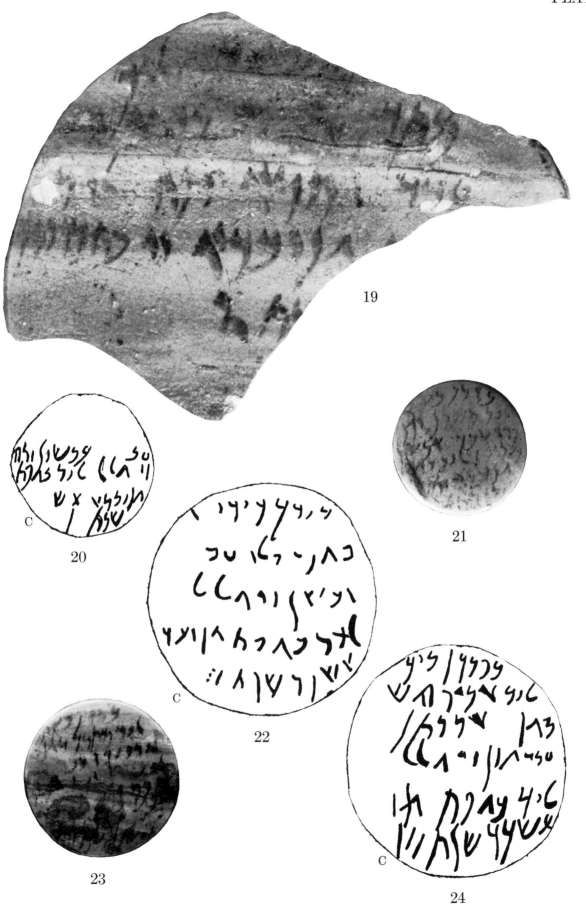

19

C

20

21

C

22

23

C

24

PLATE 8

25

26

27

29

28

30

31

PLATE 9

32

33

34

35

36

PLATE 10

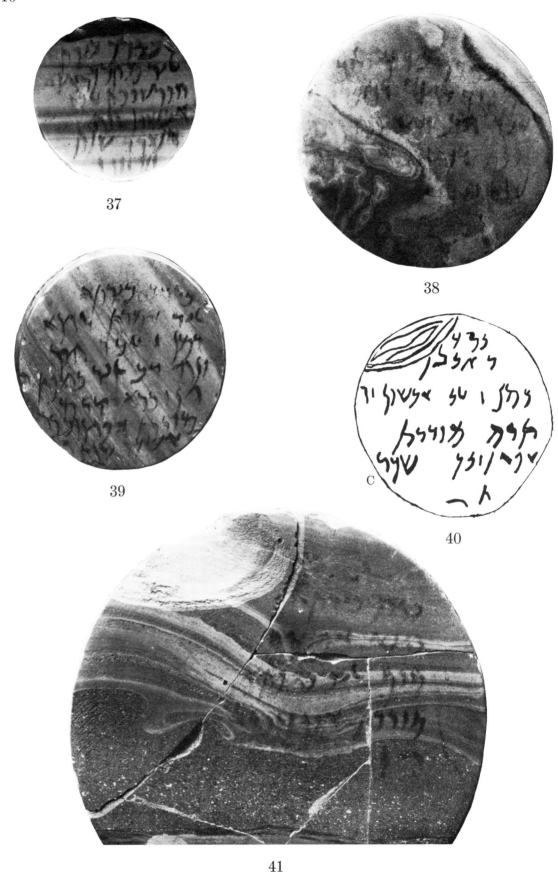

37

38

39

40

41

PLATE 11

42

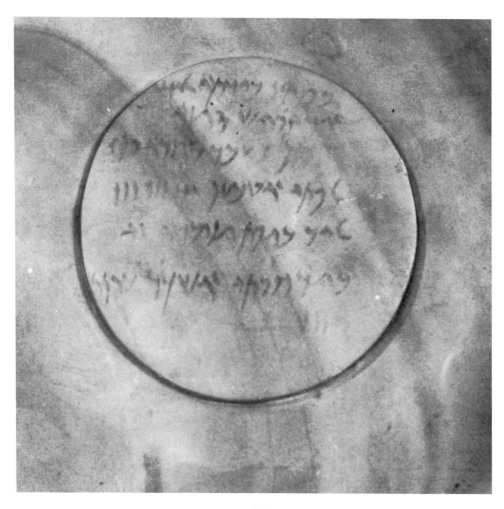

43

PLATE 12

44

45

46

PLATE 13

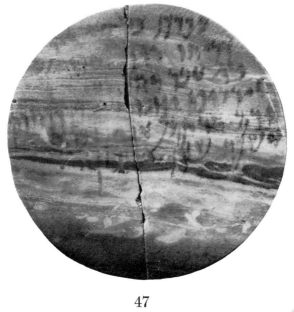

47

48

49

PLATE 14

50

C

51

52

PLATE 15

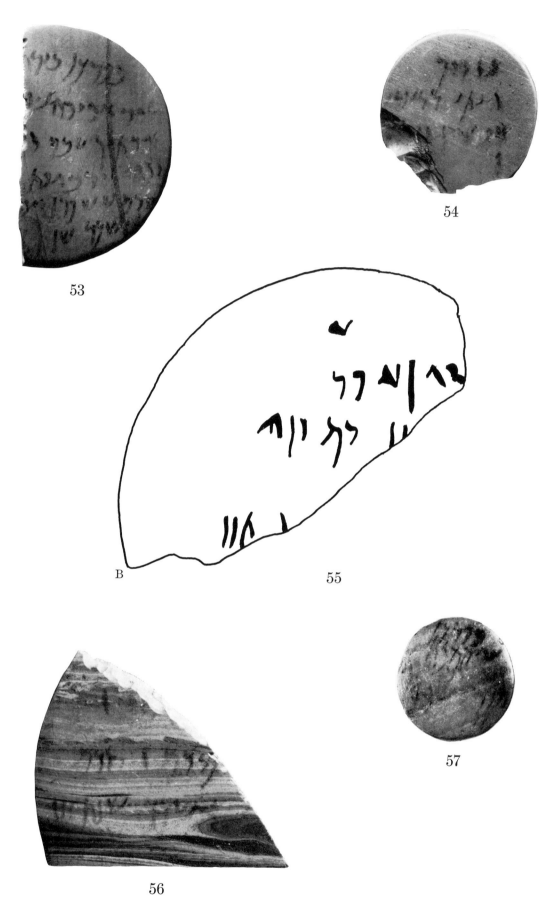

53

54

B

55

56

57

PLATE 16

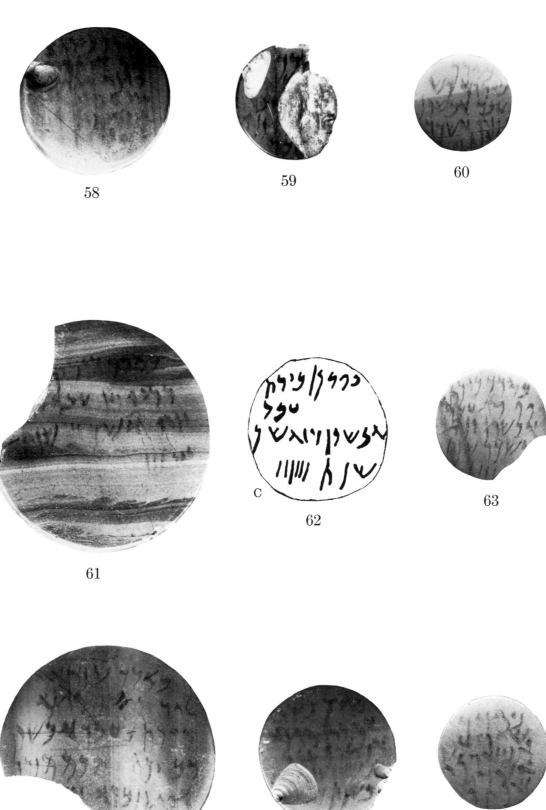

58

59

60

61

62

63

64

65

66

PLATE 17

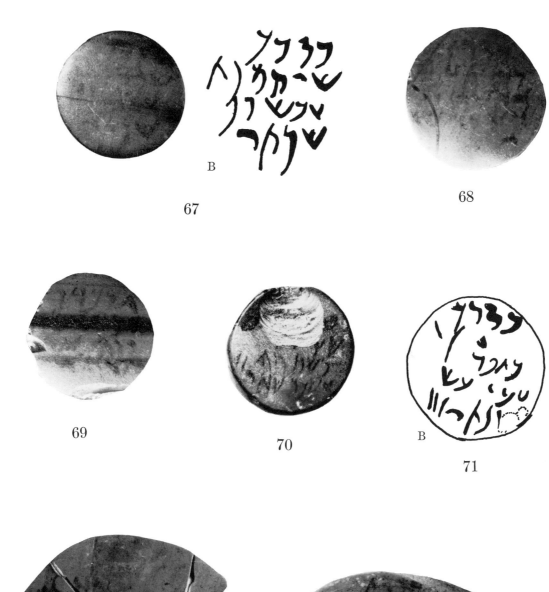

B

67

68

69

70

B

71

72

73

PLATE 18

74

75

76

77

B

78

PLATE 19

79

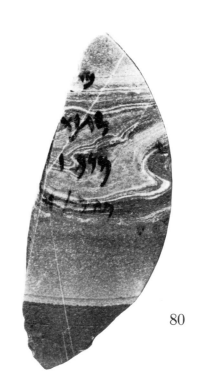

80

81

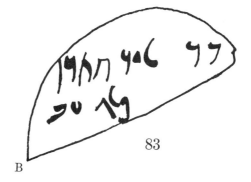

82

83

PLATE 20

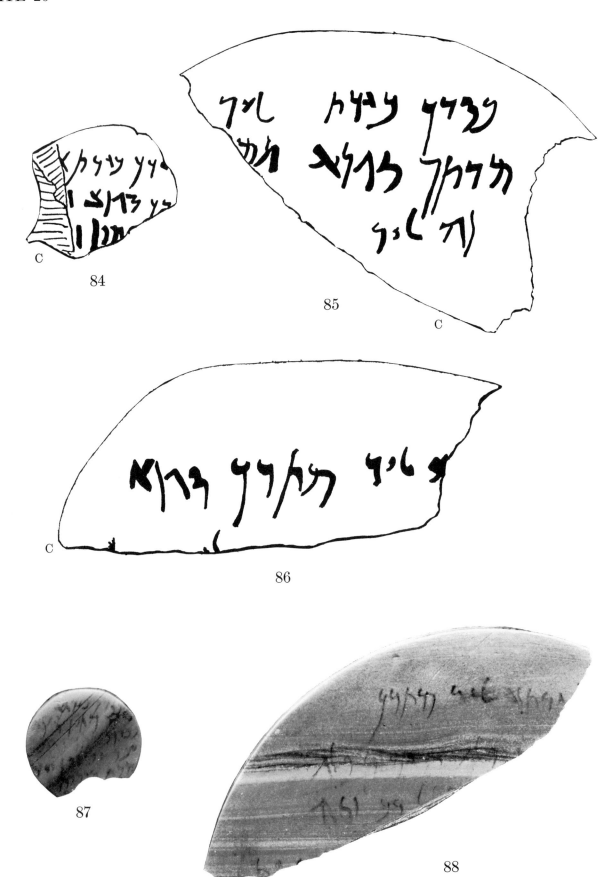

84

85

86

87

88

PLATE 21

89

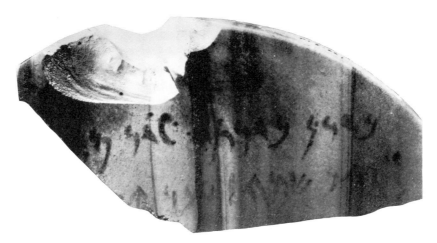

90

91

PLATE 22

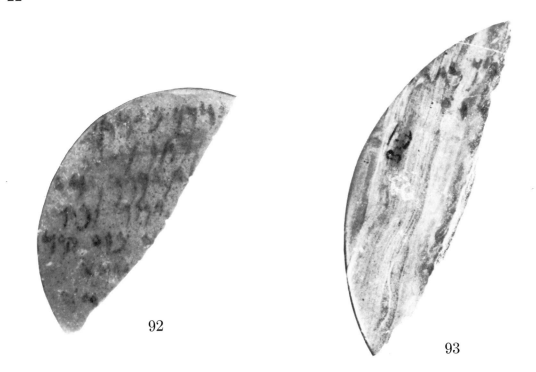

92

93

94

PLATE 23

דקי ' ע
רבני חלון '
על וו ירדן ווו
עא ית חנועיי
B ירחי שעושל

PLATE 24

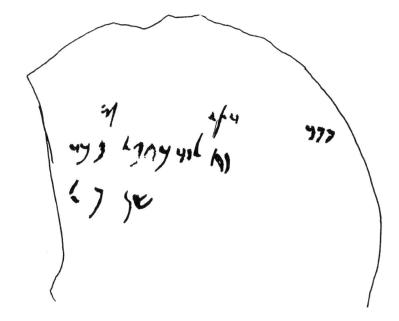

B

PLATE 25

עמנת ליר הרה

ויש תחות חומ

שיש

B

97

PLATE 26

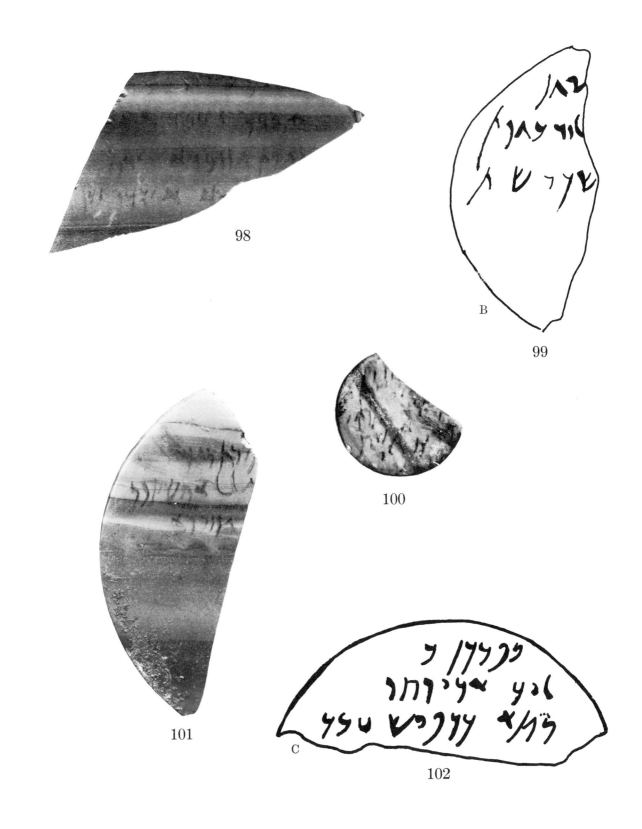

98

99

B

100

101

102

C

PLATE 27

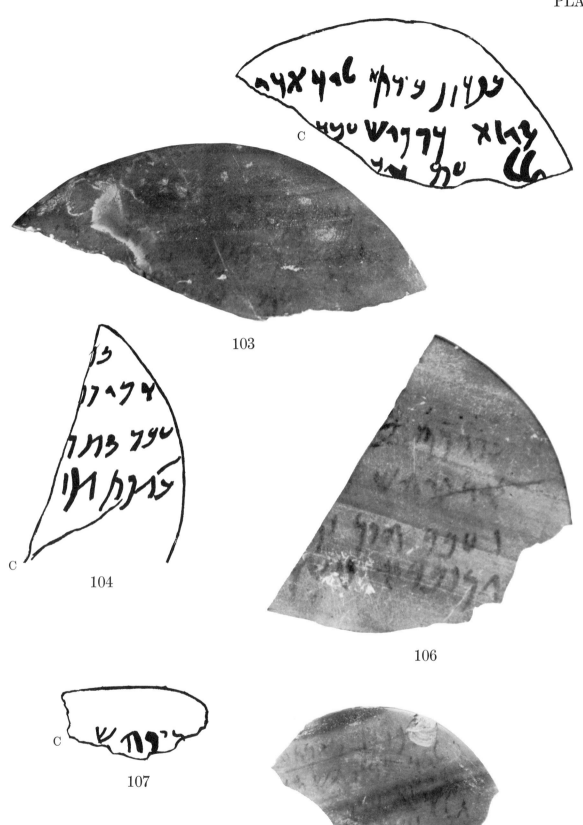

103

104

106

107

108

PLATE 28

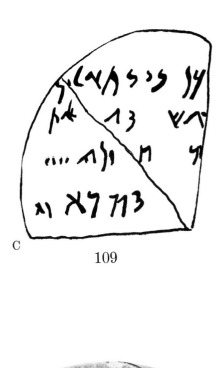

C

109

110

111

112

113

PLATE 29

114

B

115

116

117

118

119

PLATE 30

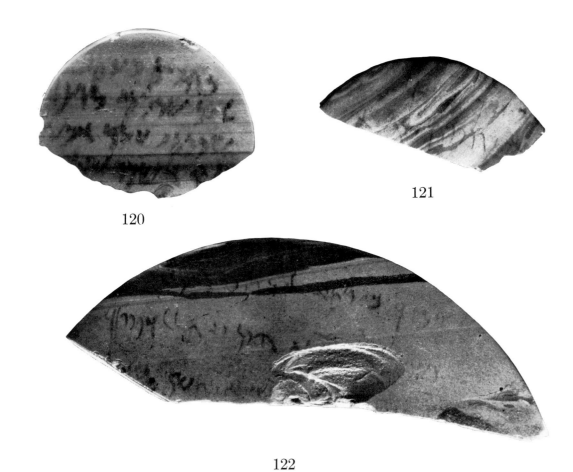

120

121

122

123

124

PLATE 31

125

126

127

128

B

129

130

PLATE 32

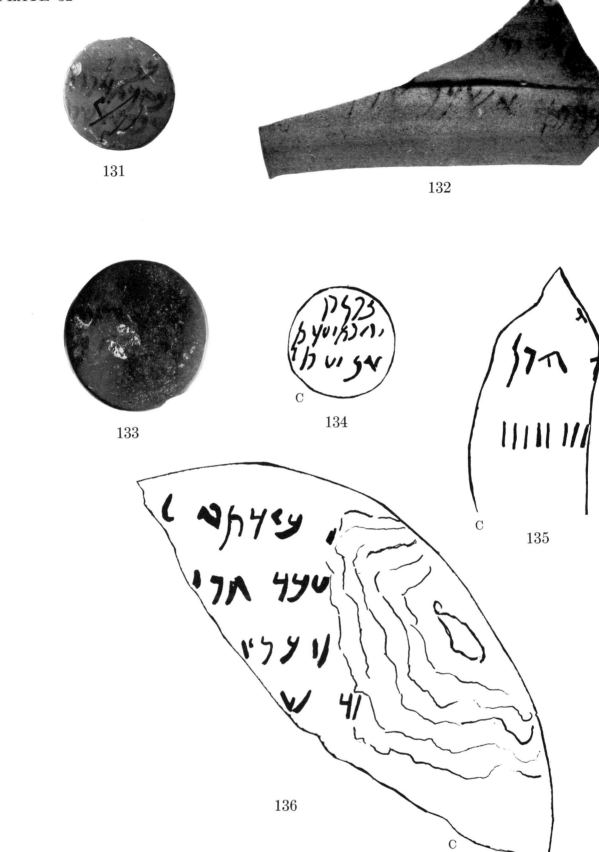

131

132

133

134

135

136

PLATE 33

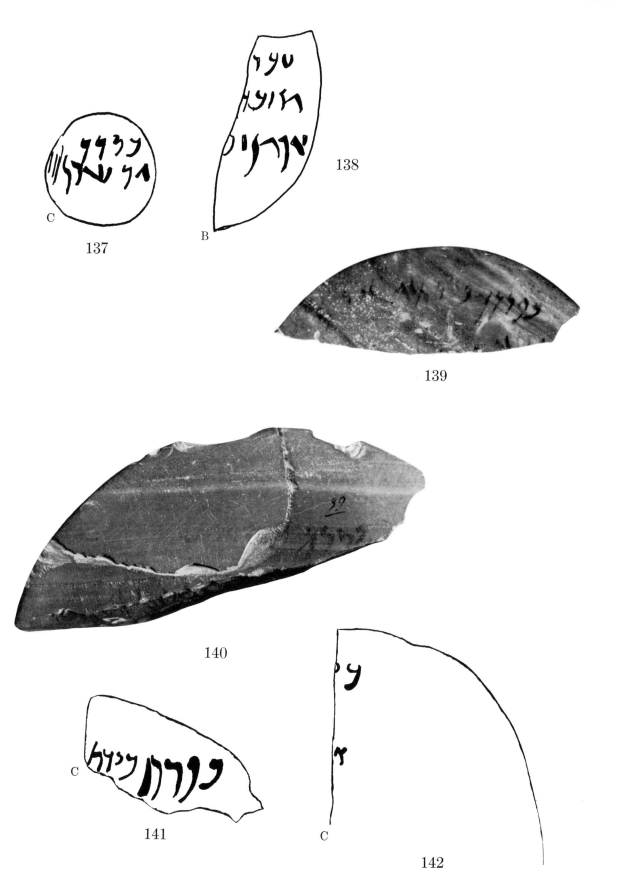

137

138

139

140

141

142

PLATE 34

143

144

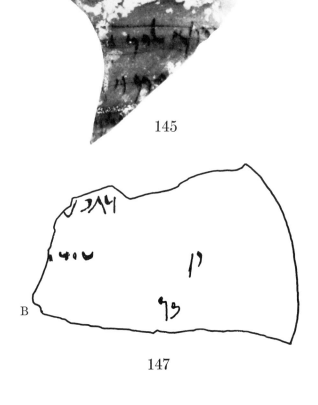

145

146

147

148

PLATE 35

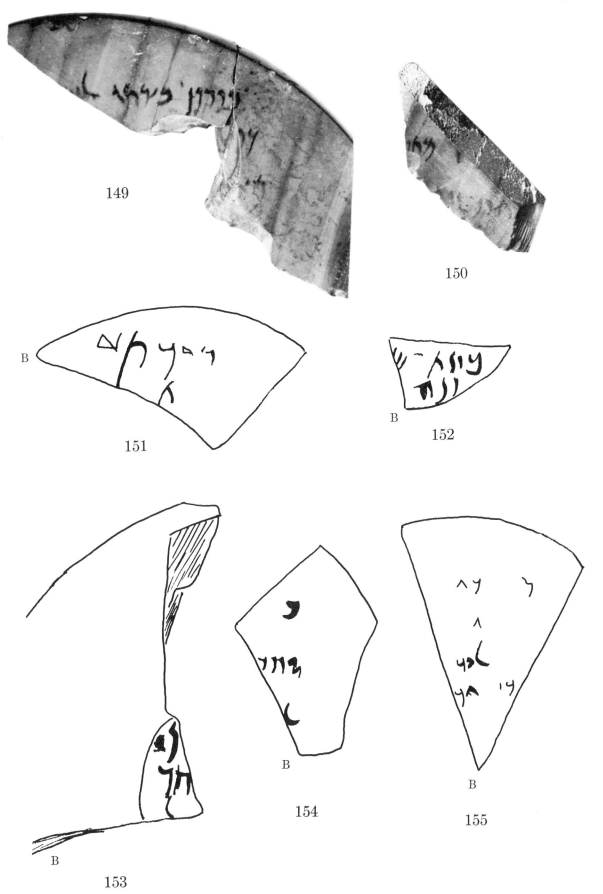

149

150

B 151

152 B

153 B

154 B

155 B

PLATE 36

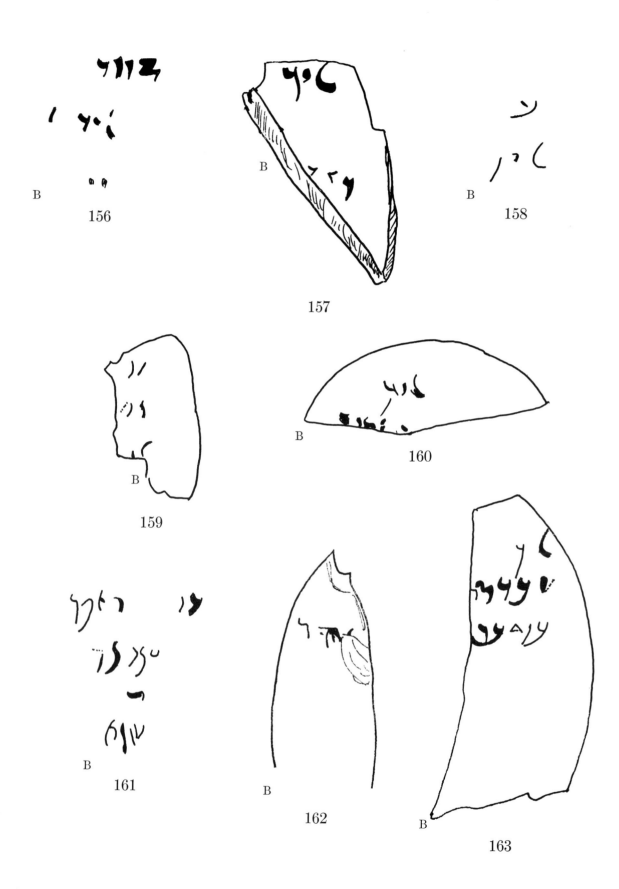

156

157

158

159

160

161

162

163